Religion
in History

Religion in History

Ernst Troeltsch

Essays translated by James Luther Adams
and Walter F. Bense

with an Introduction by James Luther Adams

T&T CLARK
EDINBURGH

T&T CLARK
59 GEORGE STREET
EDINBURGH EH2 2LQ
SCOTLAND

First Published 1991

ISBN 0 567 29192 8

Typeset by Barbers (Highlands) Ltd, Fort William
Printed and bound in Great Britain by
Billing and Sons Ltd, Worcester

Contents

PART THREE: ERNST TROELTSCH AND THE MODERN SPIRIT

Preface

The monumental work of Ernst Troeltsch stands as the twentieth century's most thorough and systematic attempt to come to terms with the historical character of culture, knowledge, and religion. This volume of his essays, only two of which have appeared previously in English, is an attempt to make more widely available his key writings on the then-emerging study of religion and its implications for theology, on the religious and social import of Christian teachings, and on the character and impact of modernity.

The volume is the fruit of more than two decades of teaching graduate students in religion and theology, through biennial seminars I offered first at the University of Chicago in the 1950s and then at Harvard Divinity School in the 1960s. To all of the students who participated in the seminars and in the process of translation that was even then underway, I am deeply grateful. Individual students who took a hand in translation of individual pieces in this volume are mentioned in the Acknowledgements. I would also like to thank Dr Walter E. Wyman for his revisions to the text and translation of Troeltsch's 1913 essay, 'The Dogmatics of the History-of-Religions School.'

Most of all I acknowledge with gratitude the contributions of the late Dr Walter F. Bense. Through close collaboration at Harvard, where he received his doctorate in 1967, and later when he was a professor of religion and chair of the department at the University of Wisconsin-Oshkosh, Dr Bense helped me to gather together the translations, revised them for consistency and style, and supplemented them with translations of his own. Unless noted otherwise in the

Acknowledgements, all of the essays were translated by me and revised by him. His skills, knowledge, and especially his conviction of Troeltsch's importance were instrumental in moving the project forward, and I and other students of Troeltsch stand in his debt.

—*James Luther Adams*

Acknowledgements

1. 'Historical and Dogmatic Method in Theology' was translated by Ephraim Fischoff, revised by Walter Bense, from 'Über historische und dogmatische Methode in der Theologie,' in *Gesammelte Schriften* 4 vols. (Tübingen, 1913 and 1922; reprinted Aalen, 1962), 2:729–53. The essay was originally published in the *Studien des rheinischen Predigervereins* (1898) as supplementary remarks to an essay by F. Niebergall, 'Über die Absolutheit des Christentums.'
2. 'On the Question of the Religious A Priori' was translated from 'Zur Frage des religiosen Apriori' (1909), in *Gesammelte Schriften*, 2:754–68.
3. '*Logos* and *Mythos* in Theology and Philosophy of Religion' was translated from 'Logos und Mythos in Theologie und Religionsphilosophie' (1913), in *Gesammelte Schriften*, 2:805–36.
4. 'Rival Methods for the Study of Religion' was translated by Joseph Mow from the first, methodological section of 'Glaube und Ethos der hebräischen Propheten' (1916), in *Gesammelte Schriften* (Tübingen, 1925, reprinted Aalen, 1966), 4:34–8.
5. 'Christianity and the History of Religions' was translated from 'Christentum und Religionsgeschichte' (1897), in *Gesammelte Schriften*, 2:328–63.
6. 'The Dogmatics of the History-of-Religions School' first appeared as 'The Dogmatics of the *Religionsgeschichtliche Schule*,' in the *American Journal of Theology* 17 (January 1913): 1–21. It has been translated by Walter E. Wyman, Jr, in light of Troeltsch's later additions in *Gesammelte Schriften*, 2:500–24.
7. 'The Separation of Church and State and the Teaching of Religion' was translated from 'Die Trennung von Staat und Kirche, der staatliche Religionsunterricht und die theologischen Fakultäten,' in *Heidelberger Akademische Rede* (Tübingen, 1906).
8. 'Faith' was translated by Eugene Peters, revised by Walter F. Bense, from 'Glaube' in *Die Religion in Geschichte und Gegenwart* (Tübingen, 1910), 2:1437–47.

9. 'Faith and History' was translated from 'Glaube und Geschichte' in *Die Religion in Geschichte und Gegenwart* (Tübingen, 1910), 2:1447–57.
10. 'Eschatology' was translated from 'Eschatologie' in *Die Religion in Geschichte und Gegenwart* (Tübingen, 1910), 2:622–32.
11. 'Christian Natural Law' was translate by P. Bon, revised by Walter F. Bense, from 'Das christliche Naturrecht' in *Die Religion in Geschichte und Gegenwart* (Tübingen, 1910), 4:697–704.
12. 'The Dispositional Ethic' was translated by Walter F. Bense from excerpts of 'Luther, der Protestantismus und die moderne Welt,' in *Gesammelte Schriften*, 4:221–4, 226–7. The essay originally was published in *Das Christentum*, vol. 50 of *Wissenschaft und Bildung* (1908).
13. 'Political Ethics and Christianity' was translated from *Politische Ethik und Christentum* (Göttingen, 1904).
14. 'The Social Philosophy of Christianity' was translated by Ernest B. Koenker, revised by Walter F. Bense, from 'Epochen und Typen der Sozialphilosophie des Christentums' (1922), in *Gesammelte Schriften*, 4:122–56.
15. 'The Essence of the Modern Spirit' was translated from 'Das Wesen des modernen Geistes' (1907), in *Gesammelte Schriften*, 4:297–338.
16. 'Modern Philosophy of History' was translated from 'Moderne Geschichtsphilosophie' (1904), in *Gesammelte Schriften*, 2:673–728.
17. 'Stoic-Christian Natural Law and Modern Secular Natural Law' was translated from 'Das stoisch-christliche Naturrecht und das profane Naturrecht' (1911), in *Gesammelte Schriften*, 4:166–91.
18. 'On the Possibility of a Liberal Christianity' was translated by Walter F. Bense from 'Über die Möglichkeit eines freien Christentums' (an address at the Fifth International Congress for Free Christianity and Religious Progress, Berlin, 1910), in *Gesammelte Schriften*, 2:837–62. The translation also appeared in *The Unitarian Universalist Christian* 29.1–2 (1974): 27–38 and a prior translation appeared as 'On the Possibility of a Free Christianity' in *Proceedings and Papers* (London, 1911), 223–49.
19. 'Max Weber' was translated from 'Max Weber' (1920), in *Deutscher Geist und Westeuropa* (Tübingen, 1925; Scientia Verlag, 1966).
20. 'My Books' was translated by Franklin H. Littell, revised by Walter F. Bense, from 'Meine Bücher' (1922), in *Gesammelte Schriften*, 4:3–18.

Introduction

James Luther Adams

'Definition is the soul of actuality.' This aphorism from the pen of Alfred North Whitehead points to a crucial task of being human, the cognitive task of grasping the pulsating actuality that confronts us in our social existence. The aphorism can point also to the vocation of the analyst or historian of culture. For this reason the aphorism is appropriate for understanding a principal concern and achievement of Ernst Troeltsch (1865–1923)—to define certain periods in Western history and especially to define the modern period. For him, then, definition of this sort is the soul of actuality.

At the beginning of his essay on 'The Essence of the Modern Spirit,' Troeltsch asserts that the task of defining a period requires the critical fact-finding of the historian united with the constructive imagination of the philosopher. 'The historian has to become the philosopher and the philosopher a historian.' For the philosopher, he says, the definition of the present epoch is 'the basis and presupposition for his delineation of norms and value judgements in terms of which he must measure the actions of an epoch against itself.' These norms are to be found in history; they are not brought to history by the historian, apart from the fact that he lives in history. Nor do they come from beyond history.

The task, moreover, is not merely an academic task, or merely contemplative. It has a practical goal. Only by means of this task can we 'find the proper basis for actions in relations to our time.' The definition of actuality, then, entails the search for relevant action.

This approach should be seen in the context of Troeltsch's life and development. He was born in 1865 in Augsburg and studied theology at Erlangen, Göttingen (where Albrecht Ritschl was at the height of his fame), and Berlin. In 1894 Troeltsch, at the age of twenty-nine, became professor of theology in Heidelberg, in 1915 he became professor of Philosophy in Berlin, where up to a thousand students attended his lectures. Simultaneously he served in the state legislature in Baden and Berlin. After the war he became Secretary of the Prussian Ministry of Public Worship from 1921 until his death in 1923. He was also a member of the *Reichsrat*. His activities as a citizen reflect in part his practical concerns.

Troeltsch has described his intellectual development in the essay 'My Books.' His reading in the various disciplines related to religion was enormous, as was his literary production—his *Social Teaching of the Christian Churches* (1908) and *The Historical Outlook and Its Problems* (1922) each was a thousand pages in length. Harnack said of his lecturing that 'he attacked an idea from all sides . . . His mind worked like a mighty catapult or like a rotating drum that shakes the object until it is cleansed of all foreign elements and appears in its own character.'[1] Troeltsch himself spoke of his writing style, sometimes difficult for the reader, as 'sailor's biscuit' (hardtack).

Ritschl had attracted a wide following in Protestant countries by his interpretation of the kingdom of God as a kingdom to be built in this world as the fulfilment of human culture. After the death of Ritschl, some scholars of the younger generation became radically critical, for example, of the Ritschlian school's tendentious use of biblical texts and also of its failure to engage in any study of comparative religion. This group became known as the 'history-of-religions school' a term first used polemically against them. (See Troeltsch's essay, 'The Dogmatics of the *Religionsgeschichtliche Schule*,' 1913). For them religion is an independent, universal phenomenon, not to be explained away by psychology or (Marxist) sociology. It exists in specific cults, whose mutual contact and influence often bring about syncretism or synthesis. It does not exist primarily in systems of theology.

According to the history-of-religion school, the dogmatic distinction between natural and revealed religion is no longer possible. Nor is any one religion complete and final, capable of supplanting all others. Through the discipline of comparative religion, one must seek not for the final truth but for analogies and differences between the world religions. Troeltsch in the decade of the 'nineties published numerous studies of psychology and epistemology. By 1897 he was writing on 'Christianity and the History of Religion.' Just before this he became associated with the eminent sociologist Max Weber, then turning his attention also to sociology of religion. In 1900 he began publication of his essays on the nature of history and of historical method, in 1902 publishing *The Absoluteness of Christianity and the History of Religion*. Here he came to grips with the problem of the relation between the historically relative and the substantively absolute, 'the key issue in all philosophy of history.' In 1903 he began to move toward a neo-Kantian position. From 1912 until his death he was concerned primarily with philosophy of history.

The essay on 'The Essence of the Modern Spirit' (1907) touches on so many themes of life-long concern for Troeltsch and is so important as a pioneering effort, that we should consider it more closely here. The essay aims not only to define modern versions of secularism in historical context but also to delineate the consequences for religion and the churches of the crisis presented by secularism.

The crisis issued from a variety of forces, sociological and psychological, but especially from the rise of modern scientific method and the rejection of the supernaturalist claims and sanctions of the churches. It arose also from the discipline of the history of religion, which viewed Christianity as one religion among many. In the essay published here, 'Christianity and the History of Religion' (1897), Troeltsch asserts that 'the rise of a comparative history of religion has shaken the Christian faith more than anything else.' In all of this Troeltsch was in part rejecting fundamental assumptions of his earlier mentor, Albrecht Ritschl.

This revolution had been aborning for two centuries. In Troeltsch's view the modern period did not originate with the Reformation but rather in the Enlightenment. The Lutheran Reformation had closer affinity with the medieval mentality than with the modern. In *Glaubenslehre*, lectures delivered four years after the appearance of the essay on the modern spirit, and published posthumously in 1925, Troeltsch would speak of this change as a shift from heteronomy to autonomy, to be transcended in 'autotheonomy' which does not abrogate autonomy but rather fulfils it. Paul Tillich, adapting these terms, has given them wide currency.

In the spirit of autonomy the modern ideal of humanity replaces the community of faith. Simultaneously the understanding of human nature passes through a radical change. The idea of total depravity is rejected, and the human being is seen as possessing 'an inalienable goodness.' Consequently, there is a new appreciation of the individual personality, 'even of women and children.'

Here Troeltsch sees a variation of a basic motif of the Christian heritage, 'the metaphysics of the person.' From this ethos emerges political individualism with its democratic tendencies and its freedom of association that had been smothered by the church and by political absolutism. But a one-sided interpretation of individualism that lacks a sense of obligation to the community gives rise to capitalism. For its part capitalism with its secularity greatly enhances economic ambition and leads not only to a phenomenal rise in the standard of living but also to a 'colossal practical materialism,' at the same time diminishing the person, reducting it to a cog and producing new forms of dependence reminiscent of the serfdom of earlier periods. Economic individualism, then, counteracts and jeopardizes the democratic thrust of political individualism. Viewing this turbid ebb and flow of historical advance and regress, one is reminded by analogy of W. C. Brownell's comment on Rousseau: 'He thought he was emancipated, he was only unbuttoned.'

This syndrome, it might be observed, has been forcefully depicted in Paul Klee's painting 'Revolution of the Viaduct' (1937). Here we see a viaduct whose arches have broken ranks in such a way that each of the arches walks away by itself on flat feet. Through individualism and independence the pathway to community was destroyed.

But in Troeltsch's view it would be an error to consider individualism as merely a poison. The modern world's great achievements were made possible only by the emancipation of the individual. Yet any ethics whatsoever requires something more, a personal sense of duty and a free community. In short, the individualism postulated by the modern spirit is the criterion by which the modern world must be judged, but this must be an individualism that intensifies the sense of social solidarity to the point of maximum participation of the individual in the highest values of life. In this formulation Troeltsch has expanded what appears in the essay of a decade before, 'Christianity and the History of Religion.' Here he views Christianity, in contrast to the previous period, as 'addressing itself exclusively to the essential inner core of the individual' and leading to 'the firmest and most comprehensive community.' This idea appears as a fundamental definition in Troeltsch's *Social Teaching of the Christian Churches* (1908). The definition of the period, it would seem, requires the definition of earlier periods.

Although he has offered severe criticism of capitalism, Troeltsch does not ask for a new social system. What is needed, he says, is an ethically disciplined individualism that would develop further the elements of greatness and would counteract the dangers with ever-vigilant self-criticism. (These admonitions, of course, were offered before the two world wars and before the advent of the welfare state.)

The idea of individualism, of course, is not the only ingredient of the modern spirit. The rise of science brought with it the social sciences and their critique of tradition. This movement helps to give rise to a specifically modern way of historical thinking, to 'a sixth sense for the apprehending of things.' Not only is tradition severely scrutinized in the search for historical fact. Everything hisorical—sacred as well as secular—is viewed as part of a closely intertwined totality. Everything is seen as related to other events and perspectives. In this sense historical thinking leads to an 'unlimited relativism' that portrays every structure as an individual and special form of the generally human (this view is not to be confused with ethical relativism). Yet no place is left for absolute rational truths and ideals that are the same everywhere. Moreover, everything in the past must find an analogy in the present if it is to be accepted as plausible. One can readily see the devastating effect of this historical way of thinking upon conventional supernaturalist theology with its reliance upon miracle, either historical or psychological. Christianity is not to be isolated from other religions as though it possesses special privilege by reason of its supernatural claims. Troeltsch spells out this contrast in his essay on 'Historical and Dogmatic Method in Theology' (1898).

In this essay Troeltsch set forth his conception of the assumptions of modern historical method. Although the essay deals mainly with contrasting methods in theology, the assumptions regarding method have broader implications than for theology alone. These assumptions figure not only in the present work but also in many of his other writings down to his monumental study on *Historicism and Its Problems* (1922) and his *Historicism and Its Overcoming* published in 1924, the year after his death, and appearing in English translation under the title *Christian Thought: Its History and Application.*

In the essay of 1898 Troeltsch emphasizes three aspects of historical method: the habit of mind associated with historical criticism, the importance of analogy in the study of history, and the correlation existing among all historical events.

The 'historical' habit of mind brings with it the view that in the realm of history only judgements of probability are possible, a view that already had been stressed by Lessing in the eighteenth century. In the sphere of the study of religion this attitude can elicit considerable antagonism and anxiety, for it entails the placing of all traditions under scrutiny and criticism.

Another aspect of the historical habit of mind is the autonomy of the historian in face of traditions and in face of authoritarianism. This conception of autonomy can be traced in part to Kant's identification of Enlightenment with cutting the apron strings of heteronomy.

The sense of probability regarding historical events depends upon the capacity of the historical critic to discern analogy between what happens before one's eyes (or within one) and events under investigation. The observation of analogy between similar events in the past entails the imputing of probability to them. Here again the autonomy of the historian comes into play, for he resolves to adopt the principle of analogy and determines how to apply it. This principle of analogy implies the essential similarity of all historical events as such. No special privilege can attach to any particular event.

So profound have been the influences of this method that Troeltsch concludes that the historical consciousness constitutes the character of our epoch. It had given a body blow to Christianity as a historical religion—historical in the sense that its revelation presupposed certain miraculous events in the past and also in the sense that it purports to interpret the very meaning and goal of history. The body blow was for the Christian churches a traumatic experience, indeed one of the greatest crises in the history of Christianity. Troeltsch held that if Christianity, along with other spheres of culture also drawn into the crisis, could not meet the challenge of the new historical consciousness and of the historical method, it would have to retreat into the stagnant darkness of obscurantism. Troeltsch approached the task of meeting the crisis with the conviction that from the historical method new truth had already become available—witness the contribution of biblical higher criticism, one of the great accomplishments of the nineteenth century (affecting also other spheres of literature). In any event, he had the confidence that truth can heal the wounds it makes.

Nor may Christianity be viewed as a pure entity immune to influences from outside. Here the relation of primitive Christianity to the surrounding world is of crucial historical significance. In the essays on natural law Troeltsch raises the question, What relation has the church to the non-Christian realities and ideals of social life? The answer is that the Christian concept of natural law (not to be confused with laws of nature) as the source of legal and social rules and institutions developed in relation to the system created by Stoicism.

This idea regarding a Stoic-Christian natural law has been set forth by a good number of scholars. Nevertheless, Emil Brunner cannot accept it; for he hold that the European notion of the 'same original right of all human beings' is derived from the Pauline doctrine that 'in faith we are all one in One, Jesus Christ.'[2] It is curious indeed that he holds this faith to be the ground of natural law in Christian history. It is curious also that Brunner does not even mention Troeltsch's view that interpretations of natural law have followed the differentiations between types of religious association, the church, the sect and the mystical orientation.

This typology probably represents the most widely adopted conception of Troeltsch, though Karl Holl's criticism of Troeltsch's presentation of natural law is worth mentioning, because it comes from Ernest Barker, an admirer and translator of Troeltsch. Barker would say that Troeltsch's essay does not sufficiently recognize the role of Roman law in natural law doctrine.[3] Natural law, he says, was a part of Roman law. The Troeltsch essay, 'Ernst Troeltsch and the ideas of Natural Law and Humanity in World Politics,' translated in the Barker volume requires mention here because in it Troeltsch expresses fear for the future of Germany by reason of the Romanticism that glorified individuality and abandoned any idea of natural law. On the one side this Romanticism produced a lofty ethereal ethos; on the other side it produced a brutal realism. We might speak of this as Romanticism on all fours. In either way natural law was abandoned. At the same time individuality, Troeltsch would add, has contributed to historical investigation and the understanding of history, indeed to the development of a historical sense as 'a specific and definite thing.'

This historical sense, however, and the search for values in history cannot suffice. The immanent standard must be found in the religious nature of the human being. For a time, therefore, Troeltsch appealed for an extension of Kant, to what he called 'a religious a priori,' a mystical relatedness linking the finite to the infinite, linking all realities and all values to absolute substance. For this reason Troeltsch can say, 'My own theology is essentially spiritualistic.'

From this mystical basis the a prioris are driven to the metaphysical presupposition of the character of spirit which before all maturing of soul and before all coming to terms with truth and reality posits the spiritual individuality and at the same time the rational universality of human being.

But, as we have seen, more even than this is a stake. From the beginning of his career Troeltsch was in search of the Absolute, the ground of being and meaning and value, the fundamental metaphysical presupposition. H. Richard Niebuhr, who wrote his doctoral dissertation on Troeltsch's philosophy of religion in 1924, in a letter to me in 1935 when I was beginning the study of Troeltsch, wrote that he considered Troeltsch to be a transitional figure, 'the beginner of new movements.' 'He was a great skeptic but one who pointed to the place where the absolute basis might be found.'

Ernst Troeltsch did this because of his fundamental interest in 'the descent of the Absolute into the finite world of sense,' that is, because of his concern for religion in history.

Notes

1. Adolf Harnack, *Erforschetes und Erlebtes* (Giessen: Alfred Topelmann, 1923), 363–4.
2. Emil Brunner, *Justice and the Social Order* (New York: Harper & Brothers, 1945), 34.
3. Ernest Barker, 'Translator's Introduction,' in Otto Gierke, *Natural Law and the Theory of Society* (Cambridge: The University Press, 1950), xxxvi.

PART ONE

Method in Theology and Religion

I

Historical and Dogmatic Method in Theology

In compliance with the kind request of Professor Niebergall and the wishes of the editorial board, I am taking the liberty of adding a few remarks to the essay of this theologian. They are intended to shed additional light on the controversy, and not only to clarify those of my views which he has attacked but also to defend my total position in the philosophy of religion and theology against his strictures. Since Niebergall is essentially espousing the ideas of his teacher, Julius Kaftan, the following remarks also represent my final word in my exchange with that distinguished Berlin theologian and member of the High Consistory.[1] I shall let this be my final word because further discussion would be of little avail in view of the fact that the opposition between us is one of principle.

I have deliberately spoken of my 'theological method.' For our primary concern here involves methodology rather than apologetics or any particular point of dogma. Apparently Niebergall, because of his presuppositions, has not quite perceived this point; for he takes the authoritarian concept of revelation for granted and regards anything beyond Christianity as merely 'natural decor.' He and others who share his view do not regard theology as such as problematical; they see only minor problems that can be patched over, and consequently they assume the same attitude on the part of everyone else. Admittedly, such an attitude has its merits and even a certain practical importance, since it reflects a common need. But it is also possible to take an entirely different approach, starting from basic principles, and my labors have more and more led me to this approach. I have not borrowed 'grounds against our supernaturalism' from any scholar in order then to meet them by my 'view of the history of religion as a continuing revelation.'

For some two hundred years these grounds have been readily available. It was not necessary for me to borrow them. Nor was my starting point the competing claims of various revelations or some 'pantheistic' concept of evolution. Such vistas are fairly obvious and have been treated often enough—however superficially—in theological apologetics. Instead, I have explicitly called attention to the much deeper ground where the disintegration of the Christian world of ideas actually originates. Though related to these other matters, this ground is still relatively independent and in any case absolutely decisive. I am referring to *the historical method as such*, to the problem of 'Christianity and history,' which is to be understood not as the defense of Christianity against particular results of historical criticism but rather as the effect of modern historical methodology on the interpretation of Christianity itself. Once applied to the scientific study of the Bible and church history, the historical method acts as a leaven, transforming everything and ultimately exploding the very form of earlier theological methods. I have clearly indicated that this was the starting point of my labors and I have developed in detail the consequences of this position.

Significantly, my efforts in this direction have made no impression whatever upon Niebergall. He proceeds as though no difficulty at all existed in this connection, and as though, with the admission that the historical context played a conditioning role, all difficulties were solved and the old dogmatic method substantially saved. He is astonishingly insensitive to the consequences flowing from the historical method. In comparison, the older apologists of the eighteenth century and the few rigid supernaturalists of the present may well be found to have attained a deeper insight.

Yet Niebergall's stance is a common one, perhaps more characteristic of contemporary theology than any other. Only particular problems raised by historical criticism are considered; one by one, they are then either rejected or designated as harmless, as the case may be. When Christianity is treated systematically, the historical-critical approach is abandoned. By focusing only on various needs, postulates, claims, theories of knowledge, or other intangible generalities, contemporary theologians attempt to validate the old authoritarian concept of revelation; and with the help of this concept they weave together a tolerable dogmatic system. Exegetes and historians are left to see for themselves how they may authenticate these purely dogmatic postulates in relation to their research. Historians, for their part, generally prefer to confine themselves to the conditioning role of the historical context and leave the theoretical questions to the dogmatists. In this sort of theology one is constantly being shuttled back and forth between the two groups.

In contrast to the foregoing, I wish most emphatically to call attention to what is signified by the historical method, the historical mode of thought, and the historical sense. I am not thinking here of the earlier historiography, which limited its criticsm to particular fragments of history, providing information about interesting foreign lands or accumulating archival material. What I have in mind is the genuine historical scholarship of the present, which involves a definite approach to the whole sphere of culture, constitutes a method of representing the past and the present, and therefore implies some extraordinary consequences. Here we are concerned principally with three essential aspects: the habituation on principle to historical criticism; the importance of analogy; and the mutual interrelation of all historical developments.

The first of these three items indicates that in the realm of history there are only judgements of probability, varying from the highest to the lowest degree, and that consequently an estimate must be made of the degree of probability attaching to any tradition. Accordingly, our overall attitude to the enormous body of material our civilization derives from memory and tradition is fundamentally changed, even when our attitude toward the particular contents of this material has not yet undergone any correction. But the latter, too, is subjected by historical criticism to analysis, correction, and transformation in a thousand ways, with the final result being never more than probably correct.

It is obvious that the application of historical criticism to religious tradition must result in a profound change in one's inward attitude to it and in one's understanding of it. Indeed, such a change has actually taken place. But the operation of historical criticism in this area signifies above all the definitive inclusion of the religious tradition with all traditions that require preliminary critical treatment. If the manner of operation of various traditions is thus shown to be in principle the same, the traditional objects and events (which must first be ascertained critically) will hardly fail to show a corresponding similarity.

The second basic postulate of the historical method is that the instrumentality that makes historical criticism possible is the employment of analogy. Analogous occurrences that we observe both without and within ourselves furnish us with the key to historical criticism. The illusions, distortions, deceptions, myths, and partisanships we see with our own eyes enable us to recognize similar features in the materials of tradition. Agreement with normal, customary, or at least frequently attested happenings and conditions as we have experienced them is the criterion of probability for all events that historical criticism can recognize as having actually or possibly happened. The observation of analogies between similar events in the past provides the possibility of imputing probability to them and of interpreting what is unkown about the one by reference to what is known about the other.

But this omnipotence of analogy implies the similarity (in principle) of all historical events—which does not, of course, mean identity. While leaving all possible room for differences, however, the analogical method always presupposes a common core of similarity that makes the differences comprehensible and empathy possible. Hence, the acceptance of historical criticism entails recognition of the significance of this analogical approach for the investigation of the history of Christianity. Biblical criticism itself is based on analogies to the ways of tradition in which other vestiges of antiquity have come down to us. Similarly, the conditions assumed by historical criticism were in numberless cases ascertainable only through the seeking out of analogies. Jewish and Christian history are thus made analogous to all other history. Actually, fewer and fewer historical 'facts' are regarded as exempt from the exigencies of the analogical principle; many would content themselves with placing Jesus' moral character and the resurrection in this category.

We have already seen that the importance of analogy as a method leveling all historical phenomena rests on the assumption of a basic consistency of the human spirit and its historical manifestations. The consequence of this position is the third basic concept of history, namely, the interaction of all phenomena in the history of civilization. This concept implies that there can be no change at one point without some preceding and consequent change elsewhere, so that all historical happening is knit together in a permanent relationship of correlation, inevitably forming a current in which everything is interconnected and each single event is related to all others. Now, the principles of historical explanation and understanding are implicit in this position. At every point there do indeed emerge unique and autonomous historical forces that, by virtue of our capacity for empathy, we perceive to be related to our common humanity. At the same time, however, these unique forces also stand in a current and context comprehending the totality of events, where we see everything conditioned by everything else so that there is no point within history which is beyond this correlative involvement and mutual influence.

There is no need for us to demonstrate that this approach constitutes the foundation of all principles of historical explanation. The historian's craft combines the art of intuiting the original import of the sources with the discovery of correlative and mutually determinative changes. The historian's ultimate problems arise from the attempt to understand the nature and basis of the whole historical context and to arrive at value judgements regarding its various forms.

The scholarly investigation of the Bible has accordingly become involved with the general political, social, and intellectual history of antiquity, and the investigation and evaluation of Christianity has at last been placed within the framework of the history of religion and culture. The exigencies of their own research have gradually compelled the scholars to elucidate the beginnings of the religion of Israel by analogies from the religions of other Semitic peoples and to relate the profound and original transformation of the religion of Yahweh to the general conditions prevailing in Western Asia, especially to its great catastrophes and its general intellectual horizon. Judaism had to be interpreted by reference to the conditions of the Exile and its institutional reorganization, and its profoundly altered conceptual framework had to be explained in terms of ideas absorbed during the Exile. The rise of Christianity had to be related to the disintegration of Judaism, to the political movements and the apocalyptic ideas of the time; and the establishment of the Christian church had to be studied in the light of the interaction of primitive Christianity with the surrounding world of the Roman empire. Indeed, no comprehensive view can any longer fail to see in the mighty movement of Christianity the culmination of antiquity. Major developments in the Near East and the West prepared the way for this culmination. Very different lines of development finally converged in it.

Now, all these necessities were entailed by the historical method itself, which, once admitted at any one point, necessarily draws everything into its train and weaves together all events into one great web of correlated effects and changes. It is not at all necessary here to adopt the distinctly Hegelian notion of Strauss that the Idea does not like to pour all its fullness into a single individual. No general philosophical theory is required to arrive at this result. The historical method itself, by its use of criticism, analogy, and correlation, produces with irresistible necessity a web of mutually interacting activities of the human spirit, which are never independent and absolute but always interrelated and therefore understandable only within the context of the most comprehensive whole.

In its origin, of course, this method was not independent of general theories. No method is. But the decisive test is the usefulness and fruitfulness of a method, its perfection through application, and its contribution to the achievement of continuity and understanding. No one can deny that wherever the historical method has been applied it has produced surprisingly illuminating results, and that confidence in its ability to illuminate previously obscure areas has been consistently vindicated. Such success is its sole—but wholly sufficient—validation.

Give the historical method an inch and it will take a mile. From a strictly orthodox standpoint, therefore, it seems to bear a certain similarity to the devil. Like the modern natural sciences, it represents a complete revolution in our patterns of thought vis-à-vis antiquity and the Middle Ages. As these sciences imply a new attitude toward nature, so history implies a new attitude toward the human spirit and its productions in the realm of ideas. Everywhere the older absolutistic or dogmatic approach, which regarded particular conditions and ideas as simply 'given' and therefore absolutized them into unchangeable norms, is being supplanted by the historical approach, which regards even those matters that are alleged to be most obviously 'given' and those powers that control the largest number of people as having been produced by the flow of history. Jurisprudence, ethics, sociology, political theory, and aesthetics have been affected to their very depths by the historical approach and have been aligned with historical viewpoints and methods. Whether this historicizing of our entire thinking should be regarded as a boon is not the question here. On this point, Nietzche's brilliant essay, 'On the Use and Abuse of History,' contains observations worth heeding. In any case, we are no longer able to think without this method or contrary to it. All our investigations regarding the nature and goals of the human spirit must be based on it. Goethe's words still apply:

> Those who will not account
> to themselves for the past thirty centuries
>   may continue to live
> in the dark, day-by-day, grossly ignorant.

Thus, the historical method has also penetrated theology, first subtly and piecemeal with all sorts of limitations and reservations, then ever more energetically and comprehensively, with the result that here also it accomplished what it had done everywhere else, namely, a transformation in principle of our entire mode of thought and our whole attitude toward the subject. To be sure, at first only particular results entered the general consciousness, and with them an uncomfortable insecurity. But subconsciously, the fundamental significance of the historical method is all-pervasive, driven by the logic of an inner necessity. The success of the method in the solution of particular problems urges its extension to the whole field, to the way the subject itself is approached. Here again, direction is not given by some theory or system but by the exigencies of the objects of historical investigation, which seem to come alive and are rendered comprehensible as soon as they are approached with the historical method. Those who expressed objections or reservations about it were compelled to retreat step by step until they were reduced to invoking, as a defense, the uncertainties engendered by deficiencies in the sources and the tradition.

The particular views that resulted from the historical treatment of Jewish and Christian religious traditions are not, however, the most decisive aspect of the development, their intrinsic importance notwithstanding. What is crucial are the consequences of the method as such, which in the nature of the case are two. In the first place, historical criticism brings a measure of uncertainty to every single fact and shows that certainty attaches only to its effects upon the present; the historical link between original fact and present influence must remain at least partly obscure. But this is to loosen the connection between religious faith and all particular facts. To be sure, the connection is not broken, but its character is changed. Now it becomes impossible to base religious faith on any single fact: faith and fact are linked by large and broad connections; their relationship is mediate, not direct.

In the second place, these connections between faith and fact are themselves not isolated and unconditioned but are most closely correlated with a much larger historical context; they arise out of this context, they share its substance, and they must be understood in relation to it. It does not follow, however, that the originality of the particular historical fact is thereby denied. What does follow is that its originality is analogous to others emerging from the common context and is neither more nor less mysterious than these. The creative significance of the personages who dominate the great life-complexes need not be denied. But the personages of Judaeo-Christian history are neither more nor less irrational than those of Greek and Persian history.

One implication of the historical method is extremely important. It follows from the univocity and the total interconnection of historical events that their evaluation and judgement no less than their explanation and description must begin with the total context. Although numerous theologians seek to persuade us that the proper starting point is the isolated claim and judgement of the Christian community, no just estimate of Christianity can be formed except by reference to the total context—even as the self-judgement of the Greeks or the Romans cannot be allowed to determine our estimate of their permanent contribution to the human spirit.

Obviously, this is how the historical method works. It relativizes everything, not in the sense that it eliminates every standard of judgement and necessarily ends in a nihilistic skepticism, but rather in the sense that every historical structure and moment can be understood only in relation to others and ultimately to the total context, and that standards of values cannot be derived from isolated events but only from an overview of the historical totality. This relativism and respect for the historical totality belong together, as indeed they are always conjoined in the practical application of the method. This spirit of historical investigation has gradually permeated every facet of historical theology; Christianity, too, must be regarded as an entity to be explained and evaluated in relation to the total context of which it forms a part. Indeed, only the investigations carried out in this spirit have produced authentic historical knowledge; all the animadversions against the historical method have represented only checks upon it or corrections of particular results, but no viable alternative. For these reasons the old dogmatic method has become untenable for anyone who has become historically sensitive. This fact, and it alone, is the starting point of all theories like the one I am proposing. Once employed, the inner logic of the method drives us forward; and all the counter-measures essayed by the theologians to neutralize its effects or to confine them to some limited area have failed, despite eager efforts to demonstrate their validity.

Indeed, no one is in a position to see these consequences more clearly than the biblical scholar, particularly in the concrete work of his speciality. Even someone who is unable to accept any of our theories is bound to be aware, after the discussions of the idea of the kingdom of God or of Jesus' messianic consciousness, that it is impossible to arrive at some supra-historical core with a method that necessarily raised such problems as these and, precisely through them, has advanced our historical understanding. Conversely, one need only survey the enormously complicated apparatus that Zahn has constructed for the purpose of annulling the results of the historical method to become aware that nothing has been accomplished in behalf of his approach; he has merely matched results with results, rather than method with method. Moreover, it will be apparent that his tortuous deductions can scarcely provide a basis for the old naively secure relationship to tradition that was the presupposition of the old dogmatic method.

If this is the situation, only one consequence appears possible. The historical method must be consistently applied. This implies not only recognition of the relative uncertainty of all historical knowledge (and consequently the awareness that the connection of religious belief with particular historical events is only mediate and relative) and the resolute subjection of the Judaeo-Christian tradition to all the consequences of a purely historical method (without fearing or seeking to bypass the results). Most importantly, it implies that Christianity should be seen in its involvement with general history. The scholarly investigation and evaluation of Christianity must begin with the general context of universal history. Now, to apply the historical method to theology with utter, uncompromising consistency means to base theology on the historical method, which is oriented to universal history; and since our concern is with Christianity as both religion and ethic, the method will have to be that of the history of religion (*religionsgeschichtliche Methode*). This idea of a theology based upon the history of religion, which was envisaged from the very beginning of historical criticism (first by the Deists and then in various forms by Lessing, Kant, Herder, Schleiermacher, DeWette, and Hegel, and finally by Baur and Lagarde), I have sought to sketch in my previous works, attempting to give it the form required since the elimination of the rationalistic concept of religion-in-general and of the Hegelian dialectic of the Absolute.

I cannot now enter again into the details. That task will have to wait for a more comprehensive work. I only desire to stress that, although many of these specific studies are important, what is decisive for me is the method. I have no doubt that even a presentation of the Christian life-world based on the method of the history of religion will fail to convince the atheist and the religious skeptic. This is not, however, my concern, which is limited to attempting to satisfy the intellectual need for consistency and uniformity of view and approach. Nor do I doubt that this method—only the details of which are my own—will attract but few followers at first, either on the right or on the left; nor does this fact concern me. What is of primary importance is that the scholar should attain a firm conviction by means of the exposition. I have the greatest confidence, however, that the implication of the historical method will necessarily lead through the present confusion and derangement of biblical studies to its full and resolute application. Only then will the worst of our fears (regarding apologetics) be lifted from our hearts, and we shall be able to behold with greater detachment and freedom the glory of God in history.

The need for a consistency that makes possible such detachment and freedom is bound to lead an increasing number of theologians, or at least people who are intellectually concerned about religion, in the direction indicated. The simple result will be, as I have already written, the following:

> All human religion is rooted in religious intuition or divine revelation, which in specifically religious personalities achieves the power to establish new communities; the faithful subsequently enter into this experience, though with diminished originality. The belief in God contained in this intuition (which is concealed in nature religion at the beginning of religious history, when the religious consciousness takes naturalistic forms) decisively breaks through these limits in the religion of Yahweh—notwithstanding many comparable beginnings elsewhere—and in the preaching of Jesus, which, emerging out of the religion of Yahweh, undergoes an infinitely rich development that was impossible to predict at the outset. But in this development the concern was always with life oriented to faith in the living God and with the interpretation of the particular situation in the light of this faith.

This new method in theology would not be adequately characterized, however, unless I contrasted it with the old method, consistently and authentically interpreted. This comparison is especially necessary in view of the remarks of Niebergall and the theologians close to him, who have claimed this method as their own even though they were not very clear about its essential nature. If the new method is to be termed the history-of-religion method, since its subjects all tradition to criticism first and, where a question of principle is involved, always starts from the total historical reality in order to derive its standards of value from this totality, the older one is to be termed the dogmatic method. It starts from a firm point of origin completely beyond the relativity of historical scholarship and thence arrives at absolutely certain positions that, at best, may subsequently be related to the insights and opinions governing the rest of human life. By its principles this method is absolutely opposed to the historical one. Its essence is that it possesses an authority that, by definition, is separate from the total context of history, not analogous to other happenings, and therefore not subject to historical criticism and the uncertainty attaching to its results. The dogmatic method seeks to commit persons to certain particular facts of history, especially insofar as these attest the authority and destroy all historical analogy to it. The dogmatic method can bring about such a commitment because its facts are not those of ordinary history and hence can be neither established nor demolished by historical criticism; they are safeguarded, rather, by a miraculous transmission and sealed by an inward testimony in the heart.

The dogmatic method accordingly lacks the main features of the method of secular historical scholarship, namely, criticism, analogy, and correlation. Indeed, it combats these features most energetically and admits them, at best, only in regard to the most immaterial details. It cannot abide historical criticism, not because it is narrow-minded but because it cannot suffer the uncertainty of results that is connected with such criticism, and because its facts possess a character that contradicts every critical presupposition—indeed, the very possibility of criticism. The dogmatic method cannot admit analogies or make use of them because it would then have to surrender its own innermost nature, which consists in the denial of any analogical similarity between Christianity and other forms of religious development. It cannot submerge itself in the total historical context because its monopoly on dogmatic truth can be recognized only in its antithesis to this context, in the assertion that its own constitutive causality is 'wholly other.'

To be sure, the dogmatic method also claims to be based upon 'history.' But this is not the ordinary, secular history reconstructed by critical historiography. It is rather a history of salvation (*Heilsgeschichte*), a nexus of saving facts which, as such, are knowable and provable only for the believer. These facts have precisely the opposite characteristics of the facts that secular, critical historians can regard, on the basis of their criteria, as having actually taken place.

When dogmatic apologetics stresses the 'historical' character of Christianity in order to appeal to the secular appreciation of historical and social forces (which generally prevails among us, as over against purely individual efforts and discoveries), this is pure obscurantism. Such apologetics has already caused enough confusion in theology. Today all kinds of things are labeled as 'historical' and as 'facts' which are nothing of the kind, and which ought not to be so labeled, since they are miraculous in nature and can only be apprehended by faith. The miracles of the Judaeo-Christian tradition are often assigned a label that sounds general and obscures their difference from the secular world. This camouflage is dropped only when the discussion has safely passed to the sphere of theology. Even Niebergall has followed this approach quite freely. Yet, it is apparent that genuine dogmatics is poorly served by such a 'historical' force that ultimately is merely fortuitous. It has need, rather, of a history that, by concentrating the necessary absolute truth at one point, sets itself apart from ordinary history, which relativizes all truths by showing their mutual interdependence. To safeguard its own uniqueness, the dogmatic method requires an open rupture with this kind of history: otherwise it would become subject to all of its conditions, the mutual limitations of its phenomena, and the continuing possibility of change.

In all these matters the traditional dogmatic method operates quite consistently and correctly. It claims an authority that is dogmatic rather than historical, intrinsic rather than based on comparison, immutable rather than sharing the conditions of historical existence. It does not seek historical greatness, based on actual strength and influence or on philosophical reflection, but rather a foundation for dogmatic truths, characterized as supernatural by special marks and thus essentially non-historical. Consequently, everything depends on the evident demonstration of this supernatural character that establishes dogma even as it vitiates history. Whether greater emphasis be placed on the internal or the external manifestations or supernaturalism, ultimately, its internal manifestation in the operations of grace always serves to prove the credibility of the external manifestation, which alone vitiates historicity. The miraculous is truly decisive, and, since a miracle confined to the psychological sphere is not sufficiently different from the life of the soul as we encounter it universally in history, such a delicate miracle only becomes useful when solid 'physical' miracles can be deduced from it. Ultimately, everything depends on this external manifestation of supernaturalism. It would be better honestly to take one's stand on it rather than to talk of a 'history' that is not history at all but rather its opposite.

Only this proof by miracle provides the dogmatic method with a firm foundation and a methodological principle. It will be recalled that the historical method issued from the metaphysical assumption that all things, including the activities of the human mind, are totally interconnected; that it achieved autonomy through elaboration; and that it then had yet again to formulate general theories regarding the essence of history and the principles by which it formed its historical judgements. Similarly, the dogmatic method possesses a general metaphysical principle that was originally only rather implicitly present but which became clearly and precisely explicit in the course of its elaboration. Only the proof for the supernatural character of its authority or for the miraculous provides the decisive metaphysical foundation for the dogmatic method, without which it could be regarded as a knife lacking both handle and blade. The division of the domain of history into one area devoid of miracles and subject to the normal working of historical criticism and another area permeated by miracles and accessible to study only through methods based on inner experiences and the humble subjection of reason is the primary theoretical basis of the dogmatic method. The construction of such a concept of history and the establishment of a separate methodology for the history of dogma or the history of salvation, with special conditions independent of ordinary history, is the basic presupposition of the dogmatic method in theology. Consequently, the theological investigations of recent centuries are replete with this special methodology geared to the history of salvation, which vitiates and distorts the methodology of secular history in various ways, and with distinctive Christian theories of knowledge supposedly based either on the principle of ecclesiastical obedience or on regeneration and inner experience. Only fatigue caused by such fruitless apologetics can excuse the astonishing habit of contemporary dogmatists who believe that they are able to pluck fruit without having a tree or who, after cutting a small, dry twig from an old trunk, expect fruit to grow from this twig.

But ultimately the essence of the problem is not exhausted by this great distinction between two realms of history and between two opposite methods corresponding to these realms. For the duality of the realms of history must be derived from a necessary ground both in the nature of God and in human nature. In the final analysis the duality of history is related to a duality in the divine nature. This duality is therefore regarded and maintained by the dogmatic method as the foundational and primary support of its concepts. God is not part of the nexus of interrelated forces continually affecting one another, nor is God involved in every vital movement only as the purposive will that produces the motion of the total system. God is also capable, rather, of extraordinary activities (as compared to regular modes of operation) which break through and abrogate the ordinary operation of the system. Everything depends on this concept of God.

No less fundamental, however, is the concept of humanity necessitating such a distinctive mode of divine operation, that is, the concept of a hereditary sinfulness due to a fall from the regular, normal, and uniform cosmic order and the concept of a salvation that requires a restoration of this order by extraordinary means. These dualistic concepts of the human and the divine are indispensable presuppositions of the dogmatic method with its dualism of two historical methods—one critical and relativistic, operative in secular history; and the other absolute and apodictically certain, appropriate to the history of salvation. Here, too, weariness with the labors of apologetics has induced many modern theologians to neglect or abandon these theories. In particular, the remarkable discovery of the irrelevance of metaphysics to theology has led to a renunciation of the proof of this dualism, even though the dualism itself necessarily continued to be recognized as valid. As though a non-metaphysical theology were not bound to eliminate this dualism and its consequences! The result would be that theology would turn into the phenomenological and historical study of religion, in which the truth-content of the religious phenomenon must first be ascertained; while a new, more cautious, and more limited metaphysics would emerge, characterized by abandonment of the miracle-dualism and based on moral certitude or sensitivity (*Gefühl*).

For the young theologian beginning to study, nothing is more astounding than the contradiction between the alleged indifference of such fundamental concepts as God, the primal state, original sin, and miracles, on the one hand, and the working assumption of their entire validity (except for some accommodating concessions regarding the influence of the pre-modern worldview), on the other. One can become accustomed to anything and make a virtue out of every necessity; but with any sense for clarity, consistency, and intellectual precision, one can hardly resign oneself to such a virtue with equanimity. For this reason most young theologians will ultimately return to the old metaphysical bases of the dogmatic method; from all their studies they will only retain the impression that the proof of these bases is a matter of no particular importance. The dogmatic method is thus pushed forward by an inner necessity towards the type of theology suggested above, just as the historical method necessarily leads to a theology that is fundamentally based on the history of religion.

It is not my intention to develop in detail the scope of the dogmatic method, but only to sketch it in its essence and to contrast it with the historical method. One might term the old method 'Catholic' because it was created by Catholic theologians and received its classic formulation from them; and one might term the new method 'Protestant' because in the last analysis it grew out of the Protestant criticism of the Catholic doctrine of authority. Yet, on the one hand, the old method is so deeply imbedded in the inclinations of human nature to dogmatism and is so necessary a product of historically unsophisticated periods that it would not make sense to term this method specifically Catholic; for it is also employed in Jewish and Muslim theology. On the other hand, Protestant historical criticism was only partial and apologetic in intent; Protestantism arose in an era that was by no means historical in its outlook. It was not until the Enlightenment that an essentially historical outlook emerged; the allegedly unhistorical outlook of the Enlightenment belongs to the realm of legend. To be sure, the Enlightenment began by critically emancipating itself from the recognized authorities and thus its first task was to put everything on one level. But its leveling efforts immediately led to a new task, the task of differentiation and graduation, which required that all the phenomena dealt with be first transformed into purely historical ones. In this transitional stage the Enlightenment made supernatural dogmatism, in part, rational; and where this was not possible, it worked out a new worldview based on history. The latter, of course, had to weave together historical data and materials of general validity, and is entitled to be termed 'historical' only a posteriori. At this very point the difference between the two methods becomes plain.

Thus, the only appropriate terms are the *dogmatic* and the *historical* method. Each has its own foundation and problems; each is consistent within itself. My concern, however, is not to detail the particular problems of each, but only, because of their respective consistencies, to insist on their incompatibility. With this insistence, the main objective of this paper is attained. I only wish to add a few remarks concerning my position in this methodological controversy. These comments will serve to defend my position against some objections of Niebergall and, incidentally, to illuminate the distorted manner in which he himself espouses the dogmatic method.

His first objection to my method is on the score of its difficulty and the subjective conditions of its implementation. It goes without saying that the production of a scale of values among the great cultural types (*Geistestypen*) of history depends on subjective judgements and can never be fully conclusive. I have always stressed this point explicitly. Nevertheless, I am convinced that, given a sharp and penetrating analysis of the nature of these types, people who are seriously concerned about ethical and religious matters—neither frivolous nor trying to be merely clever but really in earnest about finding meaning in life—may arrive at a relative degree of consensus. This conviction is based on a belief that is both religious and ethical, namely, that ultimately the essential uniformity of human nature provides a foundation for consensus in recognizing supreme standards of value and that, because of this foundation, the consensus will prevail. As for Niebergall's strictures concerning the difficulties of implementing my approach, I can say only that no amount of emphasis upon the difficulties in a method that is inherently possible can justify the adoption of a method that is inherently impossible. It only challenges us to greater devotion to the task.

Niebergall also criticizes me for connecting the scale of values I have constructed with a metaphysics of history that makes it possible to deduce values, in a logically progressive and increasingly profound sequence, from the nature of the human spirit or rather from its transcendent ground as it operates in the spirit. I am unable here to consider in detail his remarks about intellectualism and practical reason, which are completely incomprehensible to me in their present form. I only note that no one who considers history to be pure chaos will undertake to derive a scale of values from it by the exercise of reason. For the deduction of such a scale of values it is indispensable to believe in reason as operative in history and as progressively revealing itself. This belief, too, is primarily of ethical and religious origin; but it is a belief that is confirmed, in my judgement, by the deepening of personal life which is constantly taking place in history.

The third objection adduced by Niebergall is the danger of self-deception to which one is exposed in such a production of a scale of values. I do not intend to inquire whether the danger resulting from the application of the historical approach is greater than that arising from the special apologetic conditions of the dogmatic method, geared as it is to the history of salvation, whose practitioners feel no obligation to warn against such a hazard. The point I would emphasize, rather, is that I do not regard the danger as wholly insuperable. Actually, one does not always endeavor to demonstrate a preconceived thesis with all the devices of cunning, yet with the greatest possible appearance of impartiality, as many theologians believe who are absolutely unable to think otherwise. In such an intricately complex and extremely individualistic culture as our own, it is often difficult to know where to take one's stand; and it is actually possible, without any preconceived preference for Christianity, to desire to orient oneself through a comparative survey. If as a consequence one reaches the judgement that Christianity is the highest ethical and religious force, this result need not at all have been antecedently present—not even where there was a relative appreciation for Christianity from the outset, such as any serious person naturally would feel. The ultimate avowal of Christianity as the supreme religious force of history, which is the outcome for me, is something quite different from a relative and preliminary appreciation that is connected, moreover, with a serious intent not necessarily to commit oneself to this initial and immediate judgement.

Finally, Niebergall attacks me for inconsistency inasmuch as I, while ostensibly oriented to historical relativism, yet emerge at the end with the recognition of the 'absoluteness' of Christianity, a conclusion that in his judgement is quite impossible for me. It must be admitted that Niebergall has here pointed correctly to vacillations not only in my mode of expression but also in my way of thinking as they appear in various essays spread over several years. It would have been possible for him to observe that I have actually tended to draw the consequences of the historical method ever more strictly and that I have finally come to characterize the term 'absoluteness' as only a rationalized and disguised vestige of the dogmatic method. I believe, in fact, that the term is not terribly important—but only because its opposite, the much-maligned 'relativism,' is not so important to me as it would appear to be from the dogmatic point of view. Indeed, I would say that it is the essence of my view that it thoroughly combats historical relativism, which is the consequence of the historical method only within an atheistic or a religiously skeptical framework. Moreover, my view seeks to overcome this relativism through the conception of history as a disclosure of the divine reason.

It is here that we see the undeniable merits of the Hegelian doctrine, which needs only to be freed of its metaphysics of the absolute, its dialectic of opposites, and its specifically logical conception of religion. The point is that history is not a chaos but issues from unitary forces and aspires towards a unitary goal. For the believer in religion and ethics, history is an orderly sequence in which the essential truth and profundity of the human spirit rise from its transcendent ground— not without struggle and error, but with the necessary consistency of a development that has had a normal beginning. The contrasts are rather superficial and incidental. In essence, the differences among the great historical structures are not very great, and the actual ideas and values in the world are infinitely rarer than is supposed, although their manifestations and ramifications are innumerable. With the great idealists, I believe that in this apparent chaos the divine depth of the human spirit reveals itself from different directions, and that the belief in God, provided only that it is actually belief in God and not self-seeking magic, is at its core identical in all its forms. Moreover, I hold that this belief in God, by the internal consistency of the divine force that empowers it, continues to increase in energy and depth to the degree permitted by the original tie of the human spirit to nature.

Only at one point was this limitation broken through. This point, however, was located at the center of great contemporary and subsequent religious developments, namely, in the religion of the prophets of Israel and in the person of Jesus. Here a God distinct from nature produced a personality superior to nature with eternally transcendent goals and the willpower to change the world. Here a religious power manifests itself, which to anyone sensitive enough to catch its echo in one's own soul, seems to be the conclusion of all previous religious movements and the starting point of a new phase in the history of religion, in which nothing has yet emerged. Indeed, even for us today it is unthinkable that something higher should emerge, no matter how many new forms and combinations this purely inward and personal belief in God may yet enter. Clearly, this position constitutes neither dogmatic absolutism nor the confrontation of historical scholarship by Christianity, nor the exemption of Christianity from the flux, the conditioning, and the mutability of history. But it provides a stopping point that is attainable through a historical mode of thought geared to the philosophy of history, and that is adequate for the religious person. More we do not need, and more we cannot achieve. Here we find the religious support for our life and thought that has constituted the dynamic center of our European civilization, and which remains a vital power capable of further development.

It is true that the relationship of this European religion to the religions of the Orient is still a great and dark question for the future. But insofar as we recognize in the transcendence of nature, which constitutes the faith of the prophets, and in the active and lively love of God and humanity which constitutes the faith of Jesus, the decisive and elevating forces of religion, we can persevere in our traditional faith and leave further developments to the future. In this connection also, Niebergall has measured me by needs that are taken for granted by him. He has not put himself into a religious mood that really finds its rest and support in such thoughts. To his opinion that the reader of my work has to ride through a very cold land and then pass through a dark tunnel before emerging into the smiling fields of home, I might reply that the distant land is not so cold, the tunnel not so dark, nor the ultimate point of arrival so inviting as he supposes.

For my part, I have considerable misgivings about the position of Niebergall. Here again I shall forgo consideration of the epistemological explanations with which he supports his position and the formulation of which he regards as constituting the major part of difference from my own work. These matters are not crucial for the problem as a whole. For if the question to be decided is whether the scale of values in the spiritual life is to be derived from a philosophy of history or from an authoritarian judgement based on supernatural considerations, then it is quite pointless to stress factors of sentiment and will, which naturally enter into every value judgement. One can never base authoritarian supernaturalism on the practical character of all values, since this same practical character applies also to non-Christian and non-religious values. Rather, we are dealing exclusively with the basis of the authority that the dogmatic method requires as its starting point.

In this regard there is no doubt that Niebergall agrees with the intentions of the traditional dogmatic method. He desires the doctrine of a supernaturalistic authority: not a 'historical absolute but one that is dogmatic and apologetic,' an 'absolute apart from and opposed to the history of religion'; that is, apart from and opposed to the views of historical criticism in general. He wants a 'realm lying beyond the history of religion'; that is, a realm lying quite beyond secular history. He is concerned with 'absoluteness as an immediate derivation from God' in contrast to the merely mediate derivation from God of ordinary history and the history of non-Christian religions, which is based on a 'merely natural endowment.' He conceives of the absolute as a 'faith that absolute values have been supernaturally revealed at one point in history'; that is, values having an absoluteness that is primarily authenticated by their supernatural mode of revelation. Despite all Niebergall's talk about his respect for history and the practical motivation of all faith, one must not permit oneself to be deceived: what he wants is outside of and contrary to history. He wants a history of a higher order, which has different presuppositions from ordinary history and events that are distinguishable by criteria not provided by ordinary history. When he speaks of the 'autonomy of Christianity,' 'practical motivation,' or 'historical character,' such terms are euphemisms for the miraculous, which theologians of his type prefer not to call by its correct name.

The intentions of Niebergall are never fulfilled, however. His mode of thought falls far short of what he aspires to achieve, namely, a 'pure and bright supernaturalism.' One hears next to nothing from Niebergall concerning a consistent foundation for supernaturalism in the concept of God, the primal state, the Fall, and redemption. His work contains only pitiful vestiges of any other demonstration of supernaturalism actually derived from history, that is, from the miraculous character of sacred history. He intends to establish the biblical revelation as his starting point, a priori authentic and normative for his approach to history. This intention, which he emphatically proclaims, is constantly being crossed, however, by the contrary procedure of starting from general history and searching it for the possible disclosure of absolute values corresponding to human need. He acts as though he knew nothing of Christianity and were seeking, as a universal human postulate, for some absolute, redemptive revelation. From this stance he discovers the historical 'fact' of Christianity and rejoices to find it satisfying all his requirements. The historical mode of thought has here produced a deep impression after all. What should have been the starting point of the dogmatist now appears as the contingent result of a search of history. The result has been that, instead of being deduced from the concept of God and Adam's fall, theology is being authenticated by reference to human needs. Everything now depends on the legitimacy of these needs and the fact of their satisfaction, which is no more automatically guaranteed for these needs than for any others.

I do not wish to expatiate further upon these needs—the need (ostensibly demonstrated by Kant) of theoretical doubt for supernatural revelation, or the need of morality for authority, for a guarantee of victory, and for the atonement of sins. All these needs may be legitimate, but it cannot be denied that these needs themselves are in the first instance purely historical forms which do not lead beyond history. Of greater importance is the question why the satisfaction of these needs should be regarded as taking place in Christianity in an absolute manner. Here again the emphasis is not placed upon an inner necessity that enables Christianity alone to satisfy these needs, but recourse is taken—with an apparent objectivity that is very popular in contemporary theology—to the purely factual 'claim' of Christianity. Here we meet the same dialectical comedy as before. One comes upon the 'historical fact' of a tremendous claim and appears completely surprised by this fact, as though it were something astounding and overwhelming. The claim of Christianity is made into its essence, and the erstwhile theology of miracle now becomes a theology of claim. Christianity claims to be absolute truth and redemption. Without recognition of this claim Christianity is unattainable. But the assertion of claims, of course, no more proves their validity than the existence of needs guarantees their satisfaction— all the less so as various religions advance competing claims that require decision on the basis of some kind of criterion. In all of these expositions a dread of the real roots of the dogmatic method and a superficial accommodation to purely historical arguments are the only operative factors. Actually existing needs and claims are said to form the basis of the theory. But needs and claims are themselves products of history. They are to be understood in their historical context, to be illuminated, and possibly to be corrected, as have a hundred other needs and claims. By no means do needs and claims indicate some higher reality removed from historical relativity and criticism.

Thus everything depends on whether these needs are satisfied not merely by a claim but by a higher reality. In the last analysis Niebergall's views necessarily affirm this position. But how feeble and cautious is his assertion of a higher supernatural reality and causality as opposed to secular history! He stresses 'supernaturalism' and 'immediacy' as appropriate to revelation, in order to support a distinctive causality that would give special status to Christianity as the means-oriented natural causality would not. But even this emphasis is expressed only in the most general terms. To be absolute, 'Christianity must be based upon a special revelation that must somehow be made comprehensible as revelation.' This 'somehow' is typical of contemporary theology, which in its refinement disdains the concerns of the older apologetics and disposes of them 'somehow.' If one seeks clues to this 'somehow' in Niebergall, only one attempt at more precise definition will be found, along with the crude manipulation of some famous models. The personality of Jesus must be such as to break through the ordinary historical causality. But even in this context Niebergall speaks primarily of the mysterious and underivable essence of the personality, as though the same observations were not true of every personality.

> Here in the ground of the soul there remains a gap in the causal nexus which is the greater, the more unique and developed is the personality. It is this gap that provides full scope for the operation of a higher power. We believe that the revelation that we religiously apprehend and revere sets in at this point, which resists all analysis . . . Starting with Jesus, the reservoir of revelation fed both from heaven and by terrestrial streams, we proceed upwards along the course of these tributaries.

And at another point he says, 'We resolve to attribute beneficent powers that come to our assistance in deepest need to the intervention of God, because we know of no earthly source from which they could have been derived.'

What should one say to such remarks? Should one admire the modesty of a theology that has come to the point of finding its foundation ultimately in a gap? Or should one stress the uncertainty with which even this gap is asserted, in view of the fact that no clear distinction is made between the gaps in the causal nexus which characterize the personal life of ordinary human beings and the particular gap within the personality of Jesus, which is the only one that concerns us at this point? I think that one can only say that such a doctrine of authority and revelation has been deeply affected by the spirit of historical criticism, analogy, and relativity. Indeed, it has been almost destroyed. All that remain are some pathetic and quite general claims. In this respect, the older dogmatic doctrine was better and more understandable.

This judgement is made entirely from a scholarly perspective and refers only to the consistency of the ideas. Practically, such an enervation and edentulation of the old authoritarian doctrine may be a very good thing. In practical life, it is impossible to get along without such mediating positions; and in church affairs, the mediating groups may constitute a very desirable transitional form. In closing these observations, we may stress that *sub specie aeternitatis* all the differences we have noted may be quite unimportant. Consequently, they need not excessively disunite us in our earthly pilgrimage.

Note

1. See my essays 'Die Selbständigkeit der Religion' and 'Geschichte und Metaphysik' in *Zeitschrift für Theologie und Kirche*; as well as Kaftan's essay 'Die Selbstandigkeit des Christentums,' by which he means its supernatural revelation and redemptive power.

2

On the Question of the Religious A Priori

In the *Zeitschrift für Religion und Geisteskultur*, Paul Spiess has discussed my theories pertaining to the philosophy of religion and especially my concept of the religious a priori. Occupied as I am just now with something completely different, namely, purely historical studies, I can only pursue to a limited extent the thoughts suggested by this penetrating and praiseworthy critique. So a few words must suffice. Now, the nature of the objections compels me to speak of the special character of my work inasmuch as its results are determined by a combination of different lines of interests that is not widespread among systematic and dogmatic theologians, but that is nevertheless more than a juxtaposition of accidental personal preferences. In my work, as in that of of my teacher Dilthey, the historical and philosophical tendencies of the time meet; but I would like to attain stronger positions than did Dilthey. This desire has pointed me in the direction of transcendentalism and the attempt by means of it to satisfy the claims of both history and philosophy.

The essential character of my work has been its balancing of history and systematic interests, and I have always found the one to a great degree furthered by the other. My historical interests have led me to recognize the interwovenness of all human events, of the religious and the non-religious, of the Christian and the non-Christian. In view of the actual course and connection of things, it is quite impossible to ascribe to the religious life any other mode of generation or actualization than to the life of the spirit in general, with which the religious life is endlessly intertwined. Above all, it is quite impossible to show that causes operate within Christianity in a manner different from that which prevails outside Christianity. On the one hand, this axiom, basic to Christianity's self-perception until now, has crumbled under the impact of documents and philological evidence alone, without any help from speculation. But on the other hand, in the light of the determination of character that takes place under the impact of one's own religious feelings and especially under the influence of a Christian environment, it is impossible to relinquish this whole area to a mere psychologism that would derive the determination of character solely from variations in the psychical development that are connected with the environment. For the recognition of this principle would also involve the surrender of the ideal worlds of ethics, aesthetics, and pure science to the associations, variations, and transformations of the most elementary psychical properties. Such a surrender calls forth the protest of the religious feeling and of the whole self-understanding of reason with all its ideal values—values which indeed ultimately stand or fall with religion, that is, with the certainty of an absolutely rational ground of things. Thus there arises for the religious consciousness, as for the other rational functions, the problem of simultaneously recognizing, differentiating, and relating the element that is historically, psychologically, and causally determined, and the productive element that engenders valid truth by drawing upon an inner necessity.

This is the way I formulated the problem. At the same time, I think that this is the way in which the problem is posed by today's general intellectual situation, where cognitive triumphs are attained by historicizing, psychologizing, and relativizing everything actual. Yet, this very process cuts off our access to all that is normative and objective, and therefore leads to an increasing yearning for the absolute—precisely for religion. It is this present general question of life (*Lebensfrage*) which occupies me rather than the need somehow to link systematic theology to the methods of science (*Wissenschaft*) as a whole and to give it equal standing with the other disciplines. Today's systematic theology is so securely bound up with great ecclesiastical corporations, political powers, and mass instincts that it does not need to inquire at length about scientific methods and contacts with general thought, just as, conversely, no one in scientific circles pays attention to systematic theology. Contacts of systematic theology with 'science,' moreover, are of a very precarious nature. Since 'science' has no uniform methods, as soon as contact is established with one group, it is lost with another. For the pure psychologist and positivist, my theory of religion is just as grossly superstitious as the papal encyclical. Consequently, one becomes more and more indifferent to opposing philosophical schools of thought, and searches solely for ways out of the pressing difficulties. At one point only in contact with today's scientific consciousness of the necessary and possible, namely, with respect to the irrefutably given uniformity and homogeneity of human events. Herein lies the only contact with the scientific conscious- ness of the present that I am demanding and, indeed, establishing.

This whole formulation of the problem, moreover, is not that of 'science' in general but of the school in modern thought that seeks to do equal justice to both the causal-psychological and the productive- rational elements. Here Spiess rightly recognizes the approach of the Neo-Kantian school. This implies that I seek a solution of the problem in the direction of an explanation of the relationship between psychology and epistemology, and that, in the sphere of religion as well, I am led to the concept of the a priori, since epistemology has its essence precisely in the demonstration of a productive capacity of positing valid insights, a capacity that can only be analyzed, not psychologically derived. The concept of the religious a priori must, therefore, be considered in its twofold meaning: on the one hand, as the expression of the autonomy of reason, and on the other, as the universally necessary which distinguishes reason from what is variable and relative and can only be grasped psychologically. In the first case, our concept becomes a formula for the dualism between the rationally necessary and the merely factually given. In the second, it becomes a means of scholarly communication about cultural values. Such communication takes place whenever an objective cultural value is referred to a universal principle permeating the individual cases as their a priori and contained in them. The result, then, is a system of objective values or of ethics that develops the impulse towards the valid and obligatory contained in history into a system.

Now Spiess correctly notes that this application of the a priori to the religious consciousness is something different from the fundamental usage of Kant himself, where the a priori refers to theoretical reason, that is, to reason apprehending experience in the manner of the natural sciences. This theoretical reason denotes the unifying and synthesizing function of science, which is operative in the perception of time and space and in the causal understanding of reality. This is, however, in no sense the exclusive meaning of the a priori in Kant. He also recognizes an a priori in ethical, religious, and teleologic-aesthetic reason. Here, of course, the term does not denote the synthesizing and unifying function of science, but rather the rationally necessary and autonomous consideration and evaluation of the real from ethical, religious, and teleologic-aesthetic points of view. These latter types of a priori have their synthetic function, not as activities of scientific apprehension, but as elements in the formation of a unified personality that radiates out of a necessary rational core. Hence I feel justified, in aligning myself with this understanding of the Kantian a priori, to invoke his authority, even though it is incontestable that this constitutes a modification of his original concept of the a priori. Kant himself effected this modification. That certain groups of modern Neo-Kantians desire to allow as normative only the former a priori, dismissing the latter as a theological and dualistic survival, is due to a naturalistic onesidedness. The latter a priori is an essential and fundamental Kantian idea.

Now, admittedly, I go more than a little beyond Kant in this second understanding of the a priori. By stressing its synthetic function in the formation of a unified personality, and by deriving this unified personality from a rational core that lies behind the working of the soul and its foundational unity, I arrive at the metaphysic of the noumenal character. Spiess rightly recognizes here an approximation to Fichte and Schleiermacher. And, he might have alluded to Eucken and Siebeck, whose position is the same. Such a continuation and development of this idea appears to me to be unavoidable and necessary if one wishes to go beyond the cautious type of criticism that does not articulate either its presuppositions or its consequences and that dedicates itself solely to analysis. Kant's criticism could afford to restrict itself to analysis; its merit consists in having demonstrated the marvelous character of reason. The metaphysical presuppositions and consequences implied in it, however, cannot for long remain obscure. They can be put aside temporarily, but they cannot be ignored forever. They are confirmed by the independent demonstration of the a priori nature of reason, but they require further treatment. Kant's position has a metaphysical setting, a modified monadology. This presupposition is bound to reveal itself when one proceeds from the theory of experience, the understanding of causality, and an anti-utilitarian ethic to the foundation and development of a philosophy of culture.

My method of attacking the problem is, thus, correctly described by Spiess. He also rightly recognizes the difficulties which follow from it, even though in points of detail there are some misunderstandings and improperly drawn conclusions, which I feel justified in rejecting. Yet, I grant the main point: there are essential and serious difficulties inherent in my approach. But this concession is not fatal. The other possible methods have likewise organic and, in my opinion, still greater difficulties. Pure psychologism dissolves every concept of validity by portraying its origin as causally necessary and thereby ultimately destroys all validity whatsoever, even that of thought itself, to which psychologism, after all, cannot avoid being indebted for its own existence. Dogmatic supernaturalism cannot separate the divine revealedness of its propositions from the merely natural attainments of the human mind, nor can it form any conception of the process of divine communication. It destroys, furthermore, by a miracle-apologetics that gives rise to insuperable doubts, the peculiar strength that derives from certainty—a certainty that is absolute because extra-mundane and supra-human. We cannot adopt either of these alternative positions. Hence, I will not allow the difficulties inherent in my own approach to prevent me from pursuing it further. In its equal recognition of what is psychological, causal, factual, and given and what is critical, valid, autonomous, and necessary, it seems to me at least to have made the correct basic assumptions, assumptions corresponding to all real experience. Psychologism will not do; it is essentially contradictory and superficial. Supernaturalism will not do, either; it is the transparent absolutizing of a given historical element. Hence, criticism (*Kritizismus*) will need to do. Its approach at least takes into account all of the interests of genuine knowledge.

Now Spiess has formulated some of the difficulties arising from my approach to the problem and has presented these as criticisms. He appears to view Herrmann's position as alleviating these difficulties. I shall reply to his criticisms one by one with the briefest possible answers. A detailed philosophy of religion would be required to answer them definitively.

(1) Spiess raises the question of how it is possible to extract that which is valid and normative from the psychological and historical. I readily admit that this is the real difficulty in the 'critical' approach to the problem. But this is at the same time the basic difficulty of all thought whatsoever. When is a thought no longer something merely given, a product of nature, but rather an autonomous positing of the self out of a purely inward necessity? This question is difficult enough to answer theoretically; it is more difficult still with reference to the values and contents of culture. And yet no one who really understands logic questions the pure autonomy of logic, in the first case. Similarly, in the case of the contents of culture, no one has a right to question the principle by which they come into being according to their own autonomous laws (*Selbstgesetzgebung*), even if it is not possible in all particular cases to explicate the rational content with certainty and in complete independence from the psychological starting point. The

task remains from a survey of the wealth of historical values, by an hypothetical emancipation from that which is merely culturally conditioned, to acquire free insight into what is valid, stemming from the a priori of reason. Such an insight will be initially attainable only by recourse to the peculiar sense of evidence (*Evidenzgefühl*) that is the psychological concomitant of all intuitive penetrations into the realm of the valid that may finally be attained. This sense is admittedly subject to error and is threatened by relativism due to its dependence (*Haftung*) upon extremely varied types of knowledge. Practically, all one can do is to make clear to oneself, on the basis of serious comparison, deliberation, and absorption, the common thrust of these values, to enter into this thrust, and to think of particular values as approximations to an objective whose general direction is known, even though its ultimate goal is not known. It is an act of the will—not an arbitrary whim but a fully considered decision—that dares to believe that the right path has been found. This act is indirectly confirmed by the possibility it affords of interpreting life by reference to this objective. The difficult problem of the absolute, which is involved here—a problem that I have not ceased to think about since I wrote my book on the subject—cannot be further explicated here. But I believe that here also nothing is theoretically feasible beyond what is done in practice. Here the will that has become certain that its movement is correctly oriented decides by grasping what it recognizes as the truth. It can present no further theoretical proof for the correctness of its material conviction. Such a proof—were it possible—would have been found long ago.

(2) Spiess feels that the benignity of the religious phenomenon is not so easy to establish, and that, moreover, the whole psychological basis of the undertaking is questionable. I do not doubt in the least that here again great difficulties are present. But unless one is willing to dissolve the religious phenomenon into a number of purely non-religious elements and to see 'the religious' only in this chance combination—a view of 'the religious' which every religious feeling will resist as erroneous—or else to take refuge in a supernatural ecclesiastical authority that provides whatever is essential for Christianity without necessarily interesting itself in anything non-Christian, one is bound to believe that analysis will succeed in finding a universal characterization of the religious consciousness. Everything depends upon how the analysis is actually carried out, and I am not about to undertake its execution here.

(3) Spiess maintains that in all attempts to derive the religious phenomenon from an a priori that is effective in, or contained in, this

phenomenon, nothing has been demonstrated concerning the truth and validity of the religious consciousness. That is certainly true. These attempts only insure against the dissolution of the religious into the stream of psychological forces, out of which the religious would emerge solely as a product and not as a normative principle that posits requirements of its own. The validity of the ethical is no more demonstrable than that of the aesthetic, or perhaps even that of the logical. It suffices if the delusion is averted that science must analyze these functions as lacking substance and autonomy, as products of the struggle for existence and of the most elemental activities, in fine, as great human self-deceptions. The validity of each of these functions is not subject to proof because it is not derived from something superior, something more certain. It can only be acted upon, clarified, and purified in being put into practice. The certitude of their validity is not derived from any science. It is enough if these functions are able to protect themselves from destruction through the supposed consequences of science, by showing that science cannot destroy the spontaneous creative power of reason upon which science itself, after all, rests.

(4) Spiess objects to my combining the a priori with the concretely psychological to form an irrational unity of life. He maintains that religion would then no longer be distinguished from ethics, art, and science, in which a similar irrational process of combining takes place. I would not deny that. To be sure, these disciplines share a formal, mysterious character; in its act of coming into being, religion is neither more nor less of a mystery than those other functions, which are indeed mysterious enough and whose Kantian interpretation, therefore, is regarded by the pure psychologists and positivists as a superstitious, dualistic romanticism. But Spiess goes on to derive from the fact that they share a formal, mysterious character—which I concede—the conclusion that the a priori is the same in each case. And since he insists on seeing in the a priori only the synthetic unifying function that makes an empirical science possible, he concludes that the religious a priori coincides with the scientific a priori, that religion coincides with scientific understanding, and that there is, in effect, nothing uniquely specific of the religious consciousness. This is one of those deductions that I believe I am justified in rejecting, since I have already stressed the difference between the a priori of science and that of the ethical, religious, and aesthetic methods of appraising the world (*Weltbeurteilungsweisen*), and since I am by no means limited to the a priori defined by the critique of theoretical reason. If in all cases I term it 'rational,' this very word 'rational' has several shades of

meaning. It describes the nature of an ordering, evaluation, and creation of the concretely real which flows out of what is universally valid. It can be something very different in science, ethics, religion, and art. But even the latter are genuine outflowings of reason, the power working from the absolute and the unified, as opposed to the psychological flux which is united by mere continuity, apart from which it is atomistically and relativistically divided. I do not share the dread of the word 'rational' of so many theologians. It signifies autonomous validity and allows a distinction between theoretical and non-theoretical validity.

(5) Spiess rightly emphasizes the fact that in my past writing there arises above all the question of a more exact explication of the relationship between the a priori and concrete psychological actuality. It is the question that must always be asked of the Kantian approach to the problem; it is inextricably bound up with the problem of how mutually determining elements—elements separated in analysis and criticism but nevertheless always together in the consciousness—are to be reunited. To this one can no longer answer with mere criticism and analysis, since criticism has its merit precisely in separating the a priori from, and affirming it against, mere psychologism. This affirmation could only be attained through criticism; that is, through a separation. But it is precisely in such a separation that the theory has its first and most important effect, that of maintaining the autonomy of reason over against all mere physical and psychological causality and over against all mere pragmatic relativism. And since the basic interest of philsophy in the history of culture focuses upon this separation, criticism, even in its conceptually conditioned limitation, performs a decisive and basic function (*Tat*), the liberating effect of which is indeed recognized in the philosophy of religion as opposed to mere history of religion or psychology of religion.

But, admittedly, the problem of reintegration remains. Kant himself posed this problem with vigor only in the realms of theoretical and teleological-aesthetic reason. In the case of moral philosophy and philosophy of religion there was a certain vacillation, as I think I have shown in my book on Kant. Sometimes he would take on this task of reintegration; at other times he would transform the a priori into natural truth contents, like the law of nature or natural religion. In the former case he approached Hegelian ideas; in the latter he remained under the spell of the Enlightenment. There were of course good reasons why Kant did not go further here. If criticism was to remain criticism, no more could be done. For criticism can indeed analytically dissect the content of consciousness and can comprehend the separated functions in their activity. It cannot, however, investigate how this content comes into being in the first place; nor can it show how an understanding of its real, basic nature is the result only of an insight into the very process of its coming into being. Here it is necessary to enter the realm of metaphysics, as post-Kantian specul.tion has done with good reason. This step has remained unavˀidable to this day, even though, to begin with, one has every reason to isolate the work of criticism and to engage in it purely for its own sake. I myself have not hitherto proceeded beyond the work of criticism but have always recognized that it is precisely the basic question of the interrelation of the productive rational with the concrete-psychological element which leads into metaphysics. I can suggest only briefly the solution that I envisage.

The unconditioned nature of every a priori, and the continuity and logical nature of the historical forms of reason, appear to point to an active presence of the absolute spirit in the realm of the finite, to an activity of the universe, as Schleiermacher says, in individual souls. This active presence is the real ground of every a priori and of all movement that is to be understood from the standpoint of a philosophy of history. But it does not immediately coincide with the activity of the finite spirit that is determined through its connection with nature. It is rather the case that the surrender of the finite spirit to the absolute spirit demands the formation and the attainment, through freedom of the will, of a personality imbued with absolute values. It would thus be necessary to presuppose a separation in the divine life-process. This life-process would be regarded as consisting, on the one hand, of the life of the soul given in and determined by nature, and, on the other, of a rational world of historical struggle and becoming, a world that understands itself from the standpoint of this life-process, and by which the world of personality is constructed. This is Hegel's idea without the coincidence of the creaturely and the divine life-processes and therefore without dialectic, and Leibniz's idea without the determinism and the pre-established harmony. The background of Kantian thought is a vital theism, and such a theism is also the background of the philosophy of religion. But until now philosophy has been unable to make really comprehensible this interrelationship of nature and spirit, of the cosmic process and productive freedom. And it will presumably always remain impossible to do so. Presumably we shall be able to do no more than designate this interrelationship as a presupposition immanent in life. One can certainly separate its component parts, but one cannot put them together again conceptually.

(6) Spies contrasts my theory with Herrmann's and sees a sharp divergence between the two—a divergence that, according to him, is irreconcilable. That may well be. But this relationship, and the way in which I think that I am able to maintain my own position against Herrmann, I would rather not discuss here. I have the highest personal regard for Herrmann, and admire splendid passages in his books. But to this day I have been unable really to grasp his work as a whole. What I do understand in him is an exclusive supernatural church-faith, a faith that rests upon the miraculous fact of revelation in the person of Christ and upon an institution of grace (*Gnadenanstalt*) that was founded by this person: a community that posesses the assurance of the forgiveness of sins and the blessedness of redemption. This faith in its didactic development can only express, therefore, the assurance of grace that is beyond all scientific appraisal and grounded on the factuality of Jesus—a fact that cannot be explained naturally. But I still have not been able to understand how this relates to Herrmann's other fundamental positions, which are generally Kantian in their tendency. For here we have the sharpest contrast to all the basic impulses of the Kantian philosophy of religion. The only connection exists insofar as religion is grounded in the moral consciousness. But even here there is an immediate deviation from Kant, since Herrmann concedes only to Christianity the character of a moral religion and hence does not wish to recognize as religion anything outside of Christianity.

There is, then, no universal concept of religion for Herrmann, as there is for Kant. In particular, his assertion that religion is something absolutely individual, something incapable of being understood scientifically, is a view I have always been able to regard only as a further means of obviating any competition from philosophy of religion while grounding his own position simply upon the certitude of the Christian experience. At the same time, he is not disturbed by a purely mechanistic-phenomenal conception of reality and seems to deny the scientific character of history in particular. For him there is above all no philosophy of religion, because religion is not scientifically understandable and because true religion exists only in Christianity. There may be, however, a Christian scientific theology, because here revelation and not simply religion is involved, and there may be a science of revelation though none of religion. But then again, since the content of revelation belongs solely to the sphere of practical values, no theoretical science has a voice in this matter; and the faith-content of revelation can be described simply as the quintessence of the power for good which is inherent in trusting Jesus. This is my tentative understanding of Herrmann. I am unable to find the connection between this theory of revelation and his Kantian theory of knowledge, and thus I am still unable, at least at present, to cite exactly those points at which I differ from him.

(7) This, in brief, is what I have to say by way of reply to Spiess. In conclusion, I would like to touch upon just one misunderstanding. Spiess claims that I discard the way out offered by supernaturalism because 'such a way out would not be admissible.' I do not know why it should not be admissible. If its reality could be demonstrated, one would have to take it into account and personally adapt to it. But I am convinced that biblical criticism, church history, and the history of dogma have made their object so similar in all respects to other events that it could contain no miracle other than what is contained in all other events. It is the exclusiveness of Christian supernaturalism that I am combatting, because this exclusiveness is not demonstrable either on the basis of the inner experience of conversion or on the basis of the biblical traditions. But this exclusiveness is not merely incapable of proof; all history and psychology contradict it. Thus my objections are not those of Spinoza and of the popular natural science of today but rather those of Hume and Kant. According to these, however, there are only universally scientific, rather than specifically theological modes of understanding. The uniqueness of Christian theology lies, then, in the nature of its subject matter, not in special methods of research and validation.

Admittedly, one may ask whether Christianity thus understood is still Christianity and whether its normative validity for our religious consciousness can still be maintained. Today this is actually denied by a part of our admittedly not very numerous intellectual élite, and their denial is echoed by the masses of the revolutionary party, whose goal is completely to upset the whole existing order which has identified itself so closely with church and theology. But that does not happen on account of these methodological considerations; on account, that is, of the fact that a religious orientation toward life apart from the church's miracle of redemption grounded in the saving death of Christ would no longer be Christianity. It happens, rather, because the content of this orientation, God and the soul, has on so many counts become questionable for modern persons. Not until they again become certain of that content, or once again feel a hunger for it, will the indestructibility and inner power of this orientation toward life reassert itself for them. As all of our great idealistic thinkers with the exception of the radical pessimists have felt and recognized, something absolutely indispensable to our existence inheres in this orientation. This is as true today as it was a hundred years ago. The old means of proof no longer exist, and with their passing the meaning of the Christian orientation towards life has changed. But the Christian orientation contains, today more than ever, a fountain of eternal youth that offers simplicity, health, and strength to a generation languishing under capitalism, determinism, relativism, and historicism. Only we must attempt to reformulate this orientation and to develop a new structure of support for it. Our central scientific interest will then shift to the philosophy of religion, with its definition—from the viewpoint of philosophy of history—of the nature and meaning of Christianity, and to general ethics, with its elaboration of humanity's final end (*Zweckbestimmung*), an end which can only be understood from a religious perspective. Dogmatics and moral theology thus become branches of practical theology in the narrow sense. In any event, this is how the total plan of my work is to be understood; and because its main points have already been sketched by our idealistic philosophy, I generally refer to it. I continue the approach that prevailed before Hengstenberg and the Restoration.

(8) Insofar, however, as practical, religious interests are in question in all of this, I naturally do not deny that instinct and feeling can find what is right without being dependent upon this sort of religio-philosophical and ethical instruction. The latter approach becomes relevant only with the rise of a theoretical need for clarity or a practical need for a scientific composition and clarification of the struggling forces of the spirit. Then, of course, the question arises whether from this perspective the decision made by pure religious instinct can be substantiated, and if so, to what extent it is thereby changed, possibly under scientific influence. From this perspective I can answer the question which apparently occupies Spiess' mind, namely, that of my relationship to Herrmann, as far as the practical relationship is concerned. I am also clearer about this in my own mind than I am about my relationship to him as a scholar. For practical purposes, I am fully able to accept into the framework of my thinking the particular version of the Christian belief in salvation and in God that Herrmann presents with so great a power of simplification. Herrmann's faith, then, is an affirmation of the Christian orientation to life and the world, which is effectively personified in Christ interpreted and experienced as living. This affirmation is undisturbed by science and guided by strong and sure religious instincts.

From the standpoint of my general conceptual framework, many other factors would be involved in such a theology, and hence many things would have to be expressed differently. But I can only wish that everyone who learns from me would supplement and strengthen what he has learned by turning to Herrmann. He is one of our most vital authors of edifying literature, whose influence I in no wise shun. I would like expressly to emphasize what I have in common with him in the realm of the practical, whatever differences there may be in our basic religio-philosophical and non-religio-philosophical orientation. But in order to characterize the situation, even with respect to the practical, I must admit that I cannot accept the exclusiveness of making the achievement of faith dependent on the impression made by the person of Jesus. Especially with Herrmann's development of the ethical spirit of Christianity, I can agree only in part. What I miss here is the acknowledgement of the 'ascetic' element in Christianity and the feeling for the complicated relationship of this element to our rather independent this-worldly culture. But I have already discussed this problem in some detail and with reference to Herrmann in my article 'Basic Problems of Ethics' (*Grundprobleme der Ethik*).

3

Logos and *Mythos* in Theology and Philosophy of Religion

For fifteen hundred years the sole frame of reference of Christian theology was philosophy or natural theology. Within this horizon there were to be found only the obvious claim of theology that its content was derived from supernatural, divine revelation and communication, and the heritage, though philosophically transformed, of the religion of antiquity; the noetic concept of God of Aristotle, the Stoics, and the Neo-Platonists, who had been assimilated to one another and were now regarded as one. This relationship between philosophy and theology allowed philosophy to be used as the underpinning and complement of theology, by virtue of an ultimate inner identity of natural and revealed religion. But sometimes the relevance of philosophy was opposed and denied in view of the absolute validity of revelation; and sometimes the identity of the two found expression in a philosophical religion or a religious philosophy. Theology assumed, quite understandably, a structure completely analogous to scientific and objective knowledge. Only rarely did the volcanic and irrational nature of the religious imagination break through this barrier. With the collapse of the universal dominion of Christian civilization this horizon disappeared. Philosophy incorporated modern natural science. With Giordano Bruno, Descartes, and Leibniz, philosophy ceased to be natural theology in the old manner and became instead a fermentative new worldview. Theology came to question the obvious validity of its revelation. The use of philosophy as the sole frame of reference for theology was no longer possible without serious harm to both.

At this point Kant provided an alternative. He limited science to the exact classification of physical and psychic phenomena, philosophy to the transcendental doctrine of the a priori elements that effect the objectivity and validity of knowledge, and religion to the implementation, wholly apart from metaphysics, of moral postulates. That was the way to freedom for both religion and theology, and it was eagerly followed despite many relapses into the traditional confusions and identifications. Religion now appeared to be essentially autonomous. Here was the fundamental idea on which all the genuine achievements of the scientific study of religion, indeed the nineteenth century reconstruction of religion itself, have been based. Sometimes this idea is regarded as the watchword of an anti-intellectualistic theology based solely on morally necessary postulates; and sometimes this anti-intellectualism is conceived in a still more refined and poetic way so as to denote the *mythos*-character of the symbol-creating imagination borne by any strong, vital piety. Here Kant was reinforced by the influence of Herder and the Romantics, an influence that has been revived by the neo-romanticism of our own time.

Religion, however, continued to mean *our* religion, Europe's traditional faith—Christianity. This was true of Kant, who reinterpreted religion in the only manner satisfactory to himself, but who maintained the identification of religion and Christianity. It was still more true of the theologians, especially of the one who traveled the Kantian path with exceptional largeness and power of thought, Schleiermacher. On one side, then, Christianity and its theology were free. On the other, however, Christianity found itself in new relationships, connections, and frames of reference. When religious and scientific knowledge were sharply distinguished and then cut asunder, when Christianity lost its distinctive grounding, which consisted in support from reason and in the divine pronouncement of quasi-scientific propositions, then the various historical forms of the religious life naturally tended to merge. This tendency became all the stronger, the more the historical and cultural horizon expanded to include the great religious systems existing prior to, and contemporaneously with, Christianity. Instead of philosophy, the various religions now served to provide a frame of reference for Christian theology.

While these forms of the religious life neutralize or at least limit one another, there certainly was, and is, a way out of this chaos of religious structures.[1] It has been possible to look in and above these forms for the universal natural religion, in which the idea of God, which is everywhere the same, is necessitated by a universal demand of consciousness. This idea is not scientific but ethically compelling. Christianity could then be identified with such a natural religion, and a Christian theology could thus be salvaged, as Kantian theologians have shown. At the very least, if handled properly, Christianity could be regarded as a useful vehicle for this agnostic-practical religion of humanism, as was probably Kant's own intention. Such a universal, natural religion of humanism, however, did not exist. Every concrete religion, Christianity included, was found to contain an exceedingly large store of irrational peculiarities. If it was desired to fashion and promulgate such a religion of humanity, at least for future times, what was called for was not the universal agreement of ethical sentiment but rather scientific proof that only a religion of this sort was really possible and necessary. Its rational necessity (i.e., the fact that the system finds both its culmination and completion in it), its logical postulation by the moral consciousness, and finally, a scientific theory of the moral consciousness—these were bound to form the basis of the religion that was to be founded. The necessity of such a basis, however, moved this moralistic-agnostic religion back into perilous proximity to science and deprived it of its recently acquired autonomy. Moreover, this agnostic-moral religion did not speak to the emotions or the imagination. Scientific proof of its moral basis seemed lacking. The new religion appeared to be no more than an attenuation of Christian theism, and hence bound to the contingency of a religion that was actually dominant, while unable to comprehend the fullness of its imagery and vitality. In short, one was virtually back again amongst all the problems of a scientific religion, with Christianity's frame of reference but a differently grounded metaphysic.

   A different escape from the chaos of world religions was to be found in another direction. Here the stress was not laid on the quasi-scientific element of a universal validity based on moral considerations. Instead, the individual, personal, and irrational factors involved in personal affirmation were stressed. The decision here is personal and practical, and cannot be measured by any universal criteria. The affirmation of a religious life-world depends only upon personal experience and need not submit to norms of any kind. Now, if Christianity asserts that its convictions rest upon an experience wholly incapable of objective measurement, there remains no basis for opposition. The Christian believer can rely upon individual experience and upon the spirit common to Christendom which attests this experience. Foundations unassailable by science are thus attained, and it is possible to develop Christian ideals as the completely autonomous outgrowth of one's personal religious awareness and the common spirit, though objective science must not be contradicted.

Schleiermacher took this position in *The Christian Faith* after several very considerable vacillations in a relativistic-subjectivistic direction.

But such a position is tenable only so long as the Christian position remains virtually the only one that can be taken seriously in the context of our civilization. Even then, a position of this sort savors of an objectionable romantic paradoxy and arbitrariness. The clumsier theologians took this paradoxy in dead earnest. They transformed the personal-practical assurance of the purely religious spirit of Christianity into an inner experience of the supernaturally redemptive power of the Bible. Because of its subjective uniqueness, this experience was said to allow of neither comparison nor subsumption under a generalized concept. Nor could it be a clever romantic fantasy, since its supernatural character is established by experience. Whoever has a deep enough sense of sin, it was said, knows that such an experience would be impossible on the natural level; its mere occurrence guarantees its supernaturalness. A deep sense of sin is always required in order that the sinner may be dragged into the shallows of such theological sophisms. So we have once again arrived at supernatural revelation and divine authority. Consistently enough, the Christian complex of religious ideals once more becomes a quasi-scientific, objective truth with the sole advantage of no longer having to take genuine science greatly into account. Finally, even its counterpart, natural philosophy, is accorded a modest but not uninfluential place of honor, along with all the attempts at mediation between theology and philosophy.[2]

Thus the Kantian road to freedom only led back into the traditional entanglements, which became even less tolerable as under the impact of the anti-revolutionary and reactionary spirit of the period the old clerical traditionalism—Catholic, Lutheran, and Reformed—also burgeoned again. Moreover, the triumph of Romanticism's religiously oriented speculation brought about the transformation of dogma into an absolute philosophy. Trinity and Incarnation were interpreted as formulations of a logical-dialectical world process, and therefore as the quintessence of philosophical and religious knowledge. The Hegelian philosophy of religion had overcome all the theological difficulties of the orthodox Kantians and the followers of Schleiermacher and had discovered the absolute concept in the mythical forms of dogma.

It is difficult to say whether the religious life found comfort within these intricate, forced, and artificial forms and structures. Religion seems to have adopted them only under the influence of anxiety and restlessness and under the threat of impending storms and explosive forces with which the atmosphere seemed to be charged. In any event, they collapsed for us in Germany before the renewed onslaught of the French rationalistic spirit, before a methodical and objective naturalism that found new support in the empirical sciences, before the liberal and democratic anticlericalism that accompanied this naturalism, and finally, before the philosophy of socialism which linked naturalism with utopian enthusiasm. On the other side were assembled the great artistic and humanistic forces of our great literary epoch. These had previously contented themselves with the glorification of the past—of classical antiquity or of the Middle Ages—or else had retreated into the ivory tower of an unproductive and smug Goethe-cult. Now they turned to an energetic criticism of culture. Having moved beyond Schopenhauer's pessimism and idealism, they mounted a simultaneous campaign against the Christian aspects of our civilization and against democratic rationalism. With extraordinary sensitivity, Nietzsche united both of these sinister tendencies in himself. He simplified the struggle by identifying the two targets of this campaign with each other, though quite without historical justification. In any case, he has left us with the feeling that contemporary culture is not a proud achievement but only a dim expectation of a more profound, noble, powerful, and original epoch.

In our religious life, especially, Nietzsche sensed the imminence of a powerful convulsion of people's souls. He proclaimed an irreligion for the future, the development of life out of its own depths towards higher forms apart from God. But his feeling for these depths of life was so powerful that out of them religious feeling was to erupt again and again in new, groping, tentative ways. His very irrationalism, his glorifications of the sovereignty of life itself, his mythopoetic grasp of the goals of existence—all these have tended in this direction. His destiny may be that of Spinoza, who was labeled the 'philosophus atheissimus' by his contemporaries and hailed as 'entheissimus' by the Romantics. In any event, under his influence the old Kantian distinction between pure and practical reason was carried much further. Practical reason was severed from the spirit of the Enlightenment and coupled most closely with the symbolic-artistic forces of the mythos. This is why religion today often poses in the garb of aesthetics, why there is a renewed drive to understand religion as essentially different from science, as characterized by a vital imagination. We associate with this drive the separation of religious ethics from middle-class morality and a tendency to lay greater stress on the irrational character of personality. The Christian conscience, moreover, is not allowed to continue to shut its eyes to the socialist criticism of our culture.

Under the impulse of all these stimuli and threats, religious life and thought have naturally assumed new positions. Catholicism, to be sure, remained unmoved. While it more and more severed its connections with modern intellectual life, it turned its attention to political and social problems. Its adherents increasingly became a state within the state and a society within society; they were cut off from outside contact and the exchange of ideas. Catholic scholarship was content to renew and popularize its traditional apologetic, which united the authority of revelation with natural theology, and shrewdly and successfully pointed up many naturalistic inanities. The official ecclesiastical Protestantism, as a church establishment under the control of the princes and almost out of touch with parliamentary democracy, has likewise tended toward isolation and uniformity. But since the laity is not bound by its dogmas, and since the theological faculties form an integral part of the universities, Protestantism retained enough strength and spontaneity to address itself to the religious question with complete freedom. Alongside the church there exists a purely intellectual and literary Protestantism that indistinguishably blends into religious movements outside the church and includes the most diverse nuances. While it is difficult to define this purely intellectual and literary Protestantism, it is clearly present and effective, and apparently comprises the progressive and vital religious forces, at least in Germany and the Anglo-Saxon countries.[3] It maintains contact with the great historical organizations of religion, constantly wells up anew in them, and continues to exercise an influence upon them. Hence, despite its essentially academic and literary nature, it remains in touch with popular religion, which is organized along cultic and social lines.

Since this is the situation, it is only natural that there are forces within the modern religious movements that wish to break radically with Christianity, either by introducing strange, new religious elements into our European way of life or by dreaming of a great new religion that will serve the needs of the new cultural era they see dawning. Essentially it is always the influence of Nietzsche and Schopenhauer that undergirds such hopes. But there are also socialist influences and, above all, purely aesthetic tendencies that would like to create a neo-paganism out of Platonism, the Renaissance, the philosophy of identity, and the cult of sensuality. Goethe's rich, comprehensive synthesis of the classical and the Christian is abandoned here as a mere experiment in universal culture. However impressive these tokens of the religious unrest of our time may be, nobody will seriously regard them as harbingers of a true renewal and the emergence of

strong, creative, social forms of the religious life. Pessimistic Neo-
Buddhism is an alien influence among us, a combination of culture-
criticism and science, an aesthetic mood, an exceptional position for
intellectuals who deliberately separate themselves from the vital
movements of their own culture.

Aesthetic-ethical neo-paganism is no more than literature for the
literati, a wave in the fast current of metropolitan free thought
continually in quest of new moralities and worldviews. The proud,
unfeeling, aristocratic note of these writings shows how little this
movement is concerned with the souls of the masses who, struggling
with everyday problems, must have a strong, uncomplicated faith. In
the last analysis, the new religion is, by virtue of its very futurity, not
a religion at all. Nor will it ever be. By waiting for it, we overlook and
forfeit the religious resources and tasks that lie immediately at hand.
From the womb of a culture so analyzed, so conceptualized, so over-
observed and plagued by a thousand technical concerns as ours there
will never issue the simple, powerful forces of imagination and instinct,
of certitude and assurance of life, from which a religious revelation
can take its rise. Indeed, were such a revelation to make its appearance
with any considerable show of strength, hypercriticism and the absence
of a strong communal sense would prevent its establishment and
development.

The characteristic position of Christianity in world history is
precisely this, that it emerged from an unsophisticated popular base
and encountered the religious needs of a tiring superculture. Only
through this encounter did it achieve its peculiar synthesis of strict
and powerful simplicity with sublime spiritual profundity. But the
recurrence of such an historical situation does not lie within the range
of probability. The 'new religions' of which we hear will probably be
only new literary movements. We have lived through enough of them,
and yet they keep coming. They simply increase religious uncertainty
and confusion, while leaving everything else much as they found it. Or
they will be religious movements of the type we know so well—new
sects and revivals, syncretistic structures like spiritism, theosophy, and
Christian Science, or new devotions and the cult of new saints—by
means of the latter, Catholicism absorbs the 'new religions.' The
development of such religious movements does not basically aid our
progress. It constitutes merely a variation of forces already present.

Socialism is the least likely source of a religious renewal, whatever
else one may expect from it. It has decisively rejected the religious
enthusiasm of its early stages, in which it often approached the ideal
of the kingdom of God found in Christian sectarianism and in the

Bible. Today socialism relies exclusively on the deterministic evolutionary process and on human power and intelligence: the opportune moment is to be seized and exploited by purely human effort and cunning. Whatever does not contribute to the future development of the proletariat, socialism views as mere ignorance, ill-will, self-interest, and blind necessity. Any transformation of this blend of pure self-reliance and naturalistic belief in inevitability into religious reverence or a religiously grounded humanitarianism is inconceivable. At best, socialism can tolerate religion as long as religion serves its purposes, but it can never become a religion itself. In the event of its victory, the religious quest would assuredly begin once more in the new society. Yet it would certainly no longer find its motives in the idea of socialism, which would then be realized and free to develop its own inherent difficulties, but rather in its opposite. In the more likely event of a succession of partial triumphs, socialism will probably have to relinquish the passionate tension derived from its utopian ideals. The frustrated energies that had previously been devoted to the emancipation of the individual and to a future salvation will then be diverted toward the sects and similarly individualistic religious groups. These groups are already making considerable progress, which has largely remained unnoticed.

It cannot be denied that all these hopes and attempts to fashion a new religion may reflect noble intentions and genuinely religious longings. What one must deny is that modern religious needs, experiments, and promises for the future will necessarily lead beyond the religious energies that are, after all, the ancient religious resources of Western civilization. We find these inevitably in Christianity, which integrates powerful prophetic theism with the intimate Christian sense of God's presence, the infinity of the soul with the brotherhood of love, the joyous assurance of God with the heroic hope of redemption, and, finally, the Platonic-Stoic humanism with the idealistic interpretation of the universe. Christianity thus includes every ethical and religious resource of our heritage. Sober judgement will anticipate no second religious structure within our cultural horizon that could at all compare with the first. Christianity is not some fortuitous occurrence. Rather, it is the ripened fruit of every previous development of the Mediterranean peoples. If one chooses to use the customary language of the skeptic, Christianity is the ideology that is inseparably bound up with the whole future life and work of our culture. We shall not see a second Divine Comedy, nor a second Faust, which would, on the basis of a new religion, illumine and affect the problem of European life in a comparable manner.[4]

To be sure, these are only the observations of personal detachment and sober reflection. Such sober reflection, however, shows to faith and personal conviction that they need not hesitate to see more in Christianity—taking that ambiguous word for the present in the most general sense, with all the possibilities latent in it—than the mere religious destiny of our particular civilization. Quite apart from the millions who live and firmly believe in the faith of their ecclesiastical communities and who maintain this faith with all the passion of personal conviction and practical need, this same certainty exists also in the circle of free Protestantism described above. Moreover, this certainty is shared by the great religious writers who are independent of every confession—by Kierkegaard, Tolstoy, Maeterlinck, Carlyle, de Lagarde, Matthew Arnold. To these could be added, at the respectively appropriate distance, Friedrich Naumann, Rudolf Eucken, Johannes Mueller, Arthur Bonus, Wilhelm Herrmann, Friedrich Rittelmeyer, Hermann Kutter, and others. They all share the conviction, though it may be very differently expressed, that Christianity is the highest form of the religious consciousness: it reveals the depths of a soul united to God, the inner solidarity of humanity, the heroic power to overcome pain and guilt, and a full assurance for the future regarding the ultimate and supreme goals of life.

These elements constitute a supreme and final stage in the religious life of humanity. The decisive point here is that the soul is not swallowed up in the divine life. On the contrary, it returns from that vital experience to embrace again the task that translates its own eternal qualities into action, and the human relationship to God into love and the humanism of practical endeavor. No one fails to see that a deep tension still persists between this view and secular culture, the struggle for existence with its virtues, the natural common-interest groups with their ethical values, mere morality based on the sense of duty, and artistic feeling for the aesthetic dimensions of the sensual. This tension constitutes the grandeur of our life. It is resolved in countless unavoidable and constantly fresh compromises that lead to ever new cross-fertilizations, over the lonely protests of 'the salt of the earth,' the strict, radical Christians. At the same time Christianity has been able to create large, popular organizations in which the religious life can be nourished without being suffocated by dogma, ritual, and moralism. For its central symbol is not a dogma but a living, historical personality that every age can interpret anew from its own historical perspective. Hence it is not merely the sole religious resource available to us; it is the great religious resource for all humanity. Unswayed by the influences of the great alien religious systems, by naturalistic or idealistic philosophy, and by the signs of human fallibility shown in the history of Christianity, writers of this type still believe, with complete self-assurance based on a purely subjective religious decision, that the Christian life-world continues to possess unexhausted power and relevance. Its expression is not in theory or doctrine but in the imaginative and evocative exercise of its inward power. It functions not by argument but by example and stimulation of the imagination. Christianity is the great religious *mythos* of the modern world. As everywhere and always, it gives voice to religious feeling and thought, and is imperceptibly developed and transformed together with life itself. Bonus has given especially strong and effective voice to such thoughts in his essays, *Zur religiösen Krisis.*[5]

Here we are face to face with an anti-intellectualistic religiosity that sharply differentiates itself from all theologizing and all philosophical religion; far from rejecting or disregarding the findings of objective science, it merely insists that religion itself not be transformed into an objective science or compared with the objective certainties of science. It does not refuse to recognize the findings of cosmology, biology, psychology, and history, but it does not want to see religion itself turned into a scientific finding. This kind of religiosity respects science but distrusts philosophy. Insofar as it takes note of philosophy at all, it is less averse to the pragmatism of a William James or the biologism of a Bergson than to systems of all-encompassing, logical necessity. It happily seized upon Kant's famed distinction between theoretical and practical reason, but only to reinterpret the distinction completely: theoretical reason is identified with the organization of experience, which is important solely for practical purposes, while practical reason is identified with the sovereign unfolding of the will-to-live.

But these future-oriented religious movements cannot possibly stop there. Relations to science are not formed in so free and easy a manner. Science is one of the great powers in our intellectualized world. We cannot return to some primitive epoch in which religion, concealed in a living *mythos*, was proclaimed by prophets. Faith needs a firmer and clearer relationship to science. Anyone who does not personally feel this necessity need not be disturbed by science. But religion as a whole will continue to require contact with intellectual endeavors; spiritual integrity and the sense for truth cannot settle for a pure enthusiasm, a free-floating, uncontrolled *mythos*. Just as the Christian *mythos* needed to join the *logos* when it reached a higher cultural level in the second century, so the *mythos* needs the *logos* now and will continue to need it. The Logos Christology established this relationship for the early church. Modern religion cannot dispense with a comparable relationship. Only it must look for it elsewhere and in a different way. A great religious complex can exist as little without *logos* as without *mythos*.

Now this rediscovery of the *logos* is the task of theology. Instead of 'theology' one might of course say 'scientific study of religion' if one meant by this term the elaboration of normative religious ideas rather than what most people today mean by it, namely, a general theory floating above the diversity of concrete religions. But since people ordinarily see the former as the task of theology, we might as well retain this label. In any case, it is a theology that is bound to no confession and has no ready-made truths to prove. In complete freedom it seeks to give vital expression to the Christian idea. It is Protestant only to the extent that such a theology is possible only on Protestant soil, and that it shares the individualism and commitment to truth which distinguish Protestantism. It can learn from everyone, whether denominationally affiliated or not, for it is bound to no ecclesiasticism. Naturally it will be bound—and will want—to serve the churches, unless it is willing to renounce all practical relevance except to increase the general religious unrest.

But along what lines can such a theology now proceed, after the reorganization of religious philosophy on Kantian lines has had the outcome previously described? How can it include in a scientific theory an unscientific anti-intellectualism that not only represents the best contemporary religious pathos but also undoubtedly belongs to the essence of religion? How can this anti-intellectualistic thrust be simultaneously affirmed and limited? Here lies the main task of modern scientific theology. I want to try to answer this question with utmost brevity and to shed some light on the consequences flowing from this answer. Naturally I will have to refer to some major ideas expressed in my earlier writings. But I hope to proceed in a new way that will illuminate even these earlier statements.

A scientifically grounded affirmation of the Christian life-world rests either on the theory of its absolutely miraculous foundation, which renders it incomparable to anything else and ascribes to it an inerrant divine origin, or it rests upon proof of the coincidence of the Christian idea with the absolute perfection of scientific knowledge as constructible by philosophy. The former alternative is ruled out by the application of consistently historical thought to the origins of Christianity and by the compelling light thus shed upon them, even if some obscurities remain; we are convinced that these obscurities, if they can be cleared up at all, will only be removed by means of a continuing application of genuine historical research, and that it is impossible to smuggle into this twilight zone special supernatural and specifically Christian causalities. The latter alternative is eliminated both by the protest of the Christian life-world and by the impossibility of such an absolute philosophy, which would have to elaborate the ultimate and eternal truth. The same failure characterizes the more moderate attempt, which is constantly repeated, to extract a philosophical kernel of truth from Christianity. This kernel will always be too scientifically abstract for genuine religious feeling and too dependent on personal, subjective affirmation for scientific thought. Nor will it be possible to subsume Christianity under the concept of rationally necessary values because, although there is a philosophic theory concerning the rational necessity of valuation as such, there is no theory of the rational validity of specific values.

There is thus no compelling axiomatic presupposition that would establish the validity of Christianity. Without such a ready-made presupposition, however, it is necessary to trace back the more immediate presuppositions from this now questionable particular entity to the last general term that can be reached. Transcendental philosophy here teaches us to find the last and most general presuppositions attainable in the a priori functions of reason; that is, in those functions that are autonomous or self-sufficient and arise from their own inner necessity. To be sure, it is easier to demonstrate these functions of reason in the purely scientific organization of the contents of our experience than in the so-called cultural values. But these, too, as Kant has shown, have an analogous a priori, an autonomous validity emerging in accordance with an inner necessity. Religion, too, has such an a priori. We need not be concerned here with a closer and more detailed explanation. In any case, every religious person—however he or she may choose to regard Christianity in particular—will not only acknowledge it, but will understand that what is involved here is not science or morality or art. This impression is strengthened when we observe how religious thought unfolds in its own unique manner. Insofar as it seizes upon every means of stimulation and expression, religious thought most closely resembles the artistic imagination, yet it remains distinct from it by the experience of a compelling superhuman reality revealing itself everywhere. Every expression is mythical, symbolic, poetic; but in the expression something is grasped that bears within itself in a specifically religious manner its own inner necessity and compelling power. With such a theory we have attained the last presuppositions constructible by philosophy; now we understand religious truth in its own validity, which is analogous to other rational validities, and yet at the same time in its completely anti-intellectualistic singularity.

What I designated earlier as the consequence of abolishing objective-philosophical metaphysics as the frame of reference for theology drew the necessary conclusions either not at all or very hesitantly. For we are faced by a confusing abundance of concrete, historical, religious structures, and again, under the great collective labels of historical-positive religions, by a profusion of individual religiosity. This approach to religion is sufficiently anti-intellectualistic, yet it leads into the chaos of all these structures and deprives us of every intellectually constructible standard for evaluating and grading them. Kant's 'religion within the limits of reason alone' was still at least a conditionally rational standard; it rationalized and moralized religion. But now that the understanding of religion is freed from these limitations, every rational standard is eliminated. We cannot deny that this has been the result. Yet this result does not prove that every standard whatever is eliminated, only that the standard cannot be a rational one but must be a purely religious one. It must cease to refer religion to objective norms that lie outside it and are therefore irrelevant. It must learn to decide controversies on the basis of a subjectivity that asserts itself with inner power. If religion indeed includes an a priori, that is, a specifically religious consciousness of validity, then this a priori will assert itself in the conflict between different religious structures just as it asserts itself against the nonreligious spirit of secularism. If there is no controversy, judgement is unnecessary and the original certainty obtains. If a controversy does arise, the objective element that is covertly operative within the religious subjectivity will know how to decide; a decision of this kind is a personal act, an acceptance of the risk of error. The standard arises from within this vital struggle and decision; it is not available somewhere in finished form, ready for appropriation and application. The decision involved is also anti-intellectualistic: it differs from every scientific judgement, which always uses ready-made criteria, or at least standards that can be constructed from universal principles, and all too often obtrudes upon religion the deceptive desire for possession of a similar standard. Yet, however anti-intellectualistic this decision may be, it is not arbitrary or a mere matter of taste. Instead, by dint of the element of validity operative in all subjectivity, the decision takes place with a feeling of objective necessity: the decision is accompanied by the feeling that one has placed oneself in the very mainstream of the spirit as intuitively discerned.

As this objectivity is increasingly sensed to be a specifically religious one, scientific data no longer will be used as a frame of reference for religion. Religion will also cease to interfere with scientific data and, of its own accord, will fall back upon its own proper sphere of inwardness. The anti-intellectualistic attitude is not crude fantasticality or vulgar disregard of scholarship, but rather a concentration of the religious consciousness upon itself by virtue of the objective-religious element included in subjectivity. It represents a recognition of the autonomy of science and the avoidance or elimination of any conflict with it. Religion's freedom from science does not mean hostility to science.

Still more needs to be said, however. If a feeling of objective necessity is involved in such decisions, it cannot be denied that a similar feeling was present in various earlier religious structures. If necessity is not to struggle disastrously with necessity, there must be an internal connection and perceptible progress from one religious structure to the next, an advancement that can be construed as an ascending evolution, even though it may often be interrupted, opposed, and hampered. One's own decision must be set within the broadest possible horizon, within which the decision must appear as the climax of all previous development. To be sure, the development in question cannot be one whose impetus is determined by logical necessities and whose result would be a logical-theoretical proposition. The non-theoretical or anti-intellectualistic aspect must be preserved even in this construction of the development, as it obviously must be in the evolution of art and morality. In fact, the whole concept of a development and upward thrust in life cannot be understood through laws of logic. Yet the concept is replete with inner necessities and validities. There must be an immanent consistency that is not grounded in logic but can be intuitively felt and described as an ascending aspiration towards ultimate and supreme goals and thus as an inner unity. Hegelian thought has a validity that cannot be lost; indeed, it cannot be comprehended by means of a purely theoretical logic. But Hegel's logic, with its fruitful ability to create antitheses and syntheses, was itself no longer a pure logic and yet remained too purely logical to comprehend the real nature of the upward thrust. Such a thrust, non-logical yet intuitively perceptible as unity, may be the core of truth in Bergson's theory of evolution. The tremendously difficult question of the relation between the logical and alogical ideas of unity may be bypassed here. In any case, with such an alogical formulation of the evolutionary thrust it is possible to assign a place to stagnation, regression, faulty development, and side-currents in a way that was quite impossible under the dialectical-panlogical scheme.

Furthermore, through such an understanding we are able to view

individual evolutionary stages and points as more than logically
necessary places of transition that are promptly 'mediated' by the next
level of development. With this term Ranke combatted the Hegelian
dialectic, yet without wishing to contest the idea of evolution as such.
Every point has a life of its own, corresponding to the particular
moment and the total situation, as a creative expression of the driving
force that lies at the root of all things. It is valuable in and for itself,
amid the flow of activity, as an approximation to the ultimate goal;
and contains its specific value in itself even while striving towards a
dimly perceived Absolute. Thus Ranke, with the historian's instinct,
corrected the Hegelian doctrine by asserting God's immediacy to every
epoch. Yet by this assertion he did not wish to abolish the flux of
evolution and becoming. It follows from the objectivity inherent in
purely subjective decision that every profoundly and vitally
experienced moment contains in itself not only the awareness of its
own legitimacy and of its own relationship to the Absolute, but also
the consciousness that it is mere approximation to a supreme and
ultimate goal that is still in the process of becoming. Thus the decision
made at a given time is only able to designate the religious way of life
it apprehends as the highest one it has been able to attain. The
decision can provide no scientific certainty at all about the permanence
of that religious way of life or about further developments in the
future. In its approximation to the Absolute it can find its own
legitimacy and its own truth; and at the same time, by virtue of this
concept of evolution, it can claim superiority to other religious
structures because of their relationship to the basic evolutionary drive.
The total construction in itself neither validates nor executes the
decision; rather, it is only the consequence and demonstration of a
judgement already rendered by the properly autonomous religious
decision. But this judgement requires underpinning and corroboration
of this type, which provides, moreover, a kind of retroactive
illumination that is important from the practical religious standpoint.

If we now suppose that the religiously alive judgement, exercised
amidst the struggles of the present, affirms the Christian life-world,
and that this affirmation can be impressively supported by such a
doctrine of evolution, then a new series of questions presents itself.
'Christianity,' as already indicated, is an extremely ambiguous
concept. Its ambiguity is directly evident in the co-existence of the
great confessions, all of which have the historical right to identify
themselves with Christianity. It is further evident in the attempts
made to disengage the Christian life-world from its ancient and
medieval formulations and transform it through inner contact with

modern tendencies. These attempts appear in all denominations as 'Modernism,' a term coined by those experts in the labeling of heresies, the Protestant and Catholic scholastics; but they have gained a strong foothold only within Protestantism, where they pose the danger of schism.

But these obvious variations also have a real basis in the very nature of Christianity. On the one hand, Christianity is an extremely complex historical structure; on the other, through its combination of pure inwardness with vigorous activity, it has the capacity for far-reaching transformations and adjustments. It has already been shown how Christianity comprehended and molded into a vital, dynamic whole the grand and simple power of Israelite prophetism, the distinctive character of Jesus' preaching of the kingdom of God, Paul's religion of grace, the sacramental cultus of the mystery religions, Christ-cult and Christ-mysticism, the Stoic-Platonic ethic, and idealist metaphysics. Then there were the great transformations in connection with general cultural changes: Christianity's broadening out into medieval civilization, its radical personalization and individualization in Protestantism, and its amalgamation with the modern worldview and with practical-social activity today. Thus, any affirmation of a Christian view of life must always indicate the sense in which this affirmation is meant. We are once more confronted with a decision among competing claims; in fact, with the same problem we previously faced on a larger scale.

Here, too, the attempt has been made to reach a decision by purely scientific means; here, too, the attempt cannot succeed. It was thought possible to construct an 'essence of Christianity,' transcending the motley variety of actual developments and remaining ever the same, and to focus the decision upon this 'essence.' In *What Is Christianity?*—one of the most popular books of our day—Adolf von Harnack tried to define this purely historical 'essence' on the basis of the preaching of Jesus. His attempt inevitably led to a sharp modernizing and Kantianizing of the concept of the kingdom of God and, as Loisy cogently showed, failed to do justice to other facets of Christianity. The Hegelians saw the essence of Christianity in the 'idea' of Christianity, which would bring forth all of its manifestations in logical-dialectical sequence and which would fully explicate itself in the final outcome. But this is the same panlogical-dialectical error that I previously designated as the defect in their whole construction of religious development. Here the error is transferred to the 'idea of religion,' which is in principle evolved in Christianity. Moreover, the uniform outcome that should have followed has failed to appear.

Instead, diverse and contradictory tendencies prevail. Indeed, those very tendencies which have the best prospects for future growth are by no means a fulfilment of the 'idea,' or a synthesis of all earlier stages; they are rather tumultuous adaptations to a new intellectual situation, radically different from that which gave birth to Christianity.

Here, too, neither historical nor philosophical scholarship can help us with the main point. Here, too, only the anti-intellectualistic approach is viable: freely to form—as every great era has done—the Christianity of today and tomorrow, with religious sensitivity, with boldness to plunge into the depths of historical forces, and with resolute acceptance of the appropriate life-values of the present. At the same time, there is an element of religious creativity, of a new and living revelation for our time. But the objective element of inner necessity or religious conscience concealed in such a decision, loyalty and respect for the past, and the will to enlist in a vital Christian movement that grips us from within—all these create a sense of obligation or inner compulsion that lifts such decisions out of the realm of the merely arbitrary and capricious. Once again it is possible, in retrospect from the specifically religious decision, to undergird this decision with an historical view of the development of Christianity. To this view everything previously said about an evolutionary theory of this kind will apply. Every epoch of Christianity can be given its due when it is studied in its own terms rather than in any alleged relationship to modern developments. It is possible to strengthen and support one's own position by reference to history without becoming history's captive.

Certainly, anxious and dogmatic people—both opponents and proponents of Christianity, for the most part, there is no difference here—will come forward to point out that such a development might easily go beyond Christianity itself, since it will become increasingly difficult to define what Christianity really is. At this point considerations of what is 'still Christian' and what is 'no longer Christian' begin. The theologians play their trump card when they prohibit further participation on the ground that one has placed oneself outside the Christian fold. Just as though Christianity were a club that can expel members who no longer agree with the by-laws and then restrain them from further meddling with its affairs! Actually, of course, it is not so simple to establish just what Christianity is or is not, as long as it remains alive and retains the capacity for creativity. The criterion for determining whether a religious idea can rightly be called Christian must, in the first instance, be derived from that idea itself: that is, its consciousness of having been born of the Christian spirit. Above all, in the present situation, the Christian character of an idea cannot depend on whether some period in Christian history is made an object of faith and thus elevated from its historical context into the realm of the timeless and the divine. The fundamental change of attitude in the modern temper is that it sees history in continuity with the ongoing flux of events, and that consequently immediate religious experience can find its object only in the supra-historical—in God alone. This view is by no means a consequence of certain scientific discoveries; it is the whole temper of the modern mind, which assigns a different role to history than did the Middle Ages or late antiquity.

What determines what is Christian, then, is primarily the actual concept of God, the feeling for life, the attitude toward the world, the ethos, the faith in the future. Wherever the antithesis of personal existence to the world and mere nature, the task of regeneration and elevation, redemption from sin and sorrow by trusting surrender to God, the ethos of the infinite value of the person and of humanity, and hope for the kingdom of God where finite spirits find their perfection in God are asserted—that is, where the tension between personalism and pantheism is maintained, and the world is transcended rather than blissfully enjoyed—there we have the spirit of Christianity and hence Christianity itself. The historical does not lose its significance; instead, it becomes the means of education and illustration, of inculcating the sense of community, of unity, of integration. But the historical is no longer the immediate object of faith.

Whatever role or significance is then assigned to details is no longer a matter for scientific methodology but for the free religious imagination. No more need be said at this point concerning it and its relationship to what actually happened. What is of interest here is solely the general change of attitude toward the historical. This change is the most important characteristic of the Christian mentality that is taking shape in our time. Now the internal tensions and problems of this type of faith in God and the ethos corresponding to it appear much more clearly; for along with the sharp tension with the ethos of immanence and of the struggle for existence, the necessity of incorporating the latter in the specifically religious ethos is also recognized. But where such tasks are recognized and accepted, the strongly Christian orientation of religion is clearly evident; there need be no doubt at all about its Christian character.

All further development here will pertain neither to science nor to scientific theology. It may find expression, according to various needs and situations, in a completely non-scientific form; it may employ traditional Christian symbols for this purpose or it may fashion entirely new ones of its own. This is the realm of preaching, of teaching, and of literary or personal discourse, and must find its own way. A certain respect for science will be expected, to be sure, from those who are able to appreciate the results of objective research. In their religious utterances, they should avoid conflict with the scientific view of things and endeavor to give a religious perspective to it, indeed, to derive religious inspiration from it. Of course the decisive element here will always be the power of the inner life that is expressed and the skill with which this power is communicated.

A scientific theology could and should be developed along these lines. To what extent our contemporary theological faculties actually do so is a matter of relative indifference. On the one hand, contemporary theology is simply historical and philological research, having nothing at all to do with the important issues raised above but simply bypasses them. Some splendid work is being done here, although more mutual contact with general historians and philologists is desirable. On the other hand, contemporary theology is determined by the general political situation and by the relation of rulers and administrators to the political parties that are active both within and outside of the various parliamentary bodies. The theological faculties are a factor in the power politics of the state; hence they reflect the intellectual situation and its requirements only to a very limited degree. Since our theological faculties must satisfy very diverse claims that have little to do with intellectual and scholarly matters, they should not be judged solely on the basis of their scholarly attainments. Their members are appointed not for intellectual or religious reasons but for political and ecclesiastical ones, and this procedure is reflected in the level of their attainments. There is a standpoint beyond the faculties, however, which can be represented among them, and often is; namely, the one described above, which allows the combination of vigorous, anti-intellectualistic utterance with a scholarly theory of religion and its development.

It matters little whether this standpoint satisfies the requirements of today's dominant academic theology. The only question is whether it meets the requirements of the inner motives, or instinct, of faith itself. But this very question forces us to consider an objection that stems from it and has often been raised against this point of view, which has been with us ever since Schleiermacher's *Addresses on Religion*, and Herder's great *Outline of History*. For the constructions we have presented do not lead beyond the assertion of the supreme validity of the Christian life-world within our own historical horizon. They do not provide a theoretical guarantee of the permanence of Christianity or of the ultimate unification of all humanity in an understanding of religion focusing on the person of Jesus. Nor can such a guarantee be given, for there is no logical, theoretical proof of the supreme validity of Christianity.

But that is not all. The abstract possibility cannot be excluded that religion may maintain itself at high levels apart from Christianity and that it presumably would do so even if the world became nominally Christian. Nor is it logically impossible that, under certain circumstances, the whole continuity of our civilization may be broken. New ice ages and evolutionary changes might completely transform the human race or throw it back into barbarism. As purely abstract possibilities, these points must be granted. They are certainly not inconceivable. Therefore we shall stand by our conclusion: in the boundless flux of becoming, the Christian view of life is the highest form or revelation of the religious life known to us. When we now see Christianity itself in a state of flux and transformation, when we have to acknowledge that the form of Christianity peculiar to each of its great epochs has specific validity only for the general situation of that epoch, then the 'essence of Christianity' which we ourselves construct will not be the final word either. Christianity is itself in a state of flux that is theoretically illimitable, even as our own decision was not based on theory. But is this not a most hazardous subjectivism, a self-confessed relativism? Is this not the complete opposite of all orientation toward the eternal and timeless? Is it not far too complicated a conception for a simple commitment, an intolerable conditioning of the Unconditioned?

Such objections suggest themselves. We want to deal first with the charge of subjectivism, which is admitted. Subjectivism, however, does not exclude an awareness of inner necessity and validity; it only denies that these rest on logical proof. The question whether such a theory renders practice more difficult also requires little discussion at this point. For here we are not concerned with practice at all, only with a theory that will undergird it without necessarily directly affecting it at all. But the charge of complexity proves nothing against a scholarly theory. Complexity is, rather, quite appropriate to scholarship, which, by raising questions, necessarily complicates the whole situation. Plain and easy answers to complex questions are no more possible here than elsewhere. Thus the charge of relativism would appear to be the sole remaining one.

Is this whole approach actually relativism? Were it only a matter of anti-intellectualistic attitude and of the testing of all religious forces by their vitality and their embodiment in suggestive imagery, then indeed relativism would be the inevitable result; for there is no limit to the number of such systems that might be formulated. If, in addition, scientific theories are treated as no more than practical techniques for organizing empirical data, as in modern pragmatism and biologism, then there is no escape from relativism. However, insofar as the anti-intellectualistic attitude has been accepted here, it is first and foremost incorporated in a transcendental theory of the nature of spirit (*Geist*). No matter how much the a priori is drawn into the evolutionary flux, no matter how much stress is placed upon its anthropological dimension and its dependence on human sense perception and categories of space and time, the a priori will always remain a rational activity that asserts itself because of an inner logical necessity and that strives for universal logical coherence. By its very nature, transcendentalism is anti-relativistic. The theory of value indeed differs, in both method and substance, from this theory of theoretical reason. But in the spheres of art, morality, and religion, a non-theoretical validity is recognized which, together with the validity of theoretical reason, forms the unity of reason as such.

The *logos* is a system of validities, both theoretical and non-theoretical. For that very reason it is a creative vitality, not a deadly rationalization. Yet in every instance it is directed toward something ultimate, valid, and necessary; it is not a poetic chaos of motley forms. To be sure, non-theoretical validity is also drawn into the evolutionary flux and its ultimate goals have nowhere yet been disclosed. But a teleological direction is indicated, and a judgement concerning the particular formations that happen to meet and intersect within the process is possible at each point in the process of becoming. Thus it is possible for an evolutionary mainstream to emerge that can be recognized and perceived as such, as over against various eddies that dissipate their energies and sidestreams that are left behind. If we consider this stream as flowing from Hebrew prophetism, it may well be true that nothing more has been attained here than the consciousness of having most closely approximated the desired goal; yet the goal itself is always present in this approximation, and no unknown future contingencies can cancel what has been attained or uproot it by the mere phantom of some possible futurity. The present is completely filled by the immediately nearness of God, and the question of other possible revelations may well be left to the future.

All this is surely not relativism; for relativism is forced to admit the legitimacy of every point in its surroundings and hence unable to initiate a struggle for truth and depth. It is, rather, the affirmation of an ultimate and valid goal and of the ever increasing presence of that goal in every approximation to it, where individual moments are not reduced to mere intermediate stages and provisional steps that have meaning only insofar as they make the final goal possible. Such a reduction would take place if our conception were that of a process, immanent in all human history, of elaborating a logical idea. The distinctive character of these non-theoretical validities, however, is that they represent the goal in every major formation with a peculiar vigor that, although approximating the whole only in varying degrees, yet expresses it in the only manner possible. They are moments in the process of becoming; but each moment has at the same time an immediate, individual significance of its own, a direct relationship to God which belongs only to it. They are temporally discrete, and yet also approximations to the Absolute Life.

When and how this Absolute Life will reveal itself, and whether all individuals, apart from their individual participation in it in history, will ultimately participate in the full goal and the total meaning—of this we know absolutely nothing. Such matters are dealt with by doctrines of eschatology and predestination, of reincarnation and continuing development. All these notions are products of the believing imagination; they are not objects of knowledge. But neither is knowledge really indispensable here. Of course relativism, which always accompanies the stressing of life above thought, is a very present danger because of the historical vividness of its image of boundless flux, the value it places on individuality, and its rejection of every purely logical-dialectical construction. To escape this danger it is sufficient to recognize a non-theoretical validity that is operative in all these things and that enters the awakened consciousness in the form of a specifically religious assurance and decision.

This is not relativism but subjectivism. It is the renunciation of decisions based on theoretically constructed criteria, and the affirmation of decisions based exclusively on the personal sense of truth. This subjectivism, however, is of a special kind. It is, to be sure, a decision made by the subject; but by no means merely for the subject. It is a being gripped by a validity that is able to assert itself only in the personal consciousness and yet constitutes a universal inner necessity, binding on everyone capable of perceiving it and actualizing it in a personal fashion. It is set in a metaphysical background that cannot be constructed by means of a theoretically compelling logic but must be grasped, just as it is solely revealed, in personal commitments. This background consists in a vigorous

movement of reason as such, which bursts forth in ever new creations
and into whose creative teleology the soul can intuitively enter. Yet
this intuitive apprehension of the true teleology must be made in full
awareness of the risk involved, for it will be impossible to justify it by
means of speculative constructions. Something like this is intended by
Eucken's *Geistesleben* and Bergson's *intuition*. It is not possible to
pursue these concepts further at this point. We must simply emphasize
that such subjectivism is correctly understood only as the expression
of a metaphysic that is itself subjective. These thoughts lead us
ultimately into the vicinity of Meister Eckhart, of Neo-Platonism, of a
mysticism that unites the reality of becoming with the reality of
personhood; where God and the subject appear as discrete entities,
and yet the subjects act, feel, and think only in God.

From such a standpoint, the affirmation of the Christian view of
life is the affirmation of the main result of the historical evolution of
religion. The structuring of this view of life for the present marks,
then, a great step forward in the development of the religious
consciousness. We are not, therefore, merely affirming some
transitional or provisional position but the highest revelation of
religious life granted to us and known to us. We may confidently
leave to the future the question of what will be a hundred thousand
years from now, or whether this view of life will perhaps be forced to
acknowledge, in addition to the various individual forms produced
within itself, individual revelations of the highest personalistic religious
life that are quite differently conditioned. It is enough to know that
we are not mere victims of historical accident, nor of a sentimental
devotion to tradition, when we regard our foreseeable religious future
as determined by the great European religion.

Our practical outlook is determined accordingly. Few modern
philosophers of religion, to be sure, are actually concerned with the
question of practical applications. They strive for clarity in their own
thought and at most for a large sale of the books to which they
entrust their doctrines. The climate of liberalism, of an intellectual
application of the Manchester doctrine, still prevails here: everyone is
concerned with his own ideas and expects that an ultimate consensus
among the knowledgeable will result of itself. This expectation,
however, was consistently justifiable only on the intellectual
assumptions of an individualistic liberalism. Here the presupposition
that reason and its theoretical methods are identical everywhere
permitted the expectation of concurring results on the part of all
thinking persons and ultimate harmony through universal agreement.
It was believed that confessional boundaries had been transcended

and that the age of a religion of reason had arrived. In our time, however, this view has been largely abandoned, partly because the expected results have failed to appear, but primarily because of our anti-intellectualistic understanding of the sphere of values and thus of religion. Agreement and the expectation of agreement are no longer envisaged.

Just as romantic subjectivism followed the Enlightenment, compensating for its inability to form a community by a sovereign, ironic self-assurance, so a new romanticism with these same qualities has followed in the wake of liberalism with its intellectualistic conventions. The new romanticism can be no more permanent than the old, and for the same reasons. Just as Novalis, Friedrich Schlegel, Fichte, and Schleiermacher came—beginning with the most extreme individualism—to be concerned with social structures, the state, the nation, society, and the church, and worked through every possibility, from a revival of the Middle Ages to a futuristic socialism, so today the increasing attention to sociological problems points again to a similar reversal of thought. The theory of religion, therefore, must also pay attention to the sociological dimension of its problem; it cannot limit itself to purely individual and personal constructs and the manifestation of passing moods. Either it must make straight the way for the new religious community of the future, preparing for it by means of polemics and organization, or it must work out a rapprochement with existing practical organizations. The kind of theory of religion we have characterized above can be reconciled with Protestantism. Indeed, to a considerable extent it is an outgrowth of Protestantism.

The serious question arises, however, in what form this rapprochement can take place and how such a theory must influence the historical religious community. By the very nature of this theory, such a question is comparatively easy and simple to answer. The anti-intellectualistic elements of this theory, together with its recognition of the symbolic and aesthetic character of language and of a specifically religious kind of certainty, generally allow the practical sphere to operate as it will and can. Our theory provides only a general, theoretical background for the autonomy of preaching, meditation, and instruction. This background need not itself be preached; one might say that it establishes a scientific shield to protect preaching. How preaching (including worship, practical activity, teaching, and personal discussions) utilizes and shapes the treasure of Christian ideas, how it enriches, transforms, simplifies, or expands this heritage, is solely the concern of preaching itself. But preaching must strive for greater inwardness that at least avoids conflicts with objective knowledge of the world. Personal strength must form the basis of religiosity, for which all forms and symbols can serve as mere means of expression.

At this point genuine science ends, and only an indirect link to it remains. The staunchest belief in revelation and the most inward vision can now be preached, so long as one is spared the theories of both and true life is expressed. The imagination of a poor tinker like Bunyan has as much place here as the intellectual sublimity of a Schleiermacher. The anti-intellectualistic attitude looks for life and power, and accepts form as form. Thus every need, every type of intellect, every social level can be served; and yet religion is imbued with the urge to purge itself of crude contradictions of the modern knowledge of the world, and with an inclination toward productive-religious interpretation and appreciation of the new vitalities and cosmologies. The basic theory is never disturbing because it never directly interferes. In fact, it enhances religion's liveliness and interest, but solely by releasing the creative sources, not by direct affirmation. This is all that is required by the situation; and it is enough to satisfy genuinely religious needs.

At only one point does the theory directly affect the organizations. It expects them to be sufficiently magnanimous to allow the religious subjectivity the freedom, within the framework of a common will to be Christian, to revitalize the use of the Bible and of Christian history. This requirement implies a certain flexibility with respect to certain obligatory matters, especially liturgical formulations. The details need not be discussed here. Nor shall we try to decide whether the Protestant churches will take the practical steps that would constitute genuine progress. In any event, the solution that has prevailed among us now for over a century—a moderate state-church still bound to an archaic uniformity—is surely not final. Whenever this problem is taken up, it will be necessary to induce the large organizations to be sufficiently magnanimous, or else to break them up into sects and groups. The latter course would certainly create a dismal and dangerous situation. The theory developed here is designed to facilitate the avoidance of such an outcome. How far the fragmentation of the Protestant churches can be checked and overcome depends partly on the insight of church leaders and political authorities, partly on the degree to which dogmatic passions are restrained, and partly on the far-sightedness and seriousness shown by the educated laity. Fragmentation would increase the dangers that threaten our civilization from the direction of Catholicism, and would seriously jeopardize the influence of culture and science upon Protestantism. No one would gain by such fragmentation except uncultured fanaticism.

Yet even here, the theory itself remains unentangled in practical questions. It uses the *logos* as a background for the *mythos* and, as theory, does not itself take up the task of fashioning and expressing the *mythos*. The difference is still acknowledged between practical utterance, which is conditioned by circumstances and the currents of the times, and pure scientific theory, which is correspondingly less exposed to the dangers and upheavals of practical life. The difference between a more esoteric and a more exoteric religious doctrine cannot be eliminated. If the latter has the greater impact of life, the former is distinguished by its firm connection with scientific thought. This difference manifests what has underlain our whole discussion: the recognition of the polarity of life and thought, of *mythos* and *logos*.

Notes

1. In our time, this solution is valued primarily as a return to Fries, who stresses the symbolism of the religious mind and the immediacy of experience over against Kant: cf. Bousset's discussion of my views in 'Die Kantisch-Friesische Religionsphilosophie und ihre Anwendung auf die Theologie,' *Theologische Rundschau*, 1909. In reply to such rationalism I should like to illustrate my standpoint anew in this paper by defining more exactly the irrational ingredients of my theory, which Bousset has justly noted.
2. This development in theology is described in several earlier essays. I described the usual outcome in my review (*Göttinger Gelehrte Anzeigen*, 1896) of J. Köstlin, *Der Glaube und seine Bedeutung für Erkenntnis, Leben und Kirche*. The Ritschlians, too, like to operate with this individuality of the religious, which would make a comprehensive concept of religion impossible, forcing us to submit to the allegedly wholly individual claim to absoluteness made by Christianity.
3. Gaston Riou's highly interesting book *Aux écoutes de la France, qui vient*, the fourth edition of which was published in 1913 with a very pedestrian preface by Emile Faguet, indicates that the French situation appears to be much the same. The periodical *Foi et vie, Revue bimensuelle de culture chrétienne*, is also of great interest. It is neither a theological nor a church-sponsored magazine; it has general appeal and is influential. The supremacy of positivism among French youth is a thing of the past.
4. One example of such a prophetic announcement of a new religion is Alfred Weber, *Religion und Kultur*, 1912, or the aristocratic religion proclaimed by Stefan George's disciples in the *Jahrbuch für die geistige Bewegung*, edited by Gundolf and Wolters. The connection of these trends with the literati is well presented by Sörgel, *Dichtung und Dichter der Zeit*, 1911. Much closer to Christian theism are Hermann Bahr, *Inventur*, 1912, and Walter Rathenau, *Zur Kritik der Zeit*, 1912, as well as the previously cited French writer, Riou, who is primarily attacking Buddhistic and pessimistic moods of decadence.

5. Vol. 1, *Zur Germanisierung des Christentums*, 1911 (he means basically the re-formation of religion demanded by the present situation); Vol. 3, *Religiöse Spannungen*, 1912; Vol. 4, *Vom neuen Mythos, Eine Prognose*, 1911. These volumes contain much that is excellent. The present essay is an attempt to do justice to the moment of truth they contain.

4

Rival Methods for the
Study of Religion

The scholarly study of religion is today moving in two diametrically opposed directions. On the one side is the positivist-empirical school, which undertakes to explain the characteristic conceptions of religion as myth, on the basis of the conditions of primitive life understood in terms of an ingeniously reconstructed early history of humankind and of savagery. It makes to derive all cultus from the magic connected with these conceptions. Religion is the science, technology, and social philosophy of primitive man, but since the time of the Greeks it has been subjected to considerable change at the hands of a pure and independent science detaching itself from it, being thus partly spiritualized and ethicized, and partly pushed entirely into the background or even replaced. Here all the emphasis is put on the past, and within the sphere of the past the emphasis is placed on the connection with the primitive mentality. Thus all subsequent religious movements can be constructed as revivals of the primitive. The present and the future are viewed only as the weakening and eventual withering away of religion. The specifically religious elements in man's moods and feelings are interpreted as a natural consequence of these primitive conceptions, as their influence upon the imagination and the emotions, and are expected to disappear along with them. Any attempt to interpret religion as an elemental, basic expression of the soul is decried as nativism, as an unscientific escape into mysticism, or as the error of an incorrigible romanticism.

On the other side we see the idealistic-transcendental school, which attributes to the human mind the creation of the world of ideas as an essential inner process operating in history; among these ideas it points particularly to the religious idea as somehow organically related to consciousness. Here all effort is directed toward the present and the future, with the intention of distilling out of the apparent confusion of the historical religions an underlying, universal idea that is rooted in the consciousness itself and is essential for its original coherence. This idea (whether it be understood more in the sense of Kant or of Hegel) is—like all ideas—timeless, absolutely valid, and universal. In the past it has been hidden under the symbols of myth and dogma or cultus and customs; the task, accordingly, is to discern the ideal core beneath its various time-conditioned guises. For the future, then, the task is all the more to liberate this pure core—within the limits of reason alone—and thus to open the way to the religion of humanity. Since this pure idea of religion pertains to pure reason, it is equally disinterested in the differentation of individually formed convictions and organized religious groups. Such differentation, along with the cultus and the mythical world-view, belongs to the earlier, lower stages of cultural and spiritual evolution. With Plato and the Eleatics this pure idea begins the process of detaching itself from these phenomena and today, at a higher evolutionary stage, it is about to detach itself from Christianity and the other great world religions. The connection of the moral with the religious idea is of decisive significance here; it alone is eternal and truly abiding.

The contrast between the two theories is sharp and clear. Yet on one point they agree, namely, in their acceptance of the theory of evolution. They both regard this evolution as the gradual liberation of pure reason from myth and cultus, from misery, feeling and romanticism, from belief in miracles and unscientific attitudes. To be sure, reason—which itself constitutes the simple and necessary goal of evolution—is defined in opposite ways by the two schools; in the first instance, as the capacity to employ reason to render accumulated experience useful for the preservation and education of species; in the second, as the creative impulse of the mind to unfold its ideas in history, so as to to express its solidarity with the superhuman plenitude of spirit in the universe.

Undoubtedly both theories have contributed a great deal to a scholarly elucidation of the religious life and its history, even though they are both more interested in scholarship than in religion. Yet even for the understanding of religion immense contributions have been made by the school of Locke, Hume, and Comte, as well as by the school of Plato, Kant, and Hegel. Only at one point do both schools fail in dealing with actual religion, and this is precisely the point both have in common; namely, their acceptance of the theory of evolution. In both schools, this theory is supposed to explain genetically how the present state of religion has come to be, and accordingly to lay down a program for the future which will lead with logical necessity to the implied result.

But we must observe that actual religion can never be explained in this way; neither on the basis of primitive notions of causation which for the purposes of life appeal to analogies and similarities rather than to actual causal connections, nor on the basis of the working out of an ideal necessity amidst the chaos of the religious phenomena. Real life shows rather a sensitivity and susceptibility of the religious sense—as one has come to call an inner condition that cannot be further analyzed or attributed to anything else—which is present always and everywhere, although its strength varies, and which fuses with the infinitely varied objects (internal and external) that stimulate it; these fusions, in turn, have an enormous effect on the strength and the import of the religious sense. Religious susceptibility is only rarely limited to one individual; normally it is shared, both as to time and essential character, by entire groups; or it may be instantly communicated from one individual to a wider circle, so that there is always some sort of collective sense or conception in which the individual finds support and strength for the weakness and dependence of the person's own susceptibility. Indeed, the most common stimulus of this sort proceeds from the traditional religious framework of the group.

All this is certainly open to understanding and empathy, but hardly to explanation or derivation. Why the stimulus issues from a death, a dream, or the power of chieftains and ancestors, or on other occasions (among civilized peoples) from the image of the sun or from the social power of custom; why it affects one more strongly than another; why groups, nations, and epochs differ so greatly in their religious intensity—no one is able to explain. Even the theory of repression of interests can explain nothing here, since the very strength of what represses is to be explained only in terms of the weakness of what is repressed, and strength and weakness are alike inexplicable. Empathy and understanding are indeed possible—given a sufficiently clear tradition—because these manifestations of the religious sense continue to be found among us today and we do understand whatever we ourselves truly experience. But even as understanding of this type is not a deductive explanation, so the continuity implicit in all this is not an evolution in the sense of a mere continuation or consummation of something already present. Whatever the origin of a religious life-complex may have been, its significance is not exhausted by the history of its evolution and the enumeration of the elements that produced it.

Once formed by the confluence of a thousand impulses, such a complex becomes an entity with a momentary life and intrinsic significance of its own; the history of its origins is either forgotten or given an entirely new interpretation; and its contemporary form gives rise to new directions of the will and of life that were in no way contained in its original constituents. The new entity turns its back upon its own genesis, finds a new identity for itself in itself, and transforms itself beyond recognition through a thousand new relations. A completely inexplicable power of the momentary and the spontaneous, a continual generation of new elements, is found everywhere. Whatever conviction is carried by what is original and alive derives from confidence in the compelling power of its own momentary significance. All appeals to historical authority are already signs of a waning power. From the point of view of critical history, they are also as unhistorical as it is possible to be. Yet instances of such appeals are legion in the history of all religions. The history of Christianity, which we know best, is full of them.

In the light of the foregoing, even an allegedly rationally-necessary scheme for the future is a palpably transparent illusion. The evolutionary goal is not, in fact, constructed from a scientifically established law of cause and effect, but every 'law' of cause and effect is itself derived from a sense for the uniqueness of the moment—however this sense may arise—and the facts are accordingly arranged in a sequence that makes the religious life (conceived more concretely or more abstractly) of the present, or even merely of the author, appear as the evolutionary goal that may be glimpsed at any point. Hence the Jew, the Christian, the Hindu, and the Chinese (regardless of how loosely each may be identified with the group)—above all, the European and the Oriental—will inevitably have a different basic framework for his or her construction of the evolution of religion.

5

Christianity and the History of Religion

For the historian of the life of the mind, it is axiomatic that the mind is an independent potency not to be derived from nature and, more importantly, that it does not actualize itself simply in a formal adjustment to nature. It also contains independent spiritual contents, dispositions, and drives that give rise, in interaction with the demands of empirical reality, to the rich world of history. The independence, autonomy, and creative power of the mind as they develop in religion, morality, and culture become so clearly apparent in these areas that the mind can be treated as at least relatively independent.

Now, as religion is a constitutive part of historical existence, its main questions arise in the area of history. The modern scientific study of history, which has extended its sway over previously unknown areas and eras, has confronted the Christian faith with entirely new problems. In fact, the rise of a comparative history of religion has shaken the Christian faith more deeply than anything else. The application of new pragmatic and critical methods, pioneered by the Deists and energetically deepened by the German theologians of the eighteenth century, showed the mutability of Christianity by reference to its own history. It destroyed the Catholic fiction that the church simply represented the continuation of original Christianity, as well as the Protestant fiction that the Reformation represented its restoration. All the questions raised by the previously prevailing confessional view of history were replaced by new ones that involved the history of the church and of revelation in an all-compassing historical pragmatism.

What the eighteenth century had begun—still hesitantly, always in search of an immutable truth of reason, and revering the 'natural religion' in all religion but especially in Christianity—the nineteenth century continued, with growing success and ever increasing scope. Above all, it developed concrete philological-historical methods both for particular areas and for history as a whole. The pragmatic approach was replaced by the genetic approach, which rests on the assumption that the development of the life of the mind is homogeneous and continuous; and which showed, by studying the laws governing the formation of traditions in the nations of antiquity, that the actual course of events can be clearly reconstructed out of these very traditions, even though they tend to obliterate every sign of development or natural conditioning. Myths and traditions, cultures and religious laws were now perceived in their natural relationship to the whole of life. Finally, there were the researches of ethnologists and anthropologists concerning the peoples-without-history, which were found to bear many features that showed a striking similarity to the oldest traces of the cultural and religious development of the civilized nations and thus threw a wholly new light on their beginnings. Out of the co-operation of the study of antiquity, oriental philology, and ethnology there accordingly emerged a grand new discipline, the history of religion. Its methods deeply affected the investigation of the Israelite and Christian religions.

As a result, Christianity lost its exclusive-supernatural foundation. It was now perceived as only one of the great world religions, along with Islam and Buddhism, and like these, as constituting the culmination of complicated historical developments. What would become now of Christianity's exclusive truth or even of its decisive superiority? Above all, what would become of the belief in an exclusive revelation? But the consequences go even further. Not only the truth and validity of Christianity but also those of religion itself, as a unique sphere of life, disappear in this maelstrom of historical diversity. What can be true in the religious belief in God when this belief manifests itself in a thousand different forms, clearly dependent on the situation and the conditions in which they arise; and goes back to revelations that purport to be infallible and universally valid, or at least a direct, supernatural work of the Deity, yet completely contradict one another? In view of the countless number and the deep differences of the *religions* how can there still be *religion* at all, if religion is truly to mean communion with the Deity? Must we not at least follow Schiller's well-known words:

> Of the religions you name,
> You ask me which one I profess.
> Not one. And why not?
> Religion prevents me.

But—like Odin's spear—the great historical crises often heal the
very wounds they have caused. While the Enlightenment (due to the
after-effects of supernaturalism) had sought the content of history in a
rational truth that remains perpetually and rigidly the same, history
has more recently been viewed as the manifestation of manifold basic
tendencies of human nature and, in their interconnection, as unfolding
the totality of human reason in the course of the generations. This
great modern conception of history has given rise to a new conception
of religion and its historical development. Here, too, the aim is to
understand and analyze the fundamental experience, and the resulting
formation of religious groups and unfolding of the religious idea. Of
course, a thorough knowledge of the empirical history of religion is
requisite here, which up to now is only very partially available. On the
whole, however, this is the way that corresponds to the general trend
of scientific thought and has already led to many valuable insights.
We simply must learn to view religion more sympathetically; to free
ourselves from doctrinaire, rationalistic, and systematizing
presuppositions; and to focus more intently on the characteristic,
distintively religious phenomena and personages rather than on
average people. Then the deepest core of the religious history of
humanity reveals itself as an experience that cannot be further
analyzed, an ultimate and original phenomenon that constitutes, like
moral judgement and aesthetic perception and yet with characteristic
differences, a simple fact of psychic life. Everywhere the basic reality
of religion is the same: an underivable, purely positive, again and
again experienced contact with the Deity. This unity has its ground in
a common dynamism of the human spirit which advances in different
ways as a result of the mysterious movement of the divine Spirit in the
unconscious depth of the human spirit, which is everywhere the same.
Unable to attain its goal in the short span of individual life, this
movement is effected through the co-operative efforts of countless
generations as they are grasped and led by the divine activity,
surrendering to it and experiencing its true import in ever greater
fullness and profoundness.

Now, the more the great religions grasp their ultimate goal, the less
likely is their self-seclusion. Instead, they strive for the truth in its
totality and fullness, often with consuming passion. Only where the
religions are filled with such passion do they unfold a truly progressive
vitalilty of their own. What really counts, then, is to find the goal, or
the direction of the goal, of the history of religion, which can only be
found in a concrete religiosity of exceptional profundity, power, and
lucidity, not in the related areas of art and science and not in an

abstract religion derived from the multiplicity of the religions. This religiosity must comprehend, or be able to comprehend, the truth-moments of all the others. In any case, it must give living embodiment to the central idea taking shape in the evolutionary process.

The modern approach to history looks upon the history of religion as the history of God's relationship to humanity, a history of redemption which lifts both humanity as a whole and the individual person out of their bondage to mere sensual nature, with its needs and drives, into communion with God, into the freedom of the spirit transcending the mere positivity of a dull existence. Since the history of religion thus attains, or rather actualizes, the truth in varying degrees (depending on situation and conditions) and unites human beings with the deepest ground of their being and the quintessence of their spiritual goods, it is inseparable from the conviction that in it, and in it alone, there is genuine historical progress. It accordingly claims the right—a right not shared by the history of other spheres of life—to believe in the attainment of an ultimate, simple goal.

But the history of religion shows clearly that religion is not simply the direct work of God in the soul. That it is, is the theory of mysticism—that peculiar result of history of religion developments which obtains wherever particular concrete forms of the belief in God have been abandoned in favor of a completely ineffable working of God in the soul that is everywhere the same, or where the desire for a direct and inward communion with God leads to the rejection of all outward means. The self-centeredness of such piety, its lack of content and community, and its artificial concentration and withdrawal from the world, leading to over-stimulation and exhaustion, show that such phenomena cannot be regarded as normal. The religious impression or, to use a term from empirical psychology, the religious stimulus always arises from inward and outward events and experiences in nature and history, in heart and conscience. For the vast majority of people the religious stimulus is mediated by the religious tradition, with non-traditional stimuli generally playing only a minor role. The peculiar mystery of individual religious development is how traditions that are at first strange, not understood at all, or childishly misinterpreted can gradually lead to an independent, inward, and personal piety that is conscious, at least at its high-points, of an inner communion and interaction with the divine life. Where it is possible to speak of the beginnings of a religion, we encounter predominantly original personages who are less closely bound to the mediation of tradition and whose great new visions are stimulated by great events in nature or history, by the outward course of their own life, or even by the processes of their inner life. Others are then attracted by the power of their piety and personality. The seers, ecstatics, and inspired people of the ancient religions, as well as prophets, reformers, and saints, are generally personages of this kind. Their chief characteristic is an enormous one-sidedness; only by pushing everything else aside are they able to make their religious impact.

If we go beyond the accidents of time and space, personality and tradition, we find everywhere a very similar truth. We note a great sense of awe before the mystery of a supersensible world that speaks its word within the course of everyday life: whether it comforts people or frightens them, it always disrupts the slumber of a purely innerworldly existence. We also note the manifestation of divine forces in nature, and the authorization of moral and legal norms on the part of the Deity. Above all, we note the higher goods of eternal blessedness and the rise of the belief in redemption. All these phenomena are properly viewed as belonging together, as requiring a unified, comprehensive treatment.

There is also a 'religious apperception,' where the religious stimulus enters directly into the nexus of conceptions and feelings, is influenced by it, but also gives new directions to it. As the spiritual life reaches higher levels, the conditions of this apperception become correspondingly less transparent and more complicated, and religion now demands more insistently the concentration and quiet attention to the religious stimulus known as meditation and prayer. In this connection it must not be forgotten that individuals do not stand alone but that their close interaction gives certain inclinations and orientations a position of social dominance. This is why there are predominantly conservative and predominantly critical periods even in the history of religion. Periods of violent religious conflict, finally, can lead to periods where great masses of people turn against religion and prefer to concern themselves with secular, more easily ascertainable matters. Examples of this are the culture of the Roman empire, the Confucian morality of the higher classes of China, and the conditions of life in modern Europe.

Now comes the question whether this varied and partial apprehension of the truth [in the history of religion] has a point of convergence, an obviously visible high-point; or, more precisely, whether Christianity, which purports to be a such a high-point, can indeed be recognized as such. When we put the question in this way, it is because Christianity alone has made this claim with ever increasing urgency in the course of its development, and with ever more principled appeal to its own innermost essence. Sustained by the authority of its Master, it addresses itself exclusively to the essential inner core of the individual, to the most universal, profound, and simple needs for rest and peace of heart and for a positive, ultimate, absolutely valid meaning of existence. It addresses itself to every individual without exception, presupposing this essential core in everyone and with full assurance that it can educate all to recognize these needs. Peace of soul with God, overcoming the anguish of the world and all pains of conscience, living and doing the will of God, and the commandment to love the neighbor who is such because all have a common Father: this is its gospel. From it Christianity derives the firmest and most comprehensive community, by having the essential human nature originate in the divine Spirit and by pointing it to the goal of community with God and the neighbor, requiring every believer to co-operate in this universal community and the goal of a shared perfection. This is why it is the only religion to claim an absolute and unconditional universality; to have produced out of itself a philosophy of history linking the beginning, the center, and the end of human history; and to recognize in this history a coherent and unique reality promoting unconditionally worthwhile goals. Above all, Christianity does not simply assert its universal validity but derives it from an inner necessity in the being of God: creating the world out of love, the Creator *must* lead creatures out of the world, out of illusion, out of guilt and discouragement, back to the Divine Being. Both God's grace and commandments flow from this essential nature and [creatures] find their inward fulfillment through love to the God who first loved them. Here the universal tendency of religion reaches its culmination: all particular, ethnic, and worldly conditionings are eliminated; and all dependence on a merely given (and ever changing) situation is overcome through the universality of a future goal that is grounded in nature (*Wesen*) and destiny (*Bestimmung*).

Also present, to be sure, is the onesidedness of the predominantly religious type of life. But it is precisely in this onesidedness that Christianity attains full inwardness and purely human universality. Only in tension with inner-worldly cultural values does it attain the character of a higher life of the mind, where unity must be attained again and again through conscious effort. Christianity has always shown this tendency toward the individual and personal, the universally human, and the totality with all its tensions. This is confirmed by comparison with the other great universal religions that represent its only competitors. Islam—Christianity's younger sibling since both descended from Judaism—has taken over from Judaism and Christianity in a purely external manner this universalism, revelation-by-the-Book, and a fragmentary philosophy of history. Only the unity of its God and the simplicity of its few paltry moral commandments reflect universalism; which does not, however, derive from an inner necessity of the essential nature of its God, who is hard, unpredictable, arbitrary. Islam thus represents a regression from Judaism and Christianity and has never been able to conceal its characteristic ties to the Arab nation and war.

Buddhism, which shows many parallels to Christianity, originates as merely the religion of a monastic order. All who have come to understand the nothingness of the will-to-be are admittedly allowed and encouraged to enter the order, which shows a considerable missionary vitality. But its universal validity derives only from the universal validity of this understanding, not from the essential nature of a single Deity that calls all to a common goal. The Deity has here been replaced by a merely impersonal order of redemption. The physical survival of the enlightened members of the order always depends on the great mass of the unenlightened laity. The vast majority of people remain caught up in the cycle of reincarnations, a mass from which the initiates separate themselves but on which they depend for sustenance until they disappear in Nirvana. This process repeats itself in successive world periods, without linkage or goal. Life and piety lack a uniform, positive goal, as does the world itself. The order recruits members and exalts the peace of redemption, but no inner necessity requires that all of humanity ever be gathered together in it. However much here, as in Islam, the universality of religion is asserted in one way or another, the claim is less intense than that of Christianity.

Only *one* religion has completely broken out of the spell of the religion of nature and stands unique in this respect: the religion of Israel and Christianity. In view of the impending catastrophe of the nation, the religion of Israel detached itself on principle from its particularistic and natural-religious foundations and linked faith in Yahweh to purity of heart and the assurance that at the end of days all the confusions of earthly life would be resolved. Christianity, in the person of Jesus, built on this core conviction, which (as its foundation) prevents it from relapse into the pantheism and mysticism of the perfected religion of nature. While Christianity experiences God more intimately in the individual heart and in more direct activity in the world, it waits for a higher world, in the conviction that the world of the senses passes away. A purely immanent absorption in God is thus excluded. Since Christianity redeems not only from the anguish of finitude and the oppression of nature but above all from

the defiance and despondency of the human heart, from weakness and
guilt-feelings, and since it bestows not only peace of heart and
assurance concerning a supertemporal community with God but also
the power to act and to love here on earth, it is a religion of redemption
of a higher order, going equally far beyond the pessimism of Buddhism
and the mysticism of Neo-Platonism, the two final developments of
non-Christian piety. By breaking on principle with every kind of nature
religion, Christianity alone among the religions completes the tendency
towards redemption, just as it alone completes the related tendency
towards a purely intrinsic universal validity. It is because of its
empirical uniqueness and the inner coincidence of what it is with what
it demands that we recognize in the Prophetic-Christian religion the
high-point, or rather a new point of departure, in the history of religion;
not a conclusion and end calling for rest but the beginning of a new
day for the world, with new work and new struggles.

It is obvious that as the underlying view of history assumed in the
present study derives from our classical literature and philosophy, so
its view of the history of religion is close to the ideas of Lessing,
Goethe, Herder, Kant, Hegel, Schleiermacher, and similar thinkers. It
only seeks to free the understanding of religion from the all-too-great
proximity to other areas of culture in which it was placed by these
men. Lessing's 'eternal gospel' was conceived in too close an analogy
to the science of the Enlightenment. Herder brought religion too close
to the ethical concept of humaneness; by finding instances of this
humaneness everywhere, he largely obliterated the boundaries between
religions. Schleiermacher practically dissolved religion in a romatic
Spinozism that looked upon the religions as merely individually
different ways of being conscious of one's immanence in God. Hegel
likewise conformed religion too much to metaphysical monism; above
all, he derived the evolution of religion in too doctrinaire and rigid a
fashion from the logical necessity of the dialectic of the idea, thus
failing to do justice to the mysterious power of religion and the
contingency of its various movements.

More recently, of course, 'modern' science has for the most part put
a great distance between itself and these deepest foundations of our
culture. This was not so much because of scientific considerations but
because of changed external conditions resulting from the enormous
practical transformations of the nineteenth century. The all-
transforming achievements of the new technology, the burning social
questions resulting from them, the reawakening of national egoism,
and not least, the growth and improving living conditions of the
population, have diverted all interest to practical cultural questions,

focusing on the problems of innerworldly happiness. The opinion of the day is dominated by the dogma of cultural progress, or culture-optimism, and all scientific achievements are viewed in this light. From the historicizing thought of the last century or more, every effort is being made to infer the consequence of relativism, but only to devalue the ideal powers of the past and especially Christianity; faith in progress and in an absolute cultural happiness of the future remains undisturbed. The natural sciences are cultivated assiduously in order to subject all life and reality to the 'laws of nature,' but only in order to undermine spiritual values that go beyond innerworldly happiness; to the human will, on the other hand, an enormous power to manipulate these same laws of nature in the interests of cultural happiness is attributed.

Such general moods are not easily dissipated, least of all by the demonstration of their inconsistencies. Their practical consequences will have to become more clearly apparent. The desolation of the life of the mind, the continuing decline of moral strength and religious seriousness, and the deadening effects of self-gratification must show where this approach will lead us, in spite of all outward progress. It must demonstrate that a perfect innerworldly cultural happiness is the most deceptive of all illusions. Only then will recourse be had to our best cultural heritage, which will readily permit the utilization of scientific advances. The serious dangers posed by the historicizing of all science, including the scientific study of religion, will also be more readily dealt with at that time than now.

This is not the place to discuss the extent to which the views expressed here can (and will be permitted to) affect the official theology of the churches and theological faculties. Theology is not a pure science, or at not least a free science, since it is bound to the legal enactments, the actual tradition, and the conditions and goals confronting it. It is more of a compromise with science than a genuine science. Its tasks are primarily practical, given with the actual state of the institutional church. Theologians, insofar as they are scholars, may indeed make significant contributions toward the solution of the great questions. But insofar as they also have to serve ecclesiastical interests, they are bound by practical tasks and circumstances. Actually, the great scientific questions have always been settled outside of theology, despite the contributions of individual theologians, who may well be entitled to distinguish between an exoteric and an esoteric theology so long as they are conscious of having the same aim in both. But the vicious circle, that theology's self-isolation intensifies the displeasure of science while the hostility of science increases the self-isolation of theology, will not be broken so long as the extraordinary significance of the church question for national life is not perceived by enlightened indifference.

The general interest attaches to something quite different from specifically theological disquisitions. It requires that precisely in the field of religion, the historical relativism that threatens in all fields to drown us in erudition and to paralyze all creative power be recognized and overcome as the most dangerous of all opponents. Indications are multiplying on all sides that people are getting tired of it. The attempt is made to overcome it through patriotic enthusiasm, through the ideal of social justice, through futurism, through non-religious altruism; there is a thirst for simple, absolute, universally valid ideals. All this will not do it. But the recognition will come that religion is the true home of all such ideals, and that, above all, an assured and joyous faith in an absolute goal must be found again in it. To be sure, this cannot be done by a sudden turning away from history and an abjuration of its methods. But it can be done if we recall the great basic ideas of our classical literature, philosophy, and historiography and see in history the unfolding of a uniform and essentially simple spiritual import; and if we seek in the greatest and most powerful of all religions no longer merely the interesting historical phenomenon but the connection with the eternal core of the life of the mind. Then it will also be seen that the history of religion has not only parts but also a spiritual bond, and that this bond is not as difficult to find as the careful people suppose who would reserve all historical study to the specialists. Even the possibility that the end of this bond has been placed in our own hand will no longer seem frightening. If history is indeed no more than the infinitely complicated struggle for the unfolding of a simple spiritual import, then should we be amazed if in Christianity we had attained to the core of this import and were now bound to fashion our present and future by reference to it and empowered by it?

6

The Dogmatics of the History-of-Religions School

The expression 'history-of-religions school'[1] was coined in Germany or, to be precise, in German theology, in order to designate a specific conception of the tasks of religious thinking and of dogmatic theology. The writer of this article is regarded as the systematic theologian of this approach. Thus, it is appropriate for him, in answer to the request of the editors of the *American Journal of Theology* to state the meaning of a dogmatics working with the presuppositions and in the spirit of this school.

In the first place, it should be noted that the subject indicated by this expression is neither a specifically German problem in any sense of the word, nor is it really a new question, nor is it a univocal and unified axiom, upon which a 'school' in the proper sense of the word could be constructed. Rather, the expression signifies simply the recognition of the universally accepted twofold scientific conclusion that human religion exists only in multiple individual forms which develop in very complex relations of mutual contact and influence, and that a decision concerning these forms cannot be made with the old dogmatic expedient of distinguishing between a natural and a supernatural revelation. This distinction has been used by all the great monotheistic religions, by Judaism, Islam, Christianity, and in a certain sense also by Buddhism. It suffices only so long as one lives exclusively within the horizon of one's own inherited religion and is therefore able, without being contradicted by the claims made by others, naively to ascribe to it sole validity on the basis of its supernatural origin. It no longer suffices as soon as one's theoretical horizon has been expanded to include the totality of human religions, and as soon as exclusive claims to revelation collide in the practical struggle of the religions with each other. Once this situation has arisen, a shifting of horizons occurs. In place of a horizon dominated by the sole, supernatural truth of one's own religion, there appears the pluralism of rival analogous claims to truth. Today this situation has arisen practically everywhere. From the scholarly point of view the approach to the religious life of humanity is no longer a supernaturalist or philosophical apologetic for one's one religion, but rather a historical, comparative study of religions. Overwhelmingly difficult as this undertaking may be, and liable as we are to superficial self-deception, this is nevertheless the primary scholarly way in which we have to come to terms with the religious problem today.

It should be recognized that this conception is nothing new. It arose already with the collapse of the simple supernaturalistic apologetic of the Christian confessions in the eighteenth century. A number of influences led to this result. First there was the deadly conflict between the rival Christian confessions. Then came the conflict between a theology resting on supernatural foundations and the autonomous rational philosophy of the late Renaissance. Then came the period of colonial expansion with the consequent awareness of the plurality of forms of the religions of humanity. Finally appeared the idea of the development of the human spirit through different stages and forms. The English Deists, Locke, Hume, and Gibbon, Voltaire, Dupuis and the Ideologues, Herder and the German theology of the eighteenth century, and finally Lessing, Kant and Hegel, Comte and Herbert Spencer, set forth these ideas—to be sure with very different judgements concerning the religious life and the results of its development. Through the powerful countermovement to the Enlightenment which arose as Methodism, Pietism, biblicism, Catholic reaction, and political restoration, the historical conception of religion was beaten back and driven out of theology, in which it had already found a place. Today, however, the reactionary movement is on the ebb or is restricted to certain narrow sects. Thus the old statement of the problem has again come to the fore and has conquered a large portion of Protestant theology.

Since we are concerned here with the history-of-religions attitude only in so far as it has been appropriated, or can be appropriated, by theology, it, is of course, understood that we shall deal with it only insofar as it is compatible with a personal affirmation of the religious life and with the affirmation of the Christian world of ideas. We therefore exclude all purely skeptical, positivistic, and illusionistic theories that may have adopted the history-of-religions point of view. On the contrary, we affirm only those interpretations that see in religion the revelation of deepest truth, and that recognize in the development of religion progress to purified religious knowledge. The reasons for this cannot be given here. But it is self-evident that Christian theology can deal only with the latter interpretation of religion. Even with this restriction, history-of-religions thinking in theology is not unified: there is no 'school' devoted to it. In view of the widely comprehensive and far-reaching significance of this way of thinking, the formation of a 'school' is not possible. In the realm of theology in particular such thinking designates two types of interest.

The first interest is historical research directed to the history of Christianity itself. Here history-of-religions thinking does not refer to a universal philosophy of religion or to any definite dogmatics. Rather it means the concrete explanation or clarification of the rise of biblical religion out of the contact with, and in opposition to, other religions. Since we have learned that the pre-history to Genesis consists of Israelite legends, not unlike the legends of other peoples, and since we have come to know that the people of Israel entered very late into the circle of oriental history that is known to us, it is clear that the origin of the Yahweh-religion is no longer a problem to be solved purely by use of information given in the Bible. It demands for its solution a knowledge of contemporary religions, and especially an acquaintance with the religion of the Arabian nomads. It is no longer a biblical problem, but rather a problem in the history of religions. The same is true for the further development of the Yahweh-religion into prophetism, into the religion of the Law and priestly religion, and into messianism and apocalypticism. Moreover, it is especially true for the exceedingly difficult task of illuminating the rise of Christianity, which in the preaching of Jesus already presupposes the peculiarly complicated religious history of late Judaism.

In particular, the transformation of the gospel into the world-conquering Christ-religion and into the sacramental church can be made intelligible only in this way. It is superfluous to remark that the same methodological requirements hold for the study of the further development of the church and of dogma. This conception extends through all schools of exegetical and historical theology, in so far as they take historical research seriously. Even very conservative theologians find themselves compelled to acquiesce in this point of view, although they are accustomed in one way or another to blunt its point. These methods are actually used in scientific theology of every sort, though the treatment may be now more learned, now more imaginative, now more cautious, now more daring, now more consistent, now more timid. The Semitic and classical philologists have also joined in this historical work and are energetically pushing it forward. We cannot, then, speak of a history-of-religions school but only of a history-of-religions method which is more or less radically employed. At most one could use the term to designate those scholars who had given up the last remnant of a core of supernaturally revealed truths in the Bible, and who work exclusively with the universally valid methods of psychology and history. But even these scholars form no 'school' and they certainly do not have a dogmatic theology in common. We may simply mention here such diverse figures as Robertson Smith, Wellhausen, Lagarde, Gunkel, Weizsäcker, Wrede, Usener, Harnack, Holtzmann, and Bousset.

The second type of interest is concerned with the philosophy of religion or fundamental theology. It is not concerned with the concrete questions of the rise and development of biblical religion, but rather with the great question of grounding the validity of Christianity within the stream of the universal development of the history of religions and over against the entirely analogous claims to validity made by the other great religions and philosophical world-views or rational-autonomous religions. That is not an historical problem but a systematic one. But insofar as it is systematic problem, it is still not yet a dogmatic one; for it deals only in the most general terms with the question of in what sense the Christian world of ideas and of life can be acknowledged as normative after one can no longer base this normative claim upon the simple inspiration and supernatural revelation of the Bible. In this enterprise, very little is said about the dogmatic structure of Christian religious ideas. As a matter of fact, the dogmatic systems constructed on this basis differ widely from one another, if, indeed, the dogmatic task is not neglected, the impulse to constructive theology being checked by the magnitude of the general task of establishing the validity of Christianity at all. Thus we are dealing here with a general problem in the philosophy of religion that can find its solution only through adequate conceptions of the essence and the development of religion. Of course, theologians of very different tendencies are engaged in the solution of this problem, and its importance is recognized even among conservative theologians. In particular, missionaries to cultured people cannot evade it. Moreover many non-theological influences are very active at this point, since the problems of religion, of religious development and its ends have naturally been taken up by ethnologists, anthropologists, psychologists, and systematic philosophers; and theologians have received the most varied suggestions and stimuli from them.

Thus in the case of this second interest as well, it is not possible to speak of a history-of-religions school. At best, we might so designate those theologians who, renouncing all appeal to supernatural communications and foundations, seek to answer the questions that they ask purely on the basis of historical development, as, for example, Otto Pfleiderer and the author of this article have done. Simply to place together these two very different representatives of the method shows how impossible it is to speak of any 'school.' We have a modern, scientific, fundamental conception of the most general sort, capable of most fruitful development in different directions; but we have no 'school.' Let the reader simply recall such different scholars as the Caird brothers, Herrmann Siebeck, Rudolf Eucken, Wilhelm Wundt, Auguste Sabatier.

When, however, we turn from these two general applications of the fundamental approach in the realm of theology to the specific major task of theology, that is, *to the exposition of a normative, Christian world view or to so-called dogmatics*, then the two types of interest which we have noted come close together and furnish certain definite presuppositions and guiding lines for dogmatics. These are so definite that it would be possible to speak of a dogmatic based on history-of-religions principles, and in this sense to speak of a 'school,' if such a dogmatics, as a matter of fact, had been worked out. In England the dominating intellectual of the eighteenth century, John Locke, anticipated such a program. His *Reasonableness of Christianity* contains a study, elegantly grounded on psychology of religion and the history of religion, of the essence of the gospel. He saw the essence of the gospel as the ethical idea of the kingdom of God; both Paulinism and the ecclesial dogma opposed this idea, connecting it with the developmental traits of Greek ethics. Locke's view is the basis for the dogmatics of the spiritually more refined Enlightenment. In Germany, Kant also represented essentially the same standpoint. However, a very undeveloped history of religions was presupposed, and thus it was not very difficult to connect a dogmatics to it. Beyond this example we have had only preliminary attempts in this direction in the nineteenth century. They belong to German thought, whereas English thought since the rise of Methodism returned to the old pathways.

The first of these is the most famous of all. It is not less than Schleiermacher's dogmatics, which was constructed on the basis of both a general, comparative philosophy of religion and also upon a historical-critical and therefore history-of-religions investigation of Christianity. It rested on a philosophy of the history of religions according to which the highest stage of development, monotheism, resolves itself into either ethical theism or quietistic monism. Of the two, only ethical theism can stand as the final perfection of the religious idea. Now since this type of theism actually exists in the form of a world religion only in Christianity, the highest type of religious knowledge must be set forth as Christian. It must be then noted that this theism receives a unique, uplifting, and redemptive power through its historical connection with the person of Jesus and from the impression made by this personality. Thus dogmatics sets forth the essential ideas of Christianity concerning God, the world, and humanity, ideas radiating from the central personality of Jesus as a redemptive, spiritual power. In order to fulfil the practical purpose of regulating preaching and instruction in the Protestant church, it relates itself with piety but also with great freedom to the religious ideas of the Protestant ecclesiastical tradition.

The other great attempt at a dogmatics along history-of-religions lines was made by Hegel and was further developed by his theological disciples, in particular by the famous Tübingen school. Here the entire philosophy of religion, like the philosophy of history, was deduced from a definite concept of the divine nature and from the logical principles of its evolution. In this sense the world of Christian experience was not left, as it was by Schleiermacher, to be treated on the basis of a mere personal affirmation and a subjective, free formulation. Rather it was construed as a logically necessary result of the history of religion, completing the self-evolution of the Divine Spirit. Christianity is the self-realization of the Divine Spirit in a historical movement which redeems finite spirits to itself. Dogmatics coincides completely with the exposition of the content of the concept of God; it is absolute and final both as philosophy and as religion. Its Christian character rests upon the fact that in Christianity the perfect religious idea actually came to expression. The practical character of such a dogmatics was to be found for the church by expounding the content of the absolute ideal as the real inner meaning of the traditional ecclesiastical formulas.

Neither of these attempts was consistently carried through. Schleiermacher bogged down in accommodations to the ecclesiastical tradition; the result was a travesty in the shape of an ecclesiastical, biblicistic dogmatics. The Hegelian school collapsed with the dissolution of the Hegelian metaphysics; and with the critical displacement of an absolute, rational religion by the recognition of the concrete character of actual Christianity. The general scientific interest in Germany at present is not concerned with religion or theology at all. In the German churches, however, there has triumphed a more or less resolute confessional or pietistic-biblical supernaturalism that, by appealing to the inner proof of the miraculous character of Christianity exhibited in conversion, evades the questions generated by the history-of-religions perspective and leaves them to the philologists, the ethnologists, and the philosophers, with whose writings these theologians do not concern themselves. Even the Ritschlian school was and continues to be a type of biblicism which, indeed permits historical criticism of the Bible; but which declines to engage in comparative study of the history of religions.

In recent years this reaction has somewhat abated in the realm of scientific theology. The tasks of exegetical and historical theology are being conceived with a thoroughgoing recognition of the inner implications of the history-of-religions method, and are being furthered by the work of philologists in the same field. Philosophy also has become interested again in the philosophy of religion and has devoted itself with energy to the definition of the stages in the historical evolution of religion. In the nature of the case, both these attempts look toward the same end. From the perspective of the former, historical research, a comprehensive view of Christianity is possible only in the framework of the universal development of religion. From the perspective of the latter, development theory, it is, vice versa, possible to undertake research into the history of biblical religion only with a history-of-religions method. Thus the old situation of the Enlightenment, Schleiermacher, and Hegel has again appeared. But it is not precisely the same situation; it has, in the meantime, been intensified and become exceedingly complex.

On the one hand, the strictly historical interpretation of Christianity has made tremendous strides and has furnished a historical-critical picture very different from that which lay before Hegel and Schleiermacher. The relation of the Old and the New Testaments stands in a very different light. The highest development of Israel is to be found in prophetism; the religion of the Law and priestly religion constitute a later development. Between these and the preaching of Jesus late Judaism intervenes, presenting a wealth of new developments that, for the most part, can be understood only on the basis of a history-of-religions approach, and that moreover, furnish the presuppositions of Christianity itself. The preaching and the life of Jesus are to be derived only from the synoptic Gospels, and even here they can be identified only in their most general features. Jesus' life and teaching must be interpreted not by reference to later Christology and metaphysics but exclusively in the light of prophetism and late eschatological Judaism. The rise and development of the Christ-religion into a new community and church, so strikingly different from Jesus' message about the kingdom of God, constitutes as yet a much disputed but still unsolved problem. In the solution of this problem, however, interpretations derived from the history of religions play an important part. The picture is quite different from that found in Schleiermacher's *Life of Jesus* and in the expositions of the Tübingen scholars, who still believed it possible to write a genuine history of Jesus and to derive the dogmas and cultus of the church from exclusively Christian sources.

On the other hand, however, the general picture of a universal investigation in the history of religions has become much clearer and more comprehensive, but for that very reason abounding in difficulties and questions. There stretches before us the limitless, subterranean field of primitive ethnic religions. Many of the distinctly realistic and sensuous rites and conceptions of these religions have become spiritualized and sublimated in the highest forms of religion, but they show a constant tendency to revert to the original type. The polytheistic religions of cultured peoples are seen to have highly differentiated forms, so that no common schema can give adequate expression to them all; each is indissolubly bound up with specific conditions of civilization. Finally, the great world religions are found to be extraordinarily involved in similarities and in differences. The oriental religions, with their numerous analogies to Christianity and their own peculiar religious and ethical values, are even more in view; they demand that we come to terms with them practically. Under these circumstances, those constructions of the development of religion ventured by Hegel and Schleiermacher appear to us to be completely antiquated exercises of the imagination. Indeed, the very thought of setting forth any one historical religion as complete and final, capable of supplanting all others, seems to us open to serious criticism and doubt.

In view of this state of affairs, it may appear completely impossible to undertake to construct a religious world-view and a religious proclamation on the basis of the history of religions. Indeed, many scholars do judge it to be impossible. The consequence of such an attitude, however, can be only a general religious skepticism, which becomes wide-spread precisely because of such impressions. Now religious skepticism involves the complete dissolution of the religious life and its not possible for anyone who, in spite of the present confusion, has maintained a genuine religious feeling. Another possibility would be a religion completely emancipated from history and created out of the common content of all religions, or a religion based on philosophical principles. But the first is an error that an accurate knowledge of the history of religions completely refutes. The second is an illusion that is shattered by the dependence of the religious elements of philosophies on the great, historical religions, and by the impotence of every form of religion which is purely individualistic and intellectual. Thus we are thrown back upon history and upon the necessity of constructing out of history a world of ideas that shall be normative for us.

When we have said this, however, we have recognized the impulse leading to a dogmatics and, indeed, have mentioned the *first task* of a dogmatics proceeding on the basis of the history of religions. This task consists, first of all, of establishing, on the basis of a philosophy of the comparative history of religions, the fundamental and universal supremacy of Christianity for our own culture and civilization. Certainly, we cannot set Christianity forth as the religion that perfects and actualizes in final form the concept of religion—or, to use Hegel's expression, as the absolute religion. But we can juxtapose it, in the whole rich content of its historical development, to the other world religions. We can measure them all against a standard that arises in the comparison itself out of our religious and moral feelings. Such a standard is not scientifically demonstrable, but neither is it any ready-made prejudice or irresponsible bit of arbitrariness. Rather, it is a decision which grows out of a sympathetic appreciation of these groups.

This decision must be made in favor of prophetic-Christian theism, as over against the quietism and pessimism of the oriental religions. For whatever Brahmanism, Buddhism, and Confucianism may possess in terms of religious depth and ethical astuteness, they have become rigidified in problematic ways and have degenerated into external, formal structures. In comparison, Christianity possesses a much greater capacity for self-criticism and rejuvenation. In particular because of its roots in uncosmological, ethical prophetism and its assimilation of the Platonic doctrine of the soul and European-Greek science, Christianity possesses a fullness of movement and life which is lacking in the East. It may then be indirectly shown how such a decision is a result of the religious idea itself, and is compatible with the demands of other areas of life. We have no occasion to abandon the Christian foundations of the European and American world; we must develop our religious future out of this basis of our entire spiritual existence.[2]

But what do we mean by Christianity? This is the second major question. The *second task* and foundation of dogmatics lies in answering it, and again this can occur only in a way inspired by the history of religions. The first investigation leads only to Christianity in general, not exclusively to the Bible, but to the whole living, historical complexity known as Christianity. This however, represents an extraordinarily extensive world of thought and life with widely divergent periods and epochs. It cannot, just as if stands, furnish the foundation and object of dogmatics. Moreover, the interpretation of Christianity is very definitely conditioned by thinking along the lines of the history of religions. This shows us how the primitive biblical religion was bound up with very definite conditions of its age, how Platonism and Stoicism blended with Christianity until they were indistinguishable, how various national, political and social ideals determined and transformed Christianity, how Protestantism gave it a new meaning as a religion of individualistic conviction, and how modern science and humanistic ethics have drawn it into their atmosphere. Under these circumstances it is clear that for more than one reason the Christianity which is to be expounded by dogmatics is not identical with the thought-world and ethics of the New Testament. Simple biblicism is impossible.

But what, then, is Christianity? Locke and the Enlightenment already asked this question. Historical-critical thinking and historical-evolutionary thinking lead us to regard the entire range of Christian life and thought as a gradual unfolding of an immanent impulse or fundamental idea. This idea, or this 'essence' unfolding in all specific manifestations, might then be taken as the subject matter and foundation of dogmatics. Schleiermacher found the essence of Christianity to be belief in the redemption effectuated through Jesus; or to express it more accurately, in the redemptive increase of ethical-religious vigor radiating from Jesus, and in the consequent religious humanity constituting the kingdom of God. Hegel and the Tübingen school found the essence of Christianity to be the idea of the Trinity or of the Incarnation, in accordance with which the world of created beings, which had become differentiated from God, returned to him in religious knowledge. Thus universal humanity attained to divine humanity, or to unity with God, and therefore to unity with itself. Adolf Harnack, in many respects approximating the point of view of the history of religions and the philosophy of religion, in his well-known book defined the essence of Christianity by appealing to the preaching of Jesus concerning the kingdom of God. This conception of the kingdom of God consisted in brotherly love founded upon trust in God as the Father of Jesus Christ. If we take these three typical definitions, it appears that in the first case the essence of Christianity is a humanizing of the pietistic, ecclesiastical doctrine of redemption; in the second instance it is a speculative interpretation of the central ecclesiastical dogmas of the Trinity and the Incarnation; in the third instance it is a Kantian, ethical interpretation of Jesus' preaching concerning the kingdom of God. In none of these cases can the idea of Christianity be regarded as the actual unity of all the factors in its historical development.

The essence of Christianity cannot be determined in this fashion. A genuinely historical point of view reveals to us such a variety of interpretations, formulations, and syntheses that no single idea or impulse can dominate the whole. Thus the essence of Christianity can be understood only as the new interpretations and new adaptations, corresponding to each new situation, produced by Christianity's historical power. The essence of Christianity differs in every epoch, resulting from the totality of the influences in each age. The 'essence,' rather than simply the Bible or an ecclesiastical confession, must be the basis for a contemporary dogmatics. But this essence is actually the subjective, personal interpretation and synthesis which present thinking derives from the entire situation, with reference to the actual living issues and for the purpose of directing future activity. A common historical feeling and understanding, but also a subjective and creative interpretation and construction, are involved. Thus the definitions of the essence of Christianity cannot be expected even today to be in complete agreement; but will be closely related to one another only because of the determinative influences of historical development and because of the common influence of modern spiritual conditions. The definition of the essence of Christianity that I would put as the basis of dogmatics reads as follows: Christian religious faith is faith in the rebirth and higher birth of the creature who is alienated from God—a regeneration effected through the knowledge of God in Christ. The consequence of this regeneration is union with God and social fellowship so as to constitute the kingdom of God. A more detailed justification of this definition cannot be given here.[3]

At this point we are confronted by the *third task*, the properly dogmatic task in the strict sense. Under these circumstances this task is nothing other than the exposition of this 'essence' of Christianity. Dogmatics unfolds more precisely the conceptions of God, the world, humanity, redemption or spiritual elevation, community or the kingdom of God, hope or eternal life, contained in the essence. This whole conception of dogmatics as the unfolding of the essence and the amalysis of the world of ideas contained in the essence into these major concepts is conditioned by the perspective of the history of religions. These concepts are implicit in the essence of every higher or universal religion and form the schema according to which the world of Christian ideas is to be structured. Dogmatics gives a free and lively exposition of the specifically Christian meaning of these universal religious concepts. Admittedly, a certain 'school' character follows from the orientation along the lines of the history of religions. But the consequences of this orientation extend still further into the construction and into the spirit of this type of dogmatics. It is immediately evident that a historical-critical point of view brings the personalities and the facts of biblical history, particularly the person of Jesus, into the relativity of historical events and the uncertainties attached to tradition. They thus cannot be the specific and immediate object of faith. In the absence of historical-critical thinking, Jesus was naturally identified with God in order that he might be the immediate object of faith; with critical thinking, the God of Jesus becomes the object of faith, and Jesus is transformed into the historical mediator and revealer. This consequence emerged from the very beginning of historical criticism as its natural correlative. It has been strongly reinforced by the broadening of historical-critical thinking into the history of religions. Under these circumstances dogmatics has the task of setting forth Christian faith in God, or the concepts contained in the essence of Christianity, in complete uniformity without any intermingling of historical elements. It sets forth our faith in God and in the union of the creature with God as a salvation to be experienced in the present and renewed with each individual. It contains purely contemporary-religious propositions, or (if the word is not understood in a philosophical sense) purely metaphysical-religious propositions.

But this is only one aspect of the matter. These contemporary experiences receive their power, their vitality, their clarity, and especially their capacity to form communities, from the historical world which leads us to God, and particularly from the prophets and Jesus. Without these sources of power and centers of concentration, personal piety would be impoverished and crippled, and the religious community would possess no center; mere dogmatics cannot supply these. Moreover, without such sources there would be no common cultus, since such a cultus cannot consist in mere theoretical teaching, but rather in the actualization in present activity of the undogmatic, historical sources of life. Thus there arises the question of the religious meaning of historical realities and the task of maintaining them in the face of an all-destroying criticism. This is an essential task of dogmatics, next to the purely metaphysical-religious task. Dogmatics thus must be organized into the two great divisions that result from affirming the essence of Christianity: into historical-religious and metaphysical-religious propositions. The structure of the latter as deriving from the psychological character of the world of religious ideas had already been indicated.

Thus we have a characteristic outline for a dogmatics of a history-of-religions school. (1) Historical-religious propositions set forth the religious significance of the historical foundations—of the prophets, of Jesus, of the development of the Christian spirit in history. In particular, the person of Jesus here stands in the foreground, with its significance both for individual and for communal piety. (2) Metaphysical-religious propositions set forth the Christian conceptions of God, the world, the soul; the mutual relations of these in the Christian conception of redemption; and, finally, the outcome of redemption in the Christian conception of community and of the last things.

Naturally, the detailed exposition cannot be indicated here. The further question of how these conceptions may be reconciled with modern scientific conclusions in the realms of cosmology, anthropology, and the like also does not belong here, since this question has nothing to do with the specifically history-of-religions character of dogmatics. In this connection it may be simply remarked that a dogmatics of this type can proceed in a very free and resolute fashion, since it may itself be regarded as a part of religious growth and development. It is self-evident that the religious idea of the divinity of the soul to be gained from God, overcoming sin and suffering, and the idea of a kingdom of God-filled souls, must be adapted to a cosmology with its presumption that spirit has arisen on many worlds, and to a biology with its understanding of the rise of spirit out of a basis in nature. Finally, such a dogmatics will seek to illuminate its own ideas less from philosophy than from its relationship to the other great universal religions.[4]

Finally, we may call attention to a *fourth* point which, indeed, is not a specific task of this type of dogmatics but which throws light on the general character of the undertaking. A dogmatics of this sort presupposes scientific conclusions and methods; it is itself, however, not a science. It is rather a confession and an analysis of this confession for the guidance of preaching and religious instruction. For their part these are also simply confessions, but they need a carefully worked out and comprehensive primer for their work. As confessions, they need to have an underlying, fundamental scientific elucidation. The decisive affirmation of the Christian conception of the world is a personal choice. The definition of an essence of Christianity, valid for the present, is no less a matter of personal intuition. Even the exposition of the ideas of the Christian faith on this basis is an entirely free shaping of ideas out of life. Thus we are dealing here with something that is completely practical and vital; that cannot be further clarified by any unchangeably fixed, revealed standard, or by any eternally self-identical speculative principles. It is a construction and a production out of the forces of history itself; indeed, nothing else is possible in this realm. Thus dogmatics is part of practical theology and is not a scientific discipline in the strict sense.

This aspect of the matter is made even clearer when we keep in mind the practical purpose of dogmatics. This purpose is to furnish instruction to preachers and teachers in the community by offering them an outline of Christian religious ideas for their free use. Individual lay persons have no need of such a dogmatics; they can make do with a somewhat unorganized combination of practical life experiences, scientific theories, and religious affirmations, which is what they normally do anyway. But preaching and religious teaching in a community require such a primer, such an introduction to ordered religious thinking, in order to posses a clear direction of thought and a common understanding of fundamental principles. This practical purpose also explains the very general use of the forms, words, and doctrines of the tradition, which the individual lay person does not need, but which makes it possible for the community as a whole to retain a sense of historic continuity and to come to an understanding with conservative dogmatic treatises. Dogmatics, thus, like ethics (which cannot be discussed here) is a branch of practical theology; indeed, it is its most important branch. In contrast, the philosophy of religion and the history of Christianity possess a purely scientific character.[5]

This, in brief, indicates the general nature of a dogmatics that develops consistently from the point of view of the history of religions, and that derives certain principles from this point of view. It is true that the fundamental conception of the essence of Christianity and the specific development of particular doctrines may, even on this common basis, go off in quite different directions. I scarcely need to add that such a dogmatics is unquestionably capable of expressing a definitely earnest, warm, and active religious life.

I would like to respond to certain objection that may be raised against the position that has been outlined in this article. To this program it may be objected that what we propose is not a dogmatics at all, since it does not set forth permanent and unchangeable truths. This objection is valid, and it might be well to follow Schleiermacher in substituting for the term dogmatics the expression 'doctrine of faith' (*Glaubenslehre*). This title would clearly indicate the confessional and subjective character of the undertaking. But this is purely a question of terminology; the word 'dogmatics' has certain linguistic advantages and is the traditional term. In so far as the matter itself is concerned, this position frankly admits that there is no such thing as an unchangeably fixed truth. Such truth is not merely unknowable by human beings. This kind of truth is absolutely impossible because of the vital, changing character of our world, where there is no completely finished program, needing simply to be put into practice; but where, instead, there are increasingly new and vital attempts to construe the essential nature of reality, which is ever in process of evolution. But it does not follow that for this reason a dogmatics such as we have suggested is an irresponsible piece of subjectivism. Such subjectivism is avoided because a dogmatics constructs itself out of the great historical revelation and is conscious of working in the direction of the absolute goal.

It may be further objected that a dogmatics of this character is not scientific. This objection has already been admitted in what we have said. The very nature of the task precludes strictly scientific treatment. Science is concerned with that which is universally the same and universally valid. No science can determine the living values that emerge in the process of evolution; these can be grasped only by an intuition that feels, apprehends, and interprets them. These values are not universal and subject to definite law, as are the objects of science, but are always unique creations of life itself. This does not involve any depreciation of science. The recognition of the fact that matters are as they are is itself a scientific judgement. Moreover, the constant reference to the historical picture of things, exactly like the reference to the cosmological picture (which we cannot here consider), involves a genuine regard for science. Finally, the exposition of the concepts of faith requires practice in scientific method and clarity. It is true that dogmatics itself is not a science; but it presupposes scientific training.

It may be said that such a dogmatics is individualistic and anarchistic, and that it is not suited for a social religious life and for preaching in the church. The first assertion is certainly not true. A dogmatics of this kind, rather, strives constantly to make the closest possible connection with the living power of historical Christianity; and it can make the unifying significance of the personality of Jesus vitally contemporary in as warm and living a fashion as is seen, for example, in Wilhelm Herrmann's theology. But, on the other hand, it presupposes an individual diversity among different dogmatic theologies in a church, and to that extent renounces the unyielding power of a dogma to which all alike must be subject. In our day the churches are already established and no longer need the passionate insistence on conformity that was both possible and necessary in the days of their beginnings. A dogmatics for today must serve the needs of today. These needs are not those of the period of ecclesiastical beginnings, but are the needs growing out of the religious unrest and crisis due to the intellectual and ethical upheaval of our age.

Therefore, it is the duty of the churches, if they are to meet the needs of life itself, to guarantee individual freedom. Hence a dogmatics such as we have indicated can meet the needs of many believers, while the needs of different groups will be met by a different sort of dogmatics. If the churches are not able or willing to exercise this broad-mindedness, they will inevitably fall more and more into the background. They must understand that a new epoch in the spiritual development of humanity must be able to find expression in the churches or else it will pass the churches by. If they cannot actually do justice to the movement, they are essentially defeated and must content themselves with dominion over a narrow circle of reactionary believers. Such an outcome, however, would be a calamity for our religious future. The present-day crisis is not to be met through the formation of new churches but rather through the liberalization and mobilization of the existing churches.

It may be said that such a dogmatics is not suited for foreign missions. It may be contended that missions demand a fixed and definite dogma, and an unwavering certainty regarding the exclusive redemptive power of the truth to be preached. In many respects this judgement may be true. But the dogmatics proposed here is adapted not so much to actual missionary needs as to the needs of traditional Christianity, which is unquestionably finding itself involved in a difficult inner crisis. Missions are well enough cared for through the conservative ideals of the great masses of Christians: the missionary enterprise is, in any case, a task quite different from that of gaining religious clarity amid the perplexities of modern life. This task is not at all pressing in the greater part of missionary activity; consequently, missionary preaching can be much simpler and proceed along pedagogical lines. Missions, however, in the regions of the ancient religions and cultures, will certainly find themselves confronted with tasks quite like those involved in this dogmatics, and will find in such a dogmatics not a foe but a friend. In these areas, only to a limited extent will one be able to pursue direct Christian evangelizing, conversion, and acceptance into the Western churches. Rather, what is meaningful here is attaining mutual understanding, and this will rest on the basis precisely of the history of religions and the philosophy of religion. The proximate goal of missions in these cases can only be mutual understanding and mutual respect. Everything further is wide open.

Perhaps more weighty than all the above is the objection that by its emancipation from the Bible such a dogmatics would plunge all Protestantism into the greatest possible practical difficulties. Since its preaching and religious instruction are, as a matter of fact, based entirely on the Bible, a Protestantism adopting such a non-biblicistic dogmatics would be estranged from itself. It must be admitted that this difficulty is a very real one. The difficulty is not merely with dogmatics, however, but with modern religious life generally. If it is impossible to use the Bible any longer with the naive reinterpretations and accommodations current in the churches, if it is necessary now to understand the Bible in its actual, historical meaning as shown by historical criticism, then the Bible alone will no longer suffice. If a thorough-going historical-critical investigation and the point of view of the history of religions come to prevail, then it becomes entirely impossible to use the Bible as the sole means for shaping religious ideas and to ignore the history lying between the Bible and the present. The only conclusion to be drawn is that the Bible can no longer be the sole instrument employed by the church; it must be supplemented with all the riches of Christian history. The Bible is the center and point of origin, but not the sole means of edifying and nourishing the religious life. But this situation has actually existed for a long time and is not due to such a dogmatics as we have expounded.

The last objection to be mentioned is this. If we should take the essence of Christianity instead of the Bible or an ecclesiastical creed as the basis of dogmatics, it would raise the whole question of the right of such a dogmatics to call itself Christian. In answer we need only call attention to the indefinite content of the word 'Christianity' and note how impossible it is to define it in terms of any unchangeable fundamental doctrine. Even contemporary conservative theology is engaged in making new experiments. So long as Christianity is a living religion, people will be constantly quarreling with one another concerning what it is and what it ought to be; and they will constantly seek through new syntheses to meet present conditions and to adapt it to future exigencies. The dogmatics that we have portrayed is nothing more or less than such an adaptation and synthesis, and it rests on faith in the inexhaustibility of Christianity. Moreover, the Christian character of such a dogmatics is conserved in very concrete form: its entire content of life and faith remains related to the archetype found in the person of Jesus, and confession of Jesus is the sole unifying bond of the Christian community. The Christian character of such a dogmatics is conserved further by the fact that in the affirmation of the Christian view of the world it is precisely personalistic theism, the dualistic struggle of sin and redemption, and the future hope reaching out beyond the limits of this world, that are affirmed as the fundamental traits of the religious life. Now these are the very traits which go back historically to the prophets and Jesus. The essentially Christian character of such a dogmatics, therefore, cannot be questioned; and in our world of constantly changing concentrations and dissolutions of the religious life, anything more than an essential Christianity cannot be demanded. An unchangeable Christianity would mean the end of Christianity itself. An unchangeable Christianity never has been and never can be so long as it genuinely belongs to history.

But there is more in favor of a doctrinal theology (*Glaubenslehre*) of this type than the refutation of objections against it. It has positive advantages that signify a great relief and liberation for all modern thinkers who are still seeking a religious confession.

Such a theology does not as a matter of course or with ulterior motives set itself against all the feelings and instincts of the age which result from insight into the endlessly fluctuating and fluid nature of our spiritual life. Everywhere the dams that attempted to halt change through eternal, changeless truths are breaking. Eleatic, Platonic, Kantian ideas of the eternal a priori sought in vain to limit the flood and have themselves been drawn into it, becoming mere aspirations and approximations to the Absolute. All rationally necessary ideals of state and society have been swept into the vortex; there is no unchangeable code of conscience any more. The rational necessity of the classical natural science of Newton is finished; the empirical-relative point of view is even venturing upon mathematics. In the realm of applied science, every attempt to construct final possibilities and conclusions has again and again been completely refuted in practice. We reflect upon the enormous prehistoric time periods, on ice ages, changes in climate and shifts in the poles, and on the possible reoccurrence of such conditions in today's cultivated regions. We reflect on the possibly immense longevity of humanity and on the events which still lie ahead of it, and on the probable end of the human race through something like the diminishment of the energy of the sun by which we live. In this grandiose perspective we see our own existence. The mood today is certainly no longer a victorious confidence in progress; it has become rather horror in the face of the alienating and relativizing boundlessness of the fragile conditions of existence.

To the same extent that this horror is understood, thought and faith turn again to the Absolute. But we can no longer construe it as the Ready-Made (*das Fertige*). Rather we must construe the Absolute as the Goal towards which we are growing and whose eternity is already contained in all approximations to it as their driving force. We seek to situate ourselves intuitively in the forward-pressing impetus of life and are certain that we participate thereby in the Absolute in the way concretely possible in every situation. A doctrinal theology such as we have suggested here is able to feel and think its way into such a conception of the Absolute. It will do justice to the relative and believes that in its own concrete confessional structure it represents the living power of the creative Absolute in our midst. Precisely this is impossible for the absolute, traditional ecclesial or biblicistic dogmatics. Such a dogmatics either makes too many concessions to history, and is lost, or it makes only apparent concessions, and suffocates in sophistry. The ready-made, supernatural Absolute of the old dogmatics belong in the spiritual atmosphere of ready-made metaphysical truths and eternal ideals of state and society. In the atmosphere of the modern historical relativising of all things, it can no longer breath freely and unconstrainedly. We are free of these breathing difficulties and attempts at artificial respiration, and can give ourselves entirely to the task of the moment, in which we nonetheless grasp the direction towards the Eternal.

The second advantage is that such a doctrinal theology signifies an extraordinary capacity for the rejuvenation and concentration of he Christian life-world. It becomes possible to see Christianity's essence precisely in the forces that the present moment demands. Yet, at the same time, none of the earlier conceptions of the essence of Christianity becomes a mere transitional state or precondition. Above all, we remain free from the delusion of having only now arrived at the pinnacle of truth. We know that each of the great ages of Christianity has had its own living problems and answers, and that other ages will place other ideas in the center and develop other connections from that center. But we also know that in our questions the power of the living God pulses, and that in our answers the voice of eternity sounds in the manner possible for us.

Once upon a time there was a yearning for the coming kingdom of God, the new heaven and new earth, and in that yearning itself was included the holiness that alone can inherit the kingdom of God.

Later, in church, sacrament, and dogma one joyfully possessed the authority which led the way through the dangers of a declining world and made one certain of an other-worldly splendor. Still later, one knew a kingdom of universal human morality and societal order, in which nature and grace, individual and community found their place, and which imbued a cruel world with tenderness of soul. The age of the Reformation suffered under the curse of an external authority, a complicated organization of society and a fragmented ethic. So courage was taken in the simple meaning of the Bible, and the confidence and power of a plain bourgeois ethic developed out of justification through faith. Today, under the influence of naturalistic views of the soul and the world, and due to the mechanization of society and work, the greatest yearning of the age is for regaining the soul, the infinite depths of the inner life in order to regain certainty about God and a new appreciation of the contrast between nature and spirit, God and world; and to make possible a deepening of spiritual life. Today the question and the answer are focused on two fronts: on these truths of the infinite value of the soul, and on the rescuing of inner value and hope for the future. So Christianity reformulates itself as the gospel of gaining and maintaining a God-filled soul. Jesus becomes the interpreter of and guide to the mysteries of the soul. The other great religious question of the age, the question of the relationship of souls to each other and their union in a common life and a common goal, arises here as well. The kingdom of God, as distinct from the church and from the great utopian miracle of the future, the kingdom of God as the community of humanity and of the love of God, rises before us as the great hope over against all fragmenting individualism, all self-deification, all loss of community or all coerced unification.

These are the new passionate questions, while the old ones have grown cold and strange to us. We do not ask, how do I find a gracious God? We ask rather, how do I find the soul and love again? Other ages will ask other questions. However, now there is the possibility of an authentic, free doctrinal theology that can consciously formulate the questions of the present and can give the answers, as the actual contemporary content of theology, in the simplest and strongest concentration, instead of permitting an alien dogmatic tradition laboriously to speak as though it possessed the secret of how to speak with the voice of the present. We do not toil over reinterpretations and explanations; rather we decisively turn to the living central questions and hope for the answer of God, in which the old religious world gains a joyful and hopeful new resonance.

Finally, with such a doctrinal theology we will be free of the burden of history without losing the power and blessings of history. The central religious certainty is an immediate one that forms itself for us out of the world of Christian life. We do not have to bear the burden of indispensable religious claims about historical matters in order to arrive in the land of the freedom of the spirit. We do not have to pay the price of specific judgements about Jesus, the apostles, or the Bible in order to posses the pearl of great price. Rather, we perceive the heavenly Father in the living course of contemporary history as it has developed out of the past. We pay only the price of purification and self-criticism, of introspection and surrender to the eternal world, of the shattering of worldliness and self-seeking. But in so far as we pay this price and enter the kingdom of truth, its prophets and masters will become living for us, and we will seek support and community in them. An appreciation for history grows out of a freely given reverence and piety, out of a believing surrender and free interpretation that could never have risen from compulsory historical dogmas. This free appreciation will know that it is interpretation, not historical science and not dogma; that it may follow freely the inner threads without pursuing philology and scholasticism. In this way everything that is holy in Christianity's historical memories can be honored, loved and understood. But everything stands under the law of love, not that of compulsion. Different interpretations can coexist and each can be respected. What drops out is the right of the faithful to bind their brethren to a maximum or minimum of indispensable historical dogmas. This in turn should diminish the morally and aesthetically unbearable virulence which 'faith' so often has, despite all putative Christian humility and love. A healing of the disunity which fills all impartial observers with such great concern about the future of Protestantism would be possible.

Such a doctrinal theology, given a right to exist within the Christian community, would be a salvation and a liberation. It has not yet been produced. The age still lacks the courage and the drive for it; these we must have if we are to have real faith again. The only approximate example for such a theology is Schleiermacher's *The Christian Faith*, which is certainly antiquated in many respects. But presumably, many a simple pastor has been preaching such a theology for a long time without making any dogmatic noise, and many lay persons maintain such a theology in their hearts by virtue of their own faith. God bless them wherever they are in the world; they have much to say to their brothers and sisters and will not have to lament that the Word of God comes back empty.

Notes

1. The German term *religionsgeschichtlich* (rendered here as history of religions) has no exact English equivalent, but the subject matter certainly is well-known. The unfortunate expression 'comparative religion' has been coined; see Louis Henry Jordan, *Comparative Religion: Its Genesis and Growth* (Edinburgh, 1905). In this book the problems of this viewpoint are treated very superficially even though there is a very rich bibliography. Only the philosophy of religion and theology, but not religion itself, can be 'comparative.' The same is true of the German term *religionsgeschichtlich* (rendered here in the adjectival form history-of-religions).
2. See my book *Die Absolutheit des Christentums und die Religionsgeschichte* [*The Absolutness of Christianity and the History of Religions* (Richmond: John Knox, 1971)]. A similar point of view was worked out in George Burman Foster's *The Finality of the Christian Religion* (Chicago, 1909). See also my later essay, '*Logos* und *Mythos* in Theologie und Religionsphilosophie' translated in this volume.
3. See my article, 'Was heisst "Wessen des Christentums"?' ['What does "Essence of Christianity" Mean?' in Robert Morgan and Michael Pye, eds., *Ernst Troeltsch: Writings on Theology and Religion* (Atlanta: John Knox, 1977), 124–181]; and William Adams Brown, *The Essence of Christianity* (New York, 1904). My historical writings in general have been devoted to the task of indicating this synthesis or setting forth the varoius definitions of the essence of Christianity at different times. I call special attention to *Die Soziallehren der christlichen Kirchen und Gruppen*, 1912 [*The Social Teaching of the Christian Churches* (New York: The MacMillan Company, 1931)].
4. Here I can only refer to examples of my work. See the dogmatic articles in the encyclopedia *Die Religion in Geschichte und Gegenwart* (Tübingen), and my little essay, 'Die Bedeutung der Geschichtlichkeit Jesu für den Glauben,' 1911 ('The Significance of the Historical Existence of Jesus for Faith' in Morgan and Pye, *Writings*, 182–207). The former articles treat Revelation, Redemption, Grace, Faith, Church, Predestination, and Eschatology. The latter develops the significance of Jesus for the Christian community and for the individual from a purely practical and psychological point of view; the most diverse concrete applications remain open.
5. This conception was set forth by Schleiermacher in his *Brief Outline of the Study of Theology*. His program simply needs to be carried out consistently. Hardly any change is necessry. It need only be noted that since Schleiermacher's time, the methods and results of historical science have become more radical and have attained to more far-reaching conclusions. See Sueskind, *Christentum und Geschichte bei Schleiermacher* (Tübingen, 1911). See also my essays, 'Ruckblick auf ein halbes Jahrhundert der theologischen Wissenschaft' (Half a Century of Theology: a Review,' in Morgan and Pye, *Writings*, 53–81), and 'Grundprobleme der Ethik,' *Gesammelte Schriften*, 2:552–672.

7

The Separation of Church
and State and the
Teaching of Religion

The question of the state's position vis-à-vis the church evidently does not rest on arbitrary governmental decisions or purely external power relationships. Essentially, it rests on the inner position of society vis-à-vis the religious life generally and the way the nature of religious truth is instinctively—consciously or subconsciously—perceived by the great majority. The coarse and naive concept of truth recognizes only one and the same truth for all and therefore only one church, which because it has the pure truth, also has the task of subjecting everything to this truth. A more refined concept of truth recognizes various truths that carry subjective conviction, and therefore various churches and the impossibility of subjecting society to the rule of this plurality of churches. If, finally, a society is affected by both ideals of truth, there will be no lack of mediations that interpret the many truths in terms of the one truth and subject society to the rule of both.

This is easily shown by reference to the three main types that have historically solved the problem: (1) the system of *absolute establishment*, where one church assures uniformity and is most intimately and inseparably united with the whole of political life; (2) the system of *disestablishment*, where any number of different free churches are related to the state essentially on the basis of the laws governing associations in general; and finally, (3) the system of *mixed establishment*, where a fixed small number of state-churches are treated on a basis of parity, with corporate privileges grounded in public law and their essential contribution to public life; and with a considerable degree of state control, since the state provides the material base of support. This third system assumes a general consensus on the part of society regarding its essentially Christian character and its essentially

109

uniform knowledge of religious truth, but also the expression of this
unity in different historically conditioned forms that are related closely
enough to one another to be regarded as collectively making a uniform
contribution to the Christian ideal of life and truth commonly held by
state and church. Logically, the first system presupposes an absolute,
the second a relative, and the third a mixed concept of truth combining
absolutism and relativism.

The system of ecclesiastical uniformity lies far behind us but
continues to influence us even today. It is medieval system of a
church-oriented culture. Yet the church here represents, only in a
special way, the quite universally human and natural need for firm
and lasting truths and values, which are especially indispensable in
education. Thus the absoluteness of the ecclesiastical system actually
contains a moment of truth that will always continue to demand
recognition. Against it, one can only say that modern people find the
content of the worldview and ethic intended by the absolute church
for the most part unacceptable.

It is important to remember, however, that this ideal of ecclesiastical
uniformity based on a monopoly of absolute truth—and of a culture
and educational system directed by the church—is not peculiar to the
Catholic church. It is also the ideal of the Old Protestant (Lutheran or
Reformed) territorial churches, and produces the same consequences
even today wherever Old-Protestantism continues to prevail. The
consequences are a matter of course: an all-pervasive order of
Christian life and doctrine mediated by the police, and a system of
schools controlled by, and oriented toward, the church. This point
marks the primary contrast between Old Protestantism and the
Baptists, who broke through the monopoly on objective truth and the
principle of ecclesiastical uniformity. From the Lutheran emphasis on
inwardness and personal faith, Baptists inferred the possibility of
differences in the expression of faith, insisting on unity only in the
practical sphere. The result is a pluralism of religious associations,
which contrasts sharply with the teaching of the Reformers.
Ecclesiastical Protestantism (except where, under modern influences,
it has learned to re-interpret Luther's original teaching of the freedom
of faith as also the freedom to differ in doctrinal matters) still considers
itself, instinctively, as responsible (in the absolutist sense of
ecclesiastical uniformity) for the direction of all culture. Conservative
Protestantism accordingly arrives at the same results as Catholicism:
confessional schools, ecclesiastical influence on education in general,
and the demand for 'believing' universities and especially theological
faculties.

The idea of truth was relativized above all by the co-existence of different confessions in the same state. The universal dominance of the church's idea of culture, which was possible and logically necessary under ecclesiastical uniformity, is quite impossible under a plurality of confessional churches. Society as a whole must here adopt the standpoint that the value of these churches is merely relative. The truth of religion and ethics—if there is such a truth—must transcend the churches; it is a religion of tolerance, so to speak, outside and above the churches, which represents what is common to all of them and in any case does not coincide with any one of them. Most importantly, within the very core of the religious idea there is a turning away from objective external revelation to subjective internal revelation, from an absolutism identical for all to a relativism where conscientious conviction becomes the standard.

But the free-church system differs radically from country to country. Especially is there a very great difference between the American situation and the French law. Conditions in America are based on Baptist and Puritan ideas, on great diversity among the churches going back to the very beginning, on a democracy that is as individualistic as it is egalitarian, and on an enlightened relativism that genuinely appreciates the churches. There the system functions merely as the expression of a society that considers itself Christian, and of a radical respect for freedom of conscience that values highly the various systems of positive religion. The French law, in contrast, is essentially polemic, supported by a society either skeptical of, or hostile to, Christianity. Its purpose is not to give recognition to the powers ruling the religious conscience but to repress Catholicism, which had become a threat to democracy. Quite unlike the American laws, it makes the maintenance of Catholic canon law difficult by subjecting cultic organizations to the control of the laity. This law will surely not bring religious peace to France. But it illustrates most vividly how differently the separation of church and state can be interpreted.

Americans generally expect only facts to be taught; they do not require the development of an educated worldview. In contrast to the diversity and unfinished character of American education (which is prone to experiment and susceptible to local influence) and to its commitment in principle to factual knowledge, French education is highly centralized and insists on an educated disposition and worldview. Like everywhere else on the continent, one is less practical there than in the youthful America. The educational legislation of the Third Republic has now indeed removed all clerical influence and participation, along with religious instruction, from the schools. But once the voluntary principle and respect for personal conviction have been proclaimed to the churches, believers cannot be expected to send their children to a state school that ignores or combats their religiosity. More than ever, they will call for schools of their own, where even the instruction can be imbued with their life-conviction; and they will have logical consistency and moral right on their side.

The free-church system has several weak points that can only be indicated in the briefest way here. The first and most important is that the Roman church, the way it is in Germany, will never acquiesce in it. The American system is possible only in view of the special development that Catholicism has undergone there, in an absolutely democratic environment and under Protestant influence. 'Americanism' absolutely abstains from politics, plays down dogma, carries on practical charitable and social work, and encourages personal initiative. There has been no lack of attempts to transplant these same ideas to Europe, and presumably there will be even more in the future. But the transplantation of this spirit into the French church has been met with such passionate hatred, and such devastating blows on the part of the hierarchy and the theologians, that in this respect there is little to be hoped for in the foreseeable future, least of all in countries where monarchy prevails. A second difficulty is this: under this system, the state turns the churches over to their orthodox wing, which is always stronger and more aggressive, by giving up the requirement of a scientific education. The system also brings with it the danger of plutocracy in the churches, a danger that is often acualized in America. It prompted Robespierre to oppose separation in his day precisely for democratic reasons, in the interest of the masses and the poor. Moreover the businesslike competition and advertising forced upon the churches by their financial needs and their propaganda effort leads to a multitude of disagreeable practices. There are also serious legal difficulties involving property, which necessitate a constant intervention of the civil courts in the life of the churches. But it is precisely from the religious standpoint, finally, that such a division and destruction of the common religious heritage is a serious loss of traditional life-values and security.

The loss of theological faculties would apparently be the least painful in all this. People who believe that a commitment to Christianity can be combined with a scientific orientation only through gross self-deception will rejoice over such a cleansing of science; and the confessionalists will be very much pleased that the state no longer requires them [to submit to] a college and university education or above all, to the influence of modern science. But actually there is a serious loss here, too. The one organ that enjoys all the resources of science and the stimulation of a scientific environment, and is able to give a historical account of the origin and nature of the churches, would be gone. Also gone would be the one influence that puts the great social energies of the churches in touch with the whole of science, as well as the opportunity for the truly pious to attain a religiosity synthesizing a scientific truth-content with a religious spirit through well-planned, comprehensive work. A chair for church history, possibly added to the philosophical faculty, and the lectures of the philosophers on philosophy of religious and ethics, would not be sufficient in view of all the challenges and resources that present themselves. But if a Department of Religious Studies were to be created either within or alongside the philosophical faculty, as has been done in the Netherlands with a view to the separation of church and state, the result would be either a discipline bound to wander through all ages and stages of historical development, staffed by dilettantes without specialization, and committed to religious research without a religious commitment, which would bring joy to no one, least of all to itself; or, if there were a religious program, there would once again be a theological faculty under a different name, which would no less be the object of quarrels between believers and unbelievers and which would lack only the most important element of all, an assured supply of students.

Such difficulties are still unknown in Germany. The mixed establishment characterized above prevails here, along with an almost completely state-controlled and centralized educational system, which has been able, in principle, to accommodate the influence of the churches to the independence of the state school. They system is a result of the Napoleonic wars, after which the German states were re-assembled without regard to confessional differences. All states received confessionally mixed populations. The system works reasonably well. Yet it has severe defects that make themselves keenly felt and its indefinite survival doubtful. It is jeopardized, and in danger of disintegration, precisely because of its mixture of state-church and free-church elements, of absolutistic and relativistic ideas of truth.

It is the Roman church, first of all, which seeks to profit from this mixture. It demands privileges from the state on the basis of its absoluteness, and everywhere puts these privileges to good use. It also appeals, in the name of freedom, to the liberal idea of toleration and the free-church elements of the system in order to achieve recognition of all its claims; but these include, as a matter of principle, subjection (direct or indirect) of all institutions and spheres of life to the influence of the clergy. In a well-known phrase, while in the minority it demands freedom for itself in accordance with the principles of the liberals, which its own principles would compel it to deny to the liberals once it becomes the majority. There is no way out of these conflicts other than a genuine separation of church and state.

There are similar difficulties, no less serious, with respect to Protestantism. Its membership is so heterogeneous that it can be held together only with the greatest difficulty. It has an official confession and doctrine no longer shared by countless multitudes. The influence of modern science has greatly undermined its theology even where religious agreement has been essentially maintained. Here also free-church, institutional-church, and state-church principles are everywhere intermingled. The only escape from all these difficulties would be separation into more homogeneous groups, which would at the same time mean separation from the state. But these difficulties are twice as serious in our present school-struggles. Only the removal of the school from church control provides a way out of all these miseries, which in turn presupposes the separation of church and state. What is worst of all is that the system is and has been in force but is not sustained by any inner enthusiasm. It contains a deep inner dishonesty, which comes to most painful expression whenever these established churches show their dependence on political forces, social respectability, and a kind of conventional approval that is inwardly totally indifferent, or even hostile and scornful, toward their cause. Society and its ruling circles use the churches to advance goals completely alien to their inner spirit. In face of this dishonesty, honest religion feels the need to withdraw its own community from this alien world. Thus the religious spirit itself comes to demand the separation of the church from the state.

On then all sides we thus face the possibility, perhaps the probability, of a separation of church and state. The immediate present, to be sure, does not point in that direction. The relationship of church and state is essentially irrational. But the separation of church and state is only a modification of the problem. Only experience would show whether the new conditions are preferable to the old.

Neither the American nor the French solution can satisfy us; neither would have a real base of support among us. The school problem is so difficult (under the separation of church and state) precisely because society needs a strong, profound, and living religion; it cannot separate itself from this religion even when it separates the churches from the state. But among us, such a religion is solely Christianity. The famous demand of the teachers of Bremen, which is likely to be echoed throughout the teaching profession, insists that religious instruction be given only in the form of a comparative history of religion. But this is the same kind of historicist uncertainty—wandering about in all the times and places of the world—as the attempt to teach art through an 'art history of all nations and times.' One has to have a firm center, which may be reinforced and illustrated through comparison; but we must always take as our starting point the heritage that has been given us. 'Teaching', accordingly, must teach our own culture. The separation of church and state can be no separation of the state from Christianity and must not lead to an un-Christian or neutral school. Society and the state continue to be interested in teaching our youth Christianity, and may leave everyone the freedom to use this teaching in any way desired. The instruction would be essentially historical and may be clarified at the higher levels through history of religion comparisons; it should lead to a worldview of one's own, but with essential roots in Christianity. Only the state could offer such instruction, and would depend for it on the scientific study of Christianity. That is, the state would remain dependent on a theological faculty for the training of its religion teachers and as the highest resource for religious instruction.

This presupposes, of course, that the theological faculties would remain substantively Christian and would not consider themselves bound, by the principle of presuppositionlessness, to treat the value and validity of Christianity as quite questionable. Presuppositions certainly must be tested, but only in order to attain firm ones for further work. The testing of the presupposition must come to a conclusion; and in so great and simple a matter as the fundamental truth of Christianity, one must attain an undisturbed clarity. It will be realized that one can depart from the rooted religion only when a higher one presents itself; and that, if this is not the case, one must take the rooted religion as the foundation in all religious matters. The theological faculties will no longer be condemned to flutter around among the various religions of the world; nor will they be required to do the impossible, to invent a new scientific religion. The recognition will dawn that one must take one's stand on the given, and that the given is the highest religious power known to us. The freedom of the theological discipline may then be seen, not in the constant doing away with its own presupposition, but in its free development on the basis of the given presuppositions.

This would be a complete revolution, a new system. It would be the practical application of the laboriously attained differentiation between religion and church, which would then be free to find each other again and to join forces. Then would be re-established the moment of truth of the Catholic and Old-Protestant churches, that the religious idea must be universal and ruling over all because truth is one. It would be re-established by the state and by science, not as church authority, but as a common search on a common basis with a common goal. The foundation of this common religious truth would even then be a certain concept of revelation: neither the concept of a supernatural authoritative doctrinal communication for all, nor the concept of a particular illumination of the individual, but the concept of a breakthrough of the highest religious powers in history, in quest of ever new concentration and ever new fusion with the totality of life. Baptist and Independent relativism, which leaves everyone to one's own resources, would be overcome; all individual religiosity would be reminded of its common source and common goal. At the same time, modern freedom of conscience would be preserved. In terms of the three types of relationship of state, religion, and church delineated at the outset, this new system still would belong to the third type. The ideal of one truth—but as a scientific consensus regarding the formation of our religious resources—and the plurality of subjective convictions of truth would continue to coexist. This would be a solution appropriate to the nation of Kant and Goethe, which is forever set apart from America and France by its idealist philosophy.

These concerns are decisive for the answer to the question of the legitimacy of the theological faculty in the university. Our legitimacy rests now and for the foreseeable future on the mixed-establishment system and on the mission given us by the state to make purely scientific culture fruitful for the ecclesiastical and religious life of the people. Our teaching serves the established church and its ministers. We are always aware that the established church has a right to expect consideration and respect for its orders; and that our scientific instruction is not to proclaim radicalisms but gently to mediate between church and science. We are working for an established, national church, which reconciles its various wings and groups as much as possible in the practical and purely religious sphere and seeks to be a home to all its children.

But we are equally certain that our legitimacy would remain even if this connection should be severed by the separation of church and state; that is, if the various sacrifices separation would entail were to include the detachment of our faculty from the training of future clergy. We should then be charged with purely scientific, interconfessional tasks and to this extent enabled to work in a more clear-cut scientific spirit. But whatever the future may bring, the new faculty would still not be the end, in principle, of the old. For in our distinctly scientific work, in our literary researches and their publication for the scholarly and general public and not simply for the church, we are already working according to the principles of that faculty of the future, establishing the universal and basic insights that guide us in the interpretation of the teaching of the church. Even today, we understand our mission to be not merely service to the church but also a scientific contribution toward solving the general problem of the nation's religious life. This bifurcation already runs through all our work and separates our pedagogical from our purely scientific work. Yet even today, it does not destroy the inner unity of what we are and what we are charged to do. What today connects the old and the new faculty in us will also continue to connect the scientific study of religion and the cultic community in the future, namely the basic idea of Christianity. This is the same however diversely it may be expressed, and it makes Christianity the highest level of religion available to us. The Gospel of John expresses it in simple but weighty words: 'God is spirit, and those who worship him must worship in spirit and truth' (John 4:24).

PART TWO

Christian Faith and Ethics

8

Faith

A. Faith as the Totality of the Christian Religious Life

The word 'faith' is one of the most ambiguous and misunderstood words in the religious vocabulary and in the formulation of the theological concepts that have arisen from that vocabulary. In its customary sense 'faith' signifies the conceptual world of a religion that is believed in by the pious, that is regarded as present, past, or future reality. Because of its significance for the believers, this conceptual world tends to remain untouched and unaltered. It is traced back to unimpeachable authorities, and indeed generally does take its point of departure from certain particularly authoritative sources. These include revelations, inspirations, prophecies, cultic legends, priestly traditions, information that is passed on in secret, and the personal work of some Founder. From these elements all the popular conceptions of faith are derived. According to these conceptions, faith consists in an attitude of belief that is based essentially on tradition, authority, and community of conviction.

But the meaning of 'faith' is not exhausted by this customary usage. This is indicated by the usage itself, which refers the terms 'belief,' 'faith,' 'power of faith,' and 'conviction of faith' to a basic religious stance of the soul, a willing surrender to God, and an openness to divine fulfilment. Here faith is identical with religion itself. This sense of the word, and with it a religious element, applies also to one's attitude to certain objects that are not directly and properly religious.

One may believe in his country, in humanity, in another person, or in oneself.

In fact, it is doubtful whether it is appropriate to express both meanings by the same word; it might be preferable to understand faith specifically as the cognitive element of religion, while the totality of the subjective religious life would be better designated as 'piety.' Piety would then be the broader concept, within which faith would be the cognitive element that determines piety. It may be pointed out that, for the most part, non-Christian piety promotes this distinction and even adheres to it linguistically. In non-Christian piety faith, as the cognitive element, is *mythos*, while the practical element of religion consists of cultic observances and of *pietas* or *eusebeia*, the pious attitude that gives heed to the divine and otherwise pays due respect to 'the holy' in all its aspects. Or, as the case may be, speculative knowledge or *gnosis* is distinguished from practical activity and outlook, or even from ethics.

Yet there were good and profound reasons for the Christian fusion of the two senses of the word into one, a usage that is especially characteristic of Paul and the Reformers. The fusion expresses a distinctive peculiarity of Christianity, namely, that its *mythos* and its *gnosis* have religious value only as they effect a practical religious and ethical outlook; and that the Christian religious life is not directed toward cult and rite but toward a knowledge of God that determines the will, or rather toward the inner union of man's nature and will with God, which is expressed in this knowledge of God. In this union, knowledge aims spontaneously at that which is meaningful for practical religion. Christian piety is faith and Christian faith, piety.

Of course, as much can be said of the prophetic religion of Israel, the mother-religion of Christianity. Even Islam, which was in many ways influenced—and not merely in its initial stages—by the two older religions, occasionally gives rise to such views. Indeed, a sharp eye will discern the beginnings of such a fusion elsewhere, as issuing from the inner dialectic of religious thought. But only in Christianity is this fusion of fundamental significance, just as Christianity alone is driven to this fusion by its conception of a personal, ethical God. To be sure, even Christianity has by no means strictly maintained this fusion in actual history. Yet, in its classical pronouncements it has always drawn faith out of every concealment (when faith has tried to conceal itself in relationships that were not directly concerned with God) and has focused the entire religious life, both in thought and cultus, on the attaining and maintaining of a faith-relationship to the sole religious object, the holy and gracious will of God. This emphasis on faith has brought it about that for Christianity faith and piety, knowledge and the disposition of the heart, cultus and personal surrender of one's being, *gnosis* and ethics fuse; and each conditions and substantiates the other. At this point the feature distinguishing Christianity from other religions becomes explicit: the breakthrough of the pure, ethical religious life. Christianity knows only one sort of knowledge, that which has practical religious and ethical value and which bears its own witness to this value; and Christianity knows only one sort of practice, that which proceeds from pure knowledge of God. What persistently comes to view as the core of Christianity is neither the interesting, colourful *mythos* that blends into science, nor the authority of church dogma, but rather a very simple idea that give expression to the practical experience of elevation to God and that leads back to inner certainty (*Selbstgewissheit*).

In the analysis of faith, then, this involvement of faith in practice, this inner unity of faith and piety, is always to be kept in mind. Especially in Christianity, the most intimate union of both must be stressed. Nevertheless, analysis must, at least conceptually, single out faith as the cognitive element that dominates this union and, even for Christianity, must designate faith as the cognitive element of piety. Faith is a matter of trust and surrender—but surrender to a reality that is apprehended by thought. It is a matter of life and action, but on the basis of an idea. In any case, this is so in Protestantism, which for that very reason designates faith as the center of Christianity, as practical knowledge of God, and as the source of all ethical and religious motives and ideals. While Catholicism separates faith, as belief, from practical behavior, ecclesiastical sacraments, and ethics, Protestantism sees the entire Christian religion as epitomized in faith. This view represents the final emergence of Christianity as a religion of the spirit. Yet, the distinction, which is at least conceptually necessary, remains, the distinction of faith in the narrower sense from the whole of piety. It is imperative now to analyze psychologically this special quality of the idea of faith in the narrower sense.

B. Faith, in the Narrower Sense, as the Cognitive Element of Religion

All religions regard their religious life and faith as something effected and founded by God. They are impressed by the religious dependence of man on divine powers, and instinctively abridge the human role in the formation of ideas of faith. Likewise, the highest and most comprehensive levels of religion, and among them especially Christianity, regard this divine effecting and founding of religion not as something that occurs anew in each individual but as something that was given to all men at its founding and that is intended to be appropriated by all. The richer and stronger the religious content of the ideas becomes, and the richer and stronger the number of stimuli becomes in practice, the more the activity of the individual is absorbed in appropriating what is given and in conforming to it, and the less spontaneity is left to the individual's activity. Thus on this level even the cognitive element is dependent on the appropriation of what is commonly and fundamentally given for everyone. As such, the cognitive element depends upon revelation and is primarily faith in the fundamental revelation. Yet, faith is more than believing the tradition and the traditional doctrine. Since revelation itself is nothing other than intensified faith (*Gläubigkeit*) that surpasses average measure and radiates its power, by linking faith to revelation we have scarcely begun to understand faith as a cognitive mode. We must now analyze revelation as constituting an heroic and fundamental form of faith.

Revelation is the productive and original appearance of new religious power, the practical elevation of life as a whole, which communicates its powers through its bearer. Even for the bearer of revelation himself, however, such a new or preponderantly new totality entails certain novel views and conceptions about God, the world, and man, and about the divine purposes for the world and man. The imagination is here ingenuously or naively at work, giving the whole of religious existence, which is intuitively grasped, an ingenuously artistic expression that merges old and new. This is the production of *mythos*, a part of every religion. In a purely personal, spiritual, and ethical religion such as Christianity, *mythos* takes the form of an embodiment of the conception of God and his purposes for the world and man which is at the same time an image of the special mission of the bearer of revelation. This is *mythos* on a higher level, where it gives expression, in effect, only to the idea of ethical religion. For this level of *mythos* the word 'symbol' could be used, but then it should be remembered that for the productive genius himself his *mythos* is in the main an ingenuously viewed reality, while its designation as 'symbol' belongs to a scientific way of thinking which views *mythos* critically.

Thus, *heros* and *mythos* are part of faith as the specific mode of knowledge which characterizes this level of religion. The *heros* is recognized as the center of newly radiating religious powers, and the *mythos* as the conceptual expression of the religious totality living in the hero, an expression that is shaped first of all by the *heros* himself.

Trustful surrender to the religious totality appearing in the *heros* then becomes faith in the 'hero' himself and in the religious idea given through him. Faith takes the form of religious veneration of the *heros* and acceptance of his religious conceptual world, which serves as the means of transmitting his religious life. To faith in this sense the religious life and thought of the faithful add a further constantly growing body of conceptions which emphasizes the new at the expense of the old. Above all, a religious glorification of the bearer of revelation takes place, whose person and authority are initially the sole unifying bond, the basis for forming a new religious community. Out of such glorification and its substantiation, a new doctrine of faith arises, which in turn give rise to a new cultus. The new totality of religious life contained in this doctrine and made vivid by it then proceeds to function on its own. While thus establishing itself securely, the new totality's need for special formulation and substantiation remains quite secondary; but eventually it, too, becomes the object of exposition, argumentation, and enlargement. A religion that aims essentially at the ethical-personal values of life and God's relationship to them initially needs only faith in the person of the *heros*, who directly represents the connection with the intelligible world that he embodies. Even amid later changes, faith maintains its identity through its relationship to the *heros* and to the fundamental conceptual world given in him.

Faith, then, is a peculiarly religious mode of thought and knowledge deriving from the impression made by a historical personage; it is at once mythical, symbolic, and practical in character. This mode of thought and knowledge involves belief in the *mythos* for the sake of the religious powers that it conveys in practice, and that can only be expressed, objectified, and communicated by means of the *mythos*. Sometimes greater stress is put on the mythical means of expression, sometimes on the content of religious practice, sometimes the former hardens to the point of stifling the latter, sometimes the latter liquefies the former to the point of dissolution. Such faith originates only among ingenuous individuals or social strata; it becomes firmly established through authority and tradition. Yet, whenever such faith leaves the plane of naive popular life, in which alone it attains its being and its first form, and rises into the spheres of scientific formulation, then it is both scientifically attacked and scientifically defended. Out of the faith and conviction of the masses, theology arises as a combination of the ingenuous religious *mythos* with the general concepts of systematic analysis. In this connection theology first conceives of faith as what faith has become in the prevailing medium, as authoritative knowledge that is supernaturally attested and communicated, and then reconciles this supernatural knowledge so far as possible with current natural or scientific knowledge. Theology becomes rationalistic when it believes that this reconciliation can be completely effected, theology becomes supernaturalistic when it acknowledges that it contains elements inaccessible to natural, conceptual knowledge. In these encounters, however, the practical and religious nature of faith reasserts itself, which is less concerned with knowledge than with the ethical and religious life mediated by knowledge, and which tends increasingly to distinguish faith from knowledge in the proper sense as a special, religious mode of knowledge. Finally, then, the point is reached where faith is analyzed psychologically. In this analysis, what we have described as the mythical, symbolic, and practical character of faith is seen to be its special, psychological aspect. By it, faith is essentially distinguished from knowledge in the proper sense, which is the conversion of experience through general concepts into demonstrably valid judgements or as the formulations of an abstract, conceptual deduction of what is real from a fundamental principle of utmost generality.

Then come the schematization of the historical and pschological formation and development of faith, such as the one in which we have been engaged. The religions of faith are distinguished from predominantly cultic religions. They interpret the world mythically, through the significance they attach to the religious *heros* and through the crystallization of their *mythos* around the ethical-religious values made practically accessible through such a personage. This is especially true of Christianity as a whole and of special groups that are formed within it, its saints and reformers. But it is also true of Mosaic and prophetic religion, of Islam, and probably at least incipiently of all religious groups that strive to advance religion to the inwardness of personal life. Even when such groups enter upon largely philosophical considerations in the process, their religious power always depends upon mythical and personal contents, as the history of Platonism has clearly shown. In all this, however, Christianity stands out as most properly a religion of faith.

C. The Cognitive Value of Faith

Everything depends on whether faith, understood in this psychological manner, also possesses special and independent cognitive value. This is denied by the positivists, who recognize the validity of this analysis but for that very reason see in faith only an echo of the primitive, subjective activity of the imagination, which is generated by human desires and an instinctive poetry. Just as this imaginative function has been expelled from all other branches of knowledge, it is said, so it must now be expelled from its last hiding place, religion, and relegated to the realm of poetry. In that case faith, and religion itself, would be wholly devoid of any cognitive value. That faith has cognitive value is also denied by the speculative-rationalistic philosphers of religion, who can recognize a religion as affording true knowledge only in a rationally necessary and valid concept of the unity and nature of the world; and who concede truth to the *mythos* of popular religion only so far as, prompted by fortunate instinct, it approaches this idea. This attitude actually amounts to a replacement of historically positive religion by a religion of general concepts.

The reply to the positivists is twofold. First of all, the psychological indestructibility of religion actually expresses a compelling validity, an a priori that the religious consciousness experiences as obligatory and that cannot be dissolved into mere custom and training. Secondly, if the inner power and necessity of the religious life is not to be denied or explained away, then the imagination in which this life is embodied cannot be without its moment of truth. Positivism generally underrates the cognitive value of imagination.

The reply to the speculative-rationalistic philosophers of religion is as follows: Since general concepts are inadequate means for grasping the ultimate principles and the basic order of the world, every allegedly rational concept of God and the world is actually an imaginary picture borrowed from religion and retaining strong mythical elements. Consequently, there can be no acceptance of religion without acceptance of the mythical imagination of faith as a specific cognitive method. The a priori rationality and validity of religion does not lie in a completely general concept of the world, contained in religion, but solely in the inner feeling of necessity that religion shares formally with logic, ethics, and art. Such religious powers and conceptual worlds are therefore not abstract generalities, but concrete life forces issuing from intense emotional depths. Through conflicts among the different historical religions, and in counterpoise with extra-religious values, these forces strive for a generally valid form; but they are never able to attain it fully amid the complexity and incompleteness of human affairs.

The knowledge that is given to faith has its own certainty, grounded in its practical indispensability and in an inner feeling of obligation. It relates to the totality of an overall psychic force that is essentially apprehended through action and will, and that issues from strong religious individuals amid the religious impotency of the great mass of men. On the other hand, this faith-knowledge, inasmuch as it relates to the transcendental (which is wholly inaccessible to the methods of the exact sciences) and itself imparts to science the idea of absolute realities, truths, and values, is not scientific knowledge but rather a knowledge that in its basic content is specifically religious, while its conceptual elements, like those of art, are symbolic. The cognitive value of faith lies in the practical mastery of the riddle of life through the apprehension of the practically attested redeeming power of communion with God. Such knowledge, however, can only be expressed in forms that are at once mythical, poetic, and symbolic. These forms always remain mythical, no matter how much they are scientifically refined or sublimated; they never become knowledge derived from general concepts. Theology thus always remains essentially a combination of science and myth. If theology no longer juxtaposes 'supernaturally' revealed information with 'natural' knowledge in the old manner, then it must do so in the new manner: it must assure a place for the practical-symbolic mode of knowledge, which is directed toward ultimate religious truth, beside the empirical mode of knowledge of the exact sciences. Here the theologian must enter the fields of psychology and epistemology, which always contain an element of metaphysics. The basis for acknowledging an independent cognitive value of faith is an epistemology of faith which does not aim at the general concepts contained in religion but at a relationship to reality which is mediated by religion. This epistemology of faith grades the various modes of faith according to the consistency that is achieved and according to the degree to which they seek to embrace the values of the whole of life.

D. The Autonomous Dialectic of Faith

Faith-knowledge shows itself to be a cognitive principle in its own right by bearing within itself an independent law of its own movement. It has been asserted that faith-knowledge simply follows the movements in the intellectual and scientific, the ethical and legal, or even the economic and social realms. Such assertions do not command our assent. Dependencies indeed exist in all these directions, but they are reciprocal. Each case requires individual examination to determine which side is more dependent upon the other. This very fact suggests that there are independent laws of movement characteristic of faith-knowledge. More precise analysis must delineate these laws of movement, the generation of antitheses and divisions that proceed from them, and the specifically religious formations—which always remain mythical—by which these antitheses are overcome and synthesized. The Hegelian reduction of the dialectic of the religious idea to the analyses and syntheses of systematic theology obscures the nature of both the religious idea and systematic theology. Faith-knowledge carries within itself, both consciously and unconsciously, the dialectic by which religious ideas are formed. It spontaneously insists on the univocity of the divine, yet distinguishes the divine from the world; while man, as religiously related to God, is yet distinguished from both God and the world. The restoration of the inner unity of those three separated existents (*Lebensgrössen*) and the attainment of an elevation of life into the absolute by means of this restored union, constitute the dialectic of the religious idea. Thus does mythical religious thought work for the unity of God, the wholeness of the world, the religious value of man, and the integration of all these values into ideas of redemption. Two main types result, pantheistic, anti-personalist redemption and theistic, personalist redemption. Our choice today must be for one of these two. The latter is the religious idea of Christianity; it constitutes the meaning of the Christian *mythos*. The personal decision between these two types determines one's religious profession and is in turn determined by which type of redemption affords the deeper, fuller, and richer experience of the religious life.

E. The Knowledge of Faith and the Knowledge of Science

Nevertheless, there persists an influence of scientific knowledge upon faith-knowledge. We must ask of what sort this influence is. The most immediate scientific influence has already been described in the preceding pages. Faith itself is made the object of psychological and epistemological reflection, and the different modes of faith are graded from the point of view of the philosophy of history. The details of this influence belong to epistemology as well as to the philosophy of history.

But even though in this context the supreme validity of the Christian mode of faith is vindicated, there yet remains the influence of the discoveries of the exact sciences (and of the scientific cosmology based on these discoveries) upon the conceptual world of faith. This influence is twofold. On the one hand, faith will continue to adapt its *mythos* to the scientific view of the world, eliminating or re-interpreting whatever is essentially inconsistent with this view. There are, of course, limits to this adaptation. If the *mythos* is completely dissolved in the process, then the religious substance embodied in it will also be dissolved. Such a dissolution marks the transition to new formulations of religion. On the other hand, faith will assimilate the new view of the world and draw from it new religious motives with corresponding new mythical embodiments. This has actually taken place in the accommodation to such conceptions as the plurality of worlds, the infinity of the world-process, and the continuty of living creatures. Such assimilation also has its limits. When faith is completely overgrown by new mythical elements and new faith motives, its development is cut short and room is made for completely new formulations.

Analysis of these things is the most pressing task of theology today. Theology's problem at present is to determine whether the Christian faith will perhaps be dissolved in the process or transformed by new motives. This problem cannot be resolved here. It must suffice to express the conviction that the fundamental religious power of Christianity has remained completely unimpaired and efficacious throughout. This fundamental religious power is faith in the union with God, leading to God-imbued personality and a community of personalities, and to the overcoming of sin and sorrow (*Weltleid*) in the certitude of grace.

Besides this influence of science on faith, it is equally important to recognize an influence of faith on science. Every conviction of valid ultimate truths, of the existence of an unconditioned truth of ultimate validity that may not be fully attainable by man, or of ultimate, unconditioned, real values that are obligatory and are approximated by human endeavor—every such conviction partakes of the nature of religious faith, though the thinker may not be aware that this is so. In this sense faith enters into the presuppostions of the empirical sciences, which in themselves are wholly independent of faith and follow their own laws. Such a faith is an overall psychic stance that is focused on truth and validity and therefore on the Absolute, and as such it entirely avoids coming to terms with the mythical form the instant it tries to interpret itself.

In addition to this indirect effect, faith also exercises a direct influence on science whenever scientists leave the exact empirical sciences to formulate overall views of the world and of its functioning and value. The decisive positions here are always positions of faith, overall psychic stances toward the totality of existence, which is always in some way expressed mythically and artistically. These positions are sometimes influenced by one of the historical religions; sometimes they arise from spontaneously developed religious attitudes; sometimes they refuse to recognize their religious character. The belief that in such instances one is taking a purely scientific position is generally a self-deception; it may merely express opposition to a prevailing religion against which an appeal is made to the authority of science. Thus modern thought entertains certain religions or surrogates for religion that compete with Christianity. These regard themselves as having a better scientific foundation or as being simply more compatible with science, but at their core they too partake of the nature of faith and *mythos*. Faith and knowledge, in the proper sense, are neither wholly congruent nor tidily separable. Rather, mythical religious knowledge and scientific conceptual knowledge interact, they oppose each other, and yet they never cease to struggle for an accommodation that always falls short of attainment. There is no simple formula for their relationship; both alike remain incomplete in earthly existence. The idea of God or of the world from which both could be derived and in which both could be reconciled to each other, the scientific system of the universe, is for ever beyond our grasp. Every philosophy that seeks such a system resembles Saul setting out in search of a donkey and finding a kingdom instead—in this case, the kingdom of criticism.

F. Ages of Faith and Ages of Science

A proper balance between faith and knowledge is always comparatively rare. We need only consider our individual and personal limitations: how infrequently our talents and interests are directed equally towards both, how unfavorable the circumstances are for a thorough development of the question, and how complicated formulations reduce the energy with which one can act. These impediments prevailed at least up to now and presumably will always do so, since the entire task will never be completed but will always vary in its presuppostions. The result is that the convictions of the masses incline more and more exclusively to one side or the other. Furthermore, vast distinctions are thus established as between the various eras and segments of intellectual culture. Any given period or group tends to lean *en masse* toward either mythical faith or scientific thought.

The differences that result for the overall attitude are obvious. The scientific frame of mind leans toward criticism and toward the rational arrangement of all structures through human activity and insight; the believing frame of mind leans toward submission to what is above men and toward configurations based on the great forces of general history. Either attitude has its bright and its dark side. The scientific frame of mind is dominated by the creative freedom and flexibility of the experimental spirit; universally demonstrable and communicable bases of culture are secured. The believing frame of mind is dominated by the carrying power of a strong communal consciousness and the ingenuous drawing upon superhuman, and therefore firm and inexhaustible, forces. The former easily leads in the end to hypercriticism and disintegration, the latter to a lack of discrimination, of freedom, and of tolerance.

Yet such periods and groups are not completely disparate; they differ only in their preponderant emphasis. Scientific culture draws on old bases of faith and often translates faith and *mythos* into a supposedly scientific form merely to keep on living in the same way as before, by faith in a different form. In face of every need not having directly to do with faith, the believing culture for its part uses scientific forces and methods and proceeds from faith to a peculiarly comprehensive type of speculative thought. Both areas overlap; their differences vary in manifold ways. Hellenic culture at its peak was preponderantly scientific and artistic, the mother of all free, scientific culture. Yet, it also possessed a wealth, not merely of poetic, but even of genuinely religious *mythos*. Faith is especially characteristic of the peoples of the Orient, who were nevertheless the forerunners of the Greeks and the foundation for all subsequent culture, and who have evolved a rich, manifold speculation and philosophy of religion along with faith. Even in specific spheres crosscurrents are not lacking. The ancient Greeks, like all the nations of antiquity, were devout (*gläubig*). Mature Hellenism, which caused its own political disintegration, was bolder than any other culture in its freedom of reflection. Late classical antiquity returned to a rare mixture of science and faith-*mythos*. It passed this on to Christianity, which provided a stable center.

It is no wonder that this change occurs also within the Christian world, even though the Christian faith-*mythos* had from the beginning elevated the idea of faith to a higher level of clarity and inwardness, distinct from knowledge. It did this by means of its simplicity and its fundamental ethical-personal orientation. Within Christendom we first encounter the extensive culture of the Roman Catholic Church, dominated by a faith-*mythos*, and then, after sundry crises and schisms, the modern world of scientific culture. Yet even this contrast, whic is often portrayed by positivists and rationalists as absolute, is only relative. A swing of the pendulum back to faith is not impossible even now; it has often enough taken place in the past. The restoration that followed the Enlightenment and the French Revolution was not merely a reversion but rather a completely natural reaction on the part of faith against pure rationalism and the mood of mere criticism. As long as this world lasts, there will always be such swings of the pendulm. For faith and *mythos*, with its ecclesiastical basis and elements of an out-dated view of the world, the modern world indeed represents a severe crisis and an undermining of the communality and uniformity of faith. In the general confusion thus introduced, each person must seek his own faith and his own adjustment to the various types of knowledge. In this search it is of great help to see that Christian faith and *mythos* are conditioned by practical religion and ethics, and to clarify the distinction between faith and knowledge through a psychological and epistemological analysis of both.

The value of faith is measured by the degree of religious and ethical life that it produces out of its own personal, inner power; conversely, this life has the right freely to shape and to develop a *mythos* for itself according to its own conscience, since faith is an attitude of the heart toward God and since the conception of God is merely a symbolic expression to elicit this attitude. This statement—Protestant in its first part and modern in its second part—can show the way out of the confusion; first to the individual and then, hopefully, to increasingly wider circles. As the concept of faith is purified by psychological and epistemological reflection, there will be a growing unity on the basis of the 'purely religious': the *ideas* of faith will be seen as mere expressions or means of a religious relationship to God, to the world, and to man. Of course, the *mythos* has not disappeared, nor can it disappear; it has become the means and expression of the basic religious posture of the entire person. Even then the conflicts do not cease. But the area of friction is now less, and the coexistence of different forms of *mythos* is facilitated. *Mythos* knows itself for what it is, and serves only the faith of the heart.

9

Faith and History

A. The Historical Connections of Christian Faith

A particularly difficult problem for current religious thought is posed by the connection of faith with historical matters. Religion is understood and experienced as a *present* religion, as a certainty about God and the eternal world which is apprehended now through inner experience. It is felt to be a difficulty that this experience of God is supposed to depend on the mediation of historical personages and forces, and to include a religious appreciation of historical matters. When the problem is posed in this manner, the first question that arises is what historical connections are actually asserted and how these connections relate to the essential aspects of the Christian faith. From the standpoint of the psychology of religion the following points come to mind:

(a) Faith is always faith in a concrete thought-content. This thought-content never orignates solely from the individual subject. On the contrary, the richer and stronger it is, the more it is the communal work of great epochs of intellectual history and of whole generations, or of outstanding personalities that have profited from these communal achievements. Faith feels a need to gather up this whole world of ideas in its starting point and to embody it in an archetype, in order always to be able to rectify and to revitalize itself. This archetype is naturally the personality of the founding prophet or revealer. On the higher levels of religion, moreover, faith becomes increasingly the appropriation of outstanding personages. As its requirements increase, its need for support from personalities that supply direction and impetus increases also. Faith therefore depends upon history, but not only for sustenance and information; its own self-understanding depends upon history, and within history upon the embodiment of revelation to which it looks. Without a conscious relationship to Christ the Christian faith is unthinkable, even though one's faith in God may be regarded as resting upon its own inner evidence and power. The Christian faith originated in the historical disclosure of the life of God, and for the sake of clarity and power it must be constantly referred back to this foundation, which is vitally present to the imagination. Even though some individuals may be able to forego this historical referral because they are carried along by the power of the community, the community as a whole cannot forego it if the community is to retain its vital force.

(b) Christian faith is a redemption through faith in the God who reveals himself in Christ. Through the powers of faith communicated to us by Christ, the Christian faith raises men to a higher level of intellectual, moral, and religious strength, where confidence of victory prevails and where worldly sorrow (*Weltleid*) and the consciousness of guilt are overcome. This means the individual experiences something that elevates and liberates him, something that is not merely a product of his own efforts but that approaches him from the outside with a superior power. Of course, only his own living, actual faith in God himself redeems the individual, but he does not puzzle his way to this faith on his own. He receives it as a liberating and uplifting force through religious impressions that impinge upon him and that essentially have Christ as their starting point and authentication. Even in its redemptive aspect, faith must cling to the historical connection with the sources from which it derives this liberating impulse, the power to provide certainty—in short, the whole wealth of these ideas.

(c) The Christian faith has its goal in the creation of a great community of humanity which strengthened and elevated through faith, is at the same time united in a common recognition of the divine will to which it owes its existence and by which it is directed to mutual works of love. Such an ethical community requires means of solidarity and demarcation. These means can lie only in the realization and common recognition of the historical powers that have brought it into being. At any rate, such means are necessary so long as this community has to broaden itself through conflict. The situation might be different if this community were a victorious power naturally present in all and carrying all before it. Such a state of affairs, however, is unthinkable on earth. Even the ethical community of faith necessitates a conscious historical connection with the foundation that keeps the community together.

(d) Christian faith at the same time maintains, for its propagation and consolidation, a Christian cultus. This is unavoidable if religion is to stay alive. As a means of illustration and edification, and as a classical archetype, this cultus is bound, in the first instance, to cultivate the memory of the origin and personality of the founder, the revealer, the hero. However else the cultus may utilize forces of the present day, it always remains bound to the historical foundations and their realization.

(e) The faith of Christianity regards itself as the completion of revelation and redemption, and hence must take a stand regarding the faith of other circles of religious belief, which, on their higher levels, likewise depend on revelatory personalities and a content of redemptive faith. The doctrine of the church has taken such a stand by regarding the Christian revelation and redemption as the supernatural restoration of the perfect beginning of history; and by designating the non-Christian religions, insofar as they contain elements of truth, as postulates and products of vestigial reason, and insofar as they contain elements of untruth, as products of sinful human nature left to its own devices. Even when this Christian philosophy of history is abandoned, some sort of philosophy of history must be taken into account; it remains necessary to relate the Christian faith in revelation and redemption to the non-Christian religions in such a way that Christianity can maintain the conviction of its supreme validity.

All these arguments entail the essential and inseparable connection of faith with history and the necessity of a religious view of history. From time to time it may well be necessary to relax these historical connections and to make room for one's own religious creativity. But, basically, innovations will hardly be more than new positions regarding history and new fruitful applications of what was already given. To abandon history would be tantamount to faith's abandoning itself and settling for the fleeting and trivial religious stirrings produced by a subjectivity left to its own resources. The earliest Christian era established these historical connections by setting off Jesus, the church, and the Bible from the natural course of ordinary history; and secured the permanence of the connection by making these historical elements divine. The connection with history, then, was forced by psychological requirements immanent in faith itself.

B. Objections to Such Historical Relationships

Until modern times, the Christian faith was content to bear these historical connections. While interpretations differed, faith always found its strongest support in them. Even when the content of faith was transformed into a pure religion of the 'now' (*Gegenwartsreligion*), the historical connections were not abolished. The modern world first raised fundamental objections. They are the following:

(a) In every area the modern world is the world of individual autonomy. In every field, and hence in religion, compelling personal insight into the universal validity of judgements is the means by which the modern world attains certainty. Religious autonomy can lead to universal judgements and unanimous conviction only when religious truth is contained in the nature of reason itself, and hence shares the universal validity of the latter; that is, if it can be derived from reason as such. This attitude implies a departure from the historical authority: faith is put on its own. It further implies that the content of faith is a universally valid conceptual necessity that follows from the general nature of reason. If autonomous assent to that content is to be possible, faith must be a present self-apprehension of the religious content of reason. Otherwise faith would be formally an unworthy belief in authority and materially a mere attachment to accidental historical occurrences whose spheres of influence we have simply been born into. The age of autonomy and science emancipates itself from mere positive authority and from the historical accident of birth.

(b) The analysis supplied by the psychology of religion, which tries to view faith from a scientific, psychological viewpoint, shows us that in reality faith can be connected only with what is present and eternal, and never with what is merely past and transitory. Whenever faith adheres to historical facts, it alters these into non-historical realities, into miracles that proclaim the eternal purposes of God or into human incarnations of the divine, into transfigurations or resurrections of the historical in which the historical is only the veiling or revealing of the eternal. In addition to establishing historical connections, dogma pertaining to Christ, the church, and the Bible constitutes above all an abrogation of the historicity of these entities and their transformation into timeless metaphysical potencies. This procedure can be continued, however, only so long as the ostensible historical bases do not become the object of real historical research, which would show them to be, like all historical data, relative and conditioned. As soon as historical research is thus employed, the historical and the present separate. Only the latter can be a direct object of faith.

(c)A truly historical consideration of historical matters, such as was unknown to the ancient church and to the Middle Ages, not only shows that such data are relative and conditioned but even makes them objects of criticism. We do not possess the facts themselves but only the traditions concerning the facts. The task is critically to reconstruct from these traditions what probably happened in reality. But the picture of what happened becomes uncertain and shifting as a result of this critical treatment. The upshot can be an utterly unrecognizable opinion or a denial of the alleged facts themselves. A decision can be reached only through scholarly examination, which by its nature is accessible to few, and whose results are by no means assured, since it depends on religious traditions passed on from uncritical ages and social classes. Faith, however, cannot tolerate any uncertainty or dependence on erudition. Faith, therefore, retreats to positions that are not subject to historical criticism.

(d) Furthermore, modern Christianity with its various intermingled denominations is itself historically segmented. The Catholic doctrine of the sole truth of Catholicism and the Old Protestant doctrine of the sole truth of its Bible-Christianity no longer have a place in the general consciousness. They have been replaced by the demand for toleration and, consequently, by a certain relativization of all the historical forms of Christianity. In this toleration and the relativism connected with it, there is implicit a standpoint above all these particular historical forms. This standpoint lies above these particular forms only because it does not itself lie in history, but in present conviction on the basis of which relative values can be assessed and tolerated. Modern tolerance and relativism may also be due to a complete absence of conviction, which give full play to the different historical forms because there is no fixed standard by which they might be measured. At any rate, there is a tendency toward emancipation from history in the modern idea of tolerance.

(e) Difficulties arise not merely from the relation of Christianity to its own historical elements, but also from its relation to the other historical religions. Christianity appears more and more as one religion among many. This results either in complete skeptical relativism or in the attainment of a general concept of religious truth by which the different historical manifestations are measured. Such a concept derives its validity not from any historical foundation or authority, but from its own inner necessity and correctness. Here again there is a liberation of religion from history.

(f) All these difficulties, which grow out of religious thought itself, coincide with a general frame of mind that is sensitive to the oppressiveness of history and historical erudition. This historical erudition will not allow us direct, ingenuous, and living creativity; instead, it stifles every such innovation with historical comparisions and relations. As a result, the desire for freedom from history characterizes the temper of the times, in reaction to an excess of historical thought and scholarship. Add to this the effects of the temporal and spatial expansion of the historical horizon, which knows a stay of humanity on earth for more than a hundred thousand years and the prospect of a future stay of indefinite length, presumably lasting till the earth becomes uninhabitable. Christianity now appears as only another wave in the ebb and flow of the largely unknown history of mankind. Religious conviction cannot permanently attach itself to a particular historical phenomenon of this sort.

For all these reasons the problem of history is almost more difficult for faith than the problem of modern metaphysics and the modern natural sciences. History presents modern life with a truly serious and grave problem that, like both the others, works for a manifold transformation of our religious thought. The old attitude toward history can no longer be maintained. That the history of humanity reaches through immeasurable stretches of time, that all historical occurrences are alike conditioned and temporal, and that the principles of historical criticism are universally dominant—all these points must be admitted. Amid such concessions the question comes very much to the fore how the historical connections of faith are to stand their ground.

C. The Continuing Legitimacy of the Historical Connections of the Christian Faith

Yet, in face of this general trend towards the emancipation of faith, the psychological facts mentioned at the outset still persist. Strong and rich faith comes to men as the revelation of religious heroes and as the communal work of whole generations. This is all the more true if the faith, through the abundance of its ethical and religious contents, occupies the subject in appropriation and sympathetic participation and leaves him little room for his own production. Yet a faith also acts in a redeeming and liberating manner, in the measure that it assists the subject in transcending the limits of his own self through the powers of appropriation and sympathetic participation that the faith affords. Only in this way does faith bring the subject into truly complete and vital contact with the divine life. Only through such elevation and communication of power does faith become capable of autonomy. Autonomy is not the starting point but the climax of religious training. From this climax, it is often enough necessary to return to the forces that stimulate, illustrate, and authenticate faith. The same principle applies to every other sphere. Nowhere does autonomy produce the contents of modern though and life. This content derives for the most part from tradition and authorities that enable thought to strive for autonomous understanding and development—a striving never crowned with more than limited success. In religious thought, this situation prevails all the more. Religious thought especially needs tradition and authority, in view of the strength and infrequency of its great revelations and in view of the weakness and fragmentation of the average religious subjectivity. Tradition and authority are required until religious thought has passed beyond them to know the internally necessary validity of the religious ideas.

What follows emerges in reply to specific points.

(a) Modern autonomy must never be understood as the autonomous production of the contents of the mind. It only relates to the form of appropriation: the content is to be appropriated not merely on the basis of authority but on the basis of personal conviction and the demands of the individual conscience, insofar as this is practicable. Hence, modern autonomy becomes the criticism and further development of tradition. Personal conviction will of course require that the emerging world of ideas shows itself to be universally valid. But it is only possible to work toward this universal validity by proceeding from what is given. By emphasizing the elements of universal validity within this positive base, and by comparing them with the other elements, it is possible to go back to an underlying universal validity. The same applies also to religious autonomy. Only by proceeding from what is given can there be progress toward what is intrinsically necessary and valid, comparision with foreign religions, and a return to a universal validity that is contained and displayed in all these factors. If a religion fails to survive amidst such efforts and comparisons, this simply means that this religion has been transcended. If a religion maintains itself under such analyses, however, then it will be necessary to continue to build on its foundations. It is not to the point here to discuss how universally valid judgements are formed or attested. We need only stress that no degree of autonomy will ever exempt us from the necessity of dealing with the problem on the basis of the positive religion that alone is vitally grasped; that it may well be possible to maintain that Christianity represents the highest manifestation of the religious idea; and that for the sake of power, clarity, and vitality this religious idea must always retain its connection with its historical actualization and formation in the total religious understanding of countless generations. No modern autonomy can affect this state of affairs so long as the Christian faith in God is asserted and developed as a constitutive part of that autonomy. Anything else would be a rationalism tenable only to the extent that it is wholly based on inferences from the formal nature of reason—a limitation that would mean a corresponding impoverishment of religion.

(b) That everything historical is relative and conditioned doubtless applies also to the historical elements of Christianity; that is, to Jesus and the earliest Christian era. But this consideration does not preclude the possibility that these historical forces represent—and will continue to represent—the breakthrough, embodiment, and visible guarantee of the highest and purest religious powers, just as the most radical autonomy of today cannot escape historical limitation and relativity. The essential point is a correct view of the relationship of the universally valid to the historically and psychologically relative; or, if we see in history the growth of the spiritual out of the merely positive and natural, a correct view of this growth or evolution. Such a view cannot be presented here. But this much can be stressed: while in this growth the individual remains bound to previous history and to accumulated collective experience, at key historical points this collective experience receives new creative impulses—massive instances of the principle of irrational mutation that we see at work in the minutest processes. It is quite possible, then, to think of faith as contingent upon the vital realization of its historical heritage and especially of its creative foundations.

(c) Historical criticism cannot be kept off the premises of sacred history and undeniably creates serious difficulties and uncertainties for faith. Such is the fate of every faith in passing from uncritical times and social strata to a critical, scientific age; we see a comparable development in the areas of metaphysical thought and the philosophy of nature. In critical, scientific ages faith lives under other conditions than in predominantly uncritical ages; its battles differ from the ones that even an uncritical age imposes upon faith. At such a time, historical criticism can of course greatly complicate and confuse the historical connections. But this state of affairs can never be permanent. Historical criticism cannot be an end in itself and must some day arrive at results that will be generally accepted. The historical connection of faith will then attach itself all the more to major points, to the religious personalities of Jesus and Paul, of Augustine and Luther, leaving everything else to the scholars and critics. The main point, the personality of Jesus, will be interpreted in so universal a manner that faith will continue to be able to link whatever it regards as sacred and precious to it, and even future acquisitions will find room in it. The historical enters into the picture only to the extent that it can be continually transformed into present reality. These liberal interpretations of Jesus find some historical support in the preaching and personality of Jesus. Historical criticism can give us nothing more; but this is sufficient. The radical dissolution of the whole tradition and self-conception of the church, and its replacement with a history of Christian origins completely different from that entertained by the ancient church itself—this is only the expectation of a sensationalistic hypercriticism, which is one of the afflictions of critical ages.

(d) The triumph of toleration among us implies, of course, the relativization of the historical forms of traditional Christianity. Yet it can be true toleration only if at the same time it recognizes relative truth-values in those forms. Such recognition is only possible precisely on the basis of a faith that knows how to appreciate the significance of the historical and that sees manifestations of eternal religious truths in history. These truths may well be envisaged as connected with history in some way other than through the churches, but they cannot be envisaged wholly apart from historical connections of some sort. When toleration lacks such a basis, then it is mere skepticism and indolence, as in fact today it often enough is.

(e) With the enormous expansion of our knowledge of history, with the recession of the beginnings of mankind into immeasurably distant reaches of the past, and with the presumptive image of the end of humanity amidst yet remote geophyscial changes, even the position of Christianity in universal history poses new problems. The problem cannot be solved through the construction of an autonomous religion implied in non-historical reason, for every such construction is in reality conditioned by history. The most we can do is to regard Christianity as a climax in a historical evolution and actualization of the consciousness of God. Then we must either assume a further evolution of spirit that in principle continues to advance on this level; or else concede that in every large, new cultural complex, the religious consciousness has to find its high point in an analogous movement that for its part will remain similarly tied to the historical forces from which it has arisen. Every conceivable new formulation of religion, then, presupposes the demise of European-Christian culture. Yet, no new formulation could make untrue what has been religious truth in this culture; whatever truth there has been must be included in the new formulation, so that even in this most extreme case we need not doubt our religious heritage. Allotment of truth to the different epochs of history and participation by individuals in the ultimate values of history belong to a realm that transcends history and lies beyond our knowledge.

(f) Historical scholarship indeed exerts a pressure on the temper of our age, but only because historians no longer venture to interpret their material in terms of the philosophy of history. The mass of speculative and religious ideas again on the rise will above all have to deal with history on the basis of certain fundamental ideas, organizing the evaluating history from the point of view of a system of life purposes. Then the pressure of history will cease, and faith will be able once again to appreciate its historical connections, which are quite indispensable to it psychologically. A liberal and critical attitude toward history, which in its ups and downs sometimes approaches the ideal and sometimes departs from it, must free us from both skepticism and evolutionary progressivism.

D. Historical Relationships in contemporary Christian Faith

For everyone who adopts the modern attitude toward history, the conclusion will be inevitable that the historical connections of faith are to be retained but are to be formulated in a new way. It is becoming impossible to believe that the history of the world had a perfect beginning, that some six thousand years later that beginning was redemptively restored, and that there will be a speedy consummation in the return of Christ. It is further becoming impossible to separate the Bible, Jesus, and the church as supernatural entitles of an absolutely different sort from the course of history, which otherwise is natural and all-embracing. Finally, it is becoming impossible to regard redemption as an act performed by Christ and affecting God. Our present redemption is more than mere believing appropriation of this act and its benefits. More and more it becomes necessary to see the objective side of redemption in the religious experience (*Vorgang*), in the present redeeming and elevating work of God in the soul that surrenders itself to him. But this present work of

God with us and in us takes place only through a knowledge of God that comes to us from history, and through a religious power that thus works upon us, carrying us with it and uplifting us. For present faith, therefore, the historical elements of faith form the basis of revelation and knowledge, even as they communicate power and inspiration and provide attestation and illustration. Faith is disclosed directly only in statements about God, the world, man, redemption, the religious community, and hope—statements that set forth the present content of faith. In addition, faith needs the historical statements, in which its powers are indirectly revealed, confirmed, and illustrated. Theology thus contains statements that are directly, presently, or dogmatically religious. But it also contains historical statements that are seen in a religious light and regarded as religiously significant; and that are indispensable. These statements are indirectly or historically religious. Theology therefore analyzes its religious confession into historico-religious statements and presently-religious statements. Both kinds of statement must be expounded with poetic liveliness and freedom, without which dogmatic theologies are altogether unthinkable; but both kinds of statement must also find bases in actual experience. Theology can be sure that the religious life thus acquired is richer and more robust than any pure, self-contained religion of sentiment that completely emancipates itself from history. Experience shows that such sentimental religion has never had the strength to produce a religious creation similar to that which arose in Jesus and early Christianity, when the disintegration of both Eastern and Western religion marked the major turning-point in world history. Theology can also be sure that the religious truth that has grown up in this connection with Jesus and the Bible can never become truth, insofar as it is religious power and truth that actually proves itself in life. The question is solely that of working out this latter point. The future may have worries of its own.

E. Dogmatic Articles of Faith

The term 'articles of faith' refers to the particular propositions that make up the totality of the Christian faith when the attempt is made to present its thought-content. Its significance varies with the understanding of what makes up the totality of the Christian idea. If this totality is regarded, along the lines of the theology of the ancient church, as the doctrine presented once and for all by the Bible, which needs only to be re-arranged into a systematic whole with logically interconnected principles, then articles of faith are statements drawn from the Bible about God, and world, humanity, redemption, justification, the Trinity, and so forth. Their totality represents the revealed doctrine. It is possible to distinguish between main or basic articles, that is, fundamental articles of faith such as the one pertaining to justification, and subsidiary articles such as the one pertaining to angels. The three articles of the 'Apostles' Creed' are meant to be taken in this way; they are intended to be concise summaries of the Christian revelation. The assumption in this view is that the revelation is interpreted as a communication of truth which can be analyzed into specific major components. The revelation is thought to contain these components as to their matter, but not yet systematically arranged in form. If, on the other hand, revelation is understood along the lines of modern theology as the establishment of a uniform religious way of thinking and living that assumes different conceptual forms at different times and in different general contexts, then articles of faith are attempts to give conceptual expression to the totality of the Christian religious idea in its various aspects. Articles of faith, then, formulate the concepts of God, man, and the world, the concepts of redemption and the church, and the concept of last things as an expression of the Christian faith which in any such article gives a special shape to the totality by its definite and particular perspective. The expression 'article' is reminiscent of the subdivisions of a statute, and is in fact connected with the notion of a revealed law of faith. This expression is poorly suited for its task. Modern theology prefers to speak of 'ideas of faith' or of 'the expression of religious conceptions,' since there is a constant flow of new constructions and interpretations of the fundamental substance of the Christian religious life. The former view is that of conservative theology, in which theology actually commits itself to the Bible or to denominational norms. The latter is the view of modern theology. Accordingly, this interpretation is connected with a concept of the nature of revelation, of faith, and of dogmatic theology which differs from the interpretation of conservative dogmatics. Here the various 'articles' are seen as instructive for the understanding of these entities—which are decisive for the concept, 'ideas of faith.' But for modern theology they are ideas of faith and no longer articles of faith.

10

Eschatology

1. Every religiosity that seeks to achieve a clear self-understanding and self-expression has a doctrine of last things, an eschatology (to use the technical term), however mythical its form may be. More than a poetic impulse gives rise to it; it proceeds from the religious idea itself. For religion itself is, if not a *doctrine*, yet surely a *sense* of 'last things'; that is, of ultimate realities and values that are absolute and unconditioned, uniform and inherently necessary, in contrast to finite realities and values that are relativized more and more by reflexion. A highly reflective culture like the present is most acutely conscious of this contrast. It either allows the last things to be swallowed up by the flux of relative and finite realities and values that condition and produce one another and thus are dependent upon one another; or else it passionately opposes to this flux the a priori, infinite, absolute nature of ultimate realities and values.

Now, the relativizing of things constitutes the essence of science, insofar as science, in its attempt to formulate interconnections and generalities, is led farther and farther afield until the relational nexus appears to be infinite, fading off into boundlessness, with nothing firm and universal except the purely formal relational nexus itself. The natural sciences tend to look upon this relational nexus, or the prevalence of law and the elements that are found within this nexus, with naive dogmatism; but resist further division and dissolution into further nexuses as 'last things.' But then the last things are never more than a relational nexus that is only thought up by thought and can be expanded and revised *ad placitum*, ultimate facts that are phenomenal and purely given, which science ought not to avoid attempting to break down further. But this nexus and these facts must be hypostatized and mythicized in order to be turned from conceptions and notions into things or even last things; and last things of this sort can only be related to ultimate values (say, of beauty, or harmony, or the unity of life) by deliberate misrepresentation. These myths will be dissolved again, unmercifully, by every exact science, which will continue its work of ever new analysis and synthesis through relational nexuses, with the result that both fact and notion are turned into a perpetually dependent structure, conditioned by moment and situation.

All consistent historical thinking, however, leads especially to relativism. The more the notion of evolution (*ider Entwicklungsgedanke*) emancipates itself from teleological illusions and confines itself to the establishment of dependencies and transitions in the growth of historical entities, the more every link in the chain is seen to be conditioned by its context and understandable only in relation to this context; it is what it is only in relation to the other links and is constantly involved in mutations and transitions as the total situated changes. But if one wants to understand the particular that has come into being in this way (and this particular is, for that matter, equally significant for a historically interested consideration of nature), not merely in terms of a system of mutual conditionedness but in terms of a metaphysically necessary rise of the individual and autonomous (*Eigenständigem*) within the relational nexus, one is confronted by a confusing abundance of individual entities that always reveal their nature only through their effectiveness in context. Here, too, we cannot speak of last things but only of a purely formal ultimate law of individuation. But here, too, this law says nothing about last things, unless one wants to regard the empty [notion of] individuality itself as a last thing; but individuality loses its meaning and value if it does not individualize ultimate and eternal values. Gradually, then, all the last things of history—'classical' periods and eternal paradigms and revelations—have been relativized and individualized; and the cult of individuality as such, as a form of life, has become as much a self-contradictory myth as the cult of atoms and laws [of nature].

But if we confine ourselves to objective values and norms that are to be actualized and individualized in history, these, too, are recognized more and more clearly (after having been too hastily hypostatized in eternal ideals of culture) as historically conditioned and subject to historical change. The processes of psychological derivation and explanation at the end of which they appear become longer; psychology ultimately swallows up all values and norms, explaining their origin and transformation in relativistic terms. They, too, are no last things, no things-in-themselves; even if one feels compelled to ascribe to normative judgements a special psychological form, this mere form remains in and of itself only a means for establishing relationships without constituting a solid content. This form, while comprehending the most varied and changing entities, probably has a psychological origin that only lies farther back and remains more concealed.

But the relativism that is thus introduced into every sphere of life by science is also at the same time produced and encouraged by life itself. By a process of simultaneous differentiation and interrelation, society, too, is transformed into a pure relational system, based not on firm foundations of its own but on an increasingly refined exchange of goods that simply expresses the interchangeableness of all values. Even the seemingly fixed standard of interchangeableness, money, is only the symbol of the relational character of things in general, which leads from one thing to another and conditions one by the other; and the inclination to look upon money (which constitutes, after all, no more than the possibility of exchange and interchangeableness) as in itself a possession is, accordingly, symbolic of every inclination to regard mere means to the establishment of relations as last things.

Under these circumstances it is now all the more the nature of religious experience to have an ultimate, absolute reality for its object. The more the Absolute is driven out of its false identification with relative entities, and out of its premature coming to rest in incomplete chains [of reasoning], the more clearly it manifests itself in pure religious experience, which for this very reason cannot be determined, defined, and described; and which is nothing other than the experience and sense of an ultimate being and of an ultimate value that must accordingly be attributed to this ultimate being. Wherever there is an alleged coming to rest in last things of whatever kind, this very fact gives these a religious coloring; and where the Absolute at the end of all chains [of reasoning] simply breaks up and never comes to consciousness (*nie zu sich selbst kommt*), it oscillates purely within itself in order to enter the world of relative things once again, to make participation in the Absolute possible. Morality, science, and art participate in last things precisely to the degree in which they acknowledge and assert their connection with the religious idea of an Absolute manifesting itself in them. Their special dignity consists only in this, that such a connection can be acknowledged in them; how this is to take place is another question. Truly ultimate realities and values are, accordingly, unable to be thought out, because they are not relative and do not consist in relations; but they are capable of being experienced, because they constitute the reality of the divine life and the beatitude of being received into that life. Science is everywhere concerned with the relative. It knows the Absolute only as a relational form and a generality, which, for their part, are nothing more than activities of human thought. Religion, however (according to the degree of its accomplishment), seeks, divines, and experiences the Absolute; this constitutes both its ineffable meaning and its complete inaptitude ever to become a science. Religion, then, deals with last things and values; and last things and values are to be found only in religion and through religion.

2. In the first instance, last things have nothing whatever to do with time. But the expression, 'ultimate realities and values,' which we use so frequently, derives from the fact that such a notion always arises only at the conclusion of certain spiritual, practical, or theoretical movements; it is not simply part of the immediately given but always arises only by a process of transcending the immediately given in the direction of something lying behind or above it, in connection with primitive causal explanations, [or] primitive hopes and fears, which allow something to be recognized as only relative. Primitive mentality usually settles for the shortest possible chains [of reasoning] and places the Absolute at their end. But with advancing culture, these chains get longer and longer. The relative elements that must be understood relationally increase, and the Absolute recedes more and more into the unimaginable and the superhuman, or supernatural. Thence arises also the insight that the full apprehension of the Absolute can come only at the end of the whole chain [of being], at the end of earthly life or, still later, at the end of a chain of life after death, and finally, at the end of the perfection of life itself— an insight that is only facilitated by man's spontaneous cult of the spirits and the dead. Thus last things turn into eschatology, that is, into an expectation that the full disclosure of the last things comes only at the end of life. Now arise doctrines of heaven and hell, of redemption and reincarnation, of a judgement of the dead and the purgings and purifications in the Hereafter. When the last things are thus placed at the final end, as the goal of all development, they constitute the attainment and realization of the original and proper nature of man, which emerges fully realized only out of the labor of life, as the conclusion of all his labors. Thus all the great religions of culture have created a powerful eschatological myth, after embracing, together with the ethos, the principle of becoming and progress through work, and together with thought, the principle of the finitude

of all that is merely relative. In this myth, the end only actualizes the
beginning: perfection is placed both at the beginning and at the end,
and there is an instinctive preference for utilizing the myths of the
beginning for the myths of the end. But sooner or later, this myth
usually succumbs to rationalistic criticism, as is happening among us
today with the Judaeo-Graeco-Christian eschatological myth.
Eschatology then returns again to its proper *Grundmotiv*, the sense of
the Absolute, and hence elaborates two forms of the doctrine of last
things. One of these can conceive of last things only as ever present,
while the other can conceive of them only in terms of inner continuity
as the necessary conclusion of the development of life. The former is
pantheistic and immanental; that is, it focuses upon Absolute Being,
which is everywhere present and timeless. The latter is personalistic
and transcendental; that is, it rests on the ideas of freedom and
becoming. These two types of eschatology engage in lively controversy.
Between them, they divide the loyalties of our contemporary religious
life, except insofar as the old myth or complete mindlessness prevail.

3. The first type [of eschatology] sees the Absolute as the mere
unity immanent in the succession—without beginning or end—of the
relative. The religious sense of the Absolute is, accordingly, only the
breaking-through into consciousness of the sense of the quintessence of
conditions and interrelationships. This sense accompanies the life-
process of the finite spirit. It belongs to the temporal realm only
insofar as that which in itself is always equally present as an underlying
reality is also experienced by the subject at certain points; that is,
whenever the quintessence of the conditioned is for some reason raised
above the conditioned particular into consciousness. The ethical
significance of this sense is not an elevation into a new state of life
and into a new line of work but the spreading of unity, harmony, rest,
and self-limitation above the naturally given chaos of the drives and
the conditions of the soul.

The second type [of eschatology] sees the sense of the Absolute
itself coming about only through an act of freedom tearing itself away
from the course of nature. It confronts man with the ethical task of
gradually elevating himself, by devoting himself to whatever
experience indicates is conducive to concentration upon the
Unconditioned, into the [sphere of the] Absolute and the Divine,
which during this process is experienced as an active power—leading
beyond the merely relative and drawing the subject into union of life
with itself by means of his will and freedom.

The first type represents a new evaluation of the given from the
perspective of the last things working themselves out in it; the second

represents a new life-force and a new life-stance, through the self-surrender of freedom to the Absolute so as to bring about a personal life-unity. The first type is based on the concept of immanence and totality; the second is based on the concept of creation and development, with development taking place through freedom because developmental goals presuppose freedom. For the first type, the goal is fully reached in every moment of elevation; for the second, it lies at the end of freedom and of the development out of freedom. The first is pantheistic mysticism, the second is personalistic belief in creation; both, accordingly, take a radically different view of the relation between the relative and the Absolute.

For both types, the elevation above primary and relative things constitutes redemption. But for the first, redemption leads from the partial to the whole, from the changeable to the abiding, from the unreal to the real. For the second, redemption leads from bondage to freedom, from the imperfect to the perfect, from the beginning to the consummation, from conflict to victory. These are the contrasts between pantheism and Buddhism, on the one hand, and Judaism and Christianity, on the other.

A genuine choice between the two types requires a practical, ethical, and religious decision. The decisive questions would be these: Which of the two types seems to provide the more powerful religious energy and ethical training? and where is the finite more thoroughly and comprehensively taken up in to the Absolute? There can be little doubt, practically speaking, that the answer is, in the personalistic doctrine. We can only add, theoretically speaking, that the pantheistic doctrine does not fundamentally overcome relativism at all. Basically, it leaves the whole relativistic interrelationship as it is and only teaches us to view it at the same time, in a mysteriously mystical manner, under the aspect of absolute unity. But this absolute unity is nothing more than the hypostatizing of the form of the relational nexus itself; and inasmuch as it coincides with this form, it is not capable of leading us beyond it. Thus a religiosity of this type has nothing new to offer in the ethical sphere; it only teaches us to see the course of life in the light of unity, thereby breaking our selfish desires but not leading us beyond them into a higher life. If relativism is really to be broken through, this can only be accomplished by a religiosity that distinguishes the Absolute from the quintessence of the relative as a creative and living will. This will, then, leads beyond the relative also in the soul, by opening up a new life-stance in community with the divine will, which now opens up a work of progressive self-surrender to the divine will until there is complete unity of will, or perfect love.

This is the only way to overcome relativism. But whether one really wills to overcome it is again a fundamental act of freedom, for whose necessity no further proof can be given.

4. The personalistic doctrine of last things must teach an eschatology that runs its course in time and reaches its goal only through struggle and work and in dependence on grace. For it, the elevation of man out of the bondage of nature, finite egotism, and the resulting sinfulness is redemption through grace, which grasps us and leads us away from the finite-egotistical self; and this redemption must reach its consummation as the finite self is completely consumed in community with God.

But since this consummation concerns the individual, it cannot consist in a final perfection of the [human] race in its life here on earth, as it is proclaimed by the Hegelian doctrine of the state and the Socialist doctrine of society. It must go beyond the earthly life of the individual, which never gets beyond mere beginnings and never fully overcomes its sinfulness. Thus the first doctrine of personalistic eschatology is the doctrine of a life after death, or, in the very inappropriate Platonic phrase, of personal immortality. According to the whole approach of this notion, such a life after death can be nothing other than a progressive purification and development leading to the union of the creature with God. Beyond this postulate nothing more can be said; anything further is therefore imagination and myth. Objections to this doctrine arise from the fact that in our experience, all spiritual life is bound up with bodily or, more specifically, nervous processes. These objections are aggravated by references to such phenomena as mental illness, idiocy, senility, and infant mortality, as well as spiritual underdevelopment in retarded or brutalized persons and social strata. In response, one could point to our complete ignorance of the nexus between nature and spirit, as well as to the important fact that personalistic eschatology does not speak of an immortality that is naturally proper to the 'soul,' but rather of a further development of personhood or of a spiritual humanity that transcends the natural life of the soul and is perhaps endowed with hidden organs. Where nothing like this has come into being, there is nothing that needs to be developed further. The merely natural, unspiritual soul may perhaps return again and again in nature's store of energy until it succeeds in breaking into the sphere of the spirit and personality. In this respect the Buddhist doctrine of pre-existence and reincarnation has much to be said for it, and there is also deep meaning in the assertion that redemption consists in the breaking out of this ever-turning wheel of natural soul energies. But the Buddhist redemption knows no positive last things like those recognized in the Christian doctrine of freedom and redemption.

A second problem derives from the fact that personalism must naturally stress the perfection of the individual, but the individual must be viewed within the nexus of interpersonal relatedness, not in isolation. Ethical and religious development takes place only in interaction, through the mutual enrichment and elevation of individuals. These become persons only as the community assumes a collective personality; as the spirits, in their divine life, not only become one with God but equally so with one another. A growing mutual penetration of persons in love, the manifestation of their common grounding in the divine life, finally their essential identity is, consequently, an equally necessary postulate. Even as the finite self ultimately returns to God after having been a spiritual person, so the finite differentiation itself must again be overcome in the interpenetration of persons in love. The Christian ideas of the consummation of the kingdom of God, where God is ultimately all in all, provide the strongest expression here; even as, in connection with the first problem, the Christian ideas of the infinite worth of the God-filled soul gave the sharpest formulation to the concept of eschatology. The antinomy between the kingdom of God and the infinite worth of the human soul, indeed the whole enigma of our consciousness being split into an individual and a collective consciousness, would only then be overcome in this ultimate identification mediated by moral effort.

A third question, then, is the question of the participation and destination of of particular individuals with respect to this kingdom of God and this ultimate salvation (*Heil*); that is, the question to what extent all individuals in the world of finite spirits are called to participate in these last things. This question is actually twofold. In the first place, it arises from the observation that amidst the ups and downs of human history, various circles of culture and consciousness are faced with entirely different possibilities and facilities with respect to their elevation to last things; and that even within a particular circle there are extraordinary differences in these possibilities and facilities—depending on personal disposition, heredity, environment, and fate, and varying from the most favorable to the at least seemingly impossible. In the second place, this question arises out of the possibility of wickedness, which is connected with the creature's rise, through struggle, from its finite egoism and egotism to its surrender to spiritual and ideal values, and which results in an enormous sinfulness. The question here is how the wicked and vulgar, those who

consciously and completely turn their backs on the good and refuse
the divine life, stand with regard to the last things.

The first question [that of the possibility of elevation] coincides with
the dark problem of predestination. But predestination moves in sliding
transitions, not in exclusive opposites, inasmuch as it is the divine
positing of values as universally valid and thus, no doubt, as ultimately
intended for all. One is therefore inclined to see its significance only in
the distribution of the respective facility and possibility [for elevation]
not in an eternal condemnation of individuals to return again and
again on the wheel of natural energies. The situation is similar with the
second problem, that of wickedness. Since wickedness is often nothing
other than a disadvantage resulting from one's situation, disposition,
and fate; since there are certainly sliding transitions in its intensity and
consciousness; and since an actual, fully conscious and intended total
rejection of the good is difficult to establish—here, too, the notion of
purification and purging lies closer at hand than that of a self-
destruction of the wicked. For all of us are sinners, and enough of
wickedness remains even in the person who surrenders to grace, just as
in the presumably wicked person some sort of grace probably continues
to work. Thus there stands in the background, ultimately, a doctrine
of the restoration of all people; and this very doctrine has perhaps still
the broadest cosmic background, inasmuch as all products of nature
are perhaps called to spiritualization and all natural bodies are perhaps
only the bodies of spirits in the making.

At last, we come to the problem of the end itself. But here we
cannot mean the actual end of the world. As the eternal creation of
God, the world has neither temporal beginning nor temporal end.
Only what has had a temporal beginning can have an end—that is,
only the worlds that make up the world. The end that could constitute
our end can only be the end of the human world. But here we will
surely have to speak also of an end of finite spirits, who are returning
to God in the moral effort of freedom and have been transformed in
time out of natural beings into spiritual beings and persons. Their
eternity consists only in the measure of their share in the eternal
divine life; the perfection of this eternity of theirs could only be a
return to, and a re-immersion in, the divine life. Every notion of an
endless existence, on the one hand, is actually frightening and
terrifying. But a timeless existence, on the other hand, would be the
sublation of every finite existence whatever and would only be another
name for absorption in God. The actual end would thus be a complete
union of the will with the divine will, ultimately achieved in continuing
development after death and a merging into one another of the

individual finite wills in love; so that the perfection of love, the consuming of the perfected individuals, the person's rendering himself up again to the divine life, would constitute the final end. The value of this whole process would be the beatitude and the ethical and personal worth achieved through effort and reaching its culmination in the very moment of the end. The highest and most perfect beatitude would be the last moment; it would annihilate the finite being by elevating it above itself and thus destroying it. The finite being would only die of its consummate blessedness, even as in this blessedness its individual differences, too, would have been dissolved—after having expended their abundance of life and beatitude in the creative self-positing of the person and the elaboration of the divine ground of its life.

5. Such an eschatology is obviously and fundamentally connected with Christianity as the religion *par excellence* of personality, creation, freedom, and grace. It is also closely connected with the peculiar character of its notion of redemption. Conversely, the immanental eschatology is connected with pantheism and pantheistic mysticism. Buddhism occupies a peculiar middle position. With its doctrine of transmigration, reincarnation, and redemption, it indeed represents the last things or values as the culmination of a struggle of freedom; but this culmination itself as an atheistic sublation of the personality through the renunciation of the illusion of the will-to-live. Thus there remains only the Israelite-Christian eschatology as a truly personalistic eschatology. But it has undergone a rich development; numerous non-Christian but related currents have been incorporated in the Christian idea; and today especially it is faced with the task of a very profound transformation and renewal. The eschatology of Jesus, which does not coincide with his proclamation of the kingdom of God since the kingdom of God comes before the end, is simply the late-Jewish eschatology of heaven and hell, the judgement of the dead and the resurrection of the body, with only this difference—that reward and punishment are not related to good works but rather to the totality and inwardness of the disposition, and the reward does not constitute an equivalent recompense but the unmerited reward of grace. The kingdom of God proclaimed by Jesus is not yet eschatology, but rather the hope for a miraculous intervention of God in the world, with the wicked being overcome and a life under the full rule of God and in complete fulfilment of the divine will, a life of purity of heart and brotherly love without law, coercion, and conflict, possible for the pious.

Jesus himself placed the stress above all on the immediate future;

that is, on the kingdom of God. Eschatology in the proper sense played a rather minor role in his preaching. He instinctively refrained from dwelling on its anthropomorphisms. [But] since the kingdom of God, in this sense, failed to come, the church was obliged to think out and to elaborate an eschatology in the proper sense as the great doctrine of the future, while it identified itself with the kingdom of God, resolutely interpreting it as a present and immanent reality. The last things then became entirely a part of eschatology in the proper sense, but with a certain awareness of the incompatibility between the old Jewish eschatology of recompense and the Christian idea of grace and love; and also with awareness of the difficulties, suggested by experience, of making the final decision follow immediately and without further ado upon earthly existence, which is always incomplete. Probably there was an awareness, too, of the psychological necessity to derive [ultimate] weal (*Heil*) and woe (*Unheil*) from the inner movement of the spirits themselves, rather than letting them be superadded to the soul's inner worth or lack of it by a brute miracle, as a heterogenous fate. There was awareness of the crass anthropomorphism inherent in such a way of thinking. Thus the Alexandrians made the Platonic eschatology a part of Christian eschatology: the punishments of the hereafter were reinterpreted as designed to educate and purify, the path of the soul through life as a development through freedom, divine education in grace, and a punishment designed only to purge, all the way up to the last things, to the vision of God. The Greek-speaking East, to be sure, rejected this doctrine, and the West transformed it into the doctrine of purgatory, which was designed not so much to purge as to provide a provisional penal and retributive justice, along with an opportunity for the church to intervene and to mitigate these punishments. Thus purgatory only reinforced legalism, the doctrine of retribution, and the power of the church over souls. Alongside it, the Jewish retribution eschatology with all its anthropomorphisms was all the more firmly maintained.

When the Reformers liberated religion by making it consist in a right disposition, they accordingly eliminated purgatory as unbiblical and as the main citadel of churchly power and works righteousness; for the rest, however, they simply retained the Catholic eschatology. Precisely at this point, therefore, the Reformers' doctrine remained especially defective, unorganic, and external, a bare lifting of the Jewish eschatology out of the Bible without any inner connection to their interiorization of the notion of salvation or any mediation between the present possession of salvation and the wholly mythical

conceptions of eschatology. The modern world has known less what
to do with these elements of the Protestant doctrine than with all
others. With the aid of rationalist metaphysics, it first transformed all
eschatology into the belief in [personal] immortality and livened it up
with sentimentality; later, it turned largely to naturalistic notions,
interpreting immortality as the continuing influence of one's work on
earth. The deeper spirits transformed the last things into the
immanence of mysticism and connected it, in the manner of Hegel,
with freedom, but without carrying to its logical conclusion the
personalism implicit in their approach. Others did develop personalism
up to the notion of a continuous development going beyond death
and stopping only with the attainment of the goal of perfection. This
was the thought of Leibniz, Lessing, and Goethe, and probably also
of Kant and Schiller.

It is also along this line that eschatology has been developed further,
where the point of departure is the fundamental notion of personalism,
namely freedom, the eternal worth of the person, the creation of a
higher reality through the moral act, and the postulate of ultimate
realities and values. But these foundations and points of departure are
those of Christianity, and their detailed elaboration is only a modern
form of the eschatological myth in place of the Jewish form taken
over by the church. But these notions have already found their most
glorious expression under the very guise of the church's myth; namely
in Dante's great poem about humanity. Here, under the influence of
Franciscan voluntaristic mysticism and the humanistic devotion to
classical antiquity, the idea is developed that the contemplation of the
punishments of hell, the cleansing of souls in purgatory, and the
wandering through the realms of the heavenly paradise is an ascent of
freedom, beginning with the breaking of the finite self and its pride
and leading to the final union of the will with the divine will. This
great ascent is represented as constituting the meaning of human life.
In this sense, *The Divine Comedy* is the classic work of Christian
eschatology, a work of the mind and of the poetic imagination at the
same time. It instinctively turns the eschatology of the church in a
subjective direction and uses the vision of the three transcendent
realms as a means for the soul's development and ascent. In the
recognition of the self-destructive effects of wickedness, the beatifying
pains of purification, the increasing nearness to God of the purified,
and the union of all the blessed in the love of God, the destiny and
development of the soul as such are described. In this sense, *The
Divine Comedy* continues even today to be the great eschatological
textbook of Christendom. But the modern image of the world—with

the immensity of both its spatial universe and its time periods, its notion of a plurality of spiritual realms, its principle of continuity and development, [and its perception of] the organic relationship of body, soul, and spirit—requires that the eschatological myth be rewritten, with very profound changes in its traditional content. The eschatological myth will remain a myth, but its form can no longer remain bound to the biblical myth.

II

Christian Natural Law

1. *General Significance.* Christian natural law is the adoption and reinterpretation according to Christian and ecclesiastical principles of Stoic natural law, which had been developed above all by Cicero and Roman Stoicism and which later had been incorporated, in the shape of a few general expressions, in the codification of Roman law. It is this adoption which first enabled Christianity to formulate a general doctrine of state and society. Due to its own complete indifference to state and society, it had been unable to do this by its own powers. This adoption became one of the foundation-laying events in world history, not only decisive for Christian social ethics and the practice of the church but also significant for the preservation and development of the concepts of natural law originally tied to Christian individualism but separated from their Christian ties on the threshold of the modern era, thereby initiating the world-shaking process of reshaping modern society according to radical or modern natural law principles.

Now the connection with natural law is different for each different tradition, according to the general spirit of the tradition. Above all, it is necessary to note the radical dissimilarity in relationship to natural law between the concepts of the churches built on the institutional idea (*Anstaltsgedanken*), and those of the sects, built on the associational idea (*Vereinsgedanken*). In the case of the churches the relationship is always discontinuous and conditional, in the case of the sects it is radical and absolute. Today, with the ecclesiastical domination of society broken and replaced by a purely secular natural law that tends increasingly to become an independent social philosophy, only the Catholic Church has continued to maintain the old positions; it still defends them as the only structure of society that accords with Christianity, the church, and natural law. Calvinism has become permeated to a large extent by the radical, democratic natural law conception of the sects. Under the circumstances, Lutheranism has lost faith in natural law and has become generally helpless and confused in its political and social ethics, except where the conservative wing maintains the old principles. The tendencies of the sects have been passed on to the social democrats.

2. *Adoption of Stoic Natural Law by Christian Social Ethics.* The gospel of Jesus was oriented toward the coming kingdom of God; it left to God all change in the order of the present world. For the present time on earth, the gospel required only a true preparation for the coming turning-point, a preparation involving the attainment of personality, immensely precious, which enables the person to stand before God, and the solidarity of all people in the simple doing of deeds of charity as the manifestation and effect of true devotion, or love. The gospel allowed the state to remain as it was, an alien rule permitted by God to which one must submit. The gospel did not intend to reform society but only to alleviate by brotherly love specific instances of suffering. It addressed itself primarily (but not exclusively) to the poor and oppressed, because they were most receptive and presented love with its greatest opportunities. Its greatness lies in the postulate—disregarding state and society—that the personality be infused with eternal life and that people be united in a transcendental communion of love. The communities engendered by the gospel became differentiated after a time: there were those who, gathering together as believers in Jesus, wanted to keep his laws and organize a tightly-knit congregation according to the principle of love and the idea of holiness—the fundamental principles of the sect. There were others who saw in the community the institution of salvation and redemption, created by the miraculous powers of the sacraments and independent of the degree of personal achievement, and who were willing to renounce organization according to the law of Christ in favor of the monergism of grace—the fundamental principles of the church. While the sect soon receded almost entirely into the background, the church became the embodiment of Christian communal life and social thinking, a state within the state, a society within society, not interfering with the state or the social order since it believed them to be permitted by God, ordering its own internal affairs in a Christian way, conservatively and without any radicalism, insofar as this was allowed by the continuation of the secular orders.

The secular social order being thus partly accepted and partly contested, it was necessary to come to grips with it on the basis of principle. This was provided, as were nearly all the systematic concepts of Christian ethics, by the Stoic philosphy, which in its basic ideas is so closely related to Christianity. Stoicism, too, represented one of the great end-results of the religious development of antiquity; it was the reform attempt of monotheistic ethics working down from the upper classes, just as Christianity was the revolution of an ethical religion working up from below. Stoic monotheism, which eventually assumed a strongly theistic hue, also led to an individualistic morality of the free and God-filled personality that has transcended nature, and to a social morality of cosmopolitan humanitarianism and philanthropy. From these premises the Stoics constructed a social philosophy, which described the primeval age as characterized by liberty, equality, communism, and the absence of state and law, the only bond among humanity being humaneness founded in the natural law of reason, while after this Golden Age was lost (through lust for power, covetousness, and selfishness), the same reason brought forth state and law, private property and social order, as a protective reaction against evil. There existed, therefore, a twofold natural law—the *absolute natural law* of the primeval age with its liberty, equality, and common ownership; and the *relative natural law* of subsequent times with its harsh order of state and law, the protection of property by law, war, and brute force, slavery, and domination. From this latter, relative natural law there arose, according to Stoic teaching, the positive law of nations. It is the task of lawmakers and teachers of law to maintain or obtain conformity between this positive law and the natural law, despite the inevitable differences due to time and place; and Stoicism has indeed exerted considerable influence on Roman legislation.

These doctrines presented themselves to Christian ethics in very convenient form. They were used extensively by the apologists down to St. Augustine, incorporated in the Christian myth of the original state and the Fall, and assimilated to the Christian concepts. The perfect Christian morality embodied in a community of love, free from state and law, force and selfishness, is accordingly possible only in the original state. Since the Fall and the other primeval sins of mankind, the present order of society has come into being—partly as a punishment for sin, partly as a restraint against sin. This is the relative natural law, the expression of divine reason manifesting itself under the present conditions of the state of sin. This relative natural law is identical with the Decalogue, which as a model has already influenced Greek and Roman law. Its precepts with all their consequences, so harshly opposed to the Christian ideal, must be suffered as punishment and carefully preserved as remedies against sin. As far as this is possible, the always mutable positive law is to be adapted to the natural law and the Decalogue. Thus is achieved, on the basis of relative natural law, a completely conservative attitude toward society, while a radical undercurrent, which could never be completely eliminated, is maintained as a reminder of the aboslute natural law and of the true Christian ideal. The state is viewed as a product of sin and its status is reduced, in comparison with the church, to the level of the earthly and secular servant, which everywhere shows the traces of a sinful origin and cannot therefore be compared with the latter in true worth. On the other hand, however, the state also becomes a means of protection against evil and a product of divine reason: its status is raised to the position of helper of the church in the maintenance of the moral order. In the early church, state and church, the world and the spiritual community, continued to exist side by side, and there were only occasional demands by the church that the state adapt its laws to the church's spirit. The state was still too strong and too deeply rooted in the ethical traditions of antiquity. State autonomy, too, is traditional. But the foundations of a theocracy were laid for the time when the state, become weak, would need the spiritual and moral help of the church. The groundwork for the compromise had been laid. All that remained was its practical elaboration.

3. *Medieval Catholicism and Thomism.* The social doctrine of the Middle Ages became theocratic from the time of the Gregorian conflicts. In the preceding period of national churches, the institutions and interests of state and church had, in the course of centuries, overcome the initial estrangement between them by a process of mutual assimilation. By restoring the centralized, universal church, Gregory VII created the classical Catholic doctrine of the state and society. This doctrine, however, came into being only through the elaboration of the already assimilated concepts of natural law, since the direct rule of society by the church would have been a physical and moral impossibility. Under the influence of the rediscovery of Aristotle, the Thomistic doctrine of natural law then came into being, furnishing a precondition for the theocracy or universal rule of the church. This concept of natural law never lost its very conditional character. Liberty, equality, and common property were still regarded as the true Christian ideals but they pertained only to the original state. Since the Fall, relative natural law prevails as a punishment and as a restraint of sin. From this relative natural law arise the monogamous family with the patriarchal power of the man; the state

with the rule of force, war, and law; the economy with private property, the regulation of the just price and honest exchange, and the condemnation of wholesaling and usury; and the society structured according to work and profession, with guilds and estates to prevent uncharitable competition. The whole conception is the product of the natural law, of force, and of the state-constructing tendency of reason, which is obligated, however, as far as possible to respect the aboriginal human rights of the individual and to scrupulously observe the moral laws.

This organic conception is ultimately maintained by the church, which at one time conservatively protects the power structure (*Gewalt*) and at another time progressively protects the rights of the individual, demanding the adaptation of the positive laws to the natural law. The church, moreover, also claims the services of the society thus constituted for the maintenance, protection, and furtherance of its own interests, for the church is the highest authority and the central tribunal of society; its unity of faith, its financial foundation, and its jurisdiction are to be supported with all possible zeal by the society based on natural law. Thus the state, the product of sin, becomes the bulwark both of order and of liberty, and the first servant of the church. In spite of many fluctuations and upheavals, Catholic natural law has maintained this position down to the present time, with this difference that today it more strongly emphasizes the autonomy of the state in questions not directly affecting the church, and that it has abandoned in states of mixed confession the demand for exclusive support of the Catholic Church.

4. *Lutheranism.* Lutheranism has done away with the hierarchical constitution of the church and with the legal claim of the church to be the supreme guide of society, in order to give the church a completely inward character and to found its relationship to the state on voluntary mutual complementation. The assumption is that a Christian state will gladly assist in the preservation of the church and in its defense against schism, violation of its morality, etc. This state, which puts itself at the disposal of the church solely of its own free will and out of a spirit of Christian love, is in every other respect conceived entirely along the lines of Catholic natural law, which is carried over from Catholicism just as philosophical ethics is carried over. In Lutheran natural law, all the familiar features reappear: the absolute natural law of the original state; the relative natural law of the state of sin; natural law as the measure of positive law; the equation of Decalogue and natural law; the derivation of the state from sin; the compromise with the state, force, war, private property; the derivation from natural

law of the family, of the economy (including the prohibition of usury and of wholesaling), and of the social structure based on estates and professions, with the consequent reduction of social mobility and commercial competition. However, all of this is given a new aspect in that the individualistic, rationalistic, and democratic undercurrent, with it close ties to absolute natural law, is eliminated; and the natural law of the state of sin is transferred completely to the power structure (*in die Ordnung stiftende Gewalt*), which has arisen by the will of God. Inasmuch as it is instituted by God it cannot be divided or restricted but must be absolute, in keeping with the very concept of authority.

The sole duty of authority is to safeguard its office according to natural and divine law. There can be no claim on the part of the individual, however, to force the authority to perform this duty. When it fails to do so, only submission and obedience are possible. The rationalistic and individualistic aspect of Catholic natural law is thrown overboard, and in its place the right of authority is proclaimed—as the rebellious peasants learned to their sorrow.

Melanchthon and his school attempted to move back towards the rationalistic natural law of Catholicism, but with no lasting success. For the true Lutheran, there remained only the natural law embodied in the authority raised up by the will of God in the course of history—soon this authority was simply said to be 'instituted by God'—which was responsible for order and welfare, and against which there could be no resistance based on natural human rights or claims. What was still derived from natural law was the responsibility of this authority to uphold the church of the true faith, since according to Protestant principles such an obligation could not be derived from divine law. It is an exceedingly coarse, primitive, and aphoristic theory. When Pufendorf attempted to bring it into harmony with the rationalistic natural law of Grotius' legal philosophy, seeking especially to find a more subtle basis for its prime object, the safeguarding of authority, the theologians objected vehemently and retreated to the position that authority had been instituted by God since the Fall. Lutheran natural law had no deeper philosophical basis until F. J. Stahl provided one during the Lutheran Restoration. But this theory came to prevail only in the conservative wing, where it is followed to this day. Other Lutherans have been without any clear and guiding ideas in this area since their ancient doctrine of natural law was shattered by the emancipated natural law of the Enlightenment and, subsequently, by the purely scientific and critical theory of the state and society.

5. *Calvinism.* Calvinism is in its essence only an adaptation of

Lutheranism that safeguards and defines the church more strictly in relation to the state by providing it with a church law of its own, drawn from the Bible. But like Lutheranism, it relies for the rest on the voluntary and loving concord of church and state. It also took over the Lutheran-Catholic natural law—with the important difference, however, that it did not adopt the Lutheran transmutation of natural law into a law of divinely sanctioned authority. On the contrary, it adhered to the ancient Catholic natural law with its mixture of rationalistic-individualistic and irrational-authoritarian elements. Calvin exemplifies this mixture when he, too, forbids resistance against duly constituted authority; but forbids it only to the private individual, not to the subordinate authorities, who may, if the highest authority fails, step into its place and force it to carry out the natural and the divine law. Thus Calvin has made a general theory of Christian natural law out of a thesis put forward by the Lutherans in connection with the Schmalkaldic League, and formulated for the particular circumstances of German imperial law. This theory made possible the assertion of the rational and individual rights of a person against those in power. Indeed, from this theory Calvinism later developed, in the French, Dutch, and Scottish struggles, the natural law of popular sovereignty, which derives authority from the people and the interests of the people, always provided that these interests be taken care of by duly constituted corporate representatives and not by the private individual. In this way Calvinistic natural law became the law of corporate control of power, or corporate constitutionalism, and finally even the law of revolution. Calvin made a further change in Lutheran natural law with respect to economic doctrine—here deviating from Catholic natural law, too—by declaring usury and commerce to be permitted by natural law, even among Christians. Such a view was a necessity for a commercial center like Geneva; it was later set forth in scientific detail by the Dutch scholar Salmasius. The important consequence was that Calvinism could in good conscience form an intimate alliance with the countries and social classes representing the rise of the capitalist economy, while Lutheranism and Catholicism could do no more than yield reluctantly to the force of circumstances.

Yet an even more far-reaching transformation of Calvinist natural law took place in the English Revolution and in America under the influence of the Independents, whose orientation was Anabaptist and sectarian. Now the relative natural law of the sinful state was generally pushed into the background; and society as a whole was conceived along the lines of democratic equality and self-government, principles approaching those of the absolute natural law. Not even the concept of the church escaped this influence. The church, too, became a voluntary association and in full freedom took its place alongside the state, completely separated from the state, and with toleration for all forms of church organization. Calvinism has thus made the modern democratic, republican, constitutional natural law its own; and has very closely linked it to the Christian virtues of love for one's neighbor, liberty, and equality before God, yet without giving up its traditional strict and sober sense of order. The results of this development were raised by John Locke to the level of pure scholarly prose; in the process, however, he also abandoned the dogmatic character of Calvinist orthodoxy. Yet even in the course of the modern pietistic-orthodox revival, Calvinism has retained this combination of ideas, and it is precisely Puritan orthodoxy that has been democratic and liberal in England and America ever since. The natural law of Calvinism has thus followed the democratic-rational development of modern natural law, is today in accord with it, and supports it by its religious individualism and its sense of religious community. Its only reservation is the Christian demand for liberty of conscience with respect to the free formation of churches, and strict moral discipline without which no freedom is thought to be possible.

6. *The Sects.* In full accord with their character, the sects held fast to the strict Christian moral law of the Sermon on the Mount. They accordingly renounced the use of law and force, dominion and power, and clung to social equality and a communism of love without any compromises with the sinful world. They, too, appealed to natural law—not to the relative natural law of the sinful state, but to the natural law of the original state, identical with the Sermon on the Mount. They put forward their claims in the name of God, the Bible, and original nature. Now, that was something radically different from the ecclesiastical natural law. In the assertion of this divine and natural law the sects divided into two main groups, with frequent overlapping. The patient and suffering sect, on the one hand, submits to conditions but avoids state and law, oath and private property, and forms small, truly Christian groups separated from the world. The militant and reforming sect, on the other hand, attempts by force to transform the world into the genuinely Christian and natural order of life. The former appeals to the Sermon on the Mount, the latter to the Revelation of St.'John and to the Old Testament.

The movement that became by far the most important among these sects was that of the Anabaptists, which in the Netherlands proceeded to the formation of Independent, democratic congregations while dropping the communist idea. The American Pilgrim Fathers and the

English Independents absorbed these ideals from them, and thus provided the impetus for the transformation of Anglo-Saxon Calvinism. An offshoot of these sectarian movements are the Quakers, who in Pennsylavania made the memorable attempt to build up state and society according to the rules of the Sermon on the Mount and to put into practice the Christian natural law of the sects. They were successful until they foundered on the problem of war. While the sects have abundantly multiplied, the radical natural law feature [of their thought] has disappeared or at least been pushed into the background. Nevertheless, among the Christian forerunners of modern socialism the communist and egalitarian natural law of Christianity again comes to the fore. Saint-Simon and his followers combine Christianity as interpreted by the sects with a legal and social philosophy on a scientific-rational basis. The religious foundations have disappeared completely from present-day socialism, heir to the radical natural law of liberty, equality, and common property; the validity of these ideals of natural law is linked to the process of economic evolution. This process, conceived along the lines of materialistic determinism, is supposed to bring about the actualization of these ideals at a certain point, and to throw this prize into the lap of the militant proletariat at the opportune moment that makes its dictatorship possible.

7. *Christian and Secular Natural Law.* Christian natural law differs very much from modern secular natural law, which has been developed since the times of Hobbes, Locke, Grotius, Pufendorf, Thomasius, Wolf, Rousseau, and Kant. The latter was specifically oriented toward jurisprudence and social philosophy, and accordingly became a philosophical and juridical theory of modern individualism and of a societal structure based on the individual. While this secular natural law is genetically related to the natural law of antiquity and of Christianity, it has its own distinct foundations in modern philosophical and social developments and has followed its own course towards liberalism, democracy, and free competition quite independently of the Christian idea.

12

The Dispositional Ethic

[For Luther] it is the idea of religion that leads to its practice. All religious and ethical actions are motivated and sustained by it—not by some incomprehensible sacramental miracle that can affect the spirit only after laborious preparation and through some obscure magic. Religious and ethical actions can be understood because they can be logically and psychologically derived from the very meaning of the idea of religion. The connection [between the idea and the practice of religion] is made completely apparent; the connection among particular acts, their various aspects, sundry preparations, the reception of the sacraments, and the 'good works' effected by all this were not. Everything is affected by the [now] apparent ideal nature of faith, and Luther accordingly is able to show in psychologically plausible fashion how this idea gives rise to a new religious stance toward life, to trust, blessedness, love, devotion, and obedience to God; that is, how faith must be translated into action and how this action must be motivated by the union of the soul with and devotion to God's will.

Faith is an idea, yet is is also a disposition that is born of the knowledge of God and compels persons to act. What makes this conception great is that, in addition to making clear the dependence of ethics on religion, it unifies ethics by revealing the single point that gives rise to all ethics. Ethics becomes dispositional. Particular acts have value only in relation to the fundamental disposition from which they arise; action is not the sum of particular isolated 'works,' but rather the effect of a consistent disposition that expresses itself in a consistent life-style and a consistent life-work. This is the very antithesis to every possible ethic of law or of reward. The believer receives the law personally through disposition, which is directed toward the idea of God, and applies it to the particular case by freely reflecting upon it. Since the believer is only acting out a basic stance given by God, he or she is not preoccupied with the particular 'work' or the rewards or punishments that may follow from it. The whole process, rather, is a result and effect of faith that excludes all thought of reward or law.   This is the sharpest antithesis to the legal ethic of the Catholic penitential system with is authoritative moral laws, its priestly application, its constant reference to purgatory, heaven, and hell; it represents a new direction for ethical thought. Thus it signifies the abandonment, in principle, of the chief cause of fragmentation and externalism in Catholic ethics, namely the whole ethical significance of eschatology with its rewards and punishments. Blessedness is seen as intrinsically immanent in good actions that proceed even now from the certitude of faith; just as the opposite proceeds from evil actions and remoteness from God. Eschatology is thus launched on a course that would transform it so as to teach that the ultimate fate of the soul is based, by an intrinsic necessity, on its own religious and ethical character. To be sure, heaven and hell were retained in [traditional Protestant] dogmatics and only purgatory was excluded; but the connection between 'good works' and reward and punishment were, after all, most significant and practically effective in relation to purgatory.

But if the antithesis between nature and sacramental super-nature, between individual particularity and supernatural authority, between the good will and the divine law is thus everywhere cancelled, if the idea of God is something springing from man's innermost nature, and if the new disposition is a principle governing the whole of life, then the content of ethics must also be purged of the antithesis between life in the world and the world-renouncing ideal of monasticism. A religion that is able to consist in faith and idea, and that has no need to subsist in the obscurity of miraculous sacraments, cannot direct the actions of its faithful beyond the world but must permit its idea to permeate and to shape the world. The alternative would seem like a flight into special, custom-made conditions of life, instead of subjecting oneself to the natural conditions instituted by God. As the miracle of faith can only consist in the courage to grasp an idea that, in itself, is entirely clear and transparent, so the miracle of action can only be the strength to work in the given conditions and the enjoyment of doing so. As the ethical disposition uniformly leavens the entire personality, so, it must set all to work on the identical stuff of life. The consistent dispositional ethic, which recognizes no special 'good works,' makes the special sphere of the 'good works' of asceticism both redundant and impossible; just as it demands the same attitude toward life, so it demands the same motive, love of God, from everyone. Accordingly, it makes an ascetical circle based on special ascetic motives impossible. The Lutheran opposition to the special supererogatory and world-denying works of distinct monastic groups derives from all these perspectives. It leads to the rejection, as a matter of principle, of the whole ascetical renunciation of the world and of nature, and to a complete acceptance of the natural conditions of life and the cultural structures derived from history. At this point, as in faith itself, the Catholic miracle-principle is broken through. Although Luther insisted vehemently on retaining the miracle-concept itself, and even intensified it by his sharpening of the doctrine of original sin, the miracle that is retained is changed in its inmost essence. It is neither supernatural nor the effect of a divine magic upon nature, but rather the return of man to his most proper and authentic being through the revelation of the fundamental being itself, namely, gracious love, which grasps us and finds its attestation in Christ. Hence its sphere of activity is no longer a circle of super-natural accomplishments that correspond to the super-nature, but rather the simple fulfilment of the natural sphere of activities with no other miracle than the disposition to trust in God and to be one with him. In this sense, Goethe is right in celebrating Luther as the one who 'has given back to us the courage to plant our feet firmly on the God-given earth.'

The religion of faith as a reduction of religion to ideas was obscured not only through Luther's relapses into the Catholic sacramental doctrine, but even more essentially by its continuing to be strictly tied to the biblical norm, so that it never led even to relatively free and spontaneous religious thought. Luther simply assumed that God's granting of faith or the Holy Spirit's granting of insight would always be based on the Bible or on the teaching of the apostles. For him, the general validity of the idea of God was no less a matter of course. What was in question was not how one could attain certitude with respect to God, but rather how one could be sure of one's own salvation in the sight of God. His new conception of God was wholly wrapped up in the teaching of the certitude of salvation and its ethical consequences; the great ideological struggles of the modern world were not anticipated by him. He was not concerned with faith in God as such, but with the proper derivation of this faith from the Bible. All the serious problems and anxieties that face us today—our concern for the idea of God itself, our struggle with atheism and the trend towards a pantheism destructive of everything Christian—were unknown to him. Only the critical destruction of the authority of the Bible, the rise of a more discerning psychology of religion that analyzes both intellectual and practical elements, and the close connection of the religious idea with the movements of modern speculative thought have broken this spell. The consequence, to be sure, was great uncertainty and a manifold fusion of the religious idea with purely speculative and theoretical interests; but the idea of the religion of the spirit, of a faith-knowledge that produces practical religious forces by its true idea of God and the world, has nevertheless come to dominate all modern religiosity ever since. Kant and Schleiermacher used new means to give modern form—without the exclusive tie to the Bible—to Luther's idea.

Luther's often-asserted ties to German Idealism lie in this area. They are certainly not to be denied, but they are fragmentary, complicated, and very difficult to trace. One would have to begin with Leibniz, Lessing, and Goethe. What is decisive, in my opinion, is the capacity of Luther's idea of the 'spirit,' of 'freedom,' and of the 'inner motive force of faith' to become metamorphosed into that of a free spiritual evolution. This capacity is absent from Calvinism; modern ethical thought growing from the soil of Calvinism accordingly depends on sober empirical psychologism and its causality of motivation for its ideas. Upon entering on German soil, these ideas were transformed in such a way that with proper caution, one could relate them to the continuing effects of the Lutheran spirit. . . .

Protestantism's dispositional ethic remained . . . concealed for a long time. Concern for the assertion of justification by grace alone led to the assignment of ethics to the lowest possible place. Also, Lutheranism, continuing the practice of confession, moved back towards the older casuistry, while Calvinism was persuaded (with the Puritans) that the moral law of the Bible had to form the basis of its strict social-Christian community formation, to avoid dissolution in indefiniteness. Furthermore, ethics continued to be the teaching of good works rather than the teaching of a total character. Finally, heaven and hell, reward and punishment did not really relinquish their traditional position.

But since the ethics of Kant has given classical and convincing formulation to the idea of Lutheranism—in this respect in conscious dependence on the intent of the Reformation—the dispositional ethic has constituted the essence of all idealistic and religious ethics in the modern world. Even if the dispositional ethic in this formulation has repeatedly been in danger of losing its religious moorings, the presence of God in the good will and the purification and renewal of the disposition through religious devotion has nevertheless been asserted again and again. We have every right to see in it one of the great fundamental ideas of contemporary Protestantism, if only we do not overlook the new elements that are implicit in the new form of the idea. The dispositional ethic as the unfolding of the life-principle which has been adopted with the [modern] idea of religion, signifies a struggling and yet continuous development of the 'good principle' in its conflict with the 'evil principle.' Only as the evolutionary idea enters ethical thought from the sphere of natural science and mathematics do 'good works' recede. Eschatology, especially, undergoes a thoroughgoing metamorphosis in this connection. It, too, is influenced by the evolutionary idea that only thus decisively loses its effectiveness as the constant nullifier of the dispositional ethic. With the continual growth of the good, and the intrinsic connection between blessedness and the degree to which the good is actualized, eschatology now opens up vistas of continuing evolutions and developments after the death of the body. The eschatology of reward in heaven and punishment in hell, which posits an extrinsic connection between worldly value or its opposite and heterogenous joys or sufferings, fades correspondingly. Leibniz and Lessing have set the tone here; and they have been reinforced by the idea of a plurality of worlds, which would make the world of human spirits but one of many. But all this signifies a break with Jewish eschatology and apocalyptic and with the traditional anthropocentric cosmology—a break far removed from Luther's biblicism.

13

Political Ethics and Christianity

Realism dominates our present view of state and society. Ethical and cultural goals of the state, like those venerated by the generation educated by Kant, Fichte, and Hegel, are looked upon today as artificial and doctrinaire, or as mere abstract principles. Even juristic deductions of the state, and the derivation of its activities or tasks from the concept of right (*Recht*) that it embodies, are met with the same suspicion. Just to ask wherein the essence of the state might consist seems to savor of political metaphysics. For us, the state is above all a product of power, which assumes varying forms amid the conflict of various human interests; and government is above all the art of using appropriate means to assert and extend, quickly and cleverly, the power of the state in particular situations. The state is physical, intellectual, and economic power; formed in the great struggle of the nations for existence and supported by organization and military might, it establishes rules for the actual situation and its control by means of a once-for-all theory of right. Its worth as a state is no more and no less than the power it possesses and is able to exercise both within and beyond its own borders. To be initiated into politics means to be initiated into the art of forming, consolidating, extending, and protecting power against the threat of change; it does not mean to be initiated into a theory of the state and a political ethic. Statesmanship springs from a strong will to power; this instinctive, unerring will needs only to be supported by the requisite knowledge, circumspection, and coolness. Our hearts beat higher, years ago, when, as young students, Heinrich von Treitschke's glowing rhetoric so described the state for us—and poured every kind of scorn on the 'doctrinaire' advocates of an ethical and juristic concept of the state!

We took pleasure in renouncing the theoretical and ethical ideals that are so much a part of the spirit of youth; and, with the no less youthful need to show utter contempt for something, we sought to surpass his scorn in our own conversations.

There are mainly two quite different causes that have led to this mood of realism. In the first place, there is the political education that has been provided by Bismarck. (Up to now, very few Germans have learned to think politically beyond Bismarck.) The core of this education was precisely this: that the essence of the state is power, that a combat-ready army is its backbone, that the ever present domestic and international danger can be met only by use of power that is as cautious as it is ruthless, and that nothing inhibits this use of power so much as principles and theory. We must candidly admit that these proscribed principles included the principles of ethics. Not the principles of personal ethics, of course, to which his private letters bear magnificent and heart-warming testimony; but indeed the principles of public life. His actions and program manifested a complete absence of principles. He could use ethical powers and principles and appeal to them as easily as he could push them aside and scorn them. His ideal was to remain unencumbered by any prejudice; everything was to be subordinated to the one basic political idea of permanent power superiority to every possible enemy. After the long years of political misery, theoretical ideals of the state, pathetic resolutions, and the sterile demands of public opinion in the newspapers, this ideal struck us as an enormous step forward, making us aware for the first time of the elementary conditions of political life. One need only read the 'Self-Critique of German Liberalism,' published by Hermann Baumgarten immediately after the events of 1866, in order to see doctrinaire idealism coming to understand the power of facts and of political reality. What that generation, with a heavy heart, recognized as truth has today become a cheap commonplace. Our lack of principles seems to have elevated us, in our own eyes at least, high above that generation. This very lack of principles has become our theory, supported by a bit of Nietzsche's *Herrenmoral* or Darwin's struggle for existence; it combines all too readily with the ideals of military style and bureaucratic rule that largely animate the offspring of our ruling classes.

In the second place, the same lesson has been taught us by the so-called materialistic theory of history, which has nothing to do with a proper theoretical materialism. It merely teaches, rather, that the actual driving force in human affairs is the drive for food and physical survival; that all cultural constructions emerge from economic situations and conflicts; and that the state, too, is merely the work of economic forces. According to a well-known phrase, history is but the struggle for the feeding place and for the amount to be fed: all doctrines and theories are mere reflections of economic situations, all political structures mere instruments of the ruling classes, and all political revolutions merely the rise of new classes. All political theories are mere concealments of this state of affairs, and all political ethics a mere means in the class struggle with which each class idealizes its own demands. Here, too, it becomes apparent why the state must be power and cannot be anything else. In the struggle for existence, only that intensified and ruthless power survives which increases by the absorption of all that it has vanquished. [This power] can entertain sentimentalities and general principles only at the price of its own perdition. A general theory of politics and a study of social conditions can therefore be only an assessment of present tendencies—which one has deeper and stronger economic roots, or prospects of further development?—and can accordingly lead only to an accommodation of interests or, if that is no longer possible, to the jettisoning of what can no longer be maintained.

Now, we cannot think of abandoning the truth we owe to both of these educational experiences. Through them we have learned to understand the most elementary conditions of political life, and we have perceived how the economic substructure of our existence completely pervades our political ideas and institutions—indeed, even the expressions of our higher culture. Germany, which had been unpolitical before 1848 and become doctrinaire after 1848, owes the very beginnings of its political education to them. These ideas, with all their true seriousness, must become even more a part of our being than has been the case up to now. It has been, to be sure, an education for which we, in our situation—children of a system of petty principalities and of an age of philosophy and aesthetics—had a special need.

While it was a truth particularly needed in view of our political naiveté, however, it was onesided and not the whole truth. The concept of power dominates everything only so long as the state is fighting for the foundations of its existence. Once power has been attained, there always arises, besides concern for its maintenance and consolidation, the question how this power is to be used and what end is served by a powerful state. Power is the fundamental condition of political life, but it is not the whole of that life. To say that this power serves only the economic interest of the whole, the regulation of the struggles of economic parties, or the economic egotism of the ruling classes, would be strongly to contradict the intellectual and moral values we associate with the concept of the state. We indeed see the enormous importance of the relationship of population to the food supply and the linkage between the political parties and class interests, but we also feel that the state has worth and interest for us only when it also protects, furthers, and administers the values of cultural life. First of all, to be sure, we must be able to live; but once we live, we live not for the sake of mere physical existence but for the sake of ideas and ideals. They must give the state its ultimate meaning and value. Otherwise the state, with all its struggles, would only seem to signify to us that the life-energy of the European race has been overstimulated; and the rest and contemplation of Buddhism would appear to be more natural and normal.

All our political realism cannot exclude a political ethic or render it superfluous. We are in danger of letting our new insight run away with us, of turning the power-state, based on economic egoism and devoid of principle and theory, into a theory of its own. We must become aware once again that the state means much more than that, and that its possession and use of power ought to be determined, as much as possible, by the indestructible moral idea.

Now, if we inquire after an ethic of politics, we must ask about the ethical powers and convictions that are actually available to us. Just as no state was ever based merely on the power instinct or formed entirely by economic interest, so today political thought and the political struggle are still conditioned in part by the power of ideas, by ethical conceptions of the state, and by moral demands upon the state. They are not the only factors, however, or even the primary ones by which the state is built and maintained. They have their place above the massive substructure of elemental instincts and needs, forming a superstructure that ultimately throws firm braces around the substructure itself and protects it against being destroyed by the very instincts that built it. Hence we must ask: What are the ethical ideas of our people about the state today? Are they able to reinforce patriotic feeling with the conviction of their ideals?

We encounter in such a survey four general types: the ethic of the constitutional state (*Rechtsstaat*) exclusively serving a free culture, the purely nationalistic ethic of patriotism, the ethic of democracy, and the ethic of conservatism.

I can deal most briefly with the first type. It is the sort of doctrine that views the state as the means and presupposition of higher culture. It is the sort of doctrine expressed at the peak of our aesthetic culture by the young Wilhelm von Humboldt in his essay directed against

Dalberg's multi-governmentalism, the sort that again and again has been demanded, along with freedom of thought and of the press, by men of cultivation. It appears as self-evident today to innumerable people, above all to the bearers of the aesthetic culture. In its modern form this theory signifies the greatest possible reduction of state activity; namely, its limitation to the maintenance of order and of economic prosperity insofar as this is within the power of the state. The state is to provide nothing but undergirding and protection for higher culture, which is impossible without the order of the state—no more and no less. The state is expected to vouchsafe the freedom in which a rich and harmonious cultural life can grow, but is not itself to meddle with that life. This is the liberalism of Lockean vintage that proceeded from the Puritan struggles for the freedom of religion from state coercion and that made freedom of culture from the state, together with the furtherance of culture by the state, its principle. It is the liberal conception of the state in the sense of liberal education, a conception with which contemporary bourgeois liberalism of a democratic and Rousseauistic tendency is now closely connected only by reason of its distrust of an excessive growth of the power of the state.

Today we have largely escaped the spell of this idea of the state and therefore fail to appreciate its relative validity as we should. For it would continually remind us that our spiritual freedom and literary culture, which have been won in the face of great difficulties, constitute a precious possession; and that the era of Goethe represents not merely our political nursery but also the happy memory of our youth, which constantly revitalizes our idealism. This idea, however, does not generate a political ethic; it only teaches us not to allow the new attainments to become the enemy of the old, nor to neglect one value for the sake of another. It says nothing to us about the moral value of the state or the ethical regulation of patriotic sentiment. It looks upon the state as a necessary evil or as an extrinsic protective apparatus that carries no ethical idea in itself. Precisely because there is no real ethical connection between them, the state and the culture frequently move in different directions. On the one hand, the state is concerned with essentially political and social problems that only very indirectly touch upon the higher culture and quite often engulf and bury this culture or push it aside. Often, the state must sacrifice everything in the struggle for existence. If we can secure the ships that are indispensable for us in a world crisis only through an alliance with the pope, then one part of German culture after the other has to be sacrificed to such an alliance. On the other hand, culture is

comparatively independent of the state, at least of its own state. It can
thrive even under foreign domination. Renaissance Italy stood largely
under direct or indirect foreign domination; at least, its political
foundations were far from secure. If we had become a province of
France in 1806, science and art in Germany would hardly have lost in
substance. Men like Helmholz and Mommsen, Richard Wagner and
Max Klinger would have been possible even in a state that was a
member of the French-dominated Rhenish League.

A superior culture, accordingly, does not in the least guarantee an
interest in politics; nor does it give any kind of ethical value to the
institutions and laws of the state. The complete political indolence
and impotence of our contemporary aesthetes bear sufficient witness
to that. After all, higher culture as such as not a moral value of
absolutely decisive significance either for life itself or, least of all, for
politics. Higher culture does contribute something essential to the
deepening and enrichment, the harmonizing and civilizing of human
life. It demands self-denying work. But it remains *spiritually*
aristocratic, and hence differs basically from the *political* aristocracy,
which is concerned for the whole population and is remarkably
effective politically. Higher culture is peculiarly individualistic and
completely sterile in questions of human social life. It is an aristocracy
that lets the masses plow, sow, and sweat so that the few may write
poetry and carry on research. Kant confesses, with deep moral
conviction, that he was cured by Rousseau of this type of spiritual
aristocracy. A political ethic must find its support at a much deeper
level, in the very nature of the state itself.

Pure nationalism has a greater significance. It constitutes the ethical
orientation of innumerable people for whom religion is no longer a
serious reality but who nevertheless wish to devote their little ego to
some great cause. Love of country, as the devotion of the individual
to the glory of the whole, is its great ethical passion. What is especially
involved here is the idea of community honor, which turns the personal
feeling of honor into a collective feeling and, through this feeling,
regulates the relations of the individual to the whole. 'Worthless is
the nation that will not sacrifice everything for its honor.' This outlook
evokes all the powers of proud and vigorous virility, binds everyone
to the institutions of the whole, and inspires every sacrifice. The
nation wants to be respected and honored abroad; and every citizen is
elevated and ennobled by participation in a totality that can hold its
own in the world. The citizen lives for one idea, the idea of honor,
which is inscribed on the banners that fly from our buildings, our
ships, our artillery.

Nationalism thus provides a standard of ethical judgement for foreign and domestic politics. Absolutely everything must be done to maintain the state in the world, to protect it from humiliations, and to provide it internally with the organization necessary for its survival. With this objective in mind, the remnants of the genuinely national-liberal party keep demanding that the great economic differences within the nation be buried for the sake of unity in face of continuing threats to its existence. Naumann (whose politics are not so much democratic or socialistic as nationalistic, with a strong sense of solidarity with the rising classes) has the same objective in mind when he demands the abolition of the class structure as an irrevocable hindrance to the survival of a nation whose masses are becoming industrialized. And so do the Pan-Germans, who would revolutionize the map of Europe, and political dreamers, whose enthusiasm for race and nationality rises above collective egoism solely through the idea of community, honor demanding personal sacrifices.

There can be no doubt that nationalism represents a genuine ethical principle; in fact, the most direct, the most elemental, the most powerful principle of political ethics. What coercion and accident, situation and circumstances, natural kinship and the struggle for existence have created, now presents itself as a unity of consciousness and feeling, subordinating the individual to the idea of the whole and developing a sense of honor that looks upon the collective existence as so great a matter of honor that domestic troubles and even oppressive conditions are rendered bearable by it. By thus identifying oneself with the state, one no longer needs to fear any superior power, except possibly God; in this sense of inviolability, one experiences a value that transcends egoism because it relates not to the individual but to the whole, and is made possible only by an intense self-discipline and personal subjection. Only through such an identification of the individual with the state does the state become a nation, though it helps, of course, if the nation is also linguistically and anthropologically homogeneous. It is only thus, as a politically conscious nation, that the state achieves ethical value. When its power and population are increasing, the state may turn to aggression and conquest; when its needs are met or its opportunities for expansion limited, it may stress stability and the preservation of the *status quo*. In either case, the state regards itself as a source of ethical value and moral obligation. It can (and often does) invest this claim with all the pathos of moral sentiment.

Nevertheless, the idea of nationality cannot possibly be the last word in political ethics. That it is not is indicated by all the ghastly

nationalistic bunkum that has gripped the peoples of Europe with a
mixture of romantic ideas about the national spirit and the democratic
awakening of the masses, pitting one against the other in senseless
arrogance. We recognize nationality only in the larger nations; in the
smaller ones we view it as a childhood disease. But why this bias in
favor of the larger ones? Presumably because these possess something
beyond the heightened sense of honor, something that goes quite
beyond their mere numerical superiority. But what is this something?
It is commonly said that it is the higher culture of which the larger
nations are the bearers. As we have seen, however, the relation of
such culture to the state is loose; it offers no basis for a political ethic.
The science and art of a nation doubtless depend on its demographic
and geographic spread, as determining the selection of talent out of
the larger mass and affording them greater or lesser scope. But this
larger mass need not be unified as a state, nor be strongly organized
politically. The ethical value of a state, therefore, can never lie merely
in nationalism as such, nor merely in the size of the masses that are to
be organized along nationalistic lines. Whether a state is large or
small, its ethical value must, in addition, lie in the spirit of its political
institutions, in the ethical ideas permeating its organization. From the
point of view of political ethics, little Switzerland, whose higher culture
is partly German and partly French, has great value, while Turkey,
large and not lacking in nationalism, has none at all; and the Germany
of the past, organized into many small principalities and with a high
level of culture, did not have much more.

Only democracy and conservatism represent principles of political
ethics which have penetrated into the inner structure of the institutions
of the state and show how to assess and shape that structure according
to both political and ethical ideals. They alone assign to the state,
whether large or small, an intrinsic ethical value.

The democratic principle figures here as an ethical principle for the
organization and conception of the state in general, not as [the ethical
principle] of a political party, for which it would only be a cover or
tool of the interests represented by it. It may well be true that the
principle always emerges initially from specific demographic and
economic conditions; but this relationship describes only its origin,
not its essence. It properly relates to the state as such, as a whole. It is
a moral weapon even though it may originate in the class struggle and
serve plebeians or proletarians as a weapon against the ruling classes.
Its moral strength lies in the fact that even the ruling classes feel
constrained to recognize this principle, and frequently do recognize it.
The identification of democracy with the proletarian masses is only a

bad habit of the mind, which derives from the relationship just mentioned. In itself, the democratic principle stands for the transcending of the class struggle; its ideal is social peace. If a rising social class chooses to call itself 'democratic,' and the ruling class follows this usage, this is solely due to the fact that the rising class is the bearer of a principle destined to transcend the class struggle itself. However easily proletarian hatred or plebeian ambition may in practice be identified with democracy, ideally they are not part of it. The idea of democracy is an ethical one, the great idea of human rights. Human rights signify the moral right of the person to independent value, or, as Kant formulated it, the right never to be considered merely as a means but rather also always as an end. This right holds for everyone who bears a human countenance—not merely for those who, through the accident of favorable circumstances, possess refinement, authority, and property; but also for the innumerable children of the obscure masses, who are ceaselessly born from the womb of human mothers. Without their work, there would be no education, no authority, and no property. Despite their humble condition, they too are endowed with the priceless potential of personhood. This recognition arouses every ethical feeling of self-respect in the individual, and evokes every ethical feeling of justice and sympathy in the community. The declaration of human rights in the American and French constitutions is therefore a fact not only of the greatest importance for modern history, but also of the greatest significance for ethics.

While the democratic principle is purely ethical in its nature, it is at the same time capable of the most extensive political application. Everything modern in state and society—insofar as it is subject to ethical judgement—may be said to have its roots in this ethical principle. Democracy has even freed the woman from age-old fetters of absolute male domination in politics and law, so that she may not only develop an independent personality of her own but also enjoy an appropriate participation in public life. Politically, the democratic principle requires two things: first, that the organs of state power be so constituted as to emphasize the participation and responsibility of the individual; and second, that the purpose of the state be conceived, accordingly, in terms of the equal sharing by all individuals (insofar as this is possible) in the material and spiritual benefits mediated by the state. Of course, the solution of these two problems presents a great many practical and technical difficulties. Up to now, the first objective has been attained only be means of party organizations and majority rule; and since this principle necessarily leads to the two-party system, the distinctively democratic ideals have been only partially realized. Still, an active sense of freedom and of responsibility is possible. The actualization of the purpose of the state also presents considerable technical difficulties. Equal participation in the commodities of life must always be proportionate to the attainments and work of the individual. The elimination of inequality in education and wealth is no easy task. Irrespective of its degree of realization, however, the ideal is a justice that obviates envy and a distribution of goods based as much as possible on the [individual] contribution.

Since the democratic ethical principle is a political one, it is also national. Democracy does not fail to appreciate that, in the foreseeable future, humanity will continue to be divided into national groups by descent, language, economic condition, and historical relationships. The initial objective of democracy is merely to shape the nation, after it has acquired the power and might of political existence, according to this ideal. But democracy realizes that a particular nation thereby renounces many instrumentalities of power that it possessed before the democratic era, and which it can renounce only if other nations become similarly democratic. Hence originates the democratic conception of foreign policy, which revolves around an international league of nations, organized as democratic states, with the resolution of all disputes through arbitration. For the principle of personhood is valid for the community of nations as well as for the community of individuals. When the international community is established on mutual respect and the participation of the various nations in world affairs, then war, with its ingenious arts of murder and its cruel slaughter of human beings, will be no longer needed; for war can spring only from contempt for the human person. As Kant suggested, the educational benefits of war ought to be replaced by physical education, daring cultural activity, and a defensive militia. Then, of course, exploitative colonialism would also come to an end and the human rights of alien races would be protected in a program of peaceful colonization. This program does not, as is often erroneously supposed, represent some principle of unpatriotic internationalism. This supposition arises only because, in the contemporary situation, the democrats of all lands feel a community of interest in the face of the ruling undemocratic powers. Moreover, this program need not be the utopianism of idealistic enthusiasts. Democracy can and must accommodate itself to practical realities in the construction of the organs of power and in the implementation of the purposes of the state: it could likewise accommodate itself in the matter of nationhood—inasmuch as a state must first of all secure its own existence—to the realistic conditions of the existence and power of the state. It is a peculiarity of German democrats that they merely extol their theory and their ideal for the future through excited public discussion, parliamentary speeches, and party programs, while the state that is to implement their ideal is about to perish.

In this respect there is no basic difference between bourgeois and social or proletarian democracy. They differ only in the nature of the groups to which they address themselves and in the means they employ. On the one hand, the educated and economically enterprising middle class constitutes the horizon of bourgeois democracy. Thus the inauguration of equality before the law and of free competition was expected automatically to produce the ideal state through a mutual balance of interests. Social democracy, on the other hand, concerns itself with the uneducated and economically dependent masses, who are not helped by legal equality and free competition. On the contrary, their rightful share can be provided only through intensive assistance within the total organization of the state and, above all, through socialization of the means of production and of education. From the point of view of political ethics, there is no difference between bourgeois and social democracy except that the rise of a new social class appeals even more strongly to the sense of justice and to human sympathy. When social democracy claims the democratic idea as the sole property of the proletarian classes and praises their class struggle as a fight for all ethical and higher culture, such an idealization is simply a propagandistic means to create moral self-confidence or to attract moral sympathy. In itself, democracy is by no means identical with the rule of the proletarian masses. For precisely through democracy, the proletariat is supposed to lose its proletarian character.

Finally, the democratic principle implies a worldview, a metaphysics, and a religion. It implies a worldview that is teleological through and through—namely, an ardent belief in the victory of moral reason. The clash of interests and the dull condition of the masses must lead to human individuation and the autonomy of personal value-formation. Ultimately, this individuation must place its stamp also upon community life. The world must be arranged in such a way that this triumph of the ethical state becomes possible despite all hindrances of nature, unfavorable external circumstances, and differences in race, color, class, and individuality. Human beings must be organized in such a way that this ideal is bound to emerge from their nobler strivings despite all their folly, indolence, malice, and self-seeking. A metaphysics of optimism underlies this view of the world. In earlier times, there was a clear awareness of the religious foundation of this democratic metaphysics. Even today it is able to coalesce with naturalistic views and materialistic concepts of history only on the presupposition that with a firm hand, some unseen divinity directs the struggle for existence and the forms of economic life toward the manifestation of the universal and equal value of individuals.

Along with a certain metaphysics, a certain ethic is also implied here—namely, the ethic of universal love and justice. This ethic views all human beings as springing from a single root and aspiring to a single goal, and wants to see the idea of humanity actualized in every individual. The connection of this ethic with Stoic and Christian ideas also was readily acknowledged in earlier times. Only recently has it become associated with naturalistic theories that subject people to the play of chance and consider the idea of humanity an idealistic dream. In truth, however, an idealistic metaphysics and ethics continue to pervade the democratic principle. This is why Adam Smith made the theism of world harmony the basis of his doctrine, why bourgeois democracy believes in progress as the great divinity that in the course of time will automatically and irresistibly move people forward, and why social democracy believes in the law of evolution which, by an inner dialectic, drives primitive society to become feudal society, feudal society to become bourgeois society, and bourgeois society to become the collectivistic society envisaged by socialism.

Above all, the close connection of democratic ideals with Christianity springs from this common ethical concern. This is why modern democracy differs from the democracy of antiquity, which at bottom was always strongly aristocratic or oriented exclusively toward class conflict. During its formative period, modern democracy received the strongest impulses from Puritanism and the Reformed ideal of popular sovereignty. Even today, Catholicism justifies the degree of recognition it extends to democracy by the Christian belief in the [dignity of the] person. Protestant groups regard their alliance with democracy as a moral obligation for the sake of the gospel, and social democracy claims for its own the true historical Jesus. Indeed, the Christian feeling that the poor and humble must be supported in their aspirations is generally the strongest ally of contemporary democracy. More often than not, the anti-ecclesiasticism of the democrats is really hatred for the state church, which (at least among non-German democrats) by no means excludes membership in a sect. Here again, the anti-religious, officially anti-clerical dogmatism of the German democrats, which stems from French naturalism, obscures the true nature of democracy.

We find a quite different picture when we turn to conservatism. It, too, does not come into consideration as the program of a particular party or as the mere consequence of economic conditions that make the survival of a social class depend on the maintenance of traditional relationships. Rather, we are concerned with it as an ethical principle. It is a genuine and legitimate principle of political ethics, which inspires the souls of many disinterested people with genuine passion and sets at ease the conscience of many interested ones. Its essence can be expressed in a simple formula: 'Authority, not majority!' While the democratic principle rests upon the presupposition of human equality—which has not yet been actualized, but is recognized in principle—conservatism rests upon the presupposition of the inequality of human nature, which is fundamental and can never be eliminated. Moreover, this difference of native endowment and the contingency of whether or not one gets ahead is not simply an onerous and absurd fate but rather a meaningful disposition. From it proceed, together with the very possibility of community organization, all the richly varied and graded moral forces and values operative in the community. Both the formation and the preservation of the state derive from this very inequality. As a contract among atomistic individuals, the state would never have come into existence and would not hold together even today. Upon this inequality depends the ineradicable difference between leaders and followers, and amid these relationships of subordinate, co-ordinate, and superior positions originate all the various moral forces of trust and concern, modesty and responsibility, piety and loyalty. These are the ethical principles that destroy self-seeking among both leaders and followers and turn people's natural inequality into the source of the highest moral accomplishments, which are possible only amid such inequality. Only as long as thought is blinded by the illusion that all people are naturally equal will it simply insist on the intrinsic value of the person. As soon as thought perceives the indisputable fact of individual differences and of differences in power that issue not merely from the struggle for existence but rather from these individual differences themselves, it begins to appreciate the moral values that are destined to grow from these inequalities and power-based relations.

It does not follow, however, that conservatism is bound to cling to outmoded orders and social classes. It can abandon whatever has really lost its roots. But it will not abandon anything merely because people reject authorities in general, and it will always have to work toward the formation of new authorities. Thus the name 'conservatism' is only relatively justified. It is not a matter of absolutely conserving every given authority but rather of conserving

186 Religion in History

the principle of authority as such. Basically, therefore, conservatism is the principle of aristocracy, with 'aristocracy' understood solely in the political and social sense in which it signifies the power of individuals and of particular social strata—which originates in conflict and individual differences—to pass on the power to rule and the capacity for exercising this power. But in order to avoid any confusion with the purely personal and powerless aristocracy of the higher culture, it is better to avoid the term 'aristocracy,' particularly since the political impact of this kind of social aristocracy will always be preponderantly conservative.

That this ethic will be translated into political ideas goes without saying. It leads directly to a principle for the formation of the organs of state power and the objectives of state activity. The formation of the organs of state power is above all derived from history and is conditioned primarily by history. The state emerges from a preponderance of power that is either experienced as obvious or established by force. The law merely rationalizes the situation (including the continuing influence of conditions antedating the rise of the state) in such a way that a rule can be derived from it for treating every case that might occur. These primordial forces, together with whatever may later be added to them through internal or external shifts in the power structure, are the bearers of the legal power of the state and establish themselves by law in its possession. Every artistocracy is imbued with the historical spirit, because all power is regarded as the product of history. Monarchies, republics and states governed by a few leading families all share basically the same aristocratic spirit. It lies likewise in the nature of things that the core of this kind of aristocracy prides itself on its roots in landed property, which is intimately connected with the primordial forms of human society and the immobility of mother earth.

All further particulars pertain to the practical and technical sphere, which here, as for democracy, is not without difficulties if the ethical idea of conservatism is really to be carried through. But the close connection between such a construction of the state and ethical ideas is nevertheless very clear. It is less clear, perhaps, in the case of our contemporary conservatives, who, under the pressure of circumstances, have turned conservatism into a principle of class struggle based on democratic presuppositions and pursued with democratic means. But the older conservatives—F. J. Stahl and his followers—recognized and sought to implement this connection. Patriarchal care for those strata of society that need it and are best provided for by it; the historical attitude toward the state, which knows that authorities are not improvised but are received from history along with the state itself; all the ideals of loyalty, piety, faithfulness, and modesty on the part of the lower classes and the corresponding ideals of concern, responsibility, and self-sacrifice on the part of the upper classes; joyfulness on the part of those who serve and devotion to the common weal on the part of those who rule; proficiency in work and nobility of mind—all these interdependent and mutually evocative and supplementary elements together constitute the moral attitude toward the state.

The purpose of the state is to be understood in the same way. This purpose is not the compensation of individuals according to the measure of their contribution, but rather the maintenance of the whole in its organic unity and in its historically developed structures. Only in such a whole will individuals feel and find their own value; though, to be sure, this value will not be the same for everyone nor will it correspond exactly to the measure of everyone's proficiency. But in their own place and in their own way, all will be conscious of the benefits of the political order. For the realization of one's purely personal value, moreover, the sphere of each person's interior and private life remains inviolate. It is the external position and participation in the benefits of property and education that, because of the nature of things, have to remain unequal. It is a delusion to want to actualize the demand for human rights and dignity directly in the state. These are things that belong to the sphere of inwardness. The state, with its concrete power differentials and its historical distributions of power and property, can never give them unqualified and direct expression. Countries like America, to be sure, which do not have such a pre-history and therefore lack the power structures stemming from it, cannot have this kind of feeling for the state or its power. But for this very reason a historically oriented political consciousness will always find the American attitude toward the state somewhat deficient. Moreover, time will bring an aristocracy to America also. For everything historical is aristocratic, and all aristocracy entails conservatism.

In view of its strong emphasis on the historically conditioned, the nationalistic character of conservatism is a matter of course. But its nationalism only implies that the nation will always be the core of historical formations. For the rest, conservatism will accord de facto recognition to the incorporation in the state of alien national elements; or to the splintering of elements of its own nation when this is a historical datum and closely bound up with the distribution of power. Unrestrained nationalism will be suspect as Jacobinism, as it was in the days of Arndt and Jahn. The principles of conservative foreign policy also are connected with this peculiar nature of conservative nationalism. Here, too, conservatism will insist on the recognition of historically developed power relationships and will use all available resources to maintain the power of the state. War will accordingly be viewed as an unavoidable consequence of the power struggles implicit in the nature of things, and a demonstration of the discipline and authority that are necessary for waging war will be seen as a demonstration of the highest moral powers.

Moreover, conservatism will generally apply its aristocratic concept to the relationships among nations. It will sanction the domination of small states by large ones and the subjection of inferior races by those more capable of rule and richer in culture; it will regard the idea of rule by the white race as the natural consequence of the place the white race has won for itself in history. Here, too, the natural differences among human beings form the basis of the aristocratic idea, and this aristocratic idea brings to light the idea of rulership with all its conservative consequences—consequences that do not preclude the subjection and domination of those destined to be ruled by those fit to rule, or, more generally, the extension and development of power.

The ethic of conservatism also is based upon a worldview. This worldview emphasizes above all the inequalities in situations and persons, and develops its moral ideas from acceptance of these inequalities. Already the aristocratic ethic of ancient Greece was based upon racial differences. Even today, reinforced by the Darwinist struggle for existence and the Nietzschean *Herrenmoral*, the ethic of race widely serves as a basic concept that is supplemented by treating particular classes and social groups as analogous to races. Metaphysically, conservatism implies a metaphysics of realism, of sober empirical observation that is blinded neither by a precipitate teleology nor by optimistic enthusiasm but takes people and things as they are. Depending on temperament, this realism can assume a pessimistic or a resigned outlook and often does not lack even a dose of cynicism, as charmingly exemplified by Fontane in his *Junker* novels.

But when the ethical import of its doctrine is to be stressed, conservatism most frequently and most strongly identifies itself with Christianity. For only Christianity succeeds in actually deriving moral values from this realism without dissolving all naturally conceived and historically formed moral ideas; indeed, it makes the situation fruitful in terms of these ideas. Human inequality and its consequences, the formation of power structures and class distinctions, accordingly are viewed as constituting a natural order given by God in order to develop the most important elements of social morality precisely out of this situation of inequality. For the same reason, the historically developed powers are to be considered ordinances of God to which one submits as to a divine institution; they exist by the grace of God and require conformity. But this conformity is given still further moral motivation inasmuch as the Christian ethic, with its orientation toward sin and repentance, generally requires humility and resignation, inner freedom from outward possessions, a disposition to obedience and piety, modesty, and the moral, inward ennoblement of every position through proficiency and faithfulness of performance.

Thus for the Christian ethic every power struggle is in part a consequence of sin, and its misery to be borne as punishment for sin. In part, however, the powers emerging from the struggle also are to interpret their vocation morally, as a service for which they are accountable to God, thus combating the natural human tendency to self-glorification and anarchy as sinful and socially dangerous egoism. Of course, such humility is in the first instance solely humility before God; but it comes to be applied also to the ordinances established by God and requires obedience for God's sake, just as the authorities are to exercise their power as service to the community for the sake of God. If natural inequality and its consequences are thus conceived in a religious spirit, the sin that is constantly at work in the power struggle is restrained; and the result of the natural process is purified, ennobled, and sanctified. Meanwhile, the inward freedom of the religious person remains. Yet, since it is neither dependent upon one's outward position nor innate or apportioned equally to all, but rather acquired through moral efforts at self-improvement on the part of the religious person, it cannot become the principle of a political construction.

These four forms exhaust the principles of political ethics available to us. Surprisingly, perhaps, no mention has been made of a political ethic of Christianity. In view of the strong sway of Christianity over broad classes of people—especially over those classes that fail to attain literary expression—and in view of the strong power of the Christian churches, of which the Catholic Church in particular possesses a political program of the most palpable sort, this omission may appear all the more striking. Nor will it make much sense to one who, like all the friends of the Evangelical Social Congress, proceeds on the assumption that the highest standards of our life are contained in the Christian ethic. But the fact remains that there really is no political ethic that is derived directly and essentially from Christian ideas. Nor has there ever been such an ethic. The ecclesiastical ethic, especially the political ethic of the church-dominated culture of the Middle Ages, is only in part a Christian ethic; for the rest, it operates very extensively with borrowings that have been only more or less Christianized. The church has been able to enter politics in a grand style only by borrowing from natural law, Aristotelian philosophy, and Roman law. Even then the unremitting struggle between state and church and the whole conflict between the spiritual and the secular life show the deep, inner contrast. The Catholic Church basically has no political ethic that recognizes independent moral values in the state; it has only rules for subordinating the state to properly religious ideas. Protestantism, which does recognize the moral value of the state, nevertheless has no means for relating the state to the religious idea, despite all the sophistic devices and patriotic commonplaces of the average theological ethic.

In fact, then, the omission is only natural and self-explanatory. The very meaning and nature of Christianity prevent its having a direct political ethic. Christianity originally had no political ideas at all. Its moral commands address themselves in the first instance exclusively to the sphere of private morality. Even when it heals social ills with its works of love, such activity proceeds from purely religious motives or from motives of private morality. Love of God and of one's neighbors can never be a political principle. The experiment of a state that is directly and genuinely derived from Christianity has been made, only to miscarry in practice. The lessons taught by the state of the Anabaptists and of the Cromwellian saints, and of the Jesuits in Paraguay (which was different from the others but no less Christian), should not be forgotten. But it is equally erroneous to attempt theoretically to derive and construct the state from the concept of free Christian persons and their community. Such attempts already involve a rationalization and secularization of the basic Christian ideas. (The free Christian person is first of all free only in and before God, and the community of such persons is a community of love for the sake of God.) But even from this secularized idea no comprehensive political principle can be derived. Christian ethicists, to be sure, are accustomed to derive democracy from it, in the sense of a demand for love of the neighbor and compassion for the masses, the humble, and the oppressed. The greatest respect is surely due to such ethicists, especially when, as clergymen, they are driven by their conscience to put themselves in the service of this idea. For they restore to the masses, insofar as this is still possible, the belief that the church and the clergy are not merely a black-robed militia defending the egotistic hardheartedness of 'education and property.' Yet this approach is not really correct. Political democracy does not aim at love and sacrifice but rather at law (*Recht*) and a secure order; not at the gifts of subjective, personal affection or of a personal sense of duty, but rather at conditions and norms that generally and as a matter of course serve as the basis of life.

Democracy can utilize only that part of the Christian idea of the person which can pass over into the legal order or be claimed as a self-evident right; it cannot utilize the purely inward and personal element of genuine religious feeling and the idea of love. This is why modern democrats tend to react to such Christian endeavors only with distrust; they see in them only the enthusiasm of well-meaning idealists, the flabby sentimentality of 'do-gooders,' or the concealment of a far-from-selfless bid for love. However unjust this judgement generally is with respect to persons, the distrust of the theory is fully justified. For political ordinances simply do not grow directly from such purely personal factors of the life of feeling and sentiment, but rather in the first instance, only from the real organizational conditions of the political life itself. Political ordinances do not adhere to something so rare and sublime as the flight of the religious feeling or the stringency of the religious demand, but rather to the law, to the average, and to the objective structure of the state.

Nevertheless, the impression that Christianity actually possesses great significance for politics is, of course, no illusion. This significance persists even today, although the medieval ideal of a completely church-dominated culture has been transcended, and we regard the autonomous moral value of the state as beyond question. The significance of Christianity for politics is not direct but indirect. It does not derive directly from the central idea, but rather expresses itself in a variety of influences that Christianity has exercised here and there upon the life of the state. It has impressed itself deeply and indelibly upon our political sensitivities, but this has been an indirect effect of the Christian attitude toward life. These influences must first of all be sought out. The question remains open how closely these indirect influences approach the unity of a principle. But if we view the matter from this standpoint, we observe that the influences of Christianity have already been touched upon in our description of the four main types of political ethics. Only the second [the nationalistic] has absolutely nothing to do with the Christian ethic. But all the others stand in close inner connection with it. Our only task, then, is expressly to demonstrate this connection; and on this basis to arrive at a theoretical understanding of the significance of the Christian ethic for political ethics, insofar as this may be possible.

The ethic of the constitutional state limited to the service of culture requires that the life of the spirit be free from the coercive power of the state, and that the role of the state itself be confined to the service of its cultural values. Historically, it is closely connected with the demand that the church and the conscience be free from the state, even though the state is also regarded as a precondition and protection of the religious and moral life in general. The demand for freedom of the church is Catholic; the demand for freedom of the conscience is Puritan-Protestant. In fact, this demand for freedom from the state and for the subordination of the state to higher values is possible only where something is possessed that is anchored in transcendence, utterly independent of earthly power and the earthly purposes of the state. A merely intellectual and aesthetic culture would not in itself possess such independence and power of resistance. Since its aristocratic character is wholly individual and personal, it has actually shown great flexibility in politics, where it can tolerate any condition so long as it remains unmolested in its own sphere. Freedom from the state and the affirmation of spiritual values on a par with or even above the state have their strong roots rather in religion, where faith in a kingdom not of this world asserts a higher sphere of values alongside and within the kingdoms of this world. The Christian ethic is accordingly first and foremost the strong backbone of a political ethic that does not allow the purpose of human life to be identified with the state.

But this very function most clearly demonstrates the completely unpolitical nature of such an ethic. When it restricts and subordinates the state, it applies alien principles to the state. The religious ethic is ultimately international rather than national. While it limits the state, it does not seem to develop a properly political ethic or attitude. Yet the Christian ethic has not been unfruitful even in this respect, producing some genuinely political norms and views. One need only glance at our third and fourth types to realize that Christian ideas are contained in both of them and have attained considerable importance in them. The specifically political consequences of the Christian ethic, which affect the very structure of politics, are distributed between democracy and conservatism. Both camps accordingly have produced spirited defenders whose Christian commitment cannot be doubted. One side believes that the Christian ideas of freedom and of the person require them to support democracy, while the other believes that the Christian ideas of authority and order require them to support conservatism—a clear sign that the Christian idea has here undergone a bifurcation. How and why the historical development of Europe has led to this bifurcation can only be indicated by a brief historical reflection.

First of all, it is clear from the study of universal history that Christianity is the religion of personalism in the highest sense. It challenges the individual to become a person of incomparable intrinsic worth through devotion to God and the practice of God-mindedness. In God's will it sees the source of all the personal values to which the individual, struggling with error and sin, is to be raised by a pure act of trust and self-surrender. The idea of the person thus lies at the very center of Christianity. Its place is quite different in Judaism (where personality is still bound up with nationalism), in the ethnic religions, and in philosophical approaches to religion, where the individual is known but not the person, devotion to God but not the attainment of personhood through such devotion. This idea of the person established itself in a soil well prepared by Jewish ethical monotheism, by the denationalization and individualization of ancient society, by the idealistic systems of late antiquity, and by the mystical cult organizations of popular religion. Yet it introduced something new. Its revolutionary impact manifested itself immediately in conscientious opposition to the emperor-worship of the state and in the creation of a state within the state, the church, which—its authoritarian organization notwithstanding—embodied the idea of free persons, their universal and equal right of access to salvation, and their just claim to human respect and love.

With the help of ancient political and juridical philosophy, the church produced a doctrine of the state that brings the idea of the person to bear on the political sphere. Its ideal figure is Adam, the primordial man of paradise, still without sin and therefore free from all dominion, proprietary distinctions, and coercion. To be sure, in the fallen, sinful world the ideal could not longer be immediately realized; the ordinances of government and property, consecrated and confirmed by the church, had to be respected. But this qualification holds only within the world under the sway of original sin. It did not hold in the primordial state of the world and will disappear with the consummation of its redemption. Thus in the Adam of the church's political and social doctrine, the principles of personhood, freedom, equality, and individuality continued to prevail as ideals; though it should not be forgotten that this Adam had title to all this only because he was still pure and possessed of his primordial perfection, consisting in humility and submission to the will of God.

Here, then, lie the main roots of modern individualism and democracy. Certainly many other factors have made contributions—a Germanic individualism not yet broken by a centralizing culture; the urban culture of the thirteenth century; the revival of art and learning which individualized feeling as it shed its ecclesiastical fetters; the centralizing and leveling thrust of absolute monarchy; ancient natural law, especially; and finally, the enormous revolution in economic life and working conditions due to the invention of machines. But right down to the beginning of the modern world, the main lines of this intellectual evolution have been conditioned by its religious implications. The ideals of various monastic orders, mysticism, Nominalism, the Reformation, Puritanism, and Congregationalism mark stages in its evolution. The Reformed political doctrine of the Huguenots elaborated the right of the community to control the powers according to the ideal of a religious morality; thus the principle of popular sovereignty. The Congregationalists' demand for religious freedom of conscience implied the right of the free individual to participate in the power of the state. The connection between the French Declaration of the Rights of Man and American constitutions based on Congregational principles has recently been demonstrated.

Of course, in modern times the principles of natural law deriving from Stoicism have become more and more strongly linked with these religious ideas, until they have at last completely overshadowed them. Yet even this relationship is quite old; only the reversal of roles is new. The philosophy of the early church had connected the moral 'natural law' of Stoicism—that is, the doctrine of moral rights and duties that are grounded in the nature of the individual—with the law of Christ. Only by incorporating the principles of jurisprudence and the Aristotelian concept of the state into this natural law was the early church able to develop its political doctrine. The difference between Christian and pagan elements was not noticed, or rather the pagan limitations of natural law were simply dissolved through Christian interpretations and additions. Natural law regarded the autonomous individual simply as the product of a natural endowment, and the rules of natural law as the means whereby human nature maintains itself in the community and achieves its natural goals in life. The idea of human equality, therefore, predominates in natural law.

The Christian idea of the person, on the other hand, recognizes the person only as the product of fellowship with God. The goals of Christian morality lie in the world of transcendence. Equality is here only equality before God, while external relationships are characterized by freedom and equality only under conditions of sinlessness. This difference, which had already been obscured by the philosophy of the church, disappeared completely for the rationalism of the Enlightenment, which drew the Christian idea of the person down to the level of natural law; the only vestige of the Christian sensibility that remained was sympathy for the weak and oppressed, for the wretched masses. In this form, Rousseau gave to natural law its world-historical significance; he completely democratized the meaning of the gospel and sought to humanize Christians, on the assumption that the most humane Christians would also be the best Christians. Since then, the separation of democracy from Christianity—at least in Germany and the Latin nations—has made increasing progress, as is well known. But there are still always some for whom it is enough to connect the democratic idea with feelings of compassion and charity in order for it to be recognized as the essence of genuine Christianity.

There is, however, another side to this development of the political implications of Christianity. For the idea of the person is complemented by the idea of redemption. Personhood here is seen as contingent upon redemption. From the point of view of the history of religion, Christianity is characterized precisely by the close connection of personhood and redemption. It transposes the idea of redemption, which was common to the whole of late antiquity, into positive ethical terms, to signify the ascent to personhood, which is grounded in God, and the overcoming of the world through another world that is higher and morally more perfect. Now this idea of redemption involves a good deal of pessimism, both with respect to the terrestrial order in general and with respect to people in particular. People are always subject to sinful impulses; and the ethical person can develop only through struggle. Hence results the universal distinction between a higher and a lower moral status and with it, an abundance of relationships involving teaching, counselling, and subordination. A basis for aristocratic ideas is thus already laid. Even if these signify in the first instance only an inward and personal superiority, they nevertheless will lead to a hierarchical ordering of social relationships that is based on these ethical differences. To be sure, this hierarchical structure will disappear in a perfected humanity, but it is of utmost importance in a humanity that is still struggling with sin.

Another, somewhat different, basis for aristocratic ideas is laid by the pessimistic assessment of the course of the world. Here it is more a matter of submission to natural orders and relationships ordained by God, which, since they do not affect the inner person, are to be endured. The natural inequalities of the prevailing situation create a thousand differences in authority, property, status, sex, and social conditions. The powers and conditions that are formed in this natural process are to be accepted by the faithful as divinely ordained and permitted. They constitute the external framework for the exercise, in the proper place, of everyone's inner religious and moral energy. To Caesar can be rendered whatever is Caesar's according to the natural course of the world, if only one does the main thing, namely, render to God what is God's. Even though sin and egotism play an important part in the origin of the power and orders of the world, a relative value can be ascribed to these when they are viewed as permitted by God. By the ordinance of God, they wield the temporal sword of justice and create a civil discipline to which the believer should submit. Paul conceived his relation to the pagan empire in this way, and a hundred years later Bishop Melito eulogized the Augustan empire and the Christian church as twins born on the same day. Thus the church outwardly upheld the existing social stratification—including slavery; and after some opposition, even recognized soldiering as an occupation indispensable to civil order.

Here the aristocratic effect of the natural power struggles is admitted and a principle of conservatism is developed that contrasts strikingly with the revolutionary implications of the idea of the person. This aristocratic conservatism, however, develops still further after the triumph of the church and the Christianizing of state and society. Now the powers emerging from the natural power struggle with its process of selection are no longer merely endured as natural orders. Instead, there is a direct emphasis now on their having been permitted and established by God. The objective is to impress upon the rulers the obligations of meriting and sanctifying their possession of outward power through inward moral worthiness. The aristocracy of moral superiority and the aristocracy of social power are, as far as possible, to become one. The ruling powers in the spheres of sex and family, economy and society, and church and state are to be, in accordance with their position, caretakers, educators and guides; they are to consider themselves as entrusted with a divine mission for which they must account to God.

Finally, the political and social doctrine of the church undertakes to prescribe the rules according to which the exercise of such a vocation may be given Christian recognition and order. Moreover, the church undertakes to consecrate these powers and to make them inviolable if their office is conducted in the Christian way. Thus the policy of the church becomes absolutely aristocratic and conservative, yet without sacrificing the theory of popular sovereignty, of common

property, or of the origin of the state as conditioned by sin. The state
and the order of society arise solely through sin, and in manifold ways
bear the traces of their sinful origin. In this sinful world, however,
they are nevertheless divine ordinances that have only to expunge, as
far as possible, their taint of sin; and to become ever more Christian.
The political ethic of the church conserves the state as long as the
powers of the state are defined in accordance with the Christian idea.

In this respect, there is no great difference among the churches. The
Catholic political doctrine demands a direct influence on the state by
the centralized, international church; Protestantism releases the state
from the control and tutelage of the church; but it expects personal
ethical convictions from those who occupy positions of power, the
manifestation of these convictions through the discharge of their office
in the spirit of Christian paternalism, and respect for the demands of
the church. This means the subjection of the magistrate to Christian
ideas and the protection of the church by the state. The energetic
Calvinists were accordingly compelled to impose a rigid religious and
moral control on the state; in the process they lost a good many of
their conservative principles, since their base of support was the local
congregation. The Catholics, meanwhile, could appeal to the power of
an international church. Lutheranism, on the other hand, due to the
intense pessimism of its doctrine of original sin, renounced the attempt
to reform the powers along Christian lines and submitted passively
and unconditionally to the prevailing political conditions.

The Puritan Revolution and, especially, the emerging natural law
doctrine caused these theories to be thoroughly shaken, but in the
reaction to the French Revolution they reappeared among both
Catholics and Protestants. De Bonald, De Maistre, and Stahl restored
them very effectively. The circumstances of the time, however, now
gave a reactionary stamp to the aristocratic-conservative principle of
the Christian political ethic. The earlier, often contradictory
connection with the revolutionary idea of the person was almost
entirely eliminated. The question now was how to preserve the old
legitimate powers, so that they might protect the old legitimate
theology against modern science and in turn reap the gratitude of
theology, which would continue to support their prerogatives. The
result has been an alliance of all the old ruling powers against all the
new powers raised up by the natural process, even though these new
ones have much stronger roots in the total situation. This is how the
Christian conservatism of the present has become more conservative
than aristocratic, and it is already entering upon a new development:
in a difficult situation, it is capable of becoming an interested party in

the class struggle. This development, however, should not obscure the fact that the Christian ethic contains an aristocratic-conservative tendency that acquiesces in the results of the natural process of the acquisition of power as a disposition of nature; it merely requires the possessors of power to exercise it as a moral office and a divine vocation. Even today, a great many people find in this feature the ethical idealism of the conservative principle.

The political ethic of Christianity has expressed itself in these two principal tendencies. It is clear that there is from the outset a duality in the Christian ethic that is at the bottom of this bifurcation in Christian political thought. On the one hand, there is the idea of the absolute worth of the person; on the other, there is the idea of submission to God's natural ordering of the world. In the one direction lie revolutionary and democratic political tendencies; in the other, conservative and aristocratic. In both tendencies, however, something alien to Christianity has been added, namely, secular motives and viewpoints concerning the natural condition and goals of human beings. In one case natural law has been added, with its natural equality of human nature and human goals; in the other an apotheosis of traditional power relationships has taken place, which clings to property rights and would perpetuate the status quo, suppressing progress and reform. What is in question is whether the Christian ethic can get rid of these two admixtures, retain the two tendencies essentially belonging to it, and combine them with the principle of freedom from the state into a political ethic corresponding to the idea of Christianity.

Of course, this question is of vital interest only to those who are convinced that for us the Christian ethic is the highest religious and moral idea we possess. To the degree that we hold this conviction, an affirmative answer will be likely from the start. But before we can give any answer, we must dispose of a preliminary question that is closely related to it. How does it happen that such a unification, such a synthesis of the available elements, should not have been possible until now? Why has it not been achieved in the intervening period of almost two thousand years? Does not this failure indicate, rather, an intrinsic, aboriginal disunity in the idea itself and thus the improbability of such a synthesis? In my judgement this objection is not justified for the following four reasons, which are connected with more general views of ethics and the history of religion that cannot be exhaustively discussed in this essay.

The first reason is that today we know with certainty that the gospel contains no direct political and social instructions; it is fundamentally non-political. It deals only with the highest goals of personal life and of personal community, and anticipates the realization of this ideal in its expectation of the imminent end of the world and in the coming of the kingdom of God. Energized by this anticipation, the gospel wholly dismisses the world and worldly interests from its view. Political ideas are only indirectly contained in it, as implications that emerge when it is confronted by the political and social tasks of a continuing world. For in view of the continuing existence of this world, the gospel must recognize the necessity of influencing its institutions and organizations in a Christian spirit. This is why the church and theology were completely unable to grasp the political implications of the gospel so long as they retained the doctrinal standpoint of the inspiration of the Bible and clung to its very words. The New Testament was tortured and strained, but nothing was found. Church and theology accordingly were forced to confine themselves to the Old Testament and to the much lower, less developed cultural level of the Jewish state that it depicts. Only a purely historical interpretation of the gospel, which does not simply cling to the Bible but views Christianity in its broad historical development, can attempt to grasp the political implications of the Christian idea.

Second, by the same principle of historical research we have learned to discriminate more precisely between the Christian idea and the individualistic ideas of late antiquity, which confronted it and had some affinity to it but were nevertheless different. The older church doctrine merely clung to the formal difference that the ethics of late antiquity were revealed in a natural way, while the Christian ethic was revealed supernaturally. Since this external concept of revelation has been surrendered, we have come to distinguish the different forces forming the new world, beside and along with Christianity, according to their intellectual content. As a result, the profound difference between the Christian ethic of personhood and the natural law ethic of late antiquity becomes evident. We can understand why, on the one hand, the ancient church grasped this kindred force, drew upon it, and identified itself with it; for in its revelation the church possessed no means for the formation of political ideas. On the other hand, faith in its revelation certainly provided a potential corrective for the political ethics of natural law. This synthesis, however, has been disintegrating since the seventeenth century. Today we sense the deep substantive opposition between the two elements and can accordingly dissociate the Christian idea of the person from the idea of equality found in natural law.

Third, we have learned that the gospel and primitive Christianity were influenced by the expectation of the imminent end and fulfilment of all things. The doctrine of original sin—which replaced this eschatological mood—bears witness to the apologetic attempt to establish an unbridgeable gulf between Christianity and the outside world. Today we share neither the eschatological mood of primitive Christianity (even though we do not at all regard everything as ending with this earthly life) nor the blunt exclusiveness of the doctrine of original sin (even though we see good struggling with evil everywhere). Our mood, accordingly, is no longer one of mere indifference and submission to secular powers nor one of pessimistic distrust that sees in these powers only products, or at best restraints, of sin, to which the believer submits as to purely external orders that do not touch the soul. We can and must frankly acknowledge the natural process with its consequences, the struggle for existence, natural selection, and the formation of power, as the natural order—as a positive ordinance of God based on the very nature of things. But we can also demand now with greater confidence that these products of the natural process be cleansed of egoism and imbued with the ethical spirit. We can insist with much greater seriousness on the positive valuations of natural power formation that the teaching of the church has been attempting to make, and we can strive with every means to give them ethical content. We can then acknowledge the aristocratic elements of the Christian ethic without falling into a grievously pessimistic resignation or a passive conservatism that merely deifies the prevailing conditions. We can watch old aristocracies pass away and new ones rise, and find both developments equally legitimate, because both exist by virtue of the natural order and both are meant to incorporate an ethical content in their natural formation. We can demand reforms without being revolutionary, and we can acknowledge the moral values of aristocratic orders of life without deifying existing relationships. The loss of a rationale for pessimism in eschatology and original sin will not mean an underestimation of sin and evil, nor will acknowledgement of the natural life-process mean a glorification of elemental, instinctive nature not yet subjected to ethical control. Rather, ethics will accommodate itself to these presuppositions, accepting them as natural and by no means solely the products of sin, and will seek through constructive criticism to utilize and shape them for the moral life.

Fourth and above all, general ethical considerations have shown us that the Christian ethic is an essentially religious ethic whose basic idea is the perfection and purification of the person in the love of

God, together with the demonstration of God-mindedness through neighborly love. This religiously motivated love is doubtless the highest and most sublime moral ideal, but it is also primarily an ideal for the personal life and for interpersonal relations. Therefore under no circumstances can it be the one moral idea that creates all other norms. The whole range of human moral activities can never be derived from Christian love. The Christian ethic must, therefore, recognize other ethical principles beside itself. This necessity is attested by the fact that both Catholicism and the older Protestantism elaborated their ethical teaching by incorporating alien elements all along the line. While artful concealment may have obscured this fact in the past, contemporary Christianity must explicitly acknowledge it. The Renaissance, the Enlightenment, modern secular culture, and the revolutions in science, art, and technology have made this truth clear. The inner emancipation from the absolute dichotomy between Christianity and the non-Christian world, along with the turning away from the absolute pessimism of the doctrine of original sin, has made this truth inescapable. There remains only a choice between its recognition and a biblicistic-sectarian Christianity, which can consistently reject all these things because for it they simply do not exist. Of itself, Christianity cannot produce the moral values contained in art, science, economic activity, and political endeavor. The attempt, specifically, to derive the state and society from Christian love is like trying to square a circle. Yet Christianity can bring all these structures under the influence of its idea. Although it can make only minimal use in this effort of its central idea, love, it will express other basic ideas through which it can pervade these alien moral structures with its spirit and influence.

It is an utterly impossible undertaking to make the central idea of Christianity normative for political ethics. It is not the central idea of love but rather the two subsidiary ideas of personhood and submission to natural orders that enable Christianity to achieve a positive political ethic. Yet we should not expect that the influence of Christian ideas upon the state will ever exhaust the whole of political ethics. The state has an independent moral idea, the idea of nationalism, patriotism, and political honor, which is given with it and stems from its very nature. Experience indicates that not even Christianity is able to do anything directly with this idea. It must presuppose this moral idea as implicit in the state. It can only seek to show the moral inadequacy of this purely political idea. Beyond the moral ideal of the state there are still higher ideals of the inner life; these ideals provide norms that apply also to the state and are indispensable alongside those of patriotism and the political sense of honor. The state depends not merely on patriotism and the political sense of honor; it consists of persons and must accommodate itself to aristocratic orders. In both areas, the Christian ethic provides the state with a firm orientation and with ethical guidelines. What we are concerned with, therefore, is not so much a Christian political ethic as the contribution of the Christian ethic to political ethics. Once we recognize this fact, we are able to formulate this contribution more readily as a self-consistent idea. The Christian ethic stands above the state. The state is not the highest good. But the Christian ethic provides moral ideas also to the state, ideas through which the state can supplement and deepen its purely political morality.

This answer to the preliminary question brings us back again to the main question. The results of our reflection can now be drawn together and the political idea of Christianity can now be formulated. The Christian idea is strictly self-consistent only so long as it remains isolated in pure inwardness, as the love of God wrought in us by grace and resulting in purity of heart before God and in neighborly love for the sake of God. Here God as the reality of the world and God as redeeming grace are one and the same. But as soon as Christianity emerges from this isolation, its ideas necessarily move into a polarity. The God of grace is separated from the God of secular reality. Likewise, the religious inwardness of Christianity, which places the highest value on the individual soul, is separated from the natural course of the world; and the otherworldliness of the kingdom of God is separated from the natural life of this world with its law, struggles, and secular morality. Both worlds belong to God and come from God. Although the roots of sin and the arena of sin lie in the natural course of the world, it, too, comes from God. What results for the whole Christian ethic, therefore, is an oscillation between the purely religious ideals of purity of heart and neighborly love, in which the natural life is a matter of indifference, and the immanent ideals of controlling, purifying, and improving the natural world. The political ethic of Christianity is therefore the impact of its ideal upon the state. The state itself arose out of the natural flux and struggle of life and produced its own idea of political ethics. Now, however, it is being influenced by the Christian idea and its inmost structure is being conditioned by it. The Christian idea modifies our conception of the origin of state power as well as our conception of the purpose of the state. It recognizes the state as a necessary and natural form of life which, by virtue of the political idea, constitutes the framework and the presupposition for all higher life. But as the religion of personhood and submission to the divine orders, Christianity introduces something new and vital into political ethics, namely, an unconditional appreciation of the person and a respectful modesty.

Christianity thus goes about forming the will of the state out of the autonomy of individual persons. Destined to attain autonomous moral worth, these must also demand their share in public life. But from them, Christianity requires submission to the natural aristocratic orders that are simply given, along with the state and history. Christianity thus denies that the state is an end in itself, but it does not reduce the state's role to the mere maintenance of external law and order. Rather, it demands of the state the preconditions for human life on a higher moral plane, which can then reach its consummation in the religious life. These preconditions would include insistence on the idea of personhood, the fostering of feelings of authority and respect, and the opening of educational and economic opportunities to each and every individual. Christianity does away with the self-sufficiency of the state by subordinating the state to the kingdom of God. It revolutionizes the structures of the state through active support of persons, who cannot conceal their value and autonomy but press forward to participation in the shaping of public policy. It subjects individualism with its natural bent toward equality to an educative authority and to power structures based on God's natural order. It subordinates the state to God, gives human rights to men and women alike, and preaches obedience and modesty to all.

The tension between these ideas is overcome through the limitation of each by the other. The moral worth of the person is not innate but is acquired through labor and struggle. But personal ethical growth is not the automatic result of labor and struggle; it is based above all on the willingness to allow oneself to be educated, and on the moral virtues that are acquired through co-operation and subordination. Personhood is not unequivocally opposed to the aristocratic order but is developed, rather, in submission to it. Aristocratic power, however, is not a prize in the struggle for existence that is given to the winners for their own enjoyment. Rather, it is a duty to act for the common good. It involves no promise of permanence but must recede when its bearers lose their inner moral substance, or when the same flux of things that initially carried them to the top now undermines them and carries others to the top. No personhood without submission to the aristocratic orders, and no aristocratic order that does not enhance the worth of the person: this is the formula of the political outlook inspired by Christianity. Translated into political language, it means that Christianity is democratic and conservative at the same time. It is democratic in the sense that it demands an ever increasing degree of autonomy and spiritual and moral culture for people, who are also to become effective in the shaping of public policy. It is conservative in the sense that it acknowledges authority as substantiated through moral superiority and political power relationships, and sees submission to authority as a source of moral strength.

Exactly where the balance is to be struck between these two tendencies depends upon the particular situation and circumstances. Striking this balance will seem unimportant as long as the state is struggling for the foundations of its existence, but it will become important once this existence is secured and the task of organizing the state internally is faced. This organization is a problem of political technique; here, as in human affairs generally, compromises will be unavoidable. But the idea itself constitutes a thoroughly political attitude that should guide the political efforts of all who are committed to Christianity. As a political ideal it is clear and easily comprehensible.

In this formula the Christian contribution to political ethics is summarized. It is, I repeat, not a theory of the state. Such a theory would concern itself with the origin of the state in the natural processes of social evolution and its subsequent regulation through law. The formula applies only to the ethics of politics, not to the nature of the state as such. But even as an ethic of politics it is not, I repeat, the quintessence of all political ethics but only the contribution of the Christian idea to political ethics. It is clear, however, that this contribution is not merely incidental and gratuitous; it affects the inmost structure of the state and the whole temper of the political climate.

It may be objected that such a formula is much too vague and general to enable one to do anything with it in practice. At least, all its problems and difficulties come to light only in practical application. These objections are quite legitimate, but they apply to all general ethical principles. Such principles indicate no more than a fundamental attitude and orientation that serves to guide our thinking about and acting in the particular situation. These particular problems of a situation depend upon a myriad of special conditions that constitute the particular context. The ethical idea is so often shattered on the hard realities of existence that everything has to be considered from case to case, and the ethical idea can only rarely be implemented in its entire purity. The hardest feature of the human condition, after all, is that the purity of the ideal is never fully practicable, that the highest conceptions of the mind are vitiated more and more in the process of their material realization. But this feature also gives rise to the courage to decide and assume responsibility, the daring to solve the problem of the particular case in the best way possible.

Particular cases must therefore be omitted from consideration when, as here, our concern is with principles. That the principle itself, however, has a sufficiently incisive significance in practice is indicated by the first and most immediate object of its application—namely, the question of the position of the church in political and social struggles. From what has been said, it is evident that the church as a religious community has no direct political tasks. Its primary and essential social task is to foster religion and to stimulate and guide its exercise in the most immediate and most proper sphere of religious morality, namely, in the sphere of personal morality and charitable activity. A great field truly lies open for the church in the terrible conflict of modern worldviews, as skepticism, atheism, weariness with doubt, religious longing, and traditional piety struggle and compete. No less do the misery of modern overpopulation, over-work, the sins of the big city, and the demoralization of neglected youth provide the church with an abundance of objects for its charitable activity, so that the church will always have enough to do, quite apart from all organic social reforms. Religious doctrine, personal morality, and charitable activity will be its most immediate sphere of concern, and there is more than enough that can and needs to be done in this area. The Kaiser's saying, 'Political pastors are nonsense,' therefore is not unjustified in the sense presumably intended.

But the church is not on that account mute or without ideas on questions of morality in public life. It just does not have a political and social program of its own. The church is limited to the evaluation of parties and programs, as these emerge and solicit support, from the perspective of the Christian idea. In this way it can influence moral judgement in general. Here the task of the church will be to assert its democratic and aristocratic principles in complete autonomy and independence, over against both pressures from above and the instincts of the populace. The church will commit itself to the idea of personhood as its highest ideal; and will support, as in principle progressive, political demands based on this idea. The church will especially encourage and support those strata of the nation who strive to raise themselves out of the dull existence of the masses and the brutalizing struggle for existence into the light of personal life, and who demand the material preconditions without which there can be no thought of a personal life. Yet the church will also resist all the blandishments of natural law and egalitarianism, and will always recognize personhood only in terms of moral substance. It will never assent to the identification of these ideals (in the interests of the class struggle) with the spirit of the proletariat or with opposition to the ruling classes. The church will always demand that modesty and patience, humility and respect, obedience and readiness for service remain moral ideals. If it is said that political struggles are made impossible by such ideals, the church will flatly reject this allegation and demand Christian discipline even of those engaged in political struggles. At the same time, the church will be equally independent of conservatism and boldly call its truth, truth and its egotism, egotism. The church will openly recognize the necessity of authority, respect for authority, and the connection of authority with historical tradition, and will promote the moral energies that can grow only under these conditions. But the church will never take it as its task to defend an established order at any price, or to sanctify a prevailing system for the sake of authority and order.

On the whole the Catholic Church operates on these principles. Its combination of democratic and conservative elements is by no means merely a clever political stratagem but rather an expression of its nature. Only its own completely authoritarian structure keeps the Church from giving full recognition to the idea of personhood; only its own medieval mentality makes it look askance at the forces that have shaped modern history and the intellectual life of the present. The Protestant church has at its disposal the enormous energy of autonomous, subjective persons and the freedom to enter into the spirit of the modern world. If it is to have a truly historical mission as an independent force, if it is not to exhaust its best in the work of home missions, it must acquire an attitude toward questions of public morality that corresponds to its ideal of personhood and its ready acknowledgement of historical forces. It should do so—unfortunately this is all that can be said!

But all these remarks apply only to the attitude of the church as the institution that is the direct product of the religious life. It is obvious that for its political behavior the guidelines implicit in the Christian idea are normative, or should be. But it is quite a different question whether these political ideas are of any practical use from the standpoint of the state. The answer to this question is not, of course, to be given through a strict calculation of the utility that these ideas have for the state. This is one of the great questions of principle and conviction, one of the basic presuppositions or axioms on which life itself is based. Here the question is quite simply which standards should apply, those of the Christian religion or purely political ones that probably can be found only in the nationalist idea of the state. For Christian conviction the answer is obvious. It demands that the state should act according to Christian standards and recognizes an increasingly higher ethical value in the state according as the state appropriates the ideas of Christian ethics—insofar as the structure and theory of a state can assimilate Christian ideas at all. This answer obviously is not based on some hypothetical advantage to the state. What is truly useful to the state is precisely the point in question. From the Christian viewpoint, what is useful is whatever enhances the ethical substance of the state. Christian ethics will never regard the mere maintenance of the state as so valuable that it could relax its demands on this account. It may suspend its demands during periods when everything is relapsing into the natural state of flux, into the most elemental struggle for survival, but it will reserve its love and support for those developing entities that are capable of becoming vessels of ethical substance.

Nevertheless, even from the narrower viewpoint of the self-preservation and internal moral consolidation of the state, it seems to me that what the Christian ethic promises to contribute to the structure of the state is not unimportant. What is involved is a political principle that grafts upon nationalistic patriotism the higher moral ideas of service to be rendered by the state to the ideal world, the value of personhood, and submission to the natural order of history. Such grafting leaves the tree not only nobler but also stronger, and the enrichment of its sap leads to greater fruitfulness. So the structures of the state are fortified by moral convictions.

Nor can it be said that this Christian disposition is devoid of practical significance. Insofar as it is truly honest and firm, its effects will certainly be felt in politics. It would find expression in a more sensitive drawing of the boundary between the power of the state and the freedom of the individual, recognition of the idea of personhood in the constitutional sphere, the behavior of social classes toward one another, the conduct of officials and police toward the people, sympathy for the aspirations of the masses, and the just endeavor to comply (as far as possible) with their legitimate demands. It would likewise be expressed through respect and appreciation for the basic legal institutions, recognition of the importance of authorities that have come into existence in the course of history, an attitude of modesty and self-discipline, and readiness to learn and to receive guidance. It would not condemn the egotism of the social democrats more severely than that of the conservatives, but would decry both alike. It would reject the natural lack of respect for everything great, which characterizes the democrats, as well as the natural arrogance of the conservatives with respect to the masses. In all this, the Christian disposition would not merely serve the ideal of personhood and respect established orders; it would also pave the way for a reconciliation of the contending parties. Due to the real interests that are at stake here, such a reconciliation is not likely to be achieved without a severe struggle; but insofar as reconciliation is possible at all, it will be achieved only through good will and equitable understanding.

With the latitude that the combination of democratic and aristocratic principles provides, it might well seem necessary to clarify which of the two principles needs special emphasis in the present situation. This consideration may be appropriate in itself, but for our present situation in Germany it will hardly be the main concern. For the situation is such that the emphasis upon both and the interrelating of the two has become the main task. The two principles have lost touch with each other, or have never gotten touch with each other in the first place. But they must get in touch with each other.

To be sure, democracy is still far from the moral recognition and appreciation that is its due; even historically it is not yet properly understood. The caricatures of democracy drawn by arrogance, misunderstanding, fear, egotism, and the thoughtless and mindless repetition of others' opinions bear more than ample testimony to this fact. In practice, moreover, all the wisdom of the government often amounts to nothing other than the suppression and vexation of the democratic movement. But the democrats themselves are in large part responsible for this state of affairs. They are guilty of the same kind of caricatures, the same hatred and lack of understanding, of envious agitation and impassioned phrase-mongering; they have misjudged the reality of power-relationships and the unavoidability of authoritative structures; they have derided especially the moral demands of social integration and subordination. The two ideas must find each other and reach an accommodation. Morally autonomous persons may actually come to share in the power of the state; but then they will have to learn to give moral recognition to a conscious, free, and strong subordination to the indispensable powers. Conservatives may champion the historic German state and its monarchic and military foundation, but they will not have the right to do so unless they readily acknowledge the person, and personal self-affirmation and participation in the state. Only thus can there be a moral evolution of our state to a higher plane. Above all, only thus can there be a reconciliation of groups that are becoming increasingly alienated from one another.

These comments imply neither the endorsement of a political party nor even active participation in politics, which, to be effective, would indeed require a certain coming to terms with the parties. It may very well be one's duty in the present situation to vote liberal even though one is not a liberal. In practical politics, a decision may well be necessary between the liberal and conservative parties. The ideal of political ethics, however, requires a synthesis of the ideas of liberal democracy and conservatism. This ideal will undoubtedly outlive the political parties. National health and reconciliation depend on it.

This reconciliation is especially necessary in the present political situation. Internal conflicts—agrarian aristocracy vs. industrialism, population growth vs. limited resources, the incipient drive of the masses for autonomy and education vs. the old, closed circles of education and property—have brought about an uneasy ferment. Internationally, the existence of our united country is as yet not at all completely secure. No ethic can say how such antagonisms are to be resolved. This is a problem that must be worked out, above all by practicing politicians and social scientists. But if the solution is to work out for the best, it must be effected in the spirit of reconciliation between democratic and aristocratic motifs; and such a reconciliation finds its firmest support and its most profound basis in the political ideas of the Christian ethic.

14

The Social Philosophy of Christianity

There is an actual and characteristic social philosophy of Christianity that has been, and to a certain degree still is, of the greatest practical significance, and in the event of a considerable population decline in Europe could become so again. The extent to which the other great world religions have such a philosophy is still quite uncertain. Research in the history of religion has so far paid more attention to dogma, myth, and speculation, to cultus and personal ethics than to the great sociological impulses and creative powers that are present in religion and that interact at all times, either positively or negatively, with the more general conditions and trends of society. It is evident that all great religions that have a spiritual content of their own beyond their connection with national and everyday life are in possession of such impulses and powers. Yet as far as we know at present, these impulses and forces are always general and subconscious and do not constitute a systematic social philosophy. Such a philosophy seems to be characteristic of Christianity alone; and even here it is only to be explained by the close relationship that Christianity entertained with the cultural heritage of antiquity, and by the Christian adoption of theories of social philosophy evolved by antiquity. Islam, which in many respects is related to the prophetic-Hebraic roots of Christianity, displays a characteristic social principle but has not produced an analogous social philosophy. Although the ties of Islam with the cultural heritage of antiquity resemble those of Christianity, they do not extend to these matters—precisely in this lies one of the greatest differences between Islam and the Christian West.

In the Far East, the whole situation is so dissimilar that there is hardly room for comparison. To be sure, the Sino-Confucian religious

210

system is mainly a social philosophy of a very particular sort based on patriarchy and harmony, but it is inapplicable to European conditions; it lacks the tension characteristic of the Western system and has not been investigated scientifically in a manner comparable to the European. In the Indo-Brahmanic and the Buddhistic systems, a conscious social philsophy is lacking completely. Either it recedes behind a pure inwardness and contents itself with the graduations in the caste system, or else, as in Buddhism, it dissolves the caste system and leads beyond the purview of the practical-social world.

Conversely, the distinctive characteristics of our European-American civilization derive everywhere from the immediate context of the inherited Graeco-Roman organizational and theoretical rationalism, from the connection of this rationalism with the Christian ideals for the soul and society, and from the conditioning process resulting from its extension to an ever-widening circle of national cultures. Above all, the Roman Catholic Church, a world-wide organization of a type previously wholly unknown (of which the Protestant churches are the descendants and much-altered replicas), has fashioned a social theory that transcends these compounds and combinations—a social theory that has stamped on the Christian West one of its most significant features, despite all sorts of transformations and adaptations. A basic question still remains: how is the profound difference between the Christian West and the rest of the world to be accounted for? The difference is no doubt rooted in sociological relationships and impulses. But these in turn are intimately bound up with the 'Greek miracle'—a rationalism emancipating itself from instinct and nature, the contingent and the merely factual, in a wholly unique way, an unimpeded thrust towards form—with the Roman genius for organization and legal clarity, and with the Christian idea of the kingdom of God. Even though the modern world emerging from the European Middle Ages created entirely new and unparalleled economic, political, social, technical, and spiritual conditions, it could not have done so apart from this connection. Moreover, the remedies for the catastrophes and tensions arising from these conditions will be found only by taking these foundations into consideration. In our complicated system there can be no completely new, modern theory without historical foundations and without religious support from the Western metaphysics of the last two thousand years; and no borrowing from the wisdom of the Far East or from alien religions is going to be of help here. The remedies must come substantially from our own resources.

Of this enormous combination of problems only the special theme of Christian social philosophy will occupy us here, and for the most part only in its historical ramifications. But before it is possible to penetrate further into the matter, it is necessary to make two important preliminary remarks that are directly connected with the expression, 'social philosophy of Christianity.'

Christianity has a social philosophy that was derived, for the most part, from the social philosophy of late antiquity, and that has been continually modified. But it has no social theology, that is, no social theory springing directly from its religious idea, either directly as dogma or indirectly as logical consequence. Theological ethics, which might be supposed to furnish something of this sort, is of no help at all here. It concerns itself mainly with the help available from divine grace and miracles in the face of sin, damnation, and moral weakness, and centers its attention on the higher powers that are to be implanted by the religious system, especially as they apply to personal life, where casuistry finds a broad field of operation and claims the greatest interest. This point is self-evident for Catholic ethics, which is governed by the pastoral office and the confessional. What results is broad and diversified rules for life; but it is only by means of these rules that contact is made, almost incidentally, with social problems. In Protestant ethics the problem of the basic renewal of the soul through the miracle of conversion is completely dominant. Everything else then falls under the categories of what is in this case an attenuated casuistry; or else, as is more often the case—especially in modern Protestant ethics—everything comes under the sway of catchwords and general suggestions of principles.

In reality, the social philosophy of Christianity is to be found rather in works and treatises dealing with apologetics, canon law, and politics. A glance at the central religious conceptions of Christianity will show why this is, and must be, the case. All these conceptions culminate in that of the kingdom of God. But this conception was originally not a social theory applicable to earthly conditions. Nor did this conception turn into such a theory later, when the kingdom of God became the church. In the preaching of Jesus, who, generally speaking, was more the 'seed of wheat' than the founder of Christianity, the kingdom of God is understood in completely eschatological terms; while the community, awaiting the coming of the kingdom, proleptically participates in its spiritual effects. Hence the much-discussed duality of the kingdom of God. Eschatologically, the kingdom is the fulfillment of the promise, which is very earthly on the soil of Israel, and yet contingent upon a new corporeality and a new earth. The kingdom is above all the act of God at the Advent of the Son of Man, and therefore not a human act or organization. The new order will be an order of love, where the inner, spiritual values predominate and where a life of mutual service replaces the struggle for existence and the harsh law that now serves only as an external check on that struggle. Dominion will be exercised by God, whose will then will be done on earth as it is now in heaven among the angels and the heavenly hosts. The Son of Man, however, knows no further particulars; these will be revealed by the Father in heaven in his own time. These notions constitute an altogether general, futuristic utopia and can by no means be transformed into a social-philosophical or social-theological theory for modern times. At best they can be converted into rather confused chiliastic fantasies.

But even the effects of this ideal, projected into the present, can be transformed into no such theory. These effects exist in the gathering of a community that awaits and prepares for the kingdom of God. This community proleptically actualizes within itself, as far as possible, the spirit of love, having to contend all along with human weaknesses and the restraints of the existent situation on earth. Therefore the community of disciples will establish its fraternal order mainly within its own confines; and beyond that will suffer, endure, persevere, and do missionary work until the imminently expected day of the Son of Man and of the kingdom of God.

From these beginnings [at the beginning of Christian history] there evolved a missionary community, the organization of worship and missions, the experiment—at the main center in Jerusalem—of a communism of love purely for helping the poor, but no kind of social theory for the duration of the world's continuance, aiming at an adjustment to the great social institutions and activities of the world. The community was small and familial in character; for the time being it knew only the social ideas of an enlarged family. It was completely remote from the great political and social world, not suspecting the latter's existence. The possibilities of making a living in a southern climate, as well as the customs and requirements of the entire social stratum to which it belonged, spared the community any further theoretical reflection. In the transformation of the gospel of Jesus into the church, the new People of God organized along priestly-sacramental lines, the church took the place of the kingdom of God and of the apostolic 'family.' It constituted the form established by God in preparation for the coming kingdom. The church thus became a social alliance that spread throughout the Graeco-Roman world, and gradually came to be looked upon by the ruling society as a new, dangerous, and revolutionary organism.

Still, only religious ceremony, communal organization, canon law, and intra-ecclesiastical organization for social aid grew out of this creation of the church, but no theory of its own regarding the essence and objectives of social life as a whole and regarding the relation of the Christian social order to the secular orders. On the contrary, as soon as expansion and increased membership as well as penetration into the spheres of education, property, and social influence required such, the theory of social life as well as the philosophical-intellectual tools of theology were taken over from the prodigious treasury of thought of an over-ripe antiquity casting about for new sustenance. The general theory of the social order was borrowed from orientalized Platonism; the theory of the relation between the Christian and the secular orders, from popularized later Stoicism. Both theories appeared as the natural model and substructure for the supernatural revelations and powers that the church possessed. Only the theory of the relation between the Christian and the secular orders will be of interest to us here. For the attainment of a *modus vivendi* with the secular realm, a theory was needed concerning society as a whole. Certain ideas were then discovered in the treatises of the Stoics which seemed to be, and indeed were, spiritually akin to the Christian faith, and which were able to serve as a point of contact and transition to it: the original goodness, freedom, and brotherhood of man in the Golden Age; gradual corruption through passion and lust for power; reason as the goal of a cosmopolitan humanity; the unified direction of humanity in accordance with the uniformity of the law of reason; the institution of property, including the holding of slaves; and law, state, family, and the law of nations as part of the divine cosmic law of reason or of nature. State, society, economics, family, and property all derive from the natural moral code, or the law of nature.

Several things were needed to realize the possibility of union between the church and the existing institutions of the outside world: a vigorously theistic embedding of the natural moral code in the divine will; a special emphasis on the transformation of the code into power, law, and authority by reason of man's fall and his sinful state; the transformation of the cosmopolis into the church; and the establishment of the monarchical principle, as a reflection of monotheism, in the guidance of mankind by the church. The institutions of the world could then be purified and ennobled, but at the same time affirmed and continued. Christian natural law, which was reform-minded and revolutionary in certain respects and conservative and opportunistic in others, thus arose as the philosophy of the church, which could then draw further sustenance from the various writers on jurisprudence and philosophy. Best of all, it was able to provide a theoretical justification and further development for the great main event, the finally attained alliance with the holders of secular power. Just as theology found the way, through the Logos, to a combination of secular-natural wisdom with the Christ-God of the church, social ethics and practical understanding of the world discovered the same course through natural law and the natural moral code. This tendency meant compromise. The waiting for the *Civitas Dei*, for the heavenly Jerusalem, goes on, and the world remains a kingdom of sin and darkness. But in this darkness the remainder of the glory of paradise is at work—natural reason that stems from God. It is shaping the social orders of reason into potential bases and complements of the church's orders and of its highest ideal, now taking flight into asceticism.

This is how Augustine saw things at the height of Christian antiquity. At this point even a Christian state became possible, that is, the organization of society by secular rulers in accordance with the wishes of the church, or, indeed, in the service of the church. In case of emergency the church itself could take over the tasks of secular government. Such opportunities cropped up, in one form or another, after the weakening of belief in the eternity of the Roman societal and governmental order, and in the midst of the conditions created by the new barbarian kingdoms. At this time the church in Byzantium was entering into a close alliance with a self-sufficient monarchy. This marks the end of the ancient church of the spirit with its otherworldliness. But the transition took place almost imperceptibly. Christian natural law, which had been shaped during the days of the struggle with the pagan state and its society, eased the transition through its pliancy; and the relocation of the supernatural character of the church in a sacramental priesthood and a monastic asceticism relocated the dividing line between nature and super-nature.

This Christian natural law, in its various modifications, continued to exist in all Christian churches, expressing itself in the form of monarchic-monotheism in Byzantium, opportunism with respect to various constitutional possibilities in the Roman church, and reference to the modern state, absolutist at first and then liberal-democrat, in Protestantism. Social philosophy was and remained built on the foundation of Christian natural law until well into modern times. The seventeenth and eighteenth centuries, to be sure, thought that natural law was only then being re-discovered by Hobbes, Grotius, Locke, Pufendorff, and Rousseau. Though Christian natural law, as well as that of the ancient Stoics, has been largely forgotten today, these early-modern thinkers were for their part well aware of their

connections, as an examination of their writings shows. Their work is
mainly nothing but the sundering of the Christian and Stoic
constituent elements, and the reanimation of the latter in new practical
and metaphysical relationships. These men, furthermore, rediscovered
the other, Realistic-Sophistic-Epicurean form of ancient law, without
ever confining themselves to it completely. It was owing to the pride
of their successors, who wanted an absolutely brand-new modern
world, that the connection was forgotten. That connection is still
maintained in all its scope, however, and even further elaborated
among Catholics today. It is also recognized among the modern
descendants of Puritanism. Lutheranism was from the beginning less
interested in it, because of its marked social and political passivity
and its submission to divinely ordained authorities; yet the connection
continued to be affirmed as part of orthodoxy. Lutherans today,
particularly those who have been affected by modern philosophy and
speculation, have also forgotten it. When Catholics insisted, in the
name of 'natural law,' on the decisive importance of education for
those qualified, people laughed at this because they could connect the
term 'natural law' only with Newton and Darwin. In reality, however,
this 'natural law' was and is the Christian social philosophy.

I can express myself more concisely concerning my second
preliminary remark, which deals with the term 'Christianity.' The
term is unavoidable for our purposes, but misleading if used without
the necessary reservations. Before the eighteenth century there was no
'Christianity.' There were only Christian churches and sects; or at best
there was a Christendom that constituted the sum and substance of
the Christian churches. The concept 'Christianity,' as the universally-
human or the common religious element in all Christian groups, is a
product of the Enlightenment and of the religious and philosophical
development following upon it. In the Enlightenment [began the
process of] abstracting from dogmas, religious practices, churches,
and systems of government, all of which were deemed to be historical
accidents; and the 'idea,' the 'spirit,' or the 'essence' of Christianity
was sought in a purely psychical-spiritual power or even in an
essentially practical-ethical doctrine. From the historical existence of
the churches there was extracted the universal and general, which
were found in the realm of the personal-spiritual or of the universal-
humanitarian; and Jesus was believed to be the real bearer of this
humanitarianism, as opposed to the churches with their dogmas. Thus
there arose a Jesus-religion apart from the churches and dogmas, in
the place of a Christ-religion that was either of a sacramental and
priestly or of a chiliastic and conventicle type. Such Jesus-religion

may have been and may still be a necessity for modern spiritual life. But it is a considerable hindrance to the understanding of the historical and very concrete Christian social philosophy, as well as to any practical treatment of contemporary social problems to the extent that they are bound up with or touch upon religious problems. For, when considered as the generic concept and quintessence of the historical forms of life of the Christian churches, this new, universal 'Christianity,' existing apart from church and dogma, is a purely private or individual religion. It is the modern personal, individualistic religiosity, which corresponds on the whole to modern individualism. It approaches social problems with merely private charity or with very general humanitarian ideals of pacifism, philanthropy, justice, progress, and the dignity and rights of man. As a result, understanding is lost not only for the old Christian social philosophy but also, especially, for the concrete social significance and productive power of religion as such.

When religious organizations were superseded and the area of personal sentiment was broadened to include philanthropy and humanitarianism, the capacity and sense for organizational tasks were lost altogether. Any kind of definite Christian social philosophy, which is, after all, conceivable only in connection with the churches, is lacking. On the other hand, the apparent possession of general social ideals, which are presumably attained quickly through the avenues of personal disposition and assertion of the will, leads to underestimation of quite concrete doctrines of society on modern grounds. We are acquainted with these difficulties from the innumerable discussions of Christian organizations and congresses, and from the struggle of strictly realistic modern sociology with Christian idealism and utopianism. Whether and how these difficulties can be avoided is not the question we have to deal with at this point. It need only be emphasized, as a basic tenet, that the problem of a Christian social philosophy is altogether different according to whether one is thinking in this connection of the powerful and efficacious historic social philosophies of the historic churches, or of one of the social theories deriving from the modern Christian mentality for the solution of contemporary problems.

Owing to the general origin of the former types of social philosophy in Christian antiquity, and to their consequently close similarity, one can indeed speak in a certain generic sense of a social philosophy of Christianity. It is then necessary to say, however, that the expression is understood generically. It it is thought possible, though, to resolve or help resolve modern social problems in terms of the modern

Christian mentality, it must be recognized that a social theory of Christianity in this sense just does not exist but would first have to be created, even though what was understood thereby was nothing more than fixed, general influences of the Christian ideal on the shaping of society. In any case, there is no standard Christian social theory existing by itself, whose essence springs from Christian religiousness. The notion that such a theory exists is a frequent and extremely misleading error, and must be eliminated at the very beginning from any approach to our theme. Moreover, if one takes into account the arguments adduced in connection with the previous point, it is clear from the very outset that not only does such a theory not exist, but also that it could not possibly exist. All the social teachings of a religious system which deal with the secular world must be strongly conditioned by this world, and particularly by its historical vicissitudes and modifications. By their very nature these social teachings represent a compromise, and as such they are subject to changes with respect to both of their constitutive elements, provided that these elements do not so far diverge as to become incapable of re-association. A social philosophy of Christianity exists only as a historically given and historically conditioned doctrine of the great, historic church-bodies, in which the solutions arrived at in Christian antiquity are continued, altered, and adapted to new situations. There is, however, no Christian social philsophy in the form of a uniform emanation from 'Christianity-in-itself,' which is in any case difficult to define.

It follows that the social philosophy of the Christian churches is Christian natural law, which is applied now more conservatively, now more radically. The variation in its application is rendered possible by the distinction between two sorts of natural law. One is an absolute, primordial natural law of Paradise, which does not take sin into account and which envisages the possibility of continual development apart from the concept of the Fall. The other is a relative natural law which, presupposing the Fall, restrains and heals sin by means of rationally ordered organizations of coercion. In the former, freedom, equality, and brotherhood are established under the dominion of the divine spirit of love; in the latter there is the organization of force, law, coercion, power, property, defensive war either permitted or enjoined, the secular state, and the fixed social order. In contemporary societal life these last-mentioned institutions, springing from reason or natural law, prevail; but they are under the supervision and control of the church, which prevents too great a gulf between the absolute and relative natural laws, and succeeds, by means of confessional and pastoral counsel, in steering a path between contradictions and difficulties. It is quite clear that in this way the church and the world of religious conceptions achieve a very great mobility and adaptability, now to the conservative institutions of authority, now to reformatory movements for freedom; now to the power of property, now to the needs of those who possess nothing. In the past, the churches of all confessions have made the richest and most diversified applications of natural law; they continue to do so today.

Only the Byzantine church and its descendants effected a radically conservative union with the powers that be; and through the peculiar circumstances of Eastern Europe they later became simply preservers and saviors of the national vitality, identical in each instance with the existing state. By contrast, that which is peculiarly Christian in these communions has been preserved in a monasticism much less ecclesiasticized than its Western counterpart, so that in these areas monasticism has become the bearer of the truly radical Christian natural law of communism and of love. Since education and the cure of souls are in the hands of monasticism, Slavic Christianity, in spite of its total absorption of the church into the state, has preserved in monasticism the necessarily social-revolutionary ideal of absolute brotherhood, unexpectedly introducing forms of radical brotherliness into the most secular affairs and manners of society—a contradiction that has often astonished Western readers of the great Russian novelists, and that is, in reality, only another form of the oscillation between radicalism and conservatism often to be observed also in the West. But since the East lacks the Latin foundations of the West, all this does not assume the nomenclature of Christian natural law, and the analogy is concealed beneath strange terminologies.

If, after these preliminary remarks, we proceed more directly to our subject, leaving aside the question of the East, the differences among the various denominational bodes in the formation and administration of this Christian and rational natural law are, of course, revealed as altogether extraordinary. But before we can enter into these differences, we must take cognizance of an even more general difference. Only when this distinction has been clearly presented can we go to the social philosophies of the great church-bodies. The expression 'churches' does not mean—or can mean only in a very loose sense—the form of religious organizations. One cannot speak of a Muslim, of a Buddhist, or even of a Chinese church; only perhaps a Jewish or Christian church, which must always be conceived concretely in its numerous modifications and divisions. The word 'church', or *ecclesia*, itself is derived from the late-Judaic sacerdotal church of the religiously organized community of God, which found its basis in divine pledges of salvation and incorporated the populace without exception by means of circumcision. The church is an institution of salvation, a work of God and not humans, a miraculous establishment endowed with divine truths and powers of salvation that is not produced and constituted by its members. On the contrary, the church itself brings forth its members. Besides those sanctified by it, the church simultaneously embraces without further ado their entire posterity. It bestows an indelible character. The church as institution resembles an imposed condition that one is born into, not a contract through which one acquires property or binds oneself to others. The late Jewish church with its prototypes of the Christian sacraments was already something of this kind, though founded at the same time on blood-relationship. The church appeared in the full sense only with the Christian fellowship of God's children, freed from ties of blood and ancestry, refounded by Christ, and transplanted by him into the realm of the spirit. For that reason the institutionalization of Christianity, its sacramental character, and its permanent, constantly creative miracle of grace were much more strongly emphasized than previously; and became even more decisive, mysterious, and ritualistic through their sacramental character, which was absorbed from the mystery cults of late antiquity—namely, through the miracle of sacred, wonder-working, and regenerative ceremonies that implant the worshipper in Christ.

But not all Christian forms of community follow this church-type. For that reason I have been careful to speak of churches and sects. Thus, we come to a further important point that is crucial for social philosophy. The organizational type of the church, as described above, corresponds to the Christian conception of grace as divine initiative involving the establishment, election, and preparation of 'my people'. This type is the anticipation of final eschatological redemption, and its relocation in the redemption completed through the work of Christ and in the establishment and endowment of the church that were accomplished by Christ. For that very reason the idea of the forgiveness of sins in principle and of the objective holiness of all church members, even amid personal sinfulness, comes to the fore; while the idea of subjective perfection, strict conformity to the norm, and the real decision coming only at the return of Christ and his judgement, recedes into the background. The church depersonalizes to a certain extent, substituting for personal action an objective sanctification and salvation on the basis of belonging to the institution with its saving powers.

Yet the idea of personal responsibility and sanctification, as well as that of the impending ultimate eschatological decision, persists—and forms the other pole of the Christian ideal. From this pole proceed communal forms that rest on the principle of a mature, free, conscious decision by the adult individual, on the conscious union of those intent upon the service of God, on the constant control of faith and morals, and on the expectation of the deliverance yet to come. As grace was decisive at the other pole, achievement is at this one. Sacred law is more important than the sacrament, and to look forward to the coming kingdom of God is more meaningful than to look back on the founding of the church. The one pole is institution; the other is association. It is customary to be born into the former; in the latter one voluntarily joins and takes his vow. The one has sacraments of penance and the forgiveness of sins; the other congregational discipline and expulsion of the unworthy. The one allows for compromise with the world and with sin; the other makes for sharp opposition to the world and for a congregation of the subjectively sanctified. If one desires a name for the second type, only that of 'sect' offers itself— although it became common in this sense only later, after the Reformation and the emergence of sectarianism from the disintegrating church in the late Middle Ages.

The word 'heresy' (*hairesis*), that is, personally chosen association instead of submission and resignation to authority and institution, has a similar meaning, though it was applied chiefly to the willful choice of illegitimate dogmas. Following the appearance of holiness-associations, the Latin translation *secta* became more and more the expression for the phenomenon in question. Terminology and a realization of the situation actually at hand were late in coming. But the event itself is old. One might wonder whether the primitive Christian congregation, and in any case the Jewish-Christian church, did not closely approach the sectarian type. Many Gnostic-ascetic congregations belong to this category. With Montanism, that is, with the resurgence of the old spirit of holiness and the belief in the Second Coming, and with the controversy over the sacrament of penance and over the readmission or exclusion of the 'lapsed' (those who had compromised with the world), the inner opposition clearly came into the open. Monasticism found one of its motives in this opposition, and at the same time permitted that motive to be ecclesiastically neutralized. The great movement against the church-type began with the Waldensians, Franciscans, Wycliffites, and Hussites, and has continued to take on new forms down to our own times, finding better opportunities for development on the soil of the Protestant churches than on that of Catholicism, in which the religious orders have been able to arrest these tendencies again and again.

Decisive for our present context, however, is the fact that social philosophy on the soil of the church-type institution is altogether different from what it is in that of the sect-type. Basically, social philosophy as a finished theory is to be found only among the churches; for only the churches are interested in learning and its power to help rule the world. The scholarly interest of the churches, as manifested in ecclesiastical philosophy and theology, is in itself part of their relative worldliness and increases constantly together with this worldliness. Above all, however, the basic tendencies of the church and the sect are opposed. The churches seek a compromise with the world and can find it, to a great extent, with their conception of grace and of the forgiveness of sin. Therefore, they can safely acknowledge the secular organizations of relative natural law and accommodate themselves by that means to continuing labor in a continuing world. In their whole conception of institution, grace, and authority, they are in themselves conservative, perhaps more conservative than anything in the world except the Indian caste system. But the churches are also conservative in relation to the secular organizations in state and society. In general they have a natural affinity for the authority of the state and for the stability of hereditary societal structure, without being bound thereby.

The sect-type, on the other hand, focuses on constant spiritual renewal and revolution, on revolutionary opposition to the world and expectation of the end of the world, on freedom and responsibility, on equality and brotherhood. In the West, however, the sects are so implicated in the general theological and philosophical terminology, and in the formulation of ideas, that they too avail themselves of the terminology of Christian natural law. They have taken, in fact, a not inconsiderable part in spinning out these theories. But what the sects represent is the absolute natural law of the original condition of man and not the relative natural law of compromise with the state of sin.

> When Adam delved, and Eve span
> Where was then the gentleman?

Moreover, their eschatological belief is inclined more toward utopias, revolutions, imminent deliverances, and the reshaping of the world. For that reason the theologians of the Peasant Wars closely linked gospel and natural law. And where such radical applications are lacking, we are nevertheless likely to find inclination toward democracy, toward a state based on contract and association, and toward freedom and equality as natural human rights; all of which are also divine rights of the gospel.

The sturdy variety of later Calvinism or Puritanism, filled with sectarian motives of sanctification, has in this respect left the strongest mark on history. Even today the so-called sects are almost everywhere the bearers of democratic sentiments. To this last point must be added the effect of the duress exerted by the national churches, with which the sects at first had to contend everywhere. They found themselves in a situation similar to that of the Jews, who also had to put their stake in liberalism and democracy. Thus one can understand the union of the rigorous and temperate Puritan and sectarian spirit, which was mixed with a hundred other motives, with modern movements for freedom and progress, although this sectarian spirit was coupled simultaneously with distrust of secular culture in general and of 'unbelieving' modern culture in particular. But given the orientation of this type toward initiative, responsibility, and achievement, one can also understand its aversion for modern socialism and the possibility of its coming to terms with the modern business and industrial spirit, provided this spirit is compensated for by extensive charitable activity and willingness to sacrifice. The consequences, Pharisaism and certain similarities to Judaism in general, are readily understandable. Here, basically, law prevails over grace. (At Trinity Church in Boston I once heard a guest sermon by the Anglican Primate of Canterbury on the two brothers in the parable of the prodigal son. What the churchman expounded to his American audience was essentially what has been set forth above, though he naturally employed an altogether different 'spiritual' language.)

But the forms of community that have sprung from the Christian ideal are not exhausted by the enumeration of church and sect. If the former corresponds to the objective element of grace and the latter to the element of subjective, ethical holiness within the Christian ideal, then this ideal contains in addition an element of immediate conviction and feeling that cannot be entirely satisfied by church and sect, bound as these are to historical authorities and technical organizations. This third element seeks to express itself above all with the aid of pantheistic theories. To transcend everything historical and external, 'no longer to know Christ after the flesh,' to live and find blessedness immediately in Christ and in God: this impulse was present from the beginning. It attained its independence in association with Oriental-Gnostic and Greek-speculative mysticism; and gave rise to special circles, both inside and outside the church, which still lack a proper name but which nevertheless have a character all their own. These groups were strictly personal communities of mind and spirit, which formed small circles, joined by means of correspondence and social contact, that radiated into wider circles solely through the influence of Scripture. In part these interests found fulfilment in the cloisters and their environs; in part they endured as an ingredient in Oriental-Gnostic, secret religions as in those of the Paulicians and Albigensians; in part they were ecclesiasticized and became conventicles within the church, such as the centers of medieval mysticism attached to the cloisters; and in part they led to definite heresies, such as the Spiritual Franciscans' proclamation of the Third Age of the Spirit. Their great period came about with the emancipation of the individual in the late Middle Ages and with the formation of congregations through the invention of printing, when spiritual communities could be created, to a great extent, without any external organization or with the requirement only of a minimal, quite personal, and loose organizational core. Again and again, however, the general spiritual current flowed into special conventicles and reformers, as perhaps into the congregations of the Friends and the spiritualist Baptists.

Out of influences of this kind on modern philosophy and the philosophy of religion—influences not as yet sufficiently expored—the character of modern religiosity or spiritualized Christianity was shaped. Church, sect, the miracle of a finished salvation, and eschatological tension are all lacking; but the faithful enjoy unmediated, personal oneness with God, inwardness, and a union purely of the soul and the spirit. In is plain that, on the whole, a social philosophy is not possible here; and that, generally speaking, religious inwardness keeps aloof from all social and political problems and material tasks. If the religious community itself is not organized and does not in the interest of unity and immediacy as well as of freedom from the world and externals, come to terms with the decisive problem for any organization—namely that of government—then this aloofness will be all the more evident in its attitude toward the problems of society and of secular organizations. The mystical community of souls is a vital spiritual power; but in all social matters it is helpless and indifferent, if not hostile and antagonistic. The only attempt in this direction was the 'holy experiment' of the Quaker state of Pennsylvania, the religious commonwealth of tolerance and inwardness; but even this attempt was a compromise and was soon shattered by the hardships of life, that is, by the Indian Wars fanned by the French and the English. Since this type of Christianity has grown ever stronger in the age of books and since it alone has proved to be somewhat compatible with modern knowledge, the social-constructive will of contemporary Christianity has become extremely weak among the educated. In fact, it has almost disappeared.

Regardless of whether Christianity of this kind occurs in its more theistic-voluntaristic aspect, as in Kierkegaard and his followers, or in its more pantheistic-monistic form, as in Schleiermacher, Hegel, and Emerson, it either keeps entirely aloof from world and society or refrains from meddling in their management. Instead, it accompanies them as no more than a pervasive melody filling the inner life.

In this way one can account for the social indifference and unproductiveness of modern Christianity, which run deep in both churchly and sectarian circles; hence the disjunction of the inner and the outer worlds. Meanwhile the old social philosophy of the churches has been forgotten to the point that it can no longer be understood. It has to be rediscovered like Nineveh and Babylon, although it can be seen living today in the Catholic Church and in the churches of Puritanism, as well as in certain circles of provincial, small-town Lutheranism. But precisely for this reason, these churches are not understood by the contemporary religion of culture and inner feeling. The latter prefers to pick out the mystical-spiritualistic elements in the whole history of the Christian religion, the mysticism of Paul and John, of Augustine and the Greek fathers, of Eckhart and Sebastian Franck. And it even gains access to Luther through this avenue, after he had remained inaccessible to it from other directions.

There are always special motifs and instances of the Christian ideal and its thousandfold intricacies and intermixtures in the historical process. All these Christian elements are being reduced here, either radically or approximately, to the three forms of religious association we have described. This procedure is quite understandable. For Christianity is a complex phenomenon that is never universally realized and that can never be organized in its entire breadth. The situation is quite the same with respect to other spiritual forces in the world. One need only think, for example, of the presentation of antiquity in modern education!

Which of the three types of religious association steps to the fore at any particular moment depends, of course, not merely on a theoretically or psychologically grounded preference for this or that manifestation of the Christian ideal, but also, and pre-eminently, on the compatibility of one prevailing type with the more general tendencies and needs of the times. Disintegrating antiquity stood in need of the church-type and in it found the substitute for the whole idea and organization of the universal society (*oikoumenē*), for the emperor cult, and for attempts at moral renewal. The church was the saving ark into which antiquity entered with all its cultural possessions; and which, after the worst of the deluge, landed on the mountain of the Byzantine empire. The world of new peoples in the West likewise required the church-type as a comprehensive authority, as the fountain of spiritual culture, the educational medium for civilization, learning, and administration, and as support for the underdeveloped apparatus of sovereignty. In this setting the church no longer stood for deliverance from the world and the recovery of moral strength; instead, it became an educational instrument for the spread of culture and the transmitter of the traditions of antiquity. It was harbinger and shaper of the great new cultures in the West, which have been flowing into the world since the fifteenth century, away from the narrowness and manifold spiritual dependency of the Middle Ages. It laid the foundation for European intellectual and political world-dominance, which has lasted to the present day; and provided the basis for its American colonies, which have since become more than independent.

The ripening individualism of the late Middle Ages, its social crises and the development of its towns and trades were fruitful soil for sectarianism, whose radical ideas about natural law have reverberated in every revolution down to our own day. In these upheavals the church, no longer equal to the social and political conditions, went to pieces. But in the churches of the Reformation and in the Catholicism of the Counter-Reformation the church-type re-asserted itself—this time in league with the absolutism that founded the modern state— and created strong churches in Lutheranism, Calvinism, Anglicanism, and Tridentine Catholicism. These churches, in turn, revitalized the ancient and medieval Christian social philosophy and adjusted it to existing circumstances. The revolutionary uprisings against absolutism, however, turned against the new state-church, too, and against the church-type in general. Calvinism, which originally was strictly authoritarian and conservative, took a radical turn in the religious and civil wars of Western Europe; following its initially involuntary separation from the state, it succumbed to the inroads of the idea of religious association and of sectarian conceptions of holiness. With the English revolution there began a triumphant revival of the sect-type of all kinds. In the spheres in which there was now a 'separation of church and state' as a matter of principle, this revival, which continues to the present day, has in many respects wiped out the general distinction between church and sect-type.

Thus a matured Europe began its emancipation from the tutelage and rule of the church. Now that the church had fulfilled its function in this respect, it found itself obliged to retire before a powerful, independent evolution of a more secular culture and of an independent national development in political and social matters. Under these circumstances religion fell back upon philsophical and speculative problems, ethical views, and inwardness of feeling. It began to struggle with a new philsophy and adapt itself to it. This, then, was the time for the break-through and modernization of mystical-religious conception. The Cambridge Platonists, Shaftesbury, Malebranche, Fénelon, the Jansenists, Geulincx, and Spinoza; then Leibniz, Lessing, Hamann, and Herder; and finally Schleiermacher, the Romantics, Schelling, and Hegel—all contributed splendid ideas, formulas, and dogmas to this development. At the same time the political and social sphere was completely cut off from religion and forced to find support in modern theories. It is quite understandable that today one finds the roots of modern philosophy and religion in Meister Eckhart, who was interpreted by minds advancing the perspective of his own time as simply a variation on scholasticsm, as a person of singular tastes not entirely free from heresy.

Next to the mystical-spiritual Christianity of books and public opinion there stands a Christianity no less disengaged from the church and characterized by a purely intellectual moralism, as in Kant. This moralism consciously dissolved the church and the kingdom of God into the universal community of virtue, making a revived Stoic natural law the foundation for this community. In doing this, it merely perfected and ennobled the Deism that sprang from these very conflicts. But from all these thinkers and poets there emerged what the world possesses today in the way of religion, idealism, morals, and belief—except for the masses in the rural and lower-middle-class groups, which continue to live under the influence of the old ecclesiastical and sectarian conceptions. The theologians of the churches, however, find themselves in great straits between these two worlds. For the present they have lost all reliable sense of direction in matters in religious speculation as well as of social ethics.

At this point it is not possible to enter into details.[1] Only the essential point can be dealt with here, and that is the following proposition. Only in the so-called Middle Ages was there ever a real social philosophy of Christianity, of which the social philosophies of the still orthodox denominational churches of the sixteenth and seventeenth centuries are copies, though altered and adapted to fit a new situation. The ancient church, or Christian antiquity, knew and needed something of this kind [of philosophy] only in the most general outlines. It had to achieve a positive relationship to the state, and to legal and property relationships in society. It had to enlarge its own organizational structure in such a way that it could find room in that

society and achieve the most pressing moral reforms. In addition, the
initiative in these matters did not lie with the church but with the
state, with an overwhelmingly powerful society representing an
extremely old culture, and with the social philosophy of antiquity.
No one had thought as yet that this situation might be changed, that
Rome and its empire might fall before the end of the world. Here lies
the difference between an Augustine and an Orosius. Even after an
agreement had been reached with the state, it was only a matter of the
latter helping with the Christianization of society while continuing to
stand independently alongside the church, which itself was looking for
the heavenly Jerusalem. Not until the West entered the Middle Ages
did the church assume a leading and educative role, which the
weakness of the state and the immaturity of the agrarian feudal society
of the period yielded to the church. Only in this position did the
church fully work out its social philosophy, in terms of a Christian
natural law of the basically hereditary class structure. The principles
of this natural law consisted of the following: the assurance of the
food supply; the elimination, as far as possible, of the element of risk;
mutual solidarity and aid; ethical advice to the civil power from the
ecclesiastical power, and outright control by the latter in spiritual
matters; the safeguarding of all individualism under the protection of
supra-individual associations; the alleviation of the remaining injuries
by means of charity, with the monasteries serving as principle
administrants; and, finally, the international unions of the Christian
family of nations under the supreme direction of the church, which
would countenance only 'just war,' that is, war of a defensive nature,
private feuds being extinguished by the ecclesiastical Peace of God.

In the sphere of trade, which principally served as a supplement to
the agrarian economy, the 'just price' was to prevail; the guild
organization of urban industry was meant to temper and relieve the
struggle for existence by means of corporations and protective zones.
Bondsmen and dependents had to be recognized and protected in
their human and familial rights. In addition, they had to be
patriarchally supported by the lord. This system was the general
outgrowth of ecclesiastical, ancient social-philosophical, and
Germanic legal conceptions, and of the contemporary economic needs.
It suited the conditions of a period that did not suffer from
overpopulation and that was deficient in means of communication.
To what extent it was carried out in practice is another question. In
any case, it is a magnificent, meaningful system suited to the
requirements of the situation. The social-philosophical systems of
orthodox Lutheranism and of Calvinism are closely related to it. They

simply reflect the changed position of the church in its adaptation to the developing absolutistic, bureaucratic state. Primary among their precepts is the sanctity of public office as the representative of God and of his natural law. Through this precept, the basic Christian concern for the stability and peace of society was to be served. The position of Calvinism differs in this regard, as a consequence of its more limited submission to the authority of an officialdom numbering kings as well as republican oligarchs in its ranks—[a consequence] risen out of the historical process; that is, through providence. Calvinism also differs as a consequence of its uncompromising demand for the observance of the divine and natural moral law. Accordingly, that faith is in possession of a strong, forward-driving element which later facilitated its union with modern political, economic, and social developments, and even lent them an additional impetus of Calvinist energy.

In this respect perhaps one can also speak of a second great and universal type of Christian social philosophy, that of Neo-Calvinism, which comes to terms with democracy, capitalism, and the separation of church and state. Dutch, English, and American Calvinism are subsumed under this type, as are, in part, also the Calvinism of Switzerland and the Rhineland. In this development the Christian element is of course not decisive. Even in the Middle Ages its role had already been a merely co-operative one, by no means exclusively determinative. Instead, it was the situation of the modern world, the character of the peoples involved, or their social-economic conditions that was crucial. The difference is that in Neo-Calvinism there is more of realistic compromise and intuitive fusion than of well-reasoned theory. Still, there is a closely-bound conceptual unity here of the dignity of humanity, human rights, universal perspectives, democracy, tolerance, independent religious conviction, freedom of economic activity, responsibility for charitable assistance and missions, humaneness and anti-militarism, theological positivism, and the obligation to proselytize. The duration of this system for 150 years has been portrayed, somewhat eulogistically, by James Bogre in his book, *Modern Democracies*.

Whether this latter system, which undoubtedly has historic significance and efficacy, is in the long run comparable in effectiveness and comprehensiveness with the medieval-feudal-patriarchal system, is indeed more than questionable. Even in its homelands it already stands in a new social and political complex into which it no longer fits, and with which it can come to terms only by a certain *tour de force* and auto-suggestion, which frequently give the impression of hypocrisy and cant. For what is decisive for every Christian social philosophy today is the fact that in the process of outgrowing the Middle Ages the West (with its imperialism, its capitalism, and its enormous population increase), has created conditions that, because of the tremendous tensions and gigantic forces involved, can no longer be mastered by classical or Christian social philosophy, nor by a combination of both of these. The logic of the purely secular power-state, which stands opposed in its inmost essence to all Christian conceptions, has, since Machiavelli, attained an independence that is much disavowed in theory but is constantly augmented in practice. Similarly capitalism, centralized production on a grand scale, with a daring freedom of movement that draws everything into its centers of power, is the most complete antithesis to that peace, quiet, compactness, stability, and independence of personality that are the prerequisites for the nurture of Christian virtues—apart from any question of the practical realization of these virtues—and for the possibility of Christian brotherly love.

More than anything else, however, the staggering increase in population, which is connected with all these phenomena both as cause and consequence, has rendered impossible every traditional (feudal) ideal of social strata clearly integrated into a relatively constant and ordered whole. This increase in population has replaced station with class, and the balanced structure of society with free competition and class struggle. Under these circumstances, the whole range of Christian sentiment and the work of reconciliation and reunion emanating from it can thrive only with great difficulty. Closely associated with all these developments is that proud, progressive, titanic spirit so characteristic of modern Europeanism and Americanism. ('Euramerica' is the term used by some contemporary East Asian observers.) This spirit is bent on fashioning and shaping everything by its own power and intelligence. It would conquer and harness nature through a person's work and intellect. It puts unlimited faith in the miracle of its industrial and social-organizational techniques. In line with what Bacon claimed long ago, it aims to substitute the kingdom of humanity for the kingdom of God. 'Knowledge is power,' and modern science can do everything. This modern spirit is the staggering culmination of ancient rationalism. It may have absorbed the Christian notion of infinity and the Christian concept of the life of the soul, but it nevertheless forms a complete antithesis to the basic stance of the Christian. Thus it is quite natural that religion has taken refuge in mysticism and sentimentalism. For religion does not know what to do with such a society.

All these changes constitute the ripening natural development of the West, which has been educated by Christianity and antiquity and has achieved its own strength and creativity. Catholic thinkers and social philosophers may look on the Renaissance as Europe's fall into sin and see salvation in a return to the feudal-Christian social philosophy of the Middle Ages. Artistic and religious natures may bewail mechanization and rationalization and long for a return to nature, as Rousseau had prophetically done. But in the face of the throngs of Europe's population and the contemporary world-economic situation, such a return is impossible. Naturally, grievous political and social catastrophes are conceivable, so is a return to an earlier agrarian economy as a consequence of these catastrophes. Many regard the final consequences of the World War as being of this sort, and look on Russian Communism as the involuntary return to the agrarian state and feudalism. But these notions are only surmises and possibilities that a still vigorous and even undiminished zest for life contravenes. In any case, all these notions have nothing to do with Christianity and spiritual recovery. A return would be the result of elemental social catastrophes and of the starvation of millions. The only thing that will counteract such perils will be the clear-sighted and concrete awareness of statesmen and political and industrial leaders (which has been urged, for example, by H. G. Wells in his *Outline of History* and by Professor Keynes in his highly praiseworthy works), the return to recognition of solidarity among modern nations, the introduction of a planned economy of world-wide scope, the surrender of exaggerated nationalism, and suitable social reforms among all peoples. The only measures that can be of assistance here are a completely new orientation of consciousness to the situation, a scientific sociological understanding of the world and its peoples, practical co-operation among the businessmen of the world, and the creation of a public opinion cognizant of the danger and its remedies.

Not much is to be expected directly from a Christian social philosophy. Nor, for that matter, is much to be expected from a Christian social theology or social ethic, even if one could and would progress, with a generally and publicly effective program, beyond the doctrines adopted from antiquity to an independent development of the social consequences of the Christian ideal. The whole of religious life is itself in a major crisis. The Catholicism of the ancient church, which was transformed into medieval-papal religion, constituted the formative environment and the spiritual backbone of the early West. When Catholicism reached maturity in the late Middle Ages, it fragmented into a large number of denominational churches. From

232

Religion in History

these churches there eventually arose everywhere a more or less supra-
denominational religiosity. Its Christian content and basic character
are, on the whole, unquestionable. But it faces a most difficult
encounter with a completely new science peculiar to the West, a
science that in spite of hasty judgements and errors is still a force for
truth. But above all it stands in deep, inner antagonism to the
psychological import, assumptions, and effects of an enormously
burgeoning social, economic-technical, and political life. No healing
power is to be expected from the residue of social teaching of a new
religion weakened in this way.

Even so-called Christian socialism will not be able to cope with this
situation. For it is never to be inwardly reconciled with the whole
spiritual structure of contemporary socialism, the workers' movement
that presents itself as a plan for the redemption of the world through
thorough-going reform. The socialist movement strives for purely
worldly happiness and prosperity. It believes in a complete renewal of
the world, through the powers of an organizational rationalism alone.
It take part in, and even aggravates, modern Titanism—just as do the
captains of industry and the bureaucratic devisers of state-
organizations in the other camps. Moreover, the fact that this Titanism
is so prosaic, materialistic, and technical makes it doubly unfit for
fusion with the Christian reform movement. It attacks and hates
nothing so much as the churches. References to the gospel are
altogether external and are used simply for propaganda purposes. But
if one turns away from this modern socialism, whose world-redemptive
power has become, even for its own adherents, in many respects quite
questionable today, and if one repudiates its ideas, then Christian
socialism offers basically no organizational conceptions of its own for
molding society in general or modern society in particular. Christian
socialism is quite understandable among workers' pastors, but it is
still a rather one-sided orientation. After all, even neighboring
congregations will demand opposite solutions. These points do not
disqualify the claims of Christian socialism or its wholesome effects,
in some cases, on the total situation. But the transmutation of workers'
socialism into a Christian socialism and its new promise of the
salvation of the world and of the establishment of the kingdom of
God is a fantastic, dilettante notion, in comparison with which the
old Christian natural law is the very quintessence of wisdom. The
great problem of socialism that is inescapable for our generation,
namely, the control of unrestrained individual and national freedom
and the creation of a universal planned economy for the civilized
nations, simply cannot be solved by religious ideas. The problem is,

rather, a scientific and a practical-political one that only the deepest professional knowledge and superior political leadership can resolve.

This state of affairs is not strange or suprising. Basically, it is even illusory to believe that the older Christian social philosophy solved by religious means the problems presented to it in its time. It, too, was more theory than practice. The social regeneration of antiquity was only relatively successful and was based for the most part on the transformation of the declining Roman empire into the Byzantine bureaucratic state. The social order of the Middle Ages did not suppress savage feudal warfare. At bottom, it actually triumphed only in the city. It ended in the peasants' revolts and in the commercial states of early Italian capitalism. To the extent that medieval social teachings became practical realities and accomplished something significant, they stemmed by no means from religious conceptions alone but from the ancient Greek cultural heritage, the Roman art of government, Germanic law, and new conditions emerging with the times. The really significant contribution, in fact, was the relatively unified correlation of a system of life and thought, which entered the imagination and standards of the masses and created a common psychological atmosphere. Today, with our highly developed differentiation of all of life, it is indeed understandable that the religious forces and those of the political, economic, and social order have been separated from each other. The solution of the problems growing out of this situation calls for a completely secular and independent, infintely complex work of construction and reform that especially demands will-power and specialized knowledge. This is unavoidable, and should not surprise us. Enthusiasts, ideologists, and theoreticians must come to terms with this situation and find a purely sociological approach to the whole problem.

It remains true, of course, that such immense problems are not to be solved without moral renewal and deepening, without kindness and justice, without a sense of solidarity and a readiness for sacrifice, without a basically believing outlook on life and the world. In fact, this is the second great demand of the critical, historic hour in which Europe finds itself. But this task had best be kept separate from the first; and pursued with the aid of the available religious and ethical resources of the various denominations, groups, philosophies, and world-views that are being driven to rapprochement by conditions themselves. Ruthless self-deification and the drive for boundless self-assertion (under the guise of the leadership of the elite, the boldness of the entrepreneur, or the pride of nationality), must be curbed. Self-restraint, consideration for others, a feeling for the solidarity of nations, and respect for human rights, must be inculcated in people's minds; and the spirit of obligation to a more-than-human truth and justice must be aroused. That is task enough in itself, without any need for religion to embroil itself in dilettante social philosophy or amateur social ethics. The spirit it can thus awaken will then on its own redound to the benefit of social and political reconstruction, which in turn will have more and more occasion to call for such a spirit. Then, perhaps, unanticipated new syntheses will be possible. But in today's confusion, what counts is that we see our tasks and problems in their separateness and not complicate one with another. In every instance, we should do what our vocation, our talent, and our situation allow, always striving for renewed contact and renewed understanding. Otherwise the biblical myth of the Tower of Babel, the parallel of the Greek myth of the giants, may become the symbol of a European Titanism that has forgotten God: 'The winds of God blew and they were scattered abroad.'

Notes

1. For details I must refer to my book, *The Social Teaching of the Christian Churches*, 1913. The second edition is in reprint. Scholars will note that I now formulate my themes more cautiously, enlarge the general perspective, free the total interpretation still more from theological thinking, and approach a universal-historical mode of thought. With respect to the nature and intention of the latter, I call attention to my recently published book, *Der Historismus und seine Probleme*, of which the first volume is a fundamental treatment of these problems, and the second an attempt at a basic design of universal history. (The second volume was never published—Ed.)

PART THREE

Ernst Troeltsch and the Modern Spirit

15

The Essence of the
Modern Spirit

The analysis and synthesis of the synthesis of the essential spiritual content of an epoch is a task in which the critical fact-finding research of the historian and the constructive imagination of the philosopher meet; here the historian has to turn into a philosopher, the philosopher into a historian. For the historian it is the concluding climax of his scrutiny of the great structures of history. For the philosopher it is the basis and presupposition for his creation of norms and value-judgements according to which he must measure the actions of an epoch against itself. Such a task is imposed by every present that is at all complex, embracing various historic levels within itself. Now if it is much easier to solve this task in relation to a past epoch, whose perspectives have become transparent in retrospect, it is the more urgent with respect to a present such as our own, all difficulties and hesitations notwithstanding. Only in this way can we find the proper basis for our actions in relation to our own time. Where the conditions of life are simple, this self-reflection can without much hesitation have recourse to political and ethical ideals; the Hebrew prophets acted in this way. The alternative is to construct ideals of culture through speculation, purely on the basis of the concept and without reference to history; this was the course pursued by Plato and the Stoics, those great world-historic kinsmen of the prophets. Neither approach, however, is adequate for the complicated life of the white race today, where the most varied historical elements are interwoven.

When in the seventeenth century the modern way of thinking came to prevail over the medieval ecclesiastical outlook, it was considered possible to go back to the simple ideas of justice, morality, state, and society that are as old as the race. But every attempt to do this showed that what appeared to have been born with us was for the most part a product of our history; to restrict oneself to this arbitrary selection of ideas would be a violent narrowing and shortening of life. Thus it was precisely the system of 'natural truths and rights' that stimulated the study of historical evolution. Today every attempt at self-reflection and self-orientation is bound to conceive of our world primarily along purely historical lines—as a configuration brought about by certain definite historical forces, combining and fusing various levels into one. Only then can a relatively comprehensive construction based on certain fundamental ideas be attempted, which, upon completion, only can then be approached from the perspectives of ethics and cultural policy (*Kulturpolitik*).

Since the beginning of the modern age, therefore, the leading historians and philosophers have continued to analyze and reflect upon this task. If new aspects continued to push to the fore, this only indicates the extraordinary complexity of the situation. It also challenges us to synthesize ever anew the positive and valid results of these various analyses, and to pay attention to features and connections that previously may have been overlooked. There is an entire literature, pertaining to both philosophy of history and sociology, which deals with these matters. But the history of law and of civilization, of theology and of philosophy; the analyses of the problem which we find in all incisive thinkers; the poetic portrayals of life of a Stendhal, a Zola, or a Freytag—all these are working towards the solution of the problem. Nor should we forget the cultural criticism of Schopenhauer and Nietzsche: the former shook the West's faith in progress, which had previously been accepted as self-evident; the latter disjoined this very progress from all intellectualistic and rationalistic norms, thus raising the problem of norms in a very acute form. As life goes on, moreover, new symptoms, new means of interpretation emerge; and the work keeps going on, too.

The main elements constituting our present way of life are fairly clear in their general outlines. First among these elements is the civilization of ancient Greece and Rome, which has come down to us wrapped in the tradition of the Christian church. Its persistent thrusts from within this tradition have allowed it to develop into a decisive force in our language, art, institutions, ethics, and education. Today, however, its influence is obviously receding before the Nordic spirit and before what is properly the modern world.

The second basic element is Christianity, which has made the ethics and the redemptive religion of late antiquity an inseparable part of itself. But by creating a powerful new social institution, the church, and new ideological forces having to do with the metaphysics of the person, it went beyond them. By converting the Germanic peoples, Christianity brought these peoples into continuity with antiquity and colored their thinking and feeling for a millennium and a half. Christianity was always aware, moreover, that it needed to be supplemented if it were to guide civilization. Not only was the Graeco-Roman cultural heritage passed along in fact, its supplementary character and necessity were acknowledged even in principle. In every new phase of European history, the decisive factor was a new correlation of these two basic elements: antiquity and Christianity.

The third basic element is much more difficult to grasp because it nowhere developed independently; it is always bound up with the appropriation and assimilation of foreign elements. I refer here to the qualities and forces peculiar to the Germanic nations. To be sure, these nations were forced to forget their own early history and to supplant it with the Biblical and Graeco-Roman antiquities. But their peculiar spirit manifested itself again and again, and came increasingly to prevail in the sphere of law and in the forms of political and social organization. Traditional churchly Christianity was likewise given new foundations in Protestantism, which is experienced essentially along Germanic lines: Graeco-Roman classicism was confronted with an imaginative world of Nordic forms and sensitivities. (When I refer to this Germanic spirit, I am of course not thinking exclusively of the Germans but of the entire North-European and American world, including strong repercussions upon Christianity itself, which was able to emancipate itself from the Germanic influence only temporarily, during the Renaissance; the return to its own ancient traditions was a very partial one.)

The fourth basic element of the modern way of life, and the most important one, is the properly modern mentality itself, which has grown out of the inner developments of the Middle Ages, the Renaissance movement, and Protestantism. The way for this modern spirit was prepared by the culture of the late-medieval cities, of the Protestant territorial churches, and of the Catholic Counter-Reformation. It attained full independence as a result of the Enlightenment and the English, American, and French Revolutions.

All the decisive features of contemporary life have their root in the modern spirit. The positive or negative relationship of these modern elements to the traditional ones constitutes, together with the inner tensions and contradictions of the modern world of thought itself, the complicated content of contemporary life. In the spheres of state and law, society and economics, science and art, philosophy, ethics, and religion, we find now structures that have grown out of the old ones; they are ultimately only special forms of the same universally human qualities and drives that created the older forms. Yet these special forms show pronounced individuality and are of the greatest importance. To understand today's world is to understand this world of the modern spirit, enmeshed with the remaining powers of preceding epochs and with the new spiritual content which it has provided.

But in order thus to understand today's world, we have to understand its origins and its gradual growth. The modern world is an exceedingly complicated structure, even though enthusiasts of progress or conservative polemicists may portray it as a unity. While the former may wish to deck the modern spirit with flowery wreaths, like the head of a god, the latter may wish to crush it like a serpent's head. Yet the truth of the matter is that our modern world is full of inner contradictions and tensions. These are due to the fact that the modern world is the practical result of the most varied impulses and tendencies. Every attempt to represent it as a spiritual unity is in itself an attempt to forge and create this unity. Such attempts are never wholly successful; but if they gain a large following, they themselves constitute a new factor in modern intellectual life and influence its course. If one wants to understand the modern world, then one must break it down into its component parts and show how each of them has been given its modern shape, and how it, in turn, effects our total life, the spirit of the whole. Relatively unified syntheses only arise from the collaboration and interaction of these separate components, as cultural moods, programs, parties and intellectual movements. This is why the parts that are least rigid and definite, most fluid and mobile, namely, the parts that represent ethics, religion, and one's view of the world, are at the time the most variegated and mixed parts of the cultural atmosphere. In them the new and the old are most closely interwoven; hence the essence of the new will be recognized less clearly here than anywhere else. The hard and fast lines of principle lie in the practical and institutional side of life, in the political, social, and economic structures. The broad bases of opinion and feeling lie on the level of the semi-conscious and instinctive, in the forms of daily life and intercourse, and in the imagery of art that expresses and conveys the instinctive side of life even where there is a high degree of consciousness. No doubt, ideas are also involved in all this; but they have their origin in practical life, and the tendencies behind them never enter consciousness. Such ideas are quickly turned into forms and institutions that tend to keep life on this level.

We have to think in this connection of the logical needs of the various particular disciplines, which, though they too stem from general aspirations, have become bound to definite methods and tasks and thus represent an objective need—a synthesis that would be all-encompassing. But wherever great thinkers, beginning with Galileo, Hobbes, Descartes, Locke, and Spinoza, have tried to lift the driving forces to the level of consciousness and to make them the basis of an overall view; there we enter a strange subjective and personal realm. Their explanations are always more or less forced, based on a particular aspect that presses upon the attention of a particular thinker and from which he tries to deal with the rest. The history of modern philosophy is not the history of the modern spirit but the history of attempts to interpret and systematize it. Now these very attempts inject a new causality into the vast stream of modern life. The images conjured up by them dominate the imagination of large groups of people.

In seeking to understand the modern world we need to grasp its most characteristic and essential objective foundations. Only then are we in a position to throw light upon the mobile complex of world-views that forms a part of the veneer of culture and has the most manifold ties to tradition.

We are immediately, most strongly impressed by the rise and the ever increasing power of the state and the idea of the state. During the Middle Ages there was a multitude of authorities, with a supreme power above them that conditioned the inferior authorities, yet was also strongly conditioned by them. In addition, and superior to all this, there was the spiritual world-empire of the church. Since its dignitaries were part of the feudal structure, the church already shared in the exercise of authority. But in addition, all authorities were subordinated to the church as such, viewed in its entirety. The state, however, as the unitary and sovereign organization for exercising the will of the total community—we do not ask, for the present, who would exercise this sovereignty—was unknown to the Middle Ages. The idea of the sovereign state as the highest worldly power within and without is the product of a number of factors: the revival of the Roman idea of the state, the struggles of kings and emperors against the church, the example of the Norman empire of Frederick II, the succeeding Italian despotism, the unified administration of the German and Italian free cities, the revival of the classical theory of the state during the Renaissance, and the rise to power of the great European dynasties. Organized as a centralized power and supported by a modern military force, the state discovers the logic of the idea of power, which implies a thoroughgoing internal organization and a capacity for external defense that is accountable to no one. This essentially secular state emerged out of the struggle against the church, and yet had to acknowledge religion as a separate and co-ordinate power. This is a conception completely different from the classical idea of the state, which regarded the existence of the state as coinciding with the rule of law, as instituted by the gods or resulting from humanity's political instinct, where religion was recognized only as state religion. From its struggle with the church the modern state gained particularly clear and acute awareness of its own nature as a secular power. But coupled with this is the feeling that the state cannot and must not contain the fullness of human life.

From one point of view, the state is thus supreme and ultimate; from another, this is not so at all. Here lies the reason for the ambiguousness of the modern idea of the state. This ambiguousness in turn gives rise to totally divergent movements of thought. On the one hand, the sovereignty of the state expresses the principle of secularity. It is a supreme ethical value in human life—the focus of a common honor and the anti-egoistical concentration of the will upon common life-purposes. Within such a state there is really no room for a transcendent life-purpose, which is hardly allowed any longer to intrude into its sphere. To the advocates of a Christian brotherhood of humanity and of a world-church this kind of state appears—very understandably—to be a new heathenism. It is characteristic that the British, as a strictly Christian nation, instinctively transform this concept of the state into the Puritan Old Testament idea of a chosen people destined to bring religion and morality to all others.

Now, if the ethical aspects of the modern state express the principle of secularity, its juridical and administrative elements express the principle of rationalism. The state is a creation of the human intelligence, a construction of legislators and politicians who have thought up its constitutions and its laws, its technique and its organization, or else have grafted it upon the natural social structure that antedates the state. It functions like a huge insurance scheme that takes all eventualities into account. The supreme product of human art, intelligence, and foresight, it frees humanity from the elemental sense of being a mere toy of the great natural forces and drives for which the paltry powers of medieval society had been no match: only the resulting sufferings were relieved by ecclesiastical charity or monastic renunciation. The state replaces the irrational divine providence by a rational secular one.

But on the other hand, the modern state cannot forget that it had its origin in its emancipation from the church and its spiritual suzerainty. If it succeeded in shaking off this suzerainty, it also had to recognize the universal transcendental values and truths represented by this suzerainty, which it could relegate to their own sphere but which it could and would not replace by its own essence. Hence, the modern state is left with a profound sense of its inadequacy in the spiritual realm and of its limitation to external and secular matters. In the Anglo-Saxon world the state has learned to view matters in this light, largely under the influence of the ancient Germanic spirit of association and of the free churches, who had come into conflict with the state and whose Calvinism was modified by Anabaptist influence. This attitude was also brought to the Continent by the older liberalism.

But here it was sometimes felt that free rein was being given to unpredictable powers or that the state itself was being spiritually impoverished. Where this was the case, or even where the state took cognizance of the tension resulting fro the co-existence of ultimate purposes, the attempt was made to incorporate ethos and religion in their entirety into the state, and to establish the latter not only as the organization of sovereign power but also as the totality of all culture and reason. Such attempts were faciliated by the conditioning of the Lutheran state-churches and by the Catholic practice of treating all matters pertaining to one's view of the world as public concerns. The state thus rationalizes and secularizes itself, together with ethos and religion, until it becomes objective 'reason', the organization of all rational values in general. This transformation has fully taken place, up to now, only in theory—the Hegelian theory and that of the socialists. But often enough, public practice also strongly tends in this direction, as when education is brought under the control of the state. Thereby the state, which only appeared to have reached a clear insight into its nature and limitations, is drawn back into all the struggles and tensions of the intellectual world. If it seemed at first merely to radiate secularity and rationality in broad beams, it now carries within itself the great problems that ever and again dissolve secularity and pure rationalism. Otherwise it must try to pull everything down to the level of its own secularity and rationality, that is, to the level of a dreary utilitarianism. The struggle of the state with a free culture that refuses to wear its rationalistic uniform again and again makes the latter conscious of its own irrational diversity and its dependence on the purely personal. Thus the great modern creation, the state, has provided an impetus in two directions: toward the thorough rationalization of existence up to the complete absorption of all rational culture in the state; and, conversely, toward the recognition of the majestic rights of the individual and the personal, the religious and the spiritual, with their many irrational powers.

This logical reconstruction of the modern conception of the state as characterized by power implies a certain indifference to the form in which the state is organized. The modern conception developed under absolutism with its military concepts of honor, but it survived in the democracies and semi-democracies of the subsequent period. Absolutism, with its rational organization of the state, its centralizing thrust, and its victorious struggle against the church, was the indispensable prerequisite and the point of departure for the formation of such an idea of the state. Absolutism fused the peoples into nations and imbued them with this feeling for the state. But by levelling the old social structure based on states, and by radiating a secular and rationalistic spirit, absolutism ended by pulverizing the peoples into individuals. Thus it provided the impetus for the ensuing demand that the individual should participate, in a rational and orderly fashion, in the determination of the will of the sovereign state.

A number of other forces contributed to the acceleration of this movement. First among these is the individualism of Protestant piety, which rests on a most profound metaphysical basis—even though its primary stance is one of obedience and devotion to the state. Wherever Calvinism dominated, which grew to maturity in its struggles with the secular governments and did not fail to be touched by Anabaptist influences, the banner of popular sovereignty was raised. The same ideas arose also within Lutheranism after it had been abandoned by the secularized state; and though they remained comparatively weak, they are yet by no means negligible. Even within Catholicism the Christian metaphysics of the person prevails, in the form of Christian democracy, over all theories of legitimacy and authority. Another force was the natural law of antiquity, which had been conserved in ethics and public law, of whatever confession, and which governed the official social science. Natural law now ceased to be Christian and, above all, to be Biblical; returning to its ancient traditions, it undertook to base it social constructions rationally on the foundation of the individual. In all this fermentation, finally, the spirit of free association that characterized ancient Germanic law comes into its own again, after it had been smothered by the church and absolutism with the formulas of Roman Law. Beginning in England it developed, in the name of self-government (*Selbstverwaltung*), an ever-expanding freedom of association. The final consequence of this trend is that even the state appears as no more than an all-embracing free association.

Modern democracy arises out of these manifold influences and their varying combinations, in which the preponderance varies with time and place. Side by side with the notion of sovereignty and its corollary, the *raison d'Etat*, democracy becomes the truly dominant power in the modern state and thus attains fundamental importance for the modern world in general. The American colonial states are its classical example. The British constitution reconciles it with monarchy. Its radical theoretical elaboration is found in the theories of the French Revolution and its numerous daughter revolutions. We observe its compromise with absolutism in the parliamentary, military monarchies. As a principle, democracy has triumphed and is even now in the process of conquering the last center of resistance, the temporal and spiritual absolutism of Czarist Russia.

The total effect of this development on the spiritual situation is a tremendous individualization of the feeling and thinking of modern man. The point of departure of social thinking is now the individual, not the collectivity. Traditional bonds and authorities have become less stringent. All institutions need to justify their existence and function before the judgement of the individual. There is, moreover, a reciprocal relationship between political individualism and all the other individualistic forces. Those who believe themselves in need of individualism for the sake of academic freedom or for ethical reasons turn to political individualism, which thus becomes the shelter for all other individualistic tendencies. Conversely, individualism may be carried from the political sphere into all other fields of human relationship. Nevertheless, this individualism originating in a variety of motives is by no means homogeneous, and its effects are extremely diverse.

If one tries to distinguish the main types, one may note a rationalistic individualism, derived from the de-christianized natural law, and an irrationalistic individualism, which stems from the need of freedom for religion and culture over against the omnipotence of the state. The first type is motivated by the general idea of the natural equality of individuals and by the demand for a rational organization of all the functions of the state, so as to actualize the life-goals of the individual through the state, wherever possible for the individual and through the individual. The second type is motivated by the presupposition of an irrational freedom and mobility of life, which must be protected against the omnipotent state and taught to unfold itself. Such an unfolding is possible only if the individuals are always able to control and regulate the power of the state in the interest of maintaining this freedom. The first type is democracy in the spirit of

Rousseau, which for the reasons mentioned does not recognize minority rights, and which has been carried to its logical end by the Social Democrats. The second is the Anglo-Saxon type of democracy, and the principle of the older liberalism. The two types are absolutely incompatible, and this is the reason Social Democracy has found it so difficult to establish itself on Anglo-Saxon soil.

Both types of democracy accept the traditonal idea of the state as the sovereign and supreme power. but to this common ideal they give very different interpretations. Egalitarian democracy makes of the state the bearer and executor of all essential values in life. All cultural life is here absorbed by the state, because only the state can guarantee the just participation of the individual in all cultural values. Since the state is here supposed to actualize the cultural program of every respective majority, it tumbles from one crisis to another. This rationalism of equality and the acceptance of a rationally organized state apparatus distinguishes modern democratic socialism from its Christian precursors. In contrast, liberal democracy is anxious to conserve the immutability of the constitution, which guarantees freedom. From this point of view, only the strictest, most formal constitutionalism safeguards this freedom. Yet, this liberal democracy expresses its appreciation of the state as a supreme value by permitting the idea of power to realize itself externally in an ever-expanding imperialism. This policy permits the development of the greatest internal differentiations and thus favors the most irrational diversity, which is made inconspicuous by the superficial equality of democratic forms of social behavior. Modern democratic development is a powerful and incisive movement, but it is neither unchallenged nor in itself uniform. Everywhere it combats the specific characteristics of the modern state, although it presupposes this state. It opposes its bureaucracy and the militarism that has given birth to the great modern states, to which even the most democratic nations are succumbing because of their imperialism. Democracy is divided into two radically diverse branches: one rationalistic and egalitarian, which derives everything from general principles; the other, irrational, giving full scope to the forces of inequality and trusting that this freedom will lead to a harmonious adjustment. Democracy is a characteristic feature of the modern spirit, but it is neither all-pervasive nor unequivocal. It is rather a mass of new problems, many of which are mere continuations of the older ones.

The economic development is just as significant as the political, since both are of fundamental importance in the modern world. To characterize it, we need one word: capitalism. We speak of capitalism here not only as a form of banking industry, but as a form of economic organization that also embraces agriculture and the trades. It has brought about a thorough reorganization of our class structure. The new opportunities of obtaining credit and investing money for interest affect the smallest household with its savings accounts and bank balances. Parallel to these practical developments, a new economic theory has evolved, a science unknown to the simpler conditions of antiquity and the Middle Ages, it provides a theoretical examination of the foundation of the economic processes and puts them in historical perspective. Then it proceeds to formulate complicated rational programs for the economies of whole nations and continents. We need not concern ourselves here with the still very controversial question of the origins of capitalism. We are concerned here only with its significance for the modern spirit.

The essence of capitalism is that the means of production (soil, machinery, or money) are geared to produce the maximum amount of goods at the maximum rate of turnover for a free and anonymous market. The impersonal abstraction 'capital,' in which the savings and investments of thousands of individuals may be involved, grows into a gigantic force in the hands of the respective entrepreneurs. This huge, all-consuming giant works with the property of unknown owners, for unknown buyers, motivated only by the calculation of profit and favorable sales opportunities. For this purpose, the organizers of the enterprise use the mechanical and technical sciences to an ever-increasing extent and achieve a degree of progress superior to all the advances of the past two thousand years. This progress is due partly to the advancement of natural science, partly to the system of free wage labor; and also to the infinite division of labor, which destroys the worker's sense of personal involvement with his product. Between the producer and the anonymous consumer stands the agent, the middle-man who needs the greatest possible flexibility, adaptability, and freedom.

These principles form the basis of the organization of modern economic life. They have made possible fabulous economic achievements and allow everyone who saves and invests to participate in the shower of gold pouring down upon the nations. The spiritual and moral consequences, however, are as vast and overwhelming as the material consequences. The first and general effect is a tremendous enhancement of economic ambition. For this reason, work is being done with breathtaking haste and intensity. All strength and energy is directed toward the maintenance of the miraculous edifice of capitalism, which is constantly threatened by crises and yet must show no cracks. There is a growing delight in comfort and luxury, a colossal practical materialism.

All this brings about an extraordinary intensification of the secularity of all interests, thoughts, and aspirations. Closely connected with this is an exultation in the power of humanity, which owes everything to its own achievement, and which has now developed an insurance-system out of capitalism in order to protect itself against all calculable damages. Still more important, however, is the tremendous rationalization of life through the constant calculation of profit, the rational and scientific methods of applied science, the rational art of the division of labor, the ascertainability of every value in definite exchange values and the reconstruction of our whole existence according to economic laws. Secularization, self-deification, and rationalism flow into every pore of our being through a thousand channels, and induce an optimism that considers all goals and wishes within reach—if only one's economic capacities are rationally developed. This optimism seems to accord with the optimism emanating from political individualism. Its effects, however, differ greatly from those of political individualism. While the latter exalts the person and its individuality, capitalism diminishes them. Its chief effects are de-personalizing.

Capitalism presupposes political and legal individualism, the freedom of the individual to choose and change his domicile, his right freely to dispose of his person. Without these, capitalism could not have come into being, and it accordingly seeks to maintain them to the extent that it finds them useful. But it is the fate of capitalism constantly to undo its own prerequisites. It recognizes the individual only as the entrepreneur or the hired hand. Both are subjected to the inexorable abstraction 'capitalism,' which spreads its impersonal spirit everywhere and recognizes as real persons only the bold *condottieri* of capitalism. Large industrial concerns become the centers of new dependencies, creating analogues to the slavery of antiquity and the serfdom of the Middle Ages, which lack, however, the personal elements of these older forms. Entire nations and states are kept in dependency by the powers of international finance. Economic individualism thus counteracts all the tendencies of the ideas of political individualism, as well as the very essence of the sovereignty of the state as an international power. It is not surprising that in the shadow of capitalism there arose the impersonal, fatalistic philosophy of history of Social Democracy, which conceives the proces of history as kept in motion by its own abstract necessities.

Capitalism is thus initially the agent of atomization and

individualization, though even the former process serves only the conglomeration of new dependent masses out of these social atoms, perhaps with a view to securing them as a reserve army. If it actually leads to individualism, this is only by way of reaction. It is certainly understandable that the working class, which has been taught by capitalism to be intelligent, embraces democracy, which it believes to be the only power able to save the integrity of the individual. In democracy the workers find the political means for the realization of their ideas concerning the life-purposes of the individual, through pressure upon the state. It is equally understandable, however, that these democratic workers, who have as yet nothing to conserve and who strive initially only for a share of the material goods, become addicted to egalitarian democracy and fight energetically against a liberalism whose freedom makes them the objects of capitalist exploitation. Capitalism's main effect, however, is an abstract, depersonalizing rationalism, coupled with the principle that might is right.

The effects of capitalism are accordingly also quite ambiguous. Capitalism is indeed indispensable to the functioning of the complicated, gigantic machinery of the modern state and culture. As an intellectual tendency it is closely connected with all the individualistic aspirations of modern humanity. Yet as a criterion of the modern spirit it is nothing less than unitary. On the one hand it represents modern man in his secularity and rationalism; on the other hand, it brings back forms of social dependence that once seemed to belong to the past, together with all the reactions that have ever been prompted by such dependence.

The forces described above are the basic pillars of our existence, the principles by which all our life and work are guided, whether we like it or not. The strongest spiritual forces emanate from them. To these we perhaps ought to add the evolution of the law, which is generally molded by these forces and which makes of them the fundamental forms of our daily life, even if forced to compromise in various ways with the traditional legality. The humanitarian transformation of criminal law, which supplants the idea of revenge more and more with concern for education and protection, deserves special emphasis. A parallel development is taking place in the field of social welfare. Here modern humanitarians look everywhere for the good in humanity; they seek to bring about the participation of every individual, at least in one area, in the good things of our common life; they seek to obtain recognition of the collective responsibility of society for all individuals; and thus they move further and further away from the ecclesiastical conception of charity and care of the poor. Other far-reaching effects of this new tendency upon the social structure should be mentioned here, such as the appreciation of the individual personality, even of women and children. We cannot go into the details here. We can only stress the universal modern ideal of humanity which is beginning to replace the community of faith as the highest social conception and to give a different coloring to the Christian conception of brotherly love.

Even the ideal of humanity, however, springs from various sources. It is in the first instance only the old idea of love of neighbor, but without the Christian pessimism with respect to sin and without restriction to the community of faith. Man himself is possessed of an inalienable goodness which is discovered and furthered by his fellow-man. A strong optimism, coupled with an equal respect for all individuals, loves and furthers man for the sake of a common human nature, for in it the divine lies concealed. The religious motivation, through the common call to fellowship with God, is replaced by the naturalistic motivation with its concept of a common human nature. The struggle with sin is replaced by the eliciting of the fundamental goodness which is present in everyone. The contrast between the pious and the impious, the good and the bad, the elect and the reprobate, is replaced by the hope of a union of all humanity in mutual, brotherly love. Thus the meaning of the ideal humanity is changed from charity to the natural endowment of the individual with universally human truths and impulses towards the good. Humanity becomes another term for the natural endowment of man with all the forces and drives of the natural system, from which a society can be organized that satisfies the individual and brings about the actualization of all his capacities. From here on, the ideal of humanity identifies itself with all the ideas of democracy and the natural rights of man. Now, a different conception of humanity prevails wherever the aesthetic and classicist ideal is dominant. Humanity means here the full unfolding of all human capacities and potentialities into a beautiful whole. This is a truly aristocratic ideal: to form oneself into a noble and rich individuality, in purity and harmony.

The ideal of humanity finds expression in many combinations of these various elements. It finally reaches its term in the inequalities of life or the difficulties of its realization. It thus evokes the opposition of an entirely different conception that sees in nature only the fight for survival, inequality, and the triumph of force. From this point of view, the ideal of humanity appears understandable only as the product of a period of under-population. Malthusianism discovers a vicious circle: every culture is bound to try to augment its population and therefore must value man as man. The resulting over-population, however, as well as the means used to combat it, are bound to destroy all culture again. The fundamental conception of the modern idea of nature also reveals a profound ambiguity. Under the influence of Christianity or Hellenism, nature may be idealized and become an optimistic principle of the good and the beautiful. Under realistic and economic influences, however, 'nature' may express complete indifference to all spiritual values and a glorification of brutality.

In all these considerations we are already affected by the way we look at the world. Our main task is to point out the foundations of the modern view of the world (*Weltanschauung*). However important the objective and institutional powers may be (which canalize our life, so to speak), a properly conceptual effect derives always from reflection and from mobility of thought. These above all are the great common possession of the West, the ultimate basis of the triumph of its thought and of its influence in the world. Here we are immediately confronted by the second major power in the modern world, after the institutions: namely, by science (*Wissenschaft*). Its rise is no less phenomenal than that of the modern state, and of the modern economy and society. Its first period of growth came in the Age of Orthodoxy, after the Renaissance had prepared the way for it by the artistic liberation of the modern individual. Since then, the pace of its development has been such that it can claim to be the real guide of modern life. Victorious in its struggle with dogma and church, it imposes its imprint on the modern world, to a wholly unprecedented degree basing its culture on reflection. Until its advent, revelation and tradition were the decisive forces that molded human minds. Now science claims to produce the rational foundations of existence, and penetrates everywhere with the self-evidence of the logically necessary universal concept. Initially, it has no doubts about the possibility of a complete rationalization of the world or of the construction of a culture on such a rationalistic basis.

Unquestionably the leader and bearer of this genuine rationalism is the first-born among the modern sciences, natural science. Emerging from the fogs of Renaissance speculation and the jungles of scholasticism, it begins with the systematic conceptualization of experience and, even compared with the survivals of the natural science of antiquity, it attains a wholly new significance. With its more exact instruments of observation, it immeasurably enlarges the scope of experience. Giving a completely novel further development to mathematics, it creates the means for the conceptual treatment of the newly gained empirical data by subsuming them under general principles and laws that apply throughout nature's realm. In the search for the ultimate elements of nature and for the mathematical formulation of the laws of their motion, the ideal of modern natural science was formulated: to subject all natural phenomena of the world of sense to the principle of a causality that recognizes in every process no more than a transformation, in accordance with general laws, of something already existing. Nature becomes an endless line of equations. This ideal has to this day fallen far short of realization, and the principle of classical mechanics, formulated in the seventeenth century for this purpose, has in many areas been undermined by the later work of specialists. What is properly the work of natural science has indeed become so highly specialized that even the scientists communicate only with difficulty. But the ideal itself in its transparent rationality has become tremendously popular; and has carried into all realms of thought, down even to the simplest conception and fantasy, the spirit of a rationalism that explains everything by reference to its smallest units and the laws of their motion.

This formal, methodological effect is indeed far more important than the actual findings—which, for the general public, consist in the apprehension by the physical and astronomical sciences of the immensity and regularity of the universe and the doctrine of biological evolution. These are important; yet much more important in its psychological impact is the faith in the omnipotence of the method. The conviction has remained and has become all-powerful that we live in a universe that is, potentially, completely intelligible; that the never-failing key of the method of natural science will open the door to immense advances; that there is no mystery that may not be ultimately unveiled; and that with these set principles, the solution of the mystery of the universe itself is within reach. It dominates the popular mood and literature, it has had a profound effect on philosophic and speculative thinking, and it has influenced historical and social science and research. These disciplines are often thought to attain rational transparency only in the measure in which they apply the law-concepts of natural science and learn to equate all occurrences with previous ones. But the logical consequence of this line of thought is the depressing idea that humanity, with all its thought and will, is nothing but a product of natural laws. A profound and usually unsolved contradiction appears: the same natural science that, by an act of the mind, taught us to conquer nature, is after all, like humanity, also a mere product of an immense, lifeless, objective complex that now and then takes the form of spirit. The infinite massiveness of nature has consequently been felt as a heavy burden, particularly in view of the scarcity of spiritual manifestations.

This new consequence has led many into a pessimistic mood. Such moods would be even stronger if there were not one point where our conquest of nature leads ever anew to glorious successes, confirming the earlier enthusiastic faith in progress: technology. Here the natural sciences have created real miracles that have resulted in a general rise of the standard of living, first of all by enabling capitalism to make use of machines. But they also have had other profound and general effects on our way of life, through the technology of transport and press. Hence, even now an optimistic mood predominates, a faith in an all-conquering rationalism that is more than willing to overlook the gaps and inconsistencies in our knowledge of nature; and that takes comfort in the thought that every normal individual is capable of grasping these principles and, therefore, potentially able to understand the world, at least in its general principles. This rationalism is thus at the same time strongly individualistic. For inasmuch as the universal concepts remain the same, it presumes that it can engender in every individual the same kind of rational knowledge. Yet the individualism of the scientists differs markedly from political individualism; for it always tends to a certain pride in belonging to an educated aristocracy. Only the most shallow enlightenment dares to assume that all have an equal capacity for scientific attainment. The underlying reason why the less educated consider natural science their ally is that the latter has an undermining effect on authority. Nothing has advanced egalitarian and rationalistic individualism so much as comparion of the individual to the atom in the mechanical systems. All the preaching of the scientists themselves concerning the struggle for survival and the victory of the minority has availed nothing against it.

The example of the natural sciences was followed by the historical and social sciences. The new world broke with the powers of tradition and had to explain this break by a critique of tradition. It was faced everywhere by tradition—as ecclesiastical and classical authority, as legend and myth; and thus the critique turned naturally into the removal of the semblance of divinity from this tradition, and the demonstration of its human and natural character. Since the Renaissance, this has been the starting point of criticism, which was aided by the dissolution of the legend of the Catholic Church on the part of Protestantism and by general critical undertakings on the part of philology. The fundamental purpose of this criticism was the attempt to explain events that, according to the older tradition, were inexplicable and completely unique, by making them a part of the ordinary empirical world. Modern historical thinking thus arose out of this criticism. Its aim is to reconstruct actual events out of the colorful and fabulous traditions of an uncritical age. Now this reconstruction is only possible if all the events of all ages have their basis in the same psychological principles, and everything in the past can be judged as analogous to the present. But if the analogy and homogeneity of all events is thus acknowledged, the perspective is enlarged to include the totality of all events. This tendency toward universal history was reinforced by the discoveries, the travel-accounts, and the recoveries of ancient documents that characterize the period. The events of one's own historical milieu are now understood as an intergral part of the totality of human events, a constitutive part that is conditioned, however, from all sides. On this new critical foundation, which is oriented towards universal history and presupposes general and homogeneous psychological laws, the new structure of the social sciences is erected. Leaving fabulous traditions aside, the innovators begin with probable origins. From these and presupposing simple general psychological principles, 'natural' ideals of state, society, morality, law, and religion are quickly developed.

However, as beginnings are increasingly understood as much more primitive and obscure, and as origin and ideal are more and more separated by colorful formations of history, this natural system is being abandoned. The preponderant influence of the methods of natural science is replaced by growing appreciation of the rich variety of concrete historical life, which is quite past measure. Instead of the theory of simple rational beginnings, historical corruption, and rational restoration—an after-effect of the theological thought-pattern—a new conception appears. It pictures the rise of infinite historical diversities out of the universal human endowments, leaving no possibility to derive any absolute ideals and goals from history. Pre-history has been discovered. The oldest hatchet that has been found is supposed to be at least a hundred thousand years old. This shows that the 'history' of the past six thousand years, of which our knowledge is scanty enough, is but a small island in the endless ocean of human events of which we have no knowledge. All the lines of development proudly sketched by our philosophy of culture are working on one tiny fragment. All our rationalistic splendor may accordingly be no more than an ephemeral accident. All modern works on particular branches of culture drown in the flood of prehistoric introductions, which permit us to see within or behind our modernity a mere variety of uncivilized, primitive man.

The result of this new perspective is the specifically modern way of historical thinking, the historical sense which is indeed a sixth sense for the apprehension of things. It is primarily a critical sense that is suspicious of all tradition. In every case, tradition is compelled to prove its own legitimacy; usually, this cannot be done without supplanting the traditional picture with a presumably more factual substitute, which now poses as tradition. The measure of confidence in the competence of this criticism varies greatly, to be sure; indeed, it ranges from the most daring audacity to the driest precisionism and utter skepticism about history. A further effect is the immense broadening of our intellectual horizons: our conception of everything historical as part of a closely intertwined totality; a new image of humanity which in an enormous variety of experiences, assumes ever new and wholly individual forms; an extraordinarily refined individualism that, in contrast to the democratic type of individualism, is artistic and aristocratic. This broadness, this habit of comparing and relating, this refinement of individualizing perception—all these are bound up with an unlimited relativism that portrays every structure as an individual and special form of the generally human; conditioned by concrete circumstances, it leaves no room for absolute, rational truths and ideals that would be the same everywhere. While its criticism and its confidence in its own ability to reconstruct historical facts and developments seem to make history the ally of a rationalism that transforms everything supernatural into natural events, here history appears again in a decidedly anti-rationalistic role. History is the field of the infinitely manifold and particular, the boundless flux of ever new structures, where nothing is without precedent, yet everything is also unique. History teaches us to see and construe things from an infinite variety of points of view, and shows us the historical limitation of even the boldest thought that may seem to be purely rational: for every subject sees the interconnections differently. So today historical description frequently takes the place of thought. All intention and planning are burdened by the bewildering mass of comparisons and recollections. History does not favor the modern trend of mastering reality by the use of universal concepts that apply to every individual. Despite all useful lessons drawn from history, despite the strengthening of patriotic sentiment and the intensification of the sense for sober factuality, fundamentally the study of history inclines us to an anti-rationalistic contemplation, an aristocratic individualism, a resigned wisdom that everywhere seeks and honors greatness but accepts the unfathomable and unpredictable variety of human life as a dark fate.

Finally, we look at modern art. Certainly there is a specifically modern art, even though it may indeed by the offspring of classical and medieval art. However much it may also be dependent on various external accidents, such as the desires of the patron or the social status of the artist, in its unmistakable fundamentals it is the characteristic expression of a new world. This is true of painting and —above all—of poetry. We are concerned here not with the complicated story of its evolution, but with its general cultural significance. It may perhaps be said that modern art has its essence in two factors: it rediscovers and transfigures the present world, and it represents the original individual as sensing and seeking the depths of the self. On the one hand, modern art is the end and the final destroyer of the Augustinian doctrine of the absolute corruption of the present world and of sensuality. Thus modern art links up with all the other modern motives of secularism. But its argumentation is the most vivid, the most striking, the most effective one of all. On the other hand, modern art is the intensification of Christian inwardness and individuality. No longer inhibited by the objective powers of church and authority, it represents with full freedom the most personal aspects of life. This often leads to a conscious and intended originality. Using late-medieval realism as its base, it has conquered the forms of classical antiquity for the mastery and glorification of sensuality—but dissatisfied with the classical system of types, modern art has given expression at the same time to an infinite personal content. Thus modern art flows together with all the powers of modern individualism.

And yet the secularity of modern art, as well as its individualism, is fundamentally and essentially at variance with the individualism of political democracy and the secularity of state and economy. In the present secular world, art is forever searching for harmonies, ideas, spiritual backgrounds and symbols, of which only the artistic sensitivity is conscious; and its individualism is that of the personality that needs freedom precisely on account of its greater richness and intensity. Modern art has revolted energetically; but its revolutions were fundamentally against dead traditionalism and for artistic truthfulness. Art has cast its magic over all the trends and tendencies of recent centuries; but whenever it recalled its own true purpose, art was ever and again only in the service of beauty for beauty's sake. Political power, economic profit, and democratic individualism are felt as alien by artistic culture, and this mutual alienation may drive the artistic community to impassioned resistance or pessimistic resignation. Now this reaction is cause by a further phenomenon that is less important for art itself than for the cultural significance of art. This phenomenon is the theory of art and the share that the thoughts underlying it have in shaping the public's attitudes and feelings.

In thinking about its own meaning, art discovers in itself a whole system of metaphysics, a view of life. It is the metaphysics of immanence, the inclusion of everything sensual in the spritiual, of everything finite in the infinite, of everything particular in the cosmic harmony, of the life-unity of the universe in its formative principle. It is a peculiar metaphysic; spiritualistic and secular at the same time; an unscientific intuitive pantheism which nevertheless cannot rid itself of its theistic characteristics and is obscurely conscious of the spirit of the All (*Allgeist*) as the quintessence of all personal life-values. It is also the ethics of the original artistic development of the self in all directions, the majestic right of genius to impose its style on nature, the artistic expression of the ethical value of the personality in the unity of its sensual and suprasensual aspects. It is, moreover, not merely the end of Augustinianism and the doctrine of original sin but also the end of the whole anthropomorphic dualism of God and the world. It is the affirmation of the eternal and essential correlation of God and world without cosmic beginning or end; the eradication of the principles of theology from man's imagination; and its replenishing with images that illustrate how the life of God and the world are intimately and ineffably intertwined. This aesthetic unity and harmony is at one with the concept of a law of nature, and likewise the infinity of the world's existence with the widening of our historical perspective and the infinity of historical diversities.

This immanentism is by no means simply optimistic. The artist knows that sorrow is the deepest source of his creativity and that the richest profundity of his soul is not reached without the experience of guilt. But art tries to understand sorrow and guilt as components of the great unity of life, as parts of the life of the All that are necessary if life is to have depth. It opposes merely the undifferentiated dualism of good and bad, the anthropomorphic idea of a disturbance of the created world by an extraneous evil, conjured up by free-will. In this opposition it is supported by all other insights into the origin of things. Artistic creativity has thus given rise to a new and conscious spirit that is particularly hostile to the world of traditional theology. As a conscious principle for viewing the world, however, it is by no means favorably disposed towards the other fundamental elements of the modern world. It cares nothing for these political, democratic, and rationalistic elements, and wants to have nothing to do with the vulgar optimism of the egalitarians. The spirit of art is, above all, the

point of departure of continual strong reactions against abstract
rationalism and empirical positivism. Since the Renaissance, every
classicism and every artistic naturalism has turned sooner or later into
romanticism. Romanticism—the artistic approach to art—has ever
again claimed for poetry a monopoly in shaping our view of the
world. The way was thus continually prepared for mystical and
religious ideas. In ethics, however, there has not been a comparable
effect. The artistic ethic generally remains a highly refined egoism at
variance with the ethical elements of the modern spirit.

We have now entered upon the problematics of the world-view and
thus the proper domain of philosophy. Now, it is a truism that besides
ancient and medieval-ecclesiastical philosophy there is a specifically
modern philosophy. It is less commonly acknowledged however, and
most important in this context, that modern philosophy is not simply
a new evolution of the philosophical tradition, or a necessary new link
in the logical development of the idea, but a manifold and very
different attempt to master the variegated mass of new ideas. Modern
philosophy follows the lead of the world of the modern spirit; it does
not create it. Modern philosophy grows out of the new specialized
sciences and the new atmosphere of life in general—especially out of
the new natural science, but also out of history and psychology, and
finally out of art. Ever since Giordano Bruno, driven by a dark
Faustian urge, provided the prelude with his synthesis of all these
things, modern philosophy has kept on attempting to systematize the
new world of ideas, now from one and now from another point of
view. But it is nowhere a completely new creation; rather it brings the
customary ethical, religious, and philosophical traditions together with
the new motives and insights. Completely new are only the radical
breaks with traditional religiosity; but these belong always, rather, to
the realm of popular philosophy (*Halbphilosophie*). Comte excepted,
they are by no means characteristic of the leading contemporary
thinkers.

Philosophy, moreover, is difficult to understand, and as the
problems become more complicated and technically refined, it
becomes more and more a specialized science, which for this reason is
wholly incapable of exerting any considerable effect on the public.
The great cultural significance of modern philosophy consists rather
in general moods and impressions that emanate from the philosophical
effort as such, no matter what its result may be. There is, on the one
hand, the claim of working without presuppositions, which stands in
complete contrast to the bonds that have been accepted up until now
by church and convention. Descartes is right in making doubt the

principle written over the gate that leads into modern philosophy. There is, on the other hand, the assurance that all fundamental convictions of modern humanity have to be constructed anew by science on this newly leveled ground—the scientific character of the world-view, and the nullity and backwardness of everything 'unscientific.' Both ideas have become ingrained in our minds. Thought reaches back further and further; more and more it invalidates hitherto recognized postulates; deeper and deeper it digs after an ultimate foundation and self-evident presupposition.

The edifice that is reared on these newly discovered bases grows increasingly more complicated, far-flung, and comprehensive. The more philosophy devours, the more it has to produce; ever anew it tries to correct or replace with the products of scientific insight that which has grown spontaneously and instinctively. It is a grand struggle, a tonic for all strong minds. But it affects the general public above all as an excess of reflection; a skepticism that dissolves everything; an emphasis on consciousness that extinguishes all spontaneity; faith in the sole efficacy of science and scientific demonstration; and finally, as an escape from all this, the cult of the scientific authorities, which becomes the tyranny of the currently fashionable theories. The diversity of the many new and never-finished structures, however, first brings an infinite mobility to the construction-mania, and an incredible dexterity in replacing generally recognized ideas by newly invented ones. But finally, the multiplicity of the structures also brings disgust and indifference. Philosophy has tried out and exhausted all possible points of view. The resulting fatigue brings with it a readiness to be satisfied with facts and a universally plausible utilitarianism. Or philosophy becomes the history of philosophy. No one can deny that this is the present result of the past two hundred years of feverish philosophical endeavor. Whatever support philosophy, thus understood, may have given to rationalism and individualism, the final result is after all a general skepticism and flight from ideas, and a small, secret aristocracy of real thinkers.

Compared to these main effects of the general philosophical mood, the effect of the actual contents of modern philosophical ideas is relatively small. It is infinitesimal compared to the impact of politics, economic life, and art. Among these new constructions, the only popular ones have been the mechanistic theism of the eighteenth century and then, following the expulsion of God from this mechanism, the materialistic doctrine. The latter has an apparently very plausible point of departure; and, with its mechanistic rationalism, fully satisfies the need for rationality—despite the fact that it collides with every aspect of actual life and is absurd to the more profound thinker. Related ideologies that are less offensive and more cautious, pantheism and positivism, are already too complicated and are always understood by the masses in a materialistic sense. A second major form is the subjective idealism of freedom that is derived from Kant's philosophy. It owes its effect on the general public solely to the experiential nature of its point of departure, the moral consciousness. As a theory it is most difficult and complicated. The third form is objective evolutionary idealism, which culminates in the doctrine of Hegel and sees the universe as the progressive unfolding of the fundamental spiritual reality according to its own laws. This theory is based on the artistic-rhythmic sense of harmony and on the modern view of history as a totality. While the Hegelian idealism discovered the ground of the evolutionary sequence in the inner logical structure of the universe, it owed its effect on the general public solely to the optimistic idea of an ascending, logically necessary evolution. What properly constitutes the thought-content of the much richer Hegelian system was only accessible to a small élite.

Apart from these main types there is only room for a skepticism that dissolved everything, and for an underscoring of the irrational elements that still remain, a program that was throughly actualized by pessimism. There can be no thought of homogeneity in modern philosophy, except for the common attitude that our ideal world must be reconstructed wholly apart from any presuppositions. This raises, of course, the ultimate question, whether working without presuppositions is at all possible, whether all so-called presuppositionlessness is not simply the replacement of traditional presuppositions by others, which at bottom are also purely axiomatic; above all, whether the purely ethical and religious contents of our lives are at all susceptible to rational proof or rational replacement. Autonomous modern thought nowhere penetrates near so deeply into actual life as its exponents claim to do. The scholarly literature itself is clearly divided into a rationalistic and a voluntaristic branch. The guidance it provides for life is a very conditional one, and even this conditional guidance is ambiguous in its first principles.

This brings us to the last and most complicated problem, the morality and religion of the modern world. With respect to the former we note first of all a great and mighty step forward, if we recognize as such the refinement and ramification of life, and the adjustment to increasingly complex conditions, together with the attainment of both firmness and mobility. The church-oriented world used to work with an undifferentiated mixture of law, custom, and morality that was firmly held together within not very extensive, but well established conditions, by the partly secular, partly clerical authorities. The state and its system of law are extricating themselves from this confusion; their ground and existence are becoming purely secular. Their ties to the ecclesiastical order and morality, and even the ties to custom, which had been closely connected with both and had been carefully guarded, are being severed. Morality has to reflect upon itself and to differentiate itself fundamentally from both law and custom, after it has had to dissociate itself from tradition and authority. The legal orders attain a tremendous firmness and a thorough rationalization by being put on their own; they also become independent of the less tangible, flexible concerns of the inner life. The now independent morality encourages the free development of these concerns. Custom becomes a middle term between them—different from both— something that no longer binds with the force of law, nor poses in the sacred garments of morality; it becomes a mobile reflection of all elements of life.

With the attainment of independence, morality confronts the task of examining itself and working towards a new and surer understanding of itself. Modern ethics undertakes the mighty labor of probing the moral consciousness by reference to Christian morality, the ethics of antiquity, and the new ideas. Up until now these had been inextricably connected: the *jus naturale* (which includes public, criminal, and civil law, along with the fundamentals of economic theory), the moral *lex naturae*, the ethical law based on revelation, positive legislation, and the police watching over all these 'laws.' Now all these interests are becoming independent. Morality has to stand on its own. But in its newly-found independence, it is confronted by a host of completely new tasks and new conditions, by a political and economic life, a society, science, and art that were unknown to the fusion of Christian morality and the philosophy of antiquity that has prevailed until now. A new system for evaluating human life-goals and goods becomes necessary. But this is not all. With the loss of the old foundations of revelation and common sense, morality ceases to be self-evident and must look around for new foundations; these are, in truth, exceedingly hard to find. Morality therefore allies itself, now with instinctive feelings of conscience, now with the positively prevailing views, now with utilitarian considerations of permanent usefulness. Also lost is the old motivation of heaven and hell, the entire transcendental horizon. Morality must be oriented to the values of the here-and-now, or at least to immanent, inner values. Indeed, general reflection corrodes even what was hitherto regarded as obviously the innermost content of morality: the obligations of overcoming senuality and egotism. In the end, all that is left is the mere form, the frame of mind that is conscious of a general moral engagement, and a moral sophistry that abandons even this form as an illusion. All the more diligent, therefore, are the attempts to reconstruct morality. These lead to a wide variety of compromises between the old Christian morality and the new conditions and values. But they also result in countless new constructions of morality. Here the content of the older elements is sometimes largely recognized. At other times, there is the most daring transvaluation of all values. But the attempts at reconstruction may also lead to a retreat to the natural moral consciousness, which needs only to be freed from the burden of religious elements that confuse and corrupt it. Finally, they often lead to a complete moral skepticism.

Of course, all this pertains only to the educated upper strata of society, which are influenced by what they read. The great masses live largely under the influence of the old Christian morality with its unconscious adaptations; or they live by the old natural morality of conscience, as it was taught by the Enlightenment; or they base their morality on a political and social sense of honor and patriotism, or on class-solidarity. What is best here is done quietly and is never verbalized. Any attempt to pick out of this confusion the dominant traits that give a specific character to the modern moral sense is, therefore, very difficult. It involves selection and personal judgement, because those features are stressed which are related to the general state of mind and at the same time appear to have the greatest substance and inner strength, and therefore the best future.

We might say that the dominant traits are those of an autonomous morality based on sincere inner conviction, with two goals: to form one's own personality into a work of moral freedom; and to establish relations among men as moral persons, where no one is regarded merely as means, but where everyone is also regarded as always an end in the self. This is Kant's formula; but at the same time, it is also the spirit of Protestantism and of Christianity under the impact of being given a completely internal foundation and a primary sphere of activity in the here-and-now. It is also, however, the entire individualism of the modern world, modified only by the ideal of the person that no one is by nature and which everyone is to become through freedom. It is, moreover, the immanentism of the modern world, where authority and necessity are immanent in the subject. It is the secularity of the modern world, but seen as the challenge to lift human existence to the level of a higher necessity, of eternity.

But even though we may stress these features as the dominant ones, a great mass of difficult problems remains unsolved. The whole question of the evaluation (in terms of the formation of the moral personality) of the various modern cultural influences, and thus the question of the ethical significance and shaping of state, law, economy, society, science, and art, remains unanswered. The answers that have been suggested, by those who were at least conscious of the need for answers, are confusing. But the metaphyscial foundation of morality which seems to be given with its new understanding, and its relation to an ultimate and absolute meaning of existence—these likewise continue to remain obscure. The latter are questions that lead from ethics to religion. Precisely because these questions involve ethics in all the pains and enigmas of modern religion, they are very apt to be bypassed. But the unconditional and absolute, the faith in a purpose and meaning of life, which is immanent in all true morality, keeps on crying out for religion. The last question we take up is, accordingly, the question of the religion of the modern world.

Understandably enough, the picture that presents itself to us here is the most confusing one of all. To be sure, the traditonal Christian churches, Catholicism and the churches of the Reformation, and side-by-side with the latter the increasingly numerous sects that have sprung from them, continue to exist and live. While their death has often been certified, they continue as powers of significance. Just now this is clearly shown by the fact that the question of ecclesiastical influence dominates the domestic politics of almost all European states. But they are a multiplicity of powers, not one power. They constitute a multiplicity of organizations, neutralizing one another by their respective claims to be the guardian of the only and absolute truth. For this reason it is wholly impossible to give a unified picture of modern religion. But much more important is something else. These churches are the expression of religious life of the past; they are capable of existing side-by-side in their multiplicity because the modern world really does not identify itself with any one of them. The tolerance which the modern world shows to organized religions and which it expects from the state is itself only possible because of a prevalent feeling that organized religion may indeed contain important moments of truth, but that it is no longer a threat to a free intellectual world because the latter is stronger. The logical conclusion would be the separation of church and state. This conclusion was drawn by the Anglo-Saxon countries at the beginning of the modern era, to the satisfaction of all parties. On the European continent, however, this step only now begins to be taken with the ecclesiastical revolution in

France. The impetus of this revolution will affect ever wider areas, as every revolution in France has done. One is justified in pointing to the separation of church and state, or at least to the tendency towards it, as an essential characteristic of the modern religious situation. But this only means, of course, that modern religion, though it acknowledges the significance of the churches, is not wholly identical with them.

But what is this modern religion that is not identical with the churches, but maintains itself outside, alongside and above the churches? There is indeed such a religion; but it contains nothing whatever that it religiously original, no new religious idea that might kindle or shape a movement. Here the most variegated tendencies and inclinations meet. Sometimes it is merely an internalized Christianity, amalgamated in some way with the modern world of ideas, which cannot join the historic churches or believes that it cannot join them. Sometimes it is an echo of the ethical idealism of Kant and Fichte, tinged with thoughts of Goethe and Hegel, where the religious ideas also have their essential source in Christianity. Sometimes it is a syncretism of various religious elements from all over the world, assembled by the free play of the imagination and inspired by the learning of historians of religion. There are spiritistic and occultistic communities, which revive the most primitive and archaic religion, the cult of souls and ghosts. Sometimes we find a detached religion of art which identifies the aesthetic unity of the form with the natural unity of the universe. We also find the reawakening of pessimism and of the mood that looks for redemption; having renounced the Christian idea of personality, these moods prefer to lean on Buddhism rather than on Christianity. There are people with a vague yearning for religion that at once recoils, however, from all concrete religious ideas.

Here the modern world has done its work of destruction of the old religious ties with great thoroughness. But it has not produced any genuinely new force. The best thing in this extra-ecclesiastical religion is a certain Christian quality that relies on the purely internal certitude of God's revelation and that nourishes and confirms this certitude by reference to history. Faith in this revelation allows an ethically deepened and renewed individuality, a total personality to develop. This Christian quality has also penetrated deeply into the churches, but it apparently always presupposes the more robust faith of the churches, which is merely sublimated here.

Besides all this, we have to note the enormous indifference of large sections of the educated classes, as well as a passionate atheism. These factors are much stronger on the European continent than in Anglo-

Saxon countries. The policy of force in religious matters has avenged itself most bitterly here. Much of this, to be sure, is mere outward appearance, and there is no lack of religious substitutes. Social Democracy has its doctrine of original sin in the theory of the radical evil of bourgeois society, its doctrine of redemption and its 'other world' in the state of the future, and its substitute for God in an evolution that blindly drives everything forward to its logical end. Others have different substitutes: the idea of humanity, nature, conscience. What is always lacking, however, is the most essential part of religion: the sense of reverence, and personal devotion.

Thus it is quite impossible to pick out dominant traits in this confusion of mutually antagonistic forces. That the modern world constitutes a serious crisis of religion cannot be denied. The pendulum of time has swung back: an era determined essentially by religious ideas has been succeeded by a religously weak era whose essential orientation is secular. The elimination of the old objective authority and the thousandfold occasions for criticism have caused the greatest perplexities for the life of religion—which still survives, of course. The old system was broken first in the religious sphere, and here the effect has been more profound than anywhere else. We can only try, therefore, to pick out the deepest and strongest religious forces. These are to be found in Christianity in its dual form—the ecclesiastical faith, and the free fusion with elements of modern life as achieved by the poets and thinkers of German Idealism. No future development is thinkable other than that both adjust to and, instead of attacking, learn to stimulate each other. The only fundamental difference between them, after all, is that in the older form, the dualistic transcendence of the old anthropocentric cosmology and the concern for the authority and community of the church predominate; while in the newer form, the evolutionary immanence of an infinite cosmic life and the autonomy of the individual constitute the cosmology. In the former, the ideal life-values are found merely in the religious consciousness itself. In the latter, the religious value coalesces with everything that is true, good, and beautiful to form the unity of supreme spiritual value. Both forms share the main thing: the metaphysic of the person, which anchors all personal life-values in God, and the ethic of elevating the person out of mere natural conditioning to a union with God. Everything else in our society is no more than the first or last glimmer of religion, or else of religion in the negative sense—the fight against religion itself becoming a religion.

Now if all these factors are looked at together; if one consists the manifold contrasts within the modern world of ideas itself, the composite and divided character even of the older world, together with its countless concessions to the modern world; if one recalls how variously old and new are put side by side or superimposed upon each other, while the whole is everywhere penetrated by the universally human drives and passions in their eternal youth, thoughtlessness and weirdness; then one has a picture of the situation that has resulted from all these conditions. The only question we have to consider here is, whether the emergence of the world of the modern spirit in this compositeness represents the introduction of a truly new principle—of which it can be wished, by some, that it should attain uncontested power as the principle of progress, by others, that it should be extirpated as a source of disease. If the answer to this question were positive, it would allow our age to attain a certain identity by being confronted with a simple either-or.

However, the result of every penetrating analysis is that this is not so. In one respect, to be sure, there is a complete contrast. But it has its causes in the origin and emergence of the modern world itself. This is the break with a culture based on church authority, whether it be the authority of the Catholic world-church or of the Protestant territorial church. It is the elimination of the churches and their authority, based on supernatural revelation, from a position of leadership which was always fully claimed in theory but which was never fully occupied in practice. But this is something purely negative and quite evidently necessary for the rise of a new culture. For any new culture would have had to break with the established churches if it had new ideas of its own at all. Room had to be made for these; and since the church occupied whatever space there was, the new ideas could prevail only by fighting against the churches. However, this says nothing about the positive content, apart from the purely formal statement that the individual had to enact the self's freedom and that the new world had to take shape along strongly individualistic lines. Perhaps one might also say that with the breaking-away from an ecclesiastical authority based primarily on faith in the hereafter, and with the unfolding of independent powers on the part of an individualism that was seizing upon new tasks in the world, a certain secularity was a matter of course: or rather that the secular motives that had previously been inhibited but never ceased to exert influence were now set free.

It is quite natural that in such a time of of disintegration the scientific formation of universal concepts, and thus rationalism, assumes leadership as the one remaining force. But nothing is thereby said about the quality, essence, and motivation of this individualism, about the meaning, goals, and values of this secularity, about the epistemological reflections of this rationalism, or about the nature of value judgements that still continue to be made spontaneously. These factors are indeed absolutely different, as analysis shows. Only the temporary predominance of one or another tendency, and in an age of communication, the tremendous influence of mutual accommodation, may now and then obscure these differences. The very fact that the world of the modern spirit has not given rise to a great united party, but to many sharply divided groups, points up the differences. The history of German liberalism is a direct and perspicacious case in point. While every group identifies itself with the modern world, the meaning intended is different in each case. Nor will this situation change so long as these groups want to retain their ideological character, rather than unite for limited political objectives. For it is of the essence of the world of the modern spirit that it brings forth the most diverse intellectual movements.

It is above all a complete mistake to attempt to explain this new intellectual world on the basis of a consistent and essential contrast to Christianity, which dominated the older world; yet friend and foe have committed this error. The adherents of Christianity must learn to look upon this new world as largely a product of Christianity itself. Its enemies will have to realize that Christianity may be eradicated from particular moments, but never by being confronted with a unified totality of the modern world, which does not exist at all. The former group largely owes what it hates to what it considers to be the sole good, while the latter group owes all it considers worthwhile in large measure to that which it hates. The point of departure of the modern spirit is mainly an enthusiastic and believing theism and that fusion of the ideas of Christianity and ancient philosophy which was wrought by the church itself—not atheism or pantheism, as one is often told in the lead-articles of denominational papers. A theism of this kind presided over the first feeble steps of national economics and prompted the search for the wisdom of the world-mechanism. Christian individualism provided the first impulses to modern individualism and was the main cause of the breaking up of the churches, long before state and society thought of it. The greatest capitalistic business-zeal had been engendered by Puritanism. The sovereignty of the people is at least as much the work of religious enthusiasts and fighters for God as it is the accomplishment of rationalistic advocates of natural law.

Even the fundamental aversion to revelation and authority is not the root. The point of departure is merely a metamorphosis of the ideas of revelation and authority. Among the modern ideas we find both the strictest state-authority and unswerving obedience to conscience. Not even secularity is the intended and conscious point of departure. No other century has indulged in the belief in immortality as has the eighteenth; its sentimentality is only a secularization of religious exuberance, and in the writings of Spinoza and Malebranche its immanentism becomes the sublimest mysticism. If rationalism were to be regarded as the unifying characteristic, it would soon be evident that it is only the attempt of the liberated individualism to reorient itself and to replace with general, self-evident concepts what had previously been provided by authority.

Yet the points of departure and the results of the new rationalism are radically different, and the irrational elements of existence everywhere force themselves into the forefront. What appears to confront us everywhere is the replacement and transformation of a world that has outlived itself. Its own inherent forces are now under the influence of new ideas and conditions, pushing them forward everywhere—and that means at many points that are not at all interconnected. The world of the medieval church with its authority, its supernaturalism, and its cosmological philosophy of nature and history, its anthropology and psychology, its inspired books and holy traditions, has come to an end. It transforms itself, together with what it has inherited from classical antiquity, into a new world. But it lacks the unity of root and development, because unlike the medieval world it is not dominated by the idea of a single authority before which everything must give way: the religious idea of a supernatural transcendence.

There is only one point of absolute contrast: the new world's optimism, and its rejection of the Christian doctrine of sin and the pessimism to which it leads. Of course, even this optimism is not at all hostile to Christianity as it flows from its original sources. On the contrary, it is the true child of religious faith, but now emancipated from its Augustinian fetters, which it had borne for a thousand years and which had become unbearable and absurd. Initially, this optimism was animated by a thoroughly religious enthusiasm, the natural mood of a new creative dawn. In the noon-tide heat the pessimistic sighs were not lacking. Today, after the religious foundation of this optimism has been largely exhausted, it often turns into a naturalistic pessimism. Moreover, only one definite aspect of this optimism may be considered as consistently characteristic of the modern world: an aversion to the Christian consciousness of sin, and a weakness of the sense of sin in general. Though it is impossible to derive all the peculiarities of the modern world, which have their own special causes, from this feeling about sin, it is undeniable that this feeling is a fact. But it is by no means certain that the lack of a consciousness of sin is an organic part of the modern world; it may rather be the understandable reaction against a thousand years of ecclesiastical pressure that was said to be necessary because of the pressure exerted on humanity by sin. People were tired of an Augustinianism that had inhibited all initiative and self-reliance; that had been forced to serve as buttress for general subservience to the church, intellectual bondage, alienation and distrust with respect to the world; that had barred the way to everything desired by the newly-stirring spirit. People were tired of the doctrines of total depravity, absolute human inability, and the church's monopoly on saving truths. For during the Wars of Religion, people had come to feel that the churches imposed an intolerable burden; and they had learned to savor the free air of beauty and science. This reaction undoubtedly fails to recognize a profound truth, which could not have remained dominant for a thousand years without being well founded in experience, and which is not necessarily identical with its particular Augustinian form and exaggeration. But this misapprehension is necessarily linked only to the shallow optimism of the egalitarians; otherwise it constitutes by no means a necessary part of the modern spirit. The most profound thinkers—men like Kant, Hegel, and Schelling—have soberly recognized human sinfulness, and none of our great historians has failed to acknowledge it.

The result of our first impression accordingly stands: the modern world is not a unitary principle but an abundance of sometimes congenial, sometimes conflicting developments. There was room for these developments because the old world had outlived itself. The impression of unity is caused pre-eminently by this contrast; for actually the modern world diverges into the most variegated tendencies. It is not a contrast to or an aberration from ecclesiastical culture, but its successor and heir; the heir has assimilated much of the inheritance, and also acquired much that is new. Old and new elements are being mixed and crossed in a thousand ways, and formed into a relatively unified whole in modern life. Yet the inner tensions and contrasts are everywhere noticeable and continue to arise.

Another much-discussed question may be answered in this context. I refer to the question whether the modern world represents pure, absolute progress, 'progress as such' (which every new era claims to represent), a higher stage in an evolution that constantly moves upward, or whether it is perhaps the beginning of the dissolution and decay of the European peoples, comparable to the contemplative culture (*Reflexionskultur*) and individualistic disintegration that ushered in the downfall of antiquity. Both questions make sense only under very definite, dogmatic presuppositions. The first question presupposes the doctrine of an absolute, continuous, all-embracing upward evolution, a mere theory peculiar to certain branches to modern thought. But there is no doubt that this theory is a very questionable construction. Experience merely confirms the statement that all new values are purchased by the sacrifice of old ones, that no progress simply transcends the previous epoch, and that even while [progress] closes certain doors of human distress, it opens new ones. That progress is being made, and what sort of progress, cannot be established by merely pointing to the movement of history itself but only through spontaneous evaluations and constant self-criticism on the part of every age. These spontaneous value-judgements cannot be validated by the historical movement, but rather validate the evaluation of the historical movement itself. Thus there is no reason whatsoever to consider the modern world as the embodiment of progress. One may freely appreciate its achievements and yet be sensitive to its losses and dangers.

The second question, too, presupposes a theory, namely the opinion that individualism as such means decline. But there is no 'individualism as such,' just as there is no 'progress as such.' It is certainly obvious that the modern world understands its own individualism in a variety of senses. No doubt, there is much decadent individualism. But just as certainly, the modern world's greatest achievements were only made possible by the freeing of the individual, which unlocked the self's original, autonomous creative power and ability. It is, moreover, quite certain that the fundamental postulates of any ethics whatsoever are a personal sense of duty and a free community; both are expressions of an ethically developed individualism, which intensifies the sense of social solidarity to the point of maximum participation of the individual in the highest values of life. To see in individualism as such the deadly poison that kills culture would mean to despair of the fundamental demand of morality. On the contrary, it is our duty to strive with all the means at our disposal to discipline ethically and thus to transfigure the natural powers of individualism, which have become free and immensely creative. As for the frightening comparison with antiquity; the vast difference is first and above all that antiquity, with its decadent popular religion and impersonal philosophical systems, could not provide a basis such as the Christian metaphysics of the person affords for the transfiguration and ethical disciplining of individualism. It was for good reasons that Platonism and Stoicism were able to transmit their ethical and religious powers only in union with Christianity. We, for our part, can always find a firm support here for the uprooted individual and fresh strength for our disintegrating contemplative culture. Besides, it is by no means only individualism which must be considered as the cause of that obscure process of disintegration, which to this day is not fully understood. There were economic and technological causes for which there is, up to now, no analogy in our present development.

Thus it is impossible to construe the modern world as unitary by reference to any single point, whether that point be opposition to Christianity, or individualism, or secularity and immanentism, or progress as such, or the process of disintegration of aging civilizations. We have to accept the modern world as we find it, irrespective of what preceded it and what may follow. This is our epoch, from which we have no means to escape. What remains of the older world—and much is preserved and maintained among us in various political, economic, and ecclesiastical groups —is yet deeply permeated by the modern spirit. It is therefore equally impossible to construe 'conservatism' as a radical unitary principle that would be directly opposed to it. Conservatism itself is deeply and radically divided by confessional differences. Where the political and economic remains of the past invoke the religious view of the world as their own, the connection is really not organic or totally necessary and, indeed, very often is a mere pretense; modern ways have been adopted in very large measure.

If we have characterized the modern world negatively as breaking with a culture that was dominated by the authority of the church, the attempt to add a positive characterization will have to confine itself to picking out the prevailing main traits in the new conditions and tendencies. These traits are linked together only by their common origin in emancipated individualism; by the principle of order that was summoned against the latter, namely, the regulation of matters on the basis of the most universal principles; and by the gradual composition and fusion of these two factors. Now these main traits are, in essence, the following: the spaciousness of all states and relationships, together with growing populations and improved means of transportation and communication that tend to standardize everything; an individualism that aims at maximum participation of the individual in the values of life, and a corresponding independence;

a secularity that is active chiefly in the positive shaping of the world, and that amalgamates the religious values with those of civilization; the tremendous intensification of criticism and of the capacity for scholarly reflection; the astounding technological conquest of nature and its exploitation through a rationalized economy; a humane attitude that looks essentially for the good in humanity and seeks to develop it; the massive growth of the state, which encompasses every sphere of reality and aims at maximal national unity; a universal vision that stresses continuity and the intrinsic vital unity of the world-process; and, finally and above all, the freedom of an inwardly experienced necessity that opposes all purely external supernatural obligations; that is, moral and intellectual autonomy.

We are directly aware that all these signify real truths and advances. But we are just as directly aware that they also contain serious dangers. We do not seek to avert these dangers, however, by a radical combating of the modern spirit, as though it derived from some basic flaw as yet undiscovered but [conquerable] by a sober identification and explanation of the various points where dangers lurk, and by a summoning forth of the various appropriate remedies. Now that we are surely far removed from any crisis or collapse, and from any new religious ideas that are truly original, an epoch that understands itself can act concerning itself only by furthering what is great and recognizing the dangers .... Nothing remains for us but to accommodate ourselves to the given, which, according to every appearance, is still far from exhausting its vital powers and—to repeat the principle—devotedly to further the elements of greatness and counteract the dangers with ever-vigilant self-criticism. We are children of time, not its masters; we can act upon time only by acting within it. Or, according to the world of Count Egmont that Goethe places at the end of the history of his life, which is at the same time a history of German culture: 'As though driven by invisible spirits, Phoebus' horses gallop away with the light chariot of our fate. All we can do is, with steadfast courage, to hold on to the reins and to keep the wheels from hitting the rocks and going off the road, either on the right or on the left. Who knows whither we go? It is hard enough to remember whence we come.'

16

Modern Philosophy of History

Two main groups of problems have arisen for theology in its inevitable confrontation with the world of general knowledge. On the one hand, theology has to establish its position over against the scientific world-picture, a cosmology that includes biology and psychology as relating organic and psychic beings to the totality of the cosmic order. On the other hand, it has to establish the validity of faith in the truth of the Christian religion as over against ethical perspectives of life and diverse forms of faith, which have a foundation that is likewise historically positive. Patristic theology solved the first problem by combining biblical thought with Aristotelian and Neo-Platonic thought. It solved the second problem by its doctrine of a supernatural revelation and the miraculous character of the church and the Bible, and by the adoption of the Stoic doctrine of a natural religion and morality.

With the dissolution of the ancient cosmology and metaphysics, with the development of a mechanistic world-view, and above all with the new formulations of biology and psycho-physiology, the former problem has been placed upon a completely new basis in the modern world. The development of a homogenous view of history that sees all historical events as interconnected, and the growth of a historical criticism that dissolves isolating miracles, have likewise given a new perspective to the latter problem. But in spite of the different forms, the two problems remain essentially the same and continue to confront every attempt to formulate and maintain a view of life based on principles. One complex of insights arises from the formulation of concepts of nature that explain the totality of reality; the other arises from historical orientation and interconnection; both have their basis in the nature of thought and reality. Insofar as cosmology works with the general concepts that arise from the exploration of nature, and insofar as the picture of history proceeds from the peculiar character of historical thinking, the problem consists, in epistemological terms, of the unavoidable and necessary juxtaposition of concepts derived from natural science with those derived from history. Both problem areas must be given their due, either by means of a unifying metaphysics or in some other way, if norms of faith and life that have grown up and attained power by virtue of their own inherent strength are to be scientifically grounded and protected against the competition of other norms and against various doubts of a more general nature.

Modern theology has eagerly addressed itself to both problem areas. In its discussion of the former it found its first model, in the eighteenth century, in the physico-theological proofs of Newton, still greatly appreciated by Kant, and in the naturalistic idealism or 'intelligible fatalism' of Leibniz. For a long time theology remained content with this model. Then came the moral theology of Kant, which set forth within a phenomenalistic naturalism the paradoxes arising from the religious postulates of freedom. Next followed idealistic evolutionism, which incorporated natural causality into the dialectical movement of the idea. Since these systems have disintegrated, or fail any longer to satisfy a more vital religiosity, the discussion of the first problem has for the most part come to an end. The revived orthodoxy has founded, upon the inner miracle of conversion, such a robust miracle-faith that it can look upon the whole of modern natural science as a matter of indifference. Even more liberal circles no longer dare to enter upon these problems in their full depth and width so as to transform the new sense of cosmic realism into a religious mood.

The work of theologians is accordingly devoted to a thousand apologetic detail-questions; and since the conceptualism of natural science, with its idea of a unified and ordered world substance, has conquered popular metaphysics, theology conducts a purely defensive struggle against materialism—and, above all, against its idealistic counterpart, pantheistic monism. In spite of numerous fine and penetrating insights, these various discussions failed to produce a serious reorientation. Instead, disgust at apologetical pedantry and instinctive religious aversion against monism, which dissolves all individual life and hence the individual relation to God, led to a violent rejection of these problems and a blunt refusal to deal with them. It is now the fashion to stress the remoteness, even the indifference, of these problems, and of cosmology in general, for religion. They are regarded as one-sided intellectualistic fancies which men can afford to ignore. What is stressed is the practical character of the religious life, as growing out of and satisfying demands of the will.

Religion is said to be concerned with the practical value and significance of the world. Intellectuals are left to make of this whatever they want to or must, but they cannot destroy or refute these practical evaluations and interpretations.

It is not likely that this position will become permanent. The seriousness of the changes in our cosmological and biological perspective will probably exert a direct influence on the structure of religious thought, even among theologians. For the present, however, this rejection has had this beneficial result: religion is understood more properly in its own unique essence, or at least as relatively independent of all cosmology. This liberation from cosmological problems was only made possible by a more energetic attachment to the given historical reality and power of Christianity. When the validity of Christianity was based on historical arguments, it became necessary to portray its historical reality as surpassing all non-Christian religion in power; and to show that its origin in Jesus linked it firmly and redemptively to a unique historical event, in contrast to the more tenuous links to history sustained by other outlooks on life. In so doing, however, one approaches the historical problem in the degree to which one leaves the cosmological problem behind. To be sure, apologetics had had its historical side from the very beginning, but insofar as history was now forced to carry the whole burden of the proof, the historical problem became more intensified. The contradictions between the view of history presupposed by this type of argumentation and the methods and results of historical research unfettered by dogmatic considerations were the more keenly felt, as historical criticism was making great advances all along the line and exerting more and more influence on biblical scholarship and on the study of the history of dogma. History proved to be a merely temporary support. Since it was to prove the truth of Christianity, it was bound to lead to the fundamental question of how it is possible to derive absolute norms from the particularity and relativity of history. Hence on this side of the problem, too, everything is once again put into question.

Clearly this process was not limited to theology. All the norms of our intellectual and moral life evolved from a rationalistic metaphysical dogmatism, by way of Hegel's doctrine of development (which combined rationalism and history), to a purely empirical grounding in history—thus posing the larger question as to how norms can be derived from history at all. The Hegelian and empirical-historical derivation of the norms then became increasingly rare; it was replaced either by a naturalistic metaphysics that promised to ground its norms firmly in natural law, or by the radical skepticism of the individualists and anarchists of the intellectual life. Positivistic sociology and social democracy, on the one hand, and the followers of Nietzsche and Renan, on the other, represent this situation. But though this problem confronts all of contemporary thought, it is most serious for theology, since theology stands or falls with the possibility of the attainment of universal norms and standards of value. As theology relies increasingly on the historical approach, it must devote more and more of its energies to the problem of the relationship of history to the attainment of norms. Theology will accordingly be able to claim the distinction of being the battleground on which the decisive battle is being fought; the outcome of this battle, in turn, will affect every other sphere of life. Unless religious positions can be regained and strengthened, it will be impossible to establish norms in these other areas. One's religious outlook ultimately determines whether norms will be accepted and obeyed.

For quite some time I have been endeavoring, in various writings, to point up the present status of this problem together with its historical origins, in order to establish the most important starting point for our work in relation to the most general considerations. But we theologians cannot, of course, resolve this our main problem without the help of the philosophers, who deal with the general articulation of our knowledge, the significance and application of methods, and the relation of particular disciplines to the problem of a world perspective. For several years I have searched through the pertinent philosophical material that was accessible to me. To be sure the yield was rather small. This problematics, this particular task of methodological investigation, has not yet penetrated deeply enough into the general consciousness. In theology one falls back upon a somewhat diluted supernaturalism, which derives the absolute character of Christianity (which distinguishes the latter from all other human, and relative, knowledge) from the way in which Christianity came into being; or upon a continuation of the Hegelian doctrine of development (in some way stripped of its strict metaphysical foundation), which represents the universal concept of religion as realized in Christianity and derives the absolute validity of Christianity from the laws of historical development that bring about this realization. Outside of theology both of these methods are virtually obsolete.

Beginnings towards new approaches to the problem can be found in the investigations in the realms of logic and philosophy of history undertaken by Lotze, Sigwart, Dilthey, Wundt, Vierkandt, Barth, and others. But they are only beginnings, quite incapable of enabling us to attain our objective. Generally speaking, they afford us little aid towards the solution of our problem, unless one is willing to confine oneself to purely sociological theorems that work out the natural laws of the evolution of society. The presuppositions on which these theorems rest, however, definitely rule out the validity of any religious norms; if such norms are actually desired, these naturalistic presuppositions must be combated. For they reflect the naturalistic delusion that natural laws represent ideal values, or can at least take their place. Here the aristocratic law of the struggle for existence is used as the basis for the construction of a democratic society dedicated to such ideals as universal welfare. Before long, skepticism, brutality, and fatalism are bound to follow from this faith in the laws of nature, and thus the error in the presupposition will become clear.

But when one looks for other ways in which values might be established, one is only met with a shrug of the shoulders. Dilthey, in a speech on the occasion of his seventieth birthday, said that the strides taken by historical scholarship since Grimm, Böckh, and Ranke have actually led to an 'anarchy of values.' This is the underlying mood of our time. A talented philosopher, whom I asked for information concerning the literature on this problem, answered me: 'Only a charlatan gives more than he has. Questions of this kind must not be addressed to philosophy. Insofar as we can speak at all of norms for judging the values that emerge in history, we can only begin with the fact of consciousness itself, measuring the various historical forms by the degree to which they approximate the idea contained in the fundamental fact of consciousness.' He was unaware that in this statement the problem is only indicated, and by no means solved. For what is this 'idea,' and where do we encounter it? Again only in history.

I am the more delighted to be able to refer the reader to a book in which the significance of this problem is seen in all its fullness and with complete clarity. I mean the work of Heinrich Rickert, which was completed only last year: *The Limits of the Concept Formation of the Natural Sciences: A Logical Introduction to the Historical Disciplines.*[1] This book is distinguished by admirable maturity and perspective, clarity and consistency. Amid the deluge of literary over-production, this is one of the few books that are really conducive to thought and learning, to clarification and progress. Deep-rooted naturalistic and metaphysical prejudices will make it difficult for the book to establish itself. Nevertheless, it is one of a growing number of signs that philosophy is once again becoming conscious of its proper tasks. Once again, philosophy is beginning to take part in the elaboration of an idealistic view of life, and indeed at that most important point where the two problems touch: by recognizing the peculiarity of the historical world as over against nature, yet without abandoning the historical world to the anarchy of values, but rather relating it to an ideal value system. Our own work stands to benefit greatly from this contribution.

Rickert does not yet formulate the problem, however, in terms of the point of view in which we are primarily interested and which we enunciated above. He attacks the problem at an early stage of development, where the decisive issues do indeed appear, but where the ultimate questions raised by them are not yet the real objective of the investigation. According to Rickert, the relation of history to a system of values is a problem in the philosophy of history, but this problem can be resolved only if the nature of empirical historical research and its methodology are understood.

The nature of historical research, in turn, can be clarified only through being compared with and distinguished from research in the natural sciences. With this brief indication of the direction of the thought of the book, we have also suggested why its starting point is a description of the nature of the methodology of natural science.

The predominant view among the learned, as well as among the laity, as to the nature of scholarship is that the only objective and solidly founded knowledge is that which is obtained through the investigation of the natural laws of reality. This would mean that results can also be achieved in history only when human history is seen as a continuation of biological evolution; history would thus be raised to the rank of a science only by being connected with and subordinated to the laws that govern the whole of nature. This procedure would seem to make possible the attainment of norms in history; these norms, however, would be derived not from the particularities of human history, but from the natural laws that govern it together with the whole of organic and inorganic nature. What these norms usually amount to is the ideal of the greatest possible adjustment of the members of the social group to one another, and of the group itself to the natural environment that conditions it and in which it is embedded.

Since this doctrine not only seeks to overthrow the traditional methods of historical research, but also uproots most of the traditional values that have evolved out of actual history, the question naturally arises whether such a transformation of the whole view of life is really necessary. Inasmuch, moreover, as this transformation would be based on the demand for the application of the methods of natural science to history, the next and more general question is whether the use of the methodology of the natural sciences in the historical discipline is actually obligatory, or even feasible. This question, in turn, leads to an epistemological investigation of empirical historical research. Only after this fundamental question has been decided is it possible to attack the further questions of the relation of history to the formulation of norms. Rickert accordingly begins by presenting the problem in its simplest form and at its simplest stage. Is there a difference, he asks, between the methodology of natural science and that of history? And if there is, what is the basis of this difference? what consequences follow from it for the structuring of the two methodologies? and what is their value for our view of the world?

In formulating the question in this form, however, Rickert is influenced not only by the naturalistic-sociological approach to history of Comte and his English followers, but also by the constructions of their opponents, who in the interest of idealism combat these theses and seek to derive the methods and goals of history from the nature of the life of the soul, as distinct from physical events. These idealists, among whom one might mention the philosophers Dilthey and Wundt and the professional historian von Below, evade the demand of the naturalists by confining to the physical world the validity of the mechanistic-atomistic metaphysics. To this they oppose a psychological metaphysics based on certain fundamental peculiarities of the life of the soul such as personality, individuality, and freedom; from these, they construct the metaphysical peculiarities of the elements of history, which are human souls; and since elements are subject to special laws of interrelationship, our idealists feel justified in declaring historical structures to be specifically historical.

But under these circumstances, the question of the derivation of norms from history still remains obscure, unless it is answered by reference to idealistic evolutionary theories that are opposed to the naturalistic concept of evolution and cannot be derived from a psychology of the kind described above, but only from the Hegelian or some similar world-metaphysics. However much this type of psychology may avoid metaphysical terminology, it still remains a psychological metaphysics of history and rests wholly upon the distinction between a mechanistic methodology of natural science and the teleological methodology of history. But if metaphysics is thus pitted against metaphysics, then the contradictions and collisions of the two metaphysical conceptual structures must be removed; and since these contradictions are most glaring in connection with the interrelationship of brain and soul, natural causality and historical causality, a theory of this kind remains burdened with all the problems of psycho-physics and the concept of causality. The attempt to resolve the problem by positing a psycho-physical parallelism leads nowhere, for in such a parallelism the only fixity would be in the events governed by physical laws, while the psycho-historical side, although intrinsically autonomous, must nevertheless correspond to its fixed parallel.[2] Consequently such a theory, in the final analysis, again succumbs to naturalism; and through the concession of a psycho-physical parallelism it yields up the key to its own position. The state of the problem with respect to naturalism is thus precisely what it would have been in any case.

It is for this reason that Rickert approaches the problem in its purely formal and methodological sense, initially disregarding all material differences and the distinction between physical and psychical events. His sole intention is to examine the objectives of the two conceptual structures and to note their methodological implications. His first main concern is to clarify the question whether there is an essential and necessary logical difference between the objectives of the two types of research. If such a difference is established, then the reasons for it must have their foundation within our logical relation to reality; and the different objectives with their interior bases must in turn produce different methodologies and modify our thinking from opposite points of view. The belief in a universal methodology and a single form of thought would then be a prejudice and a delusion, for thought must particularize itself into two main categories with respect to the content of experience. To attain certainty in this matter, Rickert begins with a strict analysis of the approach of the natural scientist as it is generally practiced and as it has often been logically defined; having ascertained aims and methods, he asks whether such a conceptual structure allows at all for the interests and aims of history. When it is shown that the answer is decidedly negative, the logical peculiarity of the historical approach is thereby demonstrated, and the question of its particular aims and methods is now made easier by the fundamental establishment of this kind of logical contrast.

Rickert is able to confine himself entirely to the logico-methodological question, and to overlook completely all particularity in the contents of knowledge, only because he subscribes to the view that the point of departure for all philosophical orientation is epistemology, and that the central discipline in philosophy is the theory of knowledge rather than metaphysics. Rickert formulated this position in an earlier writing, *Der Gegenstand der Erkenntnis* (1892), which is indispensable for the understanding of the book under discussion and which represents, moreover, one of the best brief expositions of the problem I know.[3] It is of decisive significance for the apprehension of the principle of all scientific investigation that science is not understood as the portrayal of a true and objective world, independent of consciousness, to which science could then require the consciousness to conform. Science does not abolish experience in order to find a truer, more real world behind experience, in relation to which experience would be mere appearance or manifestation, and to which one would be required to relate, rather than to the apparent reality of experience. Objects are given only for consciousness, and indeed as the fullness of the actual, empirical, qualitative world. This standpoint, the most rigorous consciousness-immanentism, is the only possible point of departure for systematic thought. Science cannot aim at anything other than the ordering and re-arranging of this immensely broad and variegated content of consciousness, in accordance with the categories and requirement immanent in thought itself, in order to enable the consciousness to survey this content, to control it, and to evaluate it according to fixed rules. Accordingly, science does not produce a picture of the true world capable of replacing the experientially given picture of genuine reality; it merely provides the means for the mastery of the one true reality, namely, the world of experience given to consciousness. There are no representations of objects that themselves transcend consciousness; there are only these very objects as given to consciousness. Apart from these, there are only remembered images of this, the only real world, and scientific transformation of these, the only real objects, into concepts; the latter are means for the control, the ordering, and the evaluation of reality, but never the genuine reality itself. The metaphysical hypostatization of these concepts as independent realities must be thoroughly eradicated; and true realism, which is at the same time the most stringent idealism, must be introduced. This involves the acknowledgement that objects are always and only given as empirically given data of consciousness, and that no science can produce a more real reality than this one. This means that all concepts are merely means and abbreviations for the master of this, the only true and really abiding reality. All corrections of the merely apparent and the illusory are only corrections of experience by experience, and never corrections of the phenomenal through interpretation in the lights of the true, i.e. the non-apparent, reality. The whole of atomism is not the representation of a genuine reality-relationship but rather a means for the interpretation and mastery of the only true qualitative reality; a means, however, which is characterized by a conscious one-sidedness and which ignores everything qualitative. All such historical concepts as intellectual movements, the spirit of peoples, trends, and evolutionary goals do not reveal the genuine propelling power of history, of which individual and personal peculiarities and the actual course of history would be mere manifestations; they simply formulate the fullness of historical experience and memory into concepts that facilitate the surveying and the understanding of this fullness, without thereby abolishing the one true reality. There is no way of ascertaining the real and objective existence of an object through a comparison with some conceptually formed image within a transcendent world ostensibly independent of consciousness.

A judgement that something does exist can only spring from an inner necessity, and from a fundamental ethical and teleological conviction that such an existential judgement arising necessarily out of the consciousness and arranging the object in a necessary connection of some sort, must be made in order to form the basis of our ethical action in a world of existential evaluations thus made and arranged.

The objection might easily be raised that this is solipsism; and in fact, for many people solipsism constitutes a transitional stage through which they proceed to a real apprehension of the fundamental problems. In itself, however, solipsism is not only practically absurd but also logically impossible, and in no sense is it the consequence of the position delineated above. An essential part of this position is the insight that the individual self, too, is an empirically given datum within the consciousness, quite distinct from the consciousness itself, objectively given to the latter and correlated by it with the rest of the empirical world. A sharp distinction must be made between the psychological subject, which in every respect and at any moment can become the material and object of the logical consciousness, and the epistemological subject—or consciousness itself. All epistemology, and thus every attempt to formulate the fundamental philosophical concepts, proceeds not from the experimental, psychological, personal human subject, which belongs to the empirical world, but rather from an impersonal consciousness that is connected with it, but that is conceptually distinct from it. For this impersonal consciousness, the world existed long before my psychological subject was born, and will continue to exist after the latter's death. We always assume this impersonal consciousness when we speak of a history of the earth, or of the solar system, or of the world of galaxies, at a time when no human beings existed at all.

Such is the position advanced by Rickert, as a member of the school that considers the task of philosophy to be the elaboration of the teaching of Kant; and that is dominated by the Fichtean development of Kant's teaching, which was cut short by the rise of classical metaphysics. Classical speculation, with its philosophy of history and its ethics, sought too quick a solution for the problems that arose out of the incipient flowering of empirical history and out of the expansion and relativization of the concepts of cultural history to which it led. Kant himself had worked out his transcendentalism as a logic of natural science; he had placed psychology into the same framework, in principle, even though he held that little more than description was possible in this area. A transcendental logic of history did not lie within the horizon. Classical speculation, on the other hand, grasped the centrality of the problem of history and established it within the purview of philosophy. But it sought to resolve the problem directly, through a cosmic metaphysics, rather than first working out a logic of history. Scorning to logicize empirical history, it forthwith historicized God and world reason. Yet what it desired can only be attained through a careful elaboration of epistemology. Such an elaboration would require above all the development of a logic of history—which Kant and Fichte neglected in their epistemological and methodological reflections. Both only touched on the logic of history. The beginnings that were made, especially by Fichte, were not carried further because the metaphysical school of Schelling and Hegel seized upon this burning problem and absorbed all interest. But inasmuch as this attempt at a metaphysical resolution of the problem has been given up, and only a renewal of the old naturalistic Enlightenment theories has taken its place, the time has now come to return to those most pregnant ideas and to elaborate precisely that which has up to now been neglected—the logic of history.[4]

This is the position that pervades the spirit and the methodology of the whole book. A consequence of this position will be noted by readers who, perhaps influenced by Dilthey and Wundt, look upon psychology as the foundation for an independent approach to history and, especially, for an idealistic interpretation of history. Such readers will be found particularly among the theologians. Rickert, however, emphatically rejects any such psychologism as entirely inadequate for the task. This rejection is especially significant; it illuminates the fundamental idea of the book. Philosophy came to rely on psychology when the inadequacy of materialism had been recognized, when it was understood that all reality is ultimately a psychic phenomenon, and that the idea of an external world merely contemplates the psychic phenomena relating to this external world without considering the psychological subject that perceives and shapes these phenomena. Generally speaking, this procedure seemed to afford a solid foundation for an idealistic view of the world, and, above all, a basis for the autonomy of history, inasmuch as the elements of history were thought to be the particular activities of the soul that produce both the individuation of the self and the social life, and finally the state, law, art, science, and religion. So it seemed that history as the study of spirit enjoyed a certain parity with natural science as the study of matter, while the nature of the fundamental activities of the soul seemed bound somehow to yield norms and ideals for the evaluation of historical occurrences. But Rickert shows that the goal, however desirable in itself, cannot be reached in this way.

First of all, this approach does not permit a definitive differentiation of the spiritual and the physical world; the degree of differentiation it permits is not sufficient as a basis for a special logic of history. From this standpoint the physical world always remains a mass of psychic phenomena, while the spirit remains the subject of the perceptions of nature. But then the question of the relation of these natural data to the higher history-forming psychical data still remains, again giving a naturalistic twist to the problem. The more such a psychology is scientifically worked out, the more it aims at general psychological laws. But what is historically most important—whatever is special, unique and individual—is quite beyond the grasp of such general laws.

Secondly, and more significantly, the psychological approach makes it impossible in principle to conceive the essential content of history, namely, the historical values of culture, as the norm-generating values they claim to be; and it is completely impossible to regulate the relationship of these value-claims to some ultimate normative value. Psychology knows thought only as the product of psychological laws; values are likewise seen as mere products of psychological processes. But the psychological process is something purely factual, and as such quite indifferent to all norms. Whenever norms are considered as norms, they are no longer psychological products or results of processes within the psychological subject, but rather fully independent and autonomous activities of consciousness that have the process for their object. Far from being expressions of laws immanent in reality, they first postulate the idea of laws and the striving after them. All norms and all thinking proceed not from the psychological subject, which is itself a part of the process of experience and material for observation, but rather from the epistemological subject. Psychology concerns itself only with the psychological subject, which, like all experience, is precisely a datum of experience and material for thought. Psychology is itself only a result of thought. But the locus of thought and of all norms is the epistemological subject, consciousness as such, for which all factual material constitutes the data to which it applies its scientific methods and normative values, which it derives from its own a priori. The point of departure for a logic of history can therefore never be psychology or the psychological subject, but only the epistemological subject and the logical a priori which it contains. Only a self-analysis of the epistemological subject, and not psychology, can therefore resolve the problem of the methods used in ordering the data of consciousness, and hence of the relation between the logic of natural science and the logic of history.

These preliminary remarks will render comprehensible the progression of the individual studies, which, with masterful circumspection, seek in every case only to explicate the logical a priori of the scientific enterprise as it is actually carried out in the particular disciplines, and to regulate what these disciplines mean, methodologically and in principle, on the basis of this a priori.

Rickert therefore first examines the logic of the natural sciences. The procedures of natural science have indeed been adequately portrayed in a large number of splendid studies by the natural scientists themselves. Theirs is a procedure that enjoys relatively universal recognition, while the logic of history is yet to be created. Therefore it is quite natural to elucidate the latter in terms of the most familiar logical procedure. Only in this way will it be possible really to overcome the inclination to naturalize history.

The logic of the natural sciences consistently aims to conquer the intensive and extensive qualitative diversity of reality, which can never be mastered directly by our thinking. It constructs, out of the regularity of repeatable occurrences, the concept of an event that is governed by universal laws; as soon as such an event is understood in terms of the operation of laws, it can be legitimately expected to be repeated wherever these laws are operative. The idea at which this procedure aims is the comprehension of the totality of empirical reality as a single whole, in which all occurrences are absolutely calculable in terms of universally valid laws, which in turn only represent the application of a general law of relation. But in order to attain this ideal, everything, unique, individual, and qualitative must be increasingly disregarded; and the whole content of experience must be dissolved into relations of ultimate objects entirely stripped of all qualities. The absolute simplicity and absence of quality that is here required gives characteristic expression to the particular ideal of the natural sciences: the complete elimination of everything that is unique and peculiar, and the complete reduction of all the data of consciousness to universals, to that which is valid everywhere and always.

Nor is this conceptual structure limited to the physical world; it is also applied to psychic phenomena. The attempt to give to psychology the structure of a natural science is, therefore, legitimate, insofar as psychology seeks to discover general laws for the combination and interaction of elementary psychic phenomena. Even the constructs of human history can indeed be approached in this way, from the viewpoint of universal, ever recurring events and relations; but such investigations no longer have anything to do with the interests and concerns of actual history. Such investigations are the task of sociology and social psychology, insofar as they aspire to universal laws of social groups and their interaction. Here it is a question of laws of relation and of a procedure (based on these laws), which approaches reality—with conscious onesidedness—only to formulate general concepts that will be universally applicable. Now this procedure has no special relationship with 'nature' in the ordinary, narrow sense of the word, where it signifies the physical world. It has only been formulated in a peculiarly classical way with respect to the physical world, and bears the name only a posteriori. One can only say that in its application to the physical world, this procedure has produced rather worthwhile and consistent results; but that the attempt thus to comprehend physical and psychical phenomena under a common concept is as yet an unrealized ideal.

Even in the application of this procedure to the physical world, we are still far from the attainment of the idea; and the general concepts used in the investigation of the physical world are today caught up in a revolution that reminds one of the conflict of the Ptolemaic and Copernican theories. Probably it would be more fruitful not to connect this method terminologically with the ambiguous word 'nature,' but rather, following Windelband, to designate it simply as 'nomothetic.'[5] But if this is the case, then it is quite clear that it is of the essence of this method to ignore one side of the world of experience, in order thereby to discern the general, universally valid laws. The individual and qualitative aspects of experience are set aside, and experience is transformed into concepts that yield a wholly inauthentic reality—or rather no reality at all, but only the means by which reality may be ordered and controlled. These means indeed proceed from the structure of the knowing consciousness and present themselves as internally necessitated as soon as knowledge reflects upon the regularity of reality while overlooking the individual particularities of concrete experience. From this standpoint reality becomes rational, i.e., capable of being subsumed under laws that are based on general concepts.

But when one proceeds from this standpoint, everything individual and particular is seen as an irrational, purely empirical fact that is to be eliminated by conceptualization. Every particular piece of sulphur, every peculiar appearance of light, every individual organism, every human personality or community structure is, from this standpoint, something special that cannot, as such, be derived from chemical, optical, psychological, or sociological theories; the qualitative and special is accessible to these theories only insofar as in it, too, the laws that operate everywhere else are operative. Having attained this insight, we should not allow ourselves to be deceived by the common opinion, which Dubois-Reymond expressed in his famous ideal of 'the spirit of Laplace,' namely that every particular phenomenon can be derived from a complete knowledge of all ultimate things and the laws of their relations. First of all, if these non-qualitative, ultimate things were truly the elements of which reality is composed, and which would explain everything—that is to say, if their concepts were considered metaphysically as reflections of reality—they could never yield an empirical qualitative reality. Secondly, this concept of a cosmic formula presupposes that the actual structure and the conditions of movement of all the elements of the cosmos at some particular moment are known. Now this actual structure itself cannot be derived from universal concepts, but is rather the final remainder of the individual and the particular, i.e., the irrational, which falls outside the scope of even the most broadly conceived framework of the natural sciences. Even if the individual event could at least ideally be derived from the cosmic formula—which is not the case, however, even ideally, for the reasons given above—such a derivation would be possible only by virtue of a concept of the purely irrational, factual, and individual that would be included in the cosmic formula.

It is clear, then, that the formulation of natural-scientific or nomothetic concepts not only ignores but actually eliminates a part of empirical reality, or of the data of our consciousness. But this part also must be made accessible to systematic thought, and it appears that this phase of systematic thought is represented precisely by historical thinking. Historical thinking is concerned with the systematic treatment of that which is merely factual, unique, particular, and, from the standpoint of universal laws, irrational. Now this very statement implies that this second method cannot be a mere cataloguing of endless diversities. This would be as impossible as it would be unscientific. What is needed here is the formulation of concepts and judgements that will master the infinite diversity by means of general concepts. But the structuring principle of the concepts must be that which is characteristic and interesting in these diversities.

The methodology of historical thought is conditioned by its objective, the organization of what is qualitatively diverse under the viewpoints of individual, particular centers. Naturally, the principle of organization of such general concepts cannot be a concept of law, but must be a concept that integrates a succession of single occurrences into a unique, individual, and indivisible whole; namely, the concept of the value they possess for the human consciousness that becomes aware of them. Accordingly, we are not primarily concerned here with the value they possess for the historian himself, but rather, quite generally, with the value which unique, individual constructs—within the cosmos, within the evolutionary process, within the organic world—have for the origin and existence of the human race; and with the various values by reference to which the complexities of reality have actually and historically been individualized (in the judgement of the men of both the past and the present) into value units (*Wertganzen*). The personal position of the historian with respect to these values is at this point a matter of indifference. What is important is the persons structure historical reality by reference to what they consider important and essential, and that historical reality becomes history when the occurrences of the past assume their proper place in relation to these values—when they can be portrayed according to the degree in which they posit or negate these values. The concepts of individuals value units replace the law concepts of natural science. These value units may be broad collective phenomena; they may culminate in individual personalities; they may be portrayed in their widest context and in their mutual interaction; they may be examined with respect to the causal connections of their structure. All these are the actual tasks of historical scholarship as it reconstructs the historical reality after its source material has been critically secured. But the organizing principle of its activities always remains the selection of particular facts with a view to constructing individual, unique value units out of them. The historian must be entirely impartial here, setting aside personal valuations; the sole task is to set forth the organization of the particulars of history into value units that are historically effective because their value is actually experienced. We have here a completely objective, purely phenomenological teleology that has nothing to do with metaphysics; its only function is to facilitate selection from the infinity of facts, and hence 'historical conceptualization.'

The historian, then, having completed the critical investigation of sources (which does not concern us directly here), will have to gather these materials around a center that is regarded as the source of value and as the organizing principle through which the totality of the values taken up achieves an individuality of its own. Examples of such centers are humanity in its broadest sense, then civilized humanity, then nations, classes, communities, and persons. What is required here is to portray the individual value units that determine the operations and the tendencies of these centers in their historical context, in their development, in the process of their actualization. If in natural science the ultimate concept is that of a law that uniformly conditions all changes, the ultimate concept governing historiography is that of an evolution that links together all the unique facts into a chain of value constructs. Whether or not this evolution is consistently progressive and evinces a continual growth of value, and whether or not it ever leads to an absolute value, are matters of indifference for the historian at this point. The task is to structure the flow of unique events according to the objective-teleological principle of linking these events together into value units that are ever new, that form ever unique combinations and that are felt to be such, either directly or indirectly, by the historical center around which his history revolves. This concept of development wholly includes the causal interconnection of the events; but the demonstration of causal interconnections is here only a means for the construction of historical units, never an end in itself; and the causal connection between two individual facts of experience will be formulated here with due regard for the particularity of the cause, rather than in the sense of the concept of causality maintained in the natural sciences, where all particularity is excluded.[6]

All our classical histories actually follow these methodological principles. What we have done is to disclose the deeper reasons for their procedure. But at the same time it is clear that the validity of the historical method as here understood is not restricted to so-called human history in the narrower sense. It applies, rather, to all conceptual treatments of the individual and particular, wherever these may be found within the data of our experience. Only that which has no relation to human values falls outside of its scope—astronomy for instance, insofar as it goes beyond the limits of the solar system. But even the history of the solar system is, with respect to the earth, the presentation of a unique, individual value unit that is teleologically organized as interesting; and this applies still more to the history of the earth and the history of the organic world. From this point of view the presentation is in every case oriented towards the historical particular rather than the scientific-universal. It is then a matter of course that the main theme of history is properly not this procession of cosmic-telluric occurrences, but rather the occurrences that are most important to persons in their own development; hence history concerns itself essentially with humanity, and, again, with the civilized part of humanity.

The name, 'historical method,' has again only an a posteriori basis and probably here also the terminology of Windelband is to be preferred, who speaks of the 'idiographic method.' But whatever name may be used, the nature of the case is clear. The historical method aims at the individual and the particular, because only in these unique occurrences are the values of our consciousness formulated and experienced. The historical method necessarily takes its place beside that of the natural sciences, because the consciousness must, by an inner necessity, not only give a conceptual order and rationality to the world, but it must also produce values; and it achieves its orientation concerning the values of life only through objective scholarly knowledge of the historical development of human value-structures. The latter function is, in fact, more important than the former. For what meaning would it have to view the world nomothetically, if this relative ability to survey and control the world were not a necessary precondition precisely for the actualization of the values of our consciousness? But we only achieve clarity with respect to the values of the human consciousness through a historical orientation concerning their development, and through the comprehension of what has been gained by historians. This fact drives us to history and at the same time organizes its methodology.

So the two methods are, in terms of principle, worked out. But this sharp distinction applies to them only as to the two necessary poles between which our thought moves. In actual practice scholarship naturally knows countless combinations of the elements associated primarily with one of the two methods; and this situation arises from the very nature of the case. For the concept-formations of pure natural science and pure history are only the logical extremes. Between them there necessarily arise transitional and mixed forms. Natural science indeed strives to eliminate the particular but cannot fully do so even in the most universal natural science, mechanics. This striving only makes possible an approximate solution of the task and stages in the approach toward universality. Natural science is structured precisely by the degree to which the particular is eliminated, accordingly its individual disciplines are often strongly influenced by the particular. The concept-formation of the natural sciences is only relative, and contains strong historical elements; the most pronounced approximation to the historical occurs in biology. On the other hand, history likewise presupposes not only universal conditions of nature, but also universal psychological concepts and universally recurring social processes. Here also one can speak only of relatively historical disciplines, which contain strong elements of natural science. This is particularly true of sociology; and that is quite as it should be. What really matters is that the contrasting principles of the two methods are understood, and that the logical structures of these two opposite tendencies of thought are recognized. Thus these mixed forms are in no wise detrimental; since they necessarily arise out of the structure of thought, they are rather in a position to advance the cause of scholarship.

Another goal of Rickert's is thus attained. The fundamental difference between the methods of natural science and of history has been deduced epistemologically and, proceeding from this distinction between the two forms of thought through the immanent goals of the consciousness, the individual methodological procedures have been established, insofar as they are methods of empirical scholarship that treat the given data of consciousness or experience. Even Rickert's introduction had stressed that what is involved in this whole problem is not merely an epistemological distinction between two empirical disciplines, or a decision in the struggle over the 'new method' of historiography which up to now has proceeded with an instinctive sureness of touch—and with which philosophical ignorance is today interfering. Rickert is equally interested in the significance of this distinction for the general problems pertaining to one's view of the world, and in the effect of truly historical thinking on philosophy as a whole.

Now, this issue also arises immediately out of his epistemological deduction of the historical method itself. The goal that gives rise to this method, and that is set for us through the organization of consciousness, is to treat reality by reference to the values that are struggling to emerge and to assume form as life-relationships. Since these values reside only in concrete realities that can be experienced and not in abstract concepts, this investigation of values is dependent upon the sphere of the unique and particular; that is, upon history. But then some questions naturally arise. What is the relation between the knowledge of historical value-structures and the construction of one's own present values? How does one get from factual relationships, which research shows to have been organized by ideas of value, to one's own organization of a new value-oriented relationship of maximum correctness? how can the abundance of values emerging in the evolutionary process teach us something objective, which would provide objectively valid (i.e., necessary) norms for the direction of our own value constructions? In this respect, history still does not seem to be on a par with natural science. In following its essential goal, natural science arrives at objective results; not at a reproduction of the objective world, to be sure, but at a valid ordering of the world, to which, as a necessary and therefore certain truth, we can and must accommodate ourselves in our thoughts and in our actions. It is precisely this objectivity which is so passionately praised by the representatives of the natural sciences, and which is held up to the historical discipline; the latter, it is said, can never be free from entirely subjective and fluctuating judgements of historical values. If the epistemological deduction is to lead not simply to the methodology of empirical historiography but also, by means of the latter, to a philosophical grounding of the values that are recognized as valid, then must there not be an analogous 'objectivity' for history? Does the historical discipline achieve its goal if it merely presents a collection of historical value-structures, variously evaluated, for the reader to choose from? And if it does not achieve its goal, if with one of the most perceptive of historians, Renan, it plunges into the abyss of relativism and skepticism, does it then have any meaning at all that would warrant a complicated deduction of its methods?

History must be objective. This means not only that the historian must be impartial and refuse to interject private value-judgements in the representation of actual developments. History must also be objective in the sense that it permits all historically emerging values to be referred to a stable criterion of personal value, at the same time teaching its students to derive this criterion of value from the knowledge of historical developments and to attribute to it an objective and therefore unconditional validity. It is clear that under the heading 'Objectivity of History,' Rickert at last discusses as ultimately crucial the problem that constituted my point of departure in the present discussion. It is the pressing problem of the relation between history and norms, between development and standards of development—the problem that Hegelian philosophy had placed in the center of its thought and that must be solved today without the Hegelian presuppositions, which have lost much of their cogency. The teaching of Hegel was defective in that it sought to establish an immediate identity between the concepts of natural science and those of history, by making the nomothetic universal the dynamic force and the ultimate goal of the idiographic particular. In doing so, it again sacrificed the particularity and individuality of history and transformed the whole of history into a valueless preliminary stage of the realization of the universal concept; and it contributes nothing to call this concept a concrete one and to distinguish it from universality in the abstract.

Hegel's question remains; but it must be answered in another way. Here we pass from the methodology of empirical historical research to the problems of the philosophy of history. Rickert is concerned to show that these problems arise directly from empirical history, and that their resolution must be undertaken in terms of the concepts of empirical history. His book accordingly connects the logic of empirical history with the problem of the philosophy of history, i.e., the problem of an objectively valid value system. Now the connection posited by him may be too close to assure to the logic of historical thinking, which is an important and fruitful theory in its own right, its full autonomy and effectiveness. Conversely, it may also jeopardize the full appreciation of the peculiar interest of the system of recognized values that constitutes the philosophy of history, and of the special nature of this discipline, which is based on ethics. But for our purposes, since we are only concerned with the significance of the work for the philosophy of history, and with the initially raised question, these possible shortcomings are a matter of indifference.[7]

The bulk of Rickert's book deals with the problem of historical method in a purely formal and, at the same time, purely empirical manner, insofar as it establishes epistemologically the presuppositions and essence of this method in contrast to the method of natural science. Thus he continues the old struggle over the treatment of history, which has been waged since the advent of the new approach to history in the Enlightenment. This formal-rational empiricism wholly corresponds to the transcendental standpoint maintained by Rickert; thus this standpoint also becomes the means of orientation for history, as it has long been for natural science.

Since the collapse of the older Christian historiography, which had revolved completely around the four world-monarchies and the church and had operated with divine dispositions and interventions, it was necessary to construct new historical presuppositions and concepts.

Here Renaissance historiography led the way. Then the Enlightenment, which generally looked upon the conceptualization of natural
science as the ideal to be followed, atonomized history in the interplay
of individual forces. This interplay was considered to have as its goal
the realization of universal concepts; and every individual was thought
to be, intrinsically, equally qualified to achieve this realization.[8] The
reaction to this approach was led by German idealism, which
eventually gave birth to an empirical historiography that has
developed into an autonomous discipline devoted to the specifically
historical approach. While idealism provided the first impetus, this
modern historiography (which dominates, whether consciously or not,
virtually all contemporary writing of history) had either turned its
back upon the metaphysical presuppositions of idealism, or at least
ignored them. But since the natural-science ideal lost none of its
potency, there was no lack of revivals of Enlightenment
historiography. In these revivals one went far beyond the restraint
observed by the older Enlightenment historiography; history was
embedded in the grand flow of nature, in order to derive from the
latter and its laws firm rules for the comprehension and evaluation of
the small island known as history.

Thus Buckle looked upon the dependence of humanity on nature as
the central fact, the effects of which could be defined in terms of laws;
and he saw the value of history in the elaboration of a knowledge of
nature and a technology that overcomes these dependencies by
adapting to them. Similarly, Comte viewed history simply as a higher
complication of natural forces and assigned to it the task of developing
a positive knowledge of nature as the foundation of purposive social
organization. Thus it can be structured, according to the degree to
which it accomplishes this task, into the famous three stages. Going
still further, Darwinism, with its universal biological laws of
adaptation, selection, and hereditary transmission, considered itself
capable of dealing with human history as well. Naturalist psychology
then applied itself to the task and sought to discover the natural law
governing the successive stages of development. Today the name of
Lamprecht enjoys special prominence among us as of one seeking to
apply these views in the scientific treatment of history, in opposition
to the historiography that emerged out of the school of German
idealism. Rickert wants to bring clarity to this conflict; and he does so
with his distinction between nomothetic and idiographic concept
formation, both of which transform empirical reality into knowledge,
but from different points of view and for different purposes. The
reason why thought must approach the one undivided empirical reality

by means of two entirely different methods lies in the nature of the empirical world, and of the consciousness which sustains it. In order to grasp the boundless reality, consciousness must come to know. To know, however, means to simplify or to unify, and this takes place in two directions: on the one hand, there is a conceptual grasping of that which repeats itself and is everywhere the same; on the other hand, that which is ceaselessly changing, qualitative, and particular is analyzed according to its unique significance for humanity. A reduction of of one method to the other, or the attainment of a higher unity in which both methods are contained, goes beyond human power. Our ultimate point of orientation is always and only consciousness with its positive data and its dialectical requirements. But consciousness always retains its diversity, and monism remains an empty ideal.

The most important problems have not yet been settled, however; they have only been posed. To be sure, historiography first arises from the urge to know, which structures and orders the stream of diversity in order to master it. But by ordering this stream of diversity in a continuing and interrelated series of value units from the standpoint of what is valuable or essential for civilized humanity, the organizing principle of the historical disciple is shown to be its relation to human values. Inasmuch as we are confronted by a chaos of value systems, however, the need to discover an objective law arises—and not simply a law of mere causal sequences. For in the first place, such a law cannot in any case be constructed a priori; its operation can be demonstrated only case by case, through a tracing back of its particular genesis. In the second place, even if it were possible to demonstrate a universal law of consequence, such a law could only explain the consequence without providing a foundation for an objective criterion of value. Thus arises the need for relating historical constructions to an objective value system. This, however, can only be derived from historiography itself. The most intimate secret of the urge to know history is thus shown to be the relating of actual historical values to a value system that ought to be recognized as valid: this is the goal that necessitates the mastering of the stream of diversity.

The individual historian in a restricted field may wholly ignore or forget this goal; he or she may be immersed in the valuations of past generations, and order and structure the past from their standpoint. But the very fact that such a task is undertaken has meaning only if acquaintance with past and alien valuations has significance for our own valuations. The writing of universal history, above all, which transcends the horizon of individual peoples, cultures, persons, classes, and the limits of civilization, must consciously deal with this problem; it must structure and order history from the standpoint of a value that ought to be recognized as valid. But we only apprehend this obligatory value system as we look at history. By entering into alien, or semi-alien, or past value constructions and exhibiting the geographical and historical relativity of our present value constructions, we find a constant corrective for our own value constructions; that is, we supplement and broaden our own being (which is inclined to become narrow) and we dissolve all naive attempts to isolate and absolutize that which is given. But this corrective, the need for which constantly drives us to history, would attain its ideal perfection only if it allowed us in a solid scholarly way to relate the abundance of historical value constructions to a system of values that ought to be recognized as valid.

Thus the problem of historical method leads necessarily to the problem of philosophy of history in the proper sense of the term. History actually attains scientific character only when its pursuit arises from an immanent essential dialectic necessity. This necessity, however, lies in the need of the consciousness to construct ideals of value; hence the consciousness cannot be indifferent to the value constructions of the past, which must be regarded rather as realizations of this necessity, from which we have something to learn with respect to our own value constructions. There is an analogous problem for the nomothetic sciences. These sciences arisen from the drive of knowledge towards uniformity; but inasmuch as this drive towards uniformity does not afford a representation of a real world but only a simplification of the empirical world, the cognitive value of these sciences cannot ultimately be an end in itself. The mastery of experience through the discerning of uniformities must be a means to the improvement of experience, to the shaping of experience through the idea of the highest values. But this is not the place to pursue this thought further. Here our concern is only with the philosophical problem that is posed by history as an empirical discipline.

Now there are two questions that the author, in his haste to reach his conclusion, does not always keep clearly separate: first, the question under what conditions or rather through what relations to absolute dialectical requirements the character of history as an objective discipline is definitively realized; and secondly, the question, what actual relation philosophy can demonstrate between empirical history and the concept of a relation to absolute values that is implied in the methods of history, and which perfects its character as a discipline but is actually derived from ethics. Concerning the first question, the author is content to show that consciousness by its very nature urges the construction of obligatory values, and that it can therefore not be indifferent to the historical existence of actual value constructions that demand recognition; rather, it must seek to know these actual value constructs in their breadth and fullness as well as in their development and continuity. Thus Rickert establishes an epistemological need for history and for the logical concept of the historical discipline, inasmuch as this need corresponds to the epistemological peculiarity of experience, namely, that its data consist entirely of unique factualities that cannot be derived from anything else: the historical discipline constructs individual value units, makes them a part of the totality of values, characterizing the culture as a whole, and, in doing so, relates them (at least by implication) to an absolute value. What this ultimate cultural value may actually be, and what relationship may obtain between it and actually historical values, is a matter of indifference for the historian; it is sufficient that a need within the consciousness drives one towards history, and produces the methodology of history, namely, the structuring of successive and interrelated value units. History becomes objective through the implied (quite general and formal) requirement that there be this relation to an absolute value; this requirement distinguishes it, for instance, from the relativism of Renan, which would simply fall in love with its respective object.

But it is difficult to separate from these matters the second question, regarding the relation of concrete history to a materially determined value system; for only when we conceive of this second question as in some way answered do those cautious, purely formal definitions take on life. These formal definitions may leave the actual answer open, by limiting themselves to the purely formal presuppositions by virtue of which history can make the claim to be a necessary discipline. But if history is to be not simply a necessary discipline but also an actual apprehension of its intended goal, then the problem posed by these presuppositions must also be resolved. This is why Rickert repeatedly found it impossible to confine his discussion to the first problem, even though this second problem seemed to him to introduce too many properly philosophical issues into his purely methodological investigation of the empirical study of history. In our exposition of the thought content of Rickert's book, we may be allowed to bring to the fore this most important question, which is of secondary importance for the author but which, for all ethicists and philosophers of culture and religion, is of capital interest. The result of our reflections up to this point is that history proceeds from essential needs of the consciousness and relates the representations of historical value units to the concept of obligatory values. But what, then, is the relation between this obligatory ideal and historical value constructs? Or more precisely: Of what help are the historical value constructs to us in the production and structuring of the content of such an ideal, recognized as valid for us; that is, in giving content to the formal concept of absolute values? With these presuppositions, how is it possible to escape the circle of turning—because of the need for norms—to history with its merely factual and subjectively felt valuations, and then back again from the factual to the concept of empty and formal norms which it implies?

The answers to this difficult problem—a problem that clearly confronts us in Herrmann's ethics, where similar Kantian presuppositions also lead to an absolute goal that is merely formal, and which Schleiermacher sought to solve in a somewhat less formal manner through his construction of a doctrine of goods based on the relation of spirit to nature—are scattered through various parts of Rickert's book. But since this problem is particularly important for us, I would like to take the liberty of collecting these occasional statements and supplying what may be lacking out of the spirit of the whole.

The fundamental discipline is epistemology, with the logical principles that are derived from it. From the acknowledgement of these principles there arises, in the first place, a nomothetic or natural-scientific knowledge. What remains uncomprehended there, namely, the irrational particular, which is inaccessible to this type of knowledge, together with the epistemological need for value construction, requires the idiographic or historical disciplines. These disciplines point, through the teleological concepts that give them structure, to the concept of the value-unit, and hence to a third group of disciplines, the normative sciences that deal with the values and norms of the mind. But these normative concepts, which manifest the dynamic center of thinking as such, are elaborated with respect to content primarily through the consideration of historical value constructs. Their relation to the natural sciences is merely secondary, since the latter indicate the sphere, conditions, and limitations of purposeful action. The central problem is, therefore, not only for history but for systematic thought as such: What connection is there between the very concept of norms that are recognized as valid, which is the chief contribution of the theory of knowledge, and the actual, historical value constructs ascertained by historical research? Either idea requires the other, yet they also seem to exclude each other—the merely factual and individual over against the universally valid, the ought-to-be.

With his customary judiciousness, Rickert proceeds to eliminate, one after the other, the various plausible theories that resolve the problem with inadequate means. The most common popular theory, however, is not considered at all, namely the theological theory that, by grounding the norms in a divine revelation that is historically strictly isolated, achieves a solid program for the resolution of the problem. Scholarship no longer concerns itself with this theory, which has been dissolved precisely by historical criticism. In view of the preceding discussion, it is not surprising that the naturalistic theory is also quickly dispatched, together with its attempts to derive 'natural values' from its consideration of history in connection with the events and laws of nature and particularly organic evolution and the objectivity that is supposed to be unattainable by a merely subjective decision concerning anthropomorphic values, but attained by the 'natural values' in virtues of their derivation from natural law. If it is the essence of natural science to construct non-teleological concepts that operate as universally applicable laws, then it is essentially impossible for natural science to generate concepts of value; and all the values contained in the supposedly natural laws of adaptation, evolution, and differentiation are unconscious borrowings or presuppositions that are taken from the unique whole of human cultural development.

No less insoluble is the problem in terms of a purely empirical theory. Since such a theory is bound to conceive of laws of nature as mere generalizations that are empirically useful, it can also look upon valuations that have actually prevailed either in the past or in the present (or some compromise between them) as empirically general modes of procedure, and consequently must ascribe to the latter as much or as little validity as to the former. From such a standpoint, a purely empirical pursuit of both types of knowledge is certainly possible. But just as a natural science of this type does not do justice to the needs and nature of thought, so historiography that organizes and understands historical constructs only from the point of view of empirically emerging values will not do justice to the urge that drives one to pursue the knowledge of history. Both types of knowledge contain supra-empirical elements, modes of procedure that are not simply to be taken note of, but that are necessary and that point, therefore, to the supra-empirical a priori that is latent in either mode: the concept of universal law in the natural sciences, and in history, the concept of a value that is to be recognized as valid and that is to be actualized in historical individuation. Only at this point is the genuine goal of scholarship achieved: the arbitrary, accidental, and merely subjective is excluded, and a relationship is established to what is necessary and therefore objective. How such a relationship indeed exists in the metaphysical philosophy of history, which is peculiarly characteristic of German idealism, but which is also intended wherever the historical agent is seen to be, not empirical persons and their thoughts, but rather an idea or plurality of ideas manifested in them, yet not identical with them. Here the problem is resolved by positing an identity between this agent and the goal of humanity or of the world, which is constructed independently through metaphysical speculation; at the same time, a necessary procession of stages in the realization of this goal is attributed to this agent. One can accordingly attach every empirically known value construct of history to the locus that in indicated by the necessary development of the idea, assigning it a place in an objective context that is independent of short-sighted subjective judgements and, at the same time, making it possible to evaluate the construct and to adopt a position regarding it. For the locus within the necessary explication of the idea gives us exact information concerning the degree of approximation to the full realization of the idea.

But such a theory is, after all, quite impossible. First of all, because a goal for the world or for humanity cannot be metaphysically constructed and then applied to history; for truly, every such goal is always derived or abstracted from actual history. But also, and above all, because in such a viewpoint the essence of actual history is dissolved, and precisely at the decisive point where it unfolds what is essential to it and what distinguishes it from natural science. The particular and the individual, the unique and the peculiar, are destroyed; and with them also the essential organizational principle of history, which is relegated to being an instance of the realization of the universal concept, where the individual is important and essential only as long as he serves the apprehension or illustration of the universal concept. Should one, in order to avoid such a relegation, point to the significance of the individual as a link and a point of transition, this significance would still remain provisional, everything earlier being mediated through everything later.

How, then, is the problem to be solved? It is necessary to go back to the governing thought of the whole investigation. Experience or reality is the content of the epistemological subject, and this experience never becomes knowledge through representations and concepts that attempt to portray a truer reality; but only through judgements that, proceeding from a need of the consciousness, designate something as existent and then relate this existent to the thoughts that necessarily flow from the consciousness, in order thereby to lift the existent itself into the sphere of the necessary. But the resulting relations of the existent are of two kinds; inasmuch as there are no concepts of the necessary that are not of universal validity, they may be divided into concepts of laws and concepts of values. Empirical reality is dealt with from the viewpoint of laws, and in this process of abstraction everything particular, unique and qualitative vanishes; that is, the real world in which we live, hearing and seeing, groping and feeling. Or it is considered from the viewpoint of obligatory values, and under this viewpoint the abstract conformity to law vanishes, together with the empty universal; the individual qualitative reality with its particular and unique contexts comes to light, because only here, and above all in the productions of humanity, does the possibility of various valuations and the need to decide among them become apparent. In both cases, to be sure, the concept of the necessary is purely formal. We do not approach experience with a ready-made concept of law, but rather with the need to look for laws and to construct them; neither do we approach experience with a ready-made value judgement, but rather with the need to refer everything to some ultimate value.

Since we now recognize that even the determination that a thing exists presupposes the acknowledgement of the value of truth, and since we also know that the whole work of natural science is undertaken only on account of the value of this knowledge for human culture, we note immediately that knowledge rests ultimately on values and the norms to be derived from them. What ought to be is the key to what is; the acknowledgement of an absolute purpose of existence is the a priori of scholarship. This central position of the valuing consciousness, however, does not signify the subordination of the understanding of reality to subjective and arbitrary wishes. Such wishes proceed only from the psychological subject, and along with this subject are themselves objects of knowledge. The necessity of referring everything actual to an ultimate value proceeds, rather, from the epistemological subject and lies in the nature of 'consciousness in general.' when we understand what is in terms of what ought to be, and reality in terms of value, we are not elevating arbitrary and vacillating wishes above the eternal laws of being that encompass man in an infinite whole, nor are we interpreting the world anthropomorphically in terms of the perspectives of tiny and transitory creatures; this approach is actually the a priori of all knowledge and the center of the epistemological subject, which can only organize all of its knowledge from this standpoint. But if this is the case, then it is absolutely certain that there must be an ultimate value. That which is so central to all knowledge, and which, specifically, first gives meaning to all historical knowledge, must also be real; that is, it must be capable of realization. This, to be sure, is a belief and to this extent a religious thought. But this aspect of the issue cannot be pursued further here. Suffice it to say that the reference to an ultimate purpose that 'ought to be' is the a priori of all knowledge.

In this sense, as the a priori of the epistemological subject as such, the ultimate purpose indeed only signifies the necessity of a reference to something universally valid, to the ought-to-be as such, the conversion of the content of experience from a merely given diversity into a unity that is produced through submission to the necessary, the elevation of the psychological subject into the epistemological subject's sphere of necessity, the structuring of the merely nature life of the soul into a personality, the transformation (through purification) of the subjective spirit into the objective spirit. But in all this, nothing as yet is said concerning which concrete projects and the adoption of which concrete and specific goals lead to this purpose. Epistemology can only deduce the necessary as the formal purpose; it can only develop the forms of thought and the forms of goals to be adopted. The whole content of thought and of the goals to be adopted stems from experience and from the psychological subject, where the flowing stream of reality is characterized by diversity. So the content with which these forms are filled is always dependent upon experience, and the concept of absolute norms is always dependent upon history. Now the historical value-constructs, which (whether already completed or still struggling to be completed) may claim a closer or more distant relation to the necessary purpose, already present us with established connections between the empirical and the normative. We must look upon these historical value-constructs as suggestive preliminary labors toward the connection we seek to establish, and as concrete resolutions of the problems that have sprung from the necessary relation between the empirical and the supra-empirical that is concealed from us. We must, moreover, recognize the continuity between these historical value-constructs and our own partial attempt to elaborate further the idea of referring the empirical world to an absolute purpose.

But this further elaboration can only mean that we impartially comprehend, survey, and compare these historical value-constructs; and that we proceed to arrange them in a hierarchical order that does not signify the coincidence of temporal sequences and level of value, but rather the construction of a standard arising spontaneously from this comparison and carrying personal conviction. This standard is found through forging a new synthesis of the gains of the past and the living present; namely, when we take from history the ideal contents of the values of life and, for our part and in our own way, energetically refer to the idea of ultimate values whatever attests itself to our judgement as normative.[9]

To be sure, we have now once again arrived at the previously indicated circle. But insofar as we are now aware how this circle necessarily arises out of the structure of our consciousness, it can be understood in a way that contains the elements for a resolution of the problem. It is the circle that unites the epistemological and the psychological subject, the ultimate riddle of all reality and all humanity, in which all other riddles—the antinomies of fact and value, of constant change and eternal unity, of actual causal continuity and ideally necessitated freedom, of pluralism and monism—are grounded. But once it is established that this circle is the fundamental fact of our intellectual life, we are thereby assured that there must be a solution beyond human comprehension, since belief in the possibility of a solution constitutes the a priori of the dialectic that leads to the discernment of the circle in the first place. The circle thus contains an element of religious faith in the possibility of its resolution; this element keeps on urging its resolution to the extent that it is at all humanely attainable.

But for this work of resolution a number of fixed points are contained in the circle. First, there is given in it the absolute need to relate all knowledge to an ultimate purpose, and with it, the assurance of a constantly growing approximation to this ultimate purpose. Secondly, there is given in this circle the judgement that all historical value-constructs are earlier solutions to the problem, which proceed from a unity of reality unknown to us, and which connect the contents of experience with normative ideas in such a way that these connections do not simply send us back to the task; they are actual realizations of the solution and, therefore, significant materials for our own resolution. Thirdly, there is contained in this circle, and in the irrational connection between the factual and the necessary that it demands, the very concept that proved to be determinative for the understanding of history—the concept of individuality. Now it is the very essence of individuality at this point that it represents a referral to necessary values of the factually given content of the psychological subject; this referral creates complexes of value units that owe the necessity of their validity to the autonomous individual judgement, since they originate in a particular situation. While these value units thus have their universal necessary validity, they are nevertheless wholly individual and unrepeatable because they summarize particular and unique circumstances. This individuality of all such value constructs is not therefore merely a limitation and defect, as Spinoza's statement *'omnis determinatio est negatio'* suggests. It only appears this way under the rationalistic tyranny of the universal concept, whose authority is properly limited to the natural sciences. This individuality is, however, a characteristic of the finite and irrational; yet in this irrationality lies at the same time the priority of life and actuality over abstraction, as well as the ethical value of the act, which in a definite situation creates, by virtue of an inner necessity, something definite that no one else can achieve in quite the same way. This is the truth in Leibniz's objections to Spinoza, in which Leibniz advocated knowledge based on historical concept-formation in contradistinction to the natural-scientific rationalism of Spinoza. Fourthly—and this thought is for the most part only hinted at by Rickert—these individual value constructs are not unrelated structures that merely contradict one another. They are constructed in a historical context that, in its great breadth, shows a plurality of analogous structures, and in its temporal succession a development, an elaboration of previous solutions which are utilized ever anew.

This is why the developmental process does not need to mediate the individual, nor does it need to be viewed as a continuing assent to higher and higher values. All particular constructs retain their unique value. Value-constructs may sometimes become shallow and weak, they may become overly dependent on merely natural conditions, or they may even be displaced by constructs that embody no value at all. But universal-historical reflection is always able to transcend the historians' representation of the value-units of the past and to structure them in an internally cohesive hierarchy. Our own value construction is dependent, on the one hand, on these observations; but on the other hand, it also serves as the standard that gives them their structure. This paradox of the objectivity of the subject, or the synthesis of fact and idea, cannot be removed from the concept of the standard. The standard cannot be constructed as an objective law of evolution in the manner of the Hegelian metaphysic or of psychologistic naturalism. The concept of every such law must distinguish between the causal sequence and the hierarchy of values; the latter concept is to be constructed only according to one's best knowledge and conscience, on the basis of the most mature factual knowledge and the most personal commitment of faith.[10]

The implication for our own value construction is this. As all historical valuations in their time were individual, unrepeatable, unique in their structuring of the idea of value, so also every contemporary attempt at a scholarly determination of the relation between actual historical valuations and the ultimate goal is likewise an individual combination of the given moment. Through scholarly circumspection and reflection, through knowledge of the broad scope and the development of history, this assessment is protected against the arbitrariness of the judgements of merely practical life against the shortsightedness, isolation, and self-satisfaction of uncontrolled and uncompared judgements. But even the most circumspect determination remains an individual act, whose objective necessity lies, in the final analysis, only in the assurance of the one making it that, upon a careful weighting of all circumstances, conscience requires this particular judgement. The synthesis of the epistemological and the psychological subject is effected in every case by an individual act of conviction, and this very individual character belongs to its ethical worth. The circle described above is dissolved only by action, namely, by an act of forming conscientious judgements based on the greatest possible knowledge of experience. Such action never attains an absolute, pure, immutable idea of the world, unstained by historical particularity. Rather, insofar as it constitutes a decision pertaining to the continuity and comparison of historical values, it always remains an individual act, which has its particular value and its particular significance, just like all previous acts and all those that are yet to come. The endeavor to make judgements on the broadest basis, to retain the continuity with what has already been attained, and to make decisions on the basis of well-considered comparisons gives such a decision its scientific character, but this scientific character does not eliminate the individuality of the decision. For everything historical, despite all references to absolute values, remains irrational and individual. This is both our fate and our destination; nor is another world conceivable in which this would no longer be the case. In such a world, doubt and unrest might, at best, give way to clarity and certainty; but even clarity and certainty remain individual, until perchance the soul returns again into the Divine Spirit.

I believe I am justified in formulating Rickert's resolution of the problem of the philosophy of history in this way. There remains the final question—what we are to say about this piece of dialectic, about its methodology of empirical historiography as well as about its theory of a philosophy of history?

Rickert's teaching poses the same problem that German speculative idealism had already posed in the wake of the poetic, romantic, and philological expansion and relativization of the historical perspectives. Like the German idealists, Rickert closely connects historical problems with ethics when he assigns the task of solving the historical problem of culture to ethics as the doctrine of the system of values that are to be recognized as valid.[11] Among the systems that originated at that time, there is none that is closer to the thought of Rickert than that of Schleiermacher. It may be said in passing that as Schleiermacher is viewed less exclusively from a theological perspective, he is recognized more and more as one of the most astute, comprehensive, and instructive thinkers of the period. Schleiermacher also looked upon the concepts of natural science as merely introducing order and uniformity in the diversity of experience as it is given to us in consciousness; he likewise referred both history and ethics to individual valuations, in which experience is both shaped and evaluated. But Schleiermacher did not accept the plurality of principles developed by Rickert as ultimate; with the help of religion he finally welded them together in a monism oriented to feeling. He also avoided limiting himself to the merely factual values of history; ultimately he sought, although with characteristic reservations, to deduce even their content from the principle of reason.[12] Criticism, which experienced a revival after the confusions of materialism, renounced the need for a pantheistic interpretation of religion and for a deduction of the contents of absolute human values (*Geisteswerte*). Instead, the new criticism turned to the problem of history and culture, seeking to approach it epistemologically in both aspects—as the methodology of empirical historiography and as the philosophy of history. Thus Rickert and Windelband specifically posed this problem for themselves as the central task of the revived criticism. They resolved it by differentiating within thought a nomothetic and an idiographic concept-formation, and by referring the latter to an ethic that indeed formally contains the idea of the ultimate purpose but which depends for the definition of its content on history. This theory is not so much based on Kant himself, for whom the mathematic-scientific concept-formation is the self-evident ideal, both in the formulation and the resolution of the problem, and for whom ethics is grounded solely in the formal idea of autonomy; but rather on Fichte's development of the Kantian doctrine. The historical relationship of the doctrine of Rickert and Windelband to Kant is treated by Medicus and Lask in two very instructive writings.[13] But this aspect of the issue is not to be pursued further here. We only wish to point out that this school of neo-criticism is sharply opposed to the other school which, with Cohen, sees its task in stressing those elements in the Kantian doctrine that follow most closely the ideal of the concept-formation of mathematics and the natural sciences; and which thus, undoubtedly, stays much closer to Kant's own teaching. Here history remains a phenomenal natural science in the Kantian sense, which is judged by the practical postulate of the realization of freedom, and the antinomy is reconciled in the unknowable but nevertheless fundamental unity of freedom and nature.

Such a resumption and elaboration of philosophical criticism is, to be sure, urgently demanded by the needs of the intellectual life and the development of thought. The Fichtean development that eliminates the problem of the thing-in-itself, at least in that most questionable Kantian formulation as an 'affecting' moment, makes room for a purely logical approach to criticism and brings it closer to modern empirical realism, yet without abandoning the Platonic a priori motif. The distinction between the epistemological and the psychological subject eliminates, at least for the immediate needs of the system, the danger, otherwise present, of charges of psychologism and solipsism. The concept of the a priori is broadened and made pliant in a most fruitful manner, through the separation of the theoretical and the non-theoretical, practical a priori, as well as through the differentiation within the former of a nomethetic and an idiographic a priori. The system of values, or ethics, takes the place of the metaphysical absolute, and is protected against any coincidence with naturalistic concepts of evolution. Both the a priori of the natural sciences and the a priori of history are anchored in this system of values, and there is a productive interchange particularly between history and the value system, in which each supports the other but neither is absorbed by the other.

This last circumstance is especially significant. Whoever, in attempting to do justice to actual historical problems from the point of view of criticism, was detained by the purely natural-scientific treatment of the life of the soul as a succession of causally connected phenomena, could not achieve a methodology corresponding to actual historiography—and still less a philosophy of history that provides structure, takes cognizance of historical development, and penetrates to the spiritual substance. The philosopher of religion is therefore especially well-disposed to this new doctrine. The subject, religion, needs to be approached historically; and the purely Kantian concept of history never allowed the philosopher to attain standards for the evaluation of historical developments, or to apprehend a reality that has its life in history. The difficulties to which Herrmann's overall position—which developed largely out of Cohen's doctrine—constantly gives rise, especially with respect to history, derive from this deficiency in the more authentic Kantianism. But the philosopher of religion is no less well disposed to the new doctrine if the solution to the problem—insoluble for criticism—was sought through borrowings from the Hegelian evolutionary metaphysic. For this metaphysic leads away from empirical history to a universal concept of religion, which is attained and grounded independently of history and which encounters in actual history only inadequate illustrations or provisional stages that soon become superfluous. My own investigations into the significance of the historical and evolutionary for religion also have their root in critical reflections, which found both methods unsatisfactory and sought, therefore, a specifically historical logic that would culminate in a philosophy of history. My studies of 'The Absoluteness of Christianity' and of the concept of 'The Essence of Christianity' have accordingly made use of Rickert's philosophy of history, and in particular of its teaching on the connection between empirical historiography and philosophy of history as the most important means for the solution of what we felt to be serious problems.

To be sure, in stressing this significance and expressing our agreement with it, we are thinking primarily of the application of Rickert's theory to the philosophy of history, neglecting for the moment the logic of empirical history, which from another point of view would arouse the greater interest. On the one hand, however, the most important aspect of Rickert's philosophy of history is precisely the circumstance that it immediately grows out of his methodology of the empirical historical discipline and attaches itself directly to the peculiarities of a historiography that is properly source-oriented. On the other hand, the inadequacies of the older theories concerning the philosophy of history spring precisely from their inapplicability to empirical historiography. The easy construction, with which even Schleiermacher could make empirical history serve his theory of an idea of religion fulfilled in Christianity, is no longer possible. Here Strauss's devastating critique of Schleiermacher's *Life of Jesus* constitutes a warning that will continue to be instructive;[14] and modern biblical scholarship, under the influence of purely historical points of view, has completely abandoned this approach. But Hegel's evolutionary dialectic also came to grief when faced with the riches of actual history. This is why modern historians of the church and of dogma have completely turned away from the Tübingen School; the essential element in the new impulse in this area of investigation—

which proceed primarily from Ritschl—is not so much his somewhat narrow and arid moralism as his sober and realistic sense for the irrational in history. The historical achievement of Adolf Harnack, particularly, has its greatness in its sense for the individual and living, in its rejection of ideological dialectic. Dorner's most recent attempts[15] to revive the evolutionary dialectic are refuted by his own contributions as a historian, which in turn are rendered colorless and shadowlike by these philosophical efforts; his *History of Dogma* is wholly non-historical in its outlook. Now Rickert's doctrine is built precisely on a recognition of these riches and on an appreciation of exact historical research. In this sense, agreement with his philosophy of history implies agreement with his methodology of the empirical historical discipline as well.

To proceed with this matter, though its discussion falls more properly within the competence of professional historians and logicians, I would venture to state that precisely at this point the doctrine of Windelband and Rickert constitutes a certain redemption and liberation. It only formulates the principles which the most significant historical contributions have followed until now more or less instinctively. But by deducing these principles epistemologically, and freeing them from all confusing idealistic apologetics and partial concessions to the metaphysics of naturalism, Rickert and Windelband are providing the historical method with a strong backbone, consciousness of its full legitimacy, and clarity concerning its principles, together with the possibility of recognizing and using those contributions to history which proceed in terms of laws; for instance, the relatively historical concept-constructions of sociology. The direction of historical abstraction by the concept of the essential; the construction of individual unities of various sizes, from civilized humanity to the individual person; the causal interconnection of all occurrences, in the sense of causal differentiation and the introduction of new forces; the structuring of this flow according to teleological unities, as a continuing development that can be understood in terms of causation; constant awareness of the dependence of historical life on the physical world; the utilization of those universal elements of history that are capable of being dealt with in terms of laws; and the referral of every historical construct—in the first instance, exclusively—to its own particular goal; all this is genuinely historical, and it is deduced very simply and meaningfully from the fundamental logical presupposition. Other ideas, very simple and most manifestly correct, are these: caution in the hierarchical arrangement of these purposive constructs, considered in their relation to universal history, where the historical center can no longer coincide with the individuality that is being portrayed; the distinction of what is historically primary and secondary; the demarcation between the historical abstraction of the organizing principle of individuality and the details, which serve the purposes of narration and illustration. What is legitimate, moreover, in the modern naturalistic approaches to history is fully acknowledged, while the confusion in their fundamental thought is thoroughly exposed.

Now such a liberation is not as necessary for theological historiography, since a naturalistic approach to history would deprive its subject of independent existence; theologically oriented historians accordingly tend to escape from its spell. But a clarification of its principles can nevertheless be extremely beneficial even for theological history; above all, it can help in making intelligible the nature of the concept of development, so controversial among theologians; for many—and among them some who should know better—are still not able to think of this concept apart from the Darwinian concept of evolution and the Hegelian dialectic of progress. The state of fermentation in which the theological-historical disciplines find themselves at present, and which finds expression in the various methodological discussions, is indeed occasioned by the spread of the concept of development from general history into theological history. But it could also easily be shown that wherever these methodological discussions refrain from bringing in naturalistic, Hegelian, or supernatural metaphysics, they move in the paths laid out by Rickert's analysis, where they attain the freedom to recognize the new creations in the history of religion that are constantly being formed within the causal nexus.[16]

I can only express my whole-hearted agreement with the fundamental ideas of Rickert's work. This is not, however, to obscure the fact that his work also leaves us with great difficulties and problems. One would wish to broaden and supplement his observations in some respects.

The main difficulty is obvious to every reader and will be driven home with some force by Rickert's naturalistic opponents. Even after the rationalistic metaphysicizing of the abstractions of natural science has been shaken off, there will still be a strained relationship between the quality of experience that allows it to be subjected (and with the greatest success) to a quantitative approach resulting in causal equations, and the other quality of experience that, quite irrespective of the first, allows the idiographic totalities to be understood genetically in the sense of causal differentiation. It is clear that a conflict that is usually regarded as a metaphysical problem is here attributed simply to the difference in approach. But inasmuch as these approaches are, again, said to arise necessarily from the nature of the consciousness, an accommodation is needed. Rickert indeed has pursued this problem further in his incisive treatise, 'Psychophysical Causality and Psychophysical Parallelism,' which was mentioned earlier.

But even here the question is by no means answered. In my opinion, the book requires a further special treatment of the concept of causality, if it is actually to convince and to carry its point. For there will be many like myself, who at this point—and it is after all a main point—cannot fully understand and grasp Rickert's suggestions. How is it possible to understand the content of experience first nomothetically, according to the principle of causal equality and the conservation of energy, then again idiographically, according to the principle of individual causality or causal inequality? Are these really only two modes of observation with respect to the same object? Are they not rather principles of differentiation among the objects with some falling under the first principle and the rest under the second? I find it difficult to conceive of them otherwise. But then we are faced, once again, within the content of consciousness, with the difference between physical and spiritual reality; and the issue no longer simply involves differences in method but also differences in objects. Between the mechanical realm and the spiritual-productive value a line of demarcation must again be drawn. The formal differences in knowledge indicate material differences in the objects. In any case, there lies a difficulty here which I cannot master with Rickert's concepts. His whole treatment of pyschology gives rise to difficulties. In accordance with the current understanding, he designates psychology as a purely nomothetic natural science dealing with the laws of interconnection of the fundamental psychic elements. I do not believe, however, that this designation is adequate. Psychology seems to me to be an autonomous philosophic discipline that in many respects forms the presupposition of transcendentalism; since it gives a certain treatment and clarification to the empirical elements that are to be ordered by logic, it is also bound to influence logical concept-formation. But this is one of the most difficult and controversial points and cannot be pursued further here.[17]

The supplementing of Rickert's thought, in my opinion, would have to begin with a methodological point concerning the empirical historical disciplines. In the presentation of the concepts of historical interconnection and development, no account is taken of what

Ranke,[18] in an empirical sense, called the ideas. Yet from this concept is derived a series of principles for the structuring and summarizing of facts, which plays a most important role in actual historiography. We are not concerned here with the opinion that the whole of history is directed by ideas, in the sense of consciously adopted and interconnected goals; it is obvious that these are contingent and may be crossed by purely factually-given conditions and occurrences. Nor are we concerned here with hypostatized forces that would constitute the actual reality of history apart from, antecedently to, or in addition to the individual acts and events; and that would merely manifest themselves in actual occurrences. Rather, it is self-evident that our concern is with interconnected goals that emerge and are actualized only in particular, living individuals whose work establishes the interconnection. But, on the other hand, this concept of the idea is neither exhausted nor replaced by Rickert's concept of the historical individual. Rickert gives a certain characterization of the latter, insofar as such an individual is historically integrated precisely through the consistency by which all of this work will be marked, and through the unfolding of consequences that are germinally contained in the adoption of the goals. Indeed, the development of such a complex entity rests to a large extent on the manner in which the consequences of such a germinal idea either are brought to expression through circumstances or unfold according to their own inner necessity.

What is involved here is the concept of a cultural content, which Class describes phenomenologically and which Eucken characterizes as a *syntagma*.[19] Along with this, however, there are numerous other modern historical concepts which play a large role in actual history, but which are set aside by Rickert. To be sure, such a development of implications contained in the original impulse does not yield a law that works in a strictly logical manner; rather, it yields *tendencies* that, constantly reoriented, nevertheless strive for full realization in the direction given them by the original impulse. However, since a plurality of these cultural entities exist side by side with corresponding developmental tendencies, the comparison of these more or less closely related areas yields many *analogies* in the course of such tendencies; which again do not work with the force of exact law but are exceedingly important for historical understanding. Herein lies the relative moment of truth in Lamprecht's theories of stages. But the concept of analogies leads us on to the concept of the type in a sense not considered by Rickert, namely, neither in the sense of the general average applicable in every instance, nor in the sense of the ideal, but in the sense that it summarizes the characteristic processes and outcomes of the more clearly developed cultural complexes in a mediating concept around which the individual, actual entities oscillate. This is how Jellinek formulated the concept of the state in his methodological investigations, and it is clear how this concept of the type is connected with that of tendencies and analogies. In a similar way, Max Weber formulated the concept of 'ideal types' in the sphere of national economics, which makes it possible to characterize, in a general way, certain branches of economics such as handicraft, ownership of land, etc., or certain periods of economic development, such as the period of natural economy or that of capitalism.[20] The masterfully constructed universal-historical concepts of Jakob Burckhardt, such as the 'spirit of the Renaissance' and the 'Greek man' of the various centuries, also belong in this context, for they could be formulated only with the help of such an idea of tendency and type. How important these concepts are for the characterization of individual religions and their stages of development, we need only to suggest. The whole concept of 'the essence of Christianity,' like similar concepts, is only to be understood in these terms.

All of these concepts again presuppose a certain commonality and homogeneity on the part of all historical events. Breaking through the twilight of prehistory, these show marked similarities of aspiration at every point of breakthrough. This is not a matter of laws of nature or of dialectical development to be reconstructed by reference to its goal. But there is a certain uniformity of aspiration, just extensive enough to produce ideally interrelated developments, analogous and finally converging tendencies, more-than-individual frames of mind and types, and thereby to indicate common points of departure and common goals. But on the other hand, this uniformity is also sufficiently far removed from every universal concept and all natural laws to be able to produce individual peculiarities in all the particular points of departure, in all the analogous processes and results, and even in the further effects of coalescing tendencies. The specific character of historical concept-formation and abstraction lies not simply in the uniqueness and indivisibility of the value-unit that has been selected and formed but also in the concepts that express what is common. Finding expression in analogies, tendencies, and types, these indicate that civilized life, for all its particularity, also has its communal side. Here it seems to me that Rickert's theory leaves open some very important questions, which probably cannot be answered as long as one is confined to the empirical immanentism that characterizes the logical presuppositions.

These remarks lead to another point, however, which breaks

through these purely logical presuppositions and moves towards metaphysics, but which is also of importance for the historian. This is the distinction between the empirical reality confronting the investigator of nature and the investigator of culture, respectively; a distinction that retains its significance even if it is conceded that the idiographic concept-formation extends to both the physical world and the psychic world. It must certainly be granted that with respect to the physical world the only possible standpoint is consciousness-immanentism; it is a fundamental error to search for a truer reality apart from consciousness, a reality that would only appear in our experience. But this concession does not apply to the inner life of others. Here we cannot confine ourselves to interpreting experiences immanent in consciousness by analogy to our own innermost being; we must not suppose that only through our interpretaton are they constituted into a consciousness distinct from ourselves and revolving around its own center. We not only interpret these experiences by reference to ourselves, but very often we interpret ourselves by reference to these experiences. However incomprehensible this may be, in ordinary human intercourse we assume that the impression and influence we receive from the other are the manifestation of something that does not wholly coincide with our experience of it; thus we recognize a reality that is not simply empirical but the manifestation and effect of a spiritual being that can only be inferred. Historical subjects thus acquire the concept of a reality that is not merely empirical but metaphysical. Now this is intelligible enough, even from an overall point of view. If 'existence' is being-for-consciousness, then the question of the physical world's being-for-itself is meaningless. In psychophysical beings, on the other hand, where through the incomprehensible connection between the psychological and the epistemological subject a being-for-oneself is brought about, it is obvious that the concept of existence must be treated differently; psychophysical beings are more than empirical data for a perceiving consciousness. They are-for-themselves in an incomprehensible manner, and they operate as independent forces when they appear to one another. Only this insight frees history from the spectral quality of pure empirical immanentism that it retains even for Rickert. But if this is the case, then the previously stressed concepts of commonality, tendencies and analogies, the evolutionary nexus, and the convergence of different developments likewise attain a new metaphysical significance. They signify an effective principle of spiritual life that is functional, to be sure, only in particular individuals; yet it functions in them as a dominant, transcendental force. This principle rests on a common power that first arises from the natural life of the soul and it brings about an inner unity of spiritual values, whose interconnections can be discerned a posteriori even though they cannot be constructed a priori.

But we have now already entered the area of philosophy of history in the older, metaphysical sense of value, and we are approaching the ideas advanced by Eucken and his pupils.[21] The hierarchical ordering of cultural values according to their developmental stages, which is accomplished through their evaluation from a universal point of view, is then not simply a subjective arrangement for the purpose of a better orientation but rather claims, inasmuch as this ordering is based on the observer's self-immersion in the continuity of history, to apprehend an intrinsically grounded objective interrelationship. Indeed, the individual act by which such an evaluation is effected is itself a link in the evolutionary chain by which this interrelationship advances; a link, moreover, that has its origin in the inner drive of the interrelationship itself. Today this approach finds support in the daily mounting influence of Bergson, who also breaks through the mechanistic determinism of psychology from the standpoint of an experience-centered realism, and who acknowledges the *èlan vital*, the upward thrust of life, as the breaking-through of the metaphysical depths of life into the phenomenal realm with its order of space and time. To be sure, Bergson's 'upward thrust' lacks the a priori of an absolute value system, and the idea of a firm intrinsic relation of historical life to such an a priori cannot be derived from it. This is the reason why many today turn back to Hegel. But all this cannot be pursued further here. It must suffice to have shown that here lies another point where purely logical transcendentalism is inadequate. There will always have to be a metaphysic that rests on the foundation of empirical research and a value system constructed in connection with this research.

In this sense Rickert himself seems to acknowledge that his work needs to be supplemented. He writes:

> Someone might suppose that the mere assumption of a necessary relation of empirical reality to absolutely universal values, which we have encountered as a presupposition for the scientific necessity of history, and above all the conviction that all human values cannot be regarded as completely indifferent even from the scholarly standpoint, already involves a metaphysical commitment; for what is of absolute value could have a necessary relation to empirical reality only if there is also some real connection between them; and this connection, inaccessible to experience, would have to be viewed as a metaphysical reality. However this may be, the conviction of the correctness of

opinions of this sort can only arise where the validity of absolute values
is no longer doubted, and it must rest on the conviction of this validity.
A metaphysic thus grounded would therefore never be able to offer
history any support, for it is precisely 'metaphysics' that must establish
the validity of values. Nor would it belong to the kind of metaphysics
that aims at the rationalization of the universe; we were only obliged to
concern ourselves with the worthlessness of this kind of metaphysics for
the historical discipline (653 f.).

Such a metaphysic of history is, in fact, unavoidable for every
comprehensive historical comparison and evaluation, and especially for
the treatment of the problem of culture, for ethics, and for the philosophy
of religion insofar as the latter is a philosophical investigation of the
concrete historical religions and their hierarchical ordering according to
value. The difference between such a metaphysic of history and that of
Hegel is also correctly suggested by Rickert. Such a metaphysic is not a
presupposition for historical work, but rather a result of judgements,
based on intrinsic necessities, with respect to historical work. It does not
rationalize history to the point where history would simply actualize a
universal concept; rather it retains the irrationality of all individual
constructs, since it acknowledges the individual character of every
metaphysic of this sort. But this metaphysic of history is not, therefore,
reduced to a merely subjective opinion; rather, inasmuch as it proceeds
from a conscientious immersion in historical work and from the
interpretation of its meaning, its judgement seeks for continuity, which
it develops further than would a relatively creative act.[22]

A more thorough-going critique would no doubt discover further
metaphysical elements in the structure of Rickert's dialectic. The
individual cultural values are themselves bound up with metaphysical
assertions and presuppositions that would need to be pursued further.
The combination of the psychological and the epistemological subject,
moreover, remains, in spite of all careful formulations, a metaphysical
problem; it may be recalled that Fichte, in his time, subjoined
metaphysics to his theory at this very point, in connection with the
question of the individuation of the 'consciousness in general' into
particular consciousnesses. A metaphysical matter, furthermore, is
also the presupposition of the whole transcendental problematics
which, with its a priori and its transcendental center of judgement,
represents an act of the spirit as over against the mere succession of
psychic phenomena, and thus points a metaphysical, spiritual
foundation. Finally, even the problem discussed above, the question
of the relationship between the aspect of experience that warrants
nomothetic concepts and the aspect that warrants idiographic
concepts, will in some way lead to metaphysical considerations.

The purely transcendental theory, in my opinion, leaves both psychological and metaphysical problems unsettled. It provides the central foundation and the point of departure for the philosophy of culture, but by itself it cannot exhaust and regulate all the questions that arise at this point. The remaining central concern would them be to focus upon the significance that properly attaches itself to psychology and metaphysics. But the further pursuit of this concern does not lie within the scope of this exposition. Its task is accomplished if, prompted by Rickert's book, it has shed light on the present conceptual situation in this field, while pointing out the fruitful contribution made by this book to a clearer understanding; a contribution that should be especially appreciated by theologians and philosophers of religion.

Notes

1. A follow-up of a short article of H. Rickert. 'Die Grenzen der naturwissenschaftlichen Begriffsbildung: Eine logische Einleitung in die historischen Wissenschaften,' Tübingen, Mohr, 1902, X 743. One might now compare it with the summary and supplement of these ideas in the same author's shorter work: *Kulturwissenschaft und Naturwissenschaft*, 2nd ed. (1910), and the article, 'Geschichtsphilosophie' in the commemorative publication (Festschrift) for Kuno Fischer, [2]1907.
2. Cf. the thoroughly independent and instructive article of Rickert, 'Psychophysische Kausalität und psychophysischer Parallelismus,' in *Philos. Abhandlungen: Sigwart gewidmet* (1900), pp. 59–89.
3. Since then greatly expanded in a second edition (1904).
4. Cf. also Rickert's article 'Über die Aufgabe einer Logik der Geschichte,' *in Archiv f. syst. Phil.* VIII (1902). On Fichte, see the informative work of E. Lask, *Fichtes Idealismus und die Geschichte* (1902).
5. See Windelband's article, 'Geschichte und Naturwissenschaft' (1894); also in *Präludien* (1911).
6. This is the difficult concept of individual causality, in contrast to the concept of causality in the natural sciences; see Sergius Hessen, *Individuelle Kausalität: Studien zum transzendentalen Empirismus* (1909).
7. Concerning the consequences following from this empirical, historical thinking (*Geschichtsdenken*), see my article 'History,' in *Hastings' Encyclopedia of Religion and Ethics* and several writings of Max Weber, mentioned by Rickert in the Fischer-Festschrift, p. 422.
8. On this point, see Fueter's splendid book *Geschichte der neuren Historiographie* (1911) and the interesting book by Goldstein, *Die empirische Geschichtsauffassung David Humes* (1903); also Fester, *Die Säkularisation der Historie* (1909).
9. 'Empiricism and Platonism in the Philosophy of Religion,' *Harvard Theological Review*, V (1902), p. 415; cf. similar remarks by James concerning the standard for historical-philosophical judgement. It is quite evident that Rickert's experientially immanent apriorism has many points of contact with

experientially immanent empiricism and pragmatism, partly in its rejection of metaphysics, partly in its realistic tendency toward merely perceptual order and orientation within the content of experience, partly in its emphasis on the irrationality of individuality and the concomitant spontaneity. The only difference is the relation of all these concepts to an apriori, which in Rickert is certainly understood to be much more dynamic than was the case within the rigid mechanistic and formal-ethical system of Kant.

10. It is the deficiency of Wundt's stages of historical development, which he derives from Ethnic psychology, that this conditionality of the conceptual standard, and with it the whole apriori-personal background of all such conceptualization, is misunderstood. This also holds for the careful and instructive book of Vierkandt. Here the objectivity always consists in a naturalization of the idea into laws of psychological development. However, these are never at the same time critical standards, unless one has unconsciously identified one with the other. But then one would have to replace the psychological naturalism with Hegel's theory.

11. Cf. my article, 'Idealismus, deutscher,' in *PRE* 3, VIII; as well as 'Das historische in Kants Religionsphilosophie'; also my earlier article on 'Grundprobleme der Ethik.'

12. Also see Sueskind, *Christentum und Geschichte bei Schleiermarcher*, pp. 54–102. On the basis of reason, Schleiermarcher constructs the four well-known value groupings, whose historical fulfillment by individual-concrete realizations is a matter of empirical historical process. The great cadres of ethical purposes are apriori, whereas an individual fulfillment is empirical. The standard is found in the concept of the totality of reason or of spirit.

13. Medicus, *Kants Geschichtsphilosophie*, Halle (1902). Lask, *Fichtes Idealismus und die Geschichte*, Tübingen und Leipzig (1902). Cf. my short article in *Theologische Literatur-Zeitung* (1903). A third closely related work from the same school is quite valuable: Kistiakowaski, *Gesellschaft und Einzelwesen*, Berlin (1899). Here it is shown in contrast to social theories allegedly based on the natural sciences and biology, how society constitutes the object of social psychology—by and large a methodologically historical and scientific discipline. It is also shown how the communities, formed out of society and based on norms, are not to be constructed from psychology but rather from the antipsychological concepts of norms and unconditional values.

14. Cf. D. F. Strauss, *Der Christus des Glaubens und der Jesus der Geschichte*, Berlin (1865).

15. Cf. A. Dorner, 'Über den Begriff der Entwicklung in der Geschichte der christlichen Lehrbildungen,' *Prot. Monatshefte* (1901); and 'Auf welche Weise ist das Wesen des Christentums zu erkennen?' *Preuss. Jahrbuch* (1901); now also: W. Köhler, 'Idee und Persönlichkeit,' as well as my short article in *HZ*. (1913).

16. The latest summary of such methodological considerations is the work of von Schubert, *Die heutige Auffassung und Behandlung der Kirchengeschichte* (1902). This work in particular shows how much could have been learned from Rickert. Then it would have been clear how little the formulation that 'what develops is not the gospel, but its relation to the world' withdraws church history and Christianity from the concept of evolution. For the original Christian gospel is demonstrably an individual-historical construct, and during

the course of its work in the world new individual-historical constructs come forth. Nothing can develop in its relation to something else without itself changing in its nature. However, the idea or the essence of Christianity is on the whole a historical abstraction, which can only be achieved through a survey of all these individual forms and whose meaning would require the most precise definition. See my article, 'Was heisst Wesen des Christentums?' Now cf. also W. Köhler, *op. cit.*

17. This is certainly the real meaning of the objection raised by Dilthey. In his latest work, 'Der Aufbau der geschichtlichen Welt in den Geisteswissenschaften' *Abhh. d. Kgl. Preuss. Akademie d. Wiss.* (1910), his works, beginning with the brilliant *Einleitung in die Geisteswissenschaften* I (1883), are listed in their entirety. Dilthey is decidedly near to Rickert, in that he constructs history epistemologically not from psychology but rather from logic. He maintains this statement of a narrow connection between the logical goals of knowledge in history and real historical experience, and also the significance of particular historical causality over against that of the natural sciences. In my opinion there is something correct here. But of course the integration of this into Rickert's train of thought is not easy. In *Die Grundlagen der Geisteswissenschaften* (1905), Spranger follows Dilthey. Since then in his *Humboldt*, he has also drawn closer to Neo-Kantian theory. The logical goals of knowledge can only be achieved on the basis of logical principles, not on the basis of empirical fact. The latter idea is strikingly elucidated by Arvid Grotenfeld, 'Die Wertschaetzung in der Geschichte' (1903). Even more significant and profound is the work of an excellent psychologist like Simmel, who in his *Probleme der Geschichtsphilosophie* (^{3}1905) shows quite clearly how historical knowledge is a penetrating transformation of the merely experienced according to the logical principles of an apriori of history, which is perfectly parallel to the apriori of science. He also shows how our historical scientific position vis-à-vis the merely experienced—whether it is in the directly experienced, or is indirectly experienced after the fact in the imagination, or is 'hermeneutically' interpreted—is to be understood in the sense of autonomy, engendering the real only according to apriori law; herein consists our knowledge of history as well as our freedom in face of it. with Dilthey this freedom never comes to its own.

18. L. v. Ranke, *Über die Epochen der neueren Geschichtsschreibung*, Leipzig (1888), also 'Weltgeschichte,' IX.2.; cf. also the excellent book of E. Spranger, *W. v. Humboldt und die Humanitätsidee*.

19. G. Class, *Untersuchungen zur Phänomenologie und Ontologie des menschlichen Geistes*, Leipzig (1896); and Eucken, *Die Einheit des Geisteslebens in Bewusstsein und Tat der menschheit* (1888). In my previously mentioned article on German Idealism I tried to show the origin of this extremely fruitful concept and in the expansion of the historical horizon, in the poetical perception of the unconscious, in the collection of these elements through the dialectics of evolution, and finally in the work of the true historian. This concept is an essential concept of modern history, but a logical utilization of it is certainly only possible through its incorporation in a historically logical theory. Dilthey also in his already mentioned treatise and especially in his very interesting, 'Jugendgeschichte Hegels,' *Abhh. d. Berliner Akad. d. Wiss.* (1905), traces this important basic principle in a most instructive way.

20. G. Jellinek, 'Das Recht des modernen Staates', *B.I.: Allgemeine Staatslehre*, Berlin (1900), pp. 23–48. Jellinek is closely connected with the here described philosophical school, and his historical-methodological argument deserves serious attention, beyond legal circles, cf. my short article in *Z. f. Privat-und-offentl. Recht der Gegenwart* (1912). Max Weber developed his ideas in *Archiv f. Sozialwissenschaften*, XIX (1904) and XXII (1906).

21. Cf. Eucken, *Der Kampf um einen geistigen Lebensinhalt*, Leipzig (1896); Eucken, *Der Wahrheitsgehalt der Religion*[3] (1912), as well as the article 'Philosophie der Geschichte' in *Kultur der Gegenwart* I, VI (1907); Goldstein, *Kulturproblem der Gegenwart*, Leipzig (1899); Scheler, *Die transzendentale und die psychologische Methode*, Leipzig (1900). Of Bergson's works, these should be mentioned: *Essai sur les données immédiates de la conscience*, (1889); *Matière et mémoire, essai sur les relations du corps à l'esprit* (1897, German 1904); *L'évolution créatrice* (1905, German 1912). Concerning the revival of Hegel, see Windelband, *Die Erneuerung des Hegelianismus* (1910).

22. This is elaborated in my study of 'The Essence of Christianity.' In his article 'Vom Begriff der Philosophie', *Logos* (1910) Rickert himself has elaborated his replacement for this metaphysics by a theory of 'interpretation' of the subject as well as his position vis-à-vis the historical acquisition of culture. In my opinion this 'interpretation' is in truth a metaphysics of freedom.

17

Stoic-Christian Natural Law and Modern Secular Natural Law

Sociological research must from the outset make an important basic distinction between sociological natural law and the ideal types of law posited by ideologies of various kinds. To the first category belong insights concerning the relation between the size of a sociological group and the kind of ties existing among its members. There is a correlation between the smallness of a group and its personal quality, inwardness, and immediacy of relationship, and the danger of personal dissension and fragmentation. Conversely, there is a correlation between the largeness of a group and the abstract quality and impersonality of relationship (with the attendant necessity for coercion and external force), and the danger of indifference and apathy on the part of the members. This is a socio-psychological natural law, and there are countless others like it which could be classified as natural laws of society and culture.

To the second category belong those ideal laws that produce moral, political, juridical, and religious thinking; by means of these the laws endeavor to control, shape, serve, or master the group formations and antagonisms incident to the spiritual nature of humanity. The legal concept of property, once it has been construed juridically and related to the most heterogeneous ideologies—as for instance, to the idea of immortality—has a meaning and consistency of its own with which it attempts to regulate and control the economic process, even when it has accommodated itself to it. Always operative here are the basic ideals and the purely logical consequences of a concept that has in the past been laid down as principle.

Both of these laws, the natural as well as the ideal, determine the course of the history of civilization in their thousandfold commingling and interpenetration. If they are to be understood, the primary concern must be to keep in mind the different origins of these conflicting but related laws, and to analyze them in the context of their fields of operation. No history of civilization is written which deals simply with the development of the natural laws of society or with the development and dialectic of ideas. All historical understanding depends on the relatedness and conflict of these two powers. At one time the ideal laws founder on the natural laws of society or are forced by them into the most labyrinthine compromises. At another time they enhance, set in order, multiply, and harmonize the operation of natural order, utilizing it in their own favor. Often, however, the opposition between the two kinds of laws leads to utter despair of the world, hope in the future beyond, quietistic pessimism, or mystical indifference.

The attempts to merge these two conflicting forces or to resolve them in a higher synthesis can be passed over. Such attempts always are mere philosophizing and at the most provide a logical postulate, but they are not a requirement for the historical understanding of the facts themselves. Particularly the economic theory of history, with its attempt to see the ideal bodies of law as pure reflections and outgrowths of the sociological laws of nature, is based on highly dubious speculation. No doubt, there are connections. But the relationship between the two is reciprocal: just as the sociological situation determines the formation of ideas, so, conversely, the ideology impinges upon the sociological circumstances. Furthermore, the relationship is not merely one of reflection and dependence. The fact that an ethical, artistic, or religious idea takes a certain form cannot be explained exclusively by the background from which it arises. The whole conditioning relationship must be studied and ascertained case by case. Finally, an ideal body of laws, even if its origin is closely related to natural, sociological grounds contains so much that is peculiar to itself, so much that transcends its origin, that it leads an existence that is at least relatively independent and can for that reason influence its surroundings through its own initiative. This existence can really be recognized only in its historical context, and through appreciative awareness of the inner significance of ideas that sometimes take on one form and sometimes another. Only thus is it possible to understand the almost never-ending (though constantly modulated) conflict between the goals of the ideal body of laws and the conditions of life posited by the sociological natural laws.

The social ideal that springs from the religious idea of Christianity offers an example of just such contrariety and complementarity, compromise and repudation—an example that is extremely important for our whole culture. This ideal, as it arises in its basic configuration from the religious idea of Christianity, can be determined easily and simply. It is the radical religious individualism of a faith that dedicates itself to God by moral obedience and thus provides the individual with a metaphysical ground, rendering him indestructible. This inclusion in the will of God, however, is not merely a matter of the elevation and concentration of the individual, since all individuals meet and find one another in God. In this suprahuman medium, all ordinary human conflict, rivalry, selfishness, and egoism are extinguished and transformed into mutual relations of love for the sake of God. Since Jesus shares Israel's concept of God he recognizes as a matter of course a living and creative will of God and, consequently, the unity of souls in a people or kingdom of God. The correlate to Jesus' thought, therefore, is not a quietistic mysticism but a transcendent kingdom of love, made up of souls that have the ground of their being in God.

This love should make all law, power, and force superfluous, since togetherness based on the personal sense of fellowship overcomes all the usual conflicts and formalities. In particular, it should free people from the desire for pleasure and possessions, and direct them toward contentment, humility, and unconditional willingness to help one another. Jesus' word shows him to be very much aware of the contrast between this ideal and the ways and demands of the world. What he has in mind, therefore, is a complete fulfillment that will not take place until a new world order is established. Then the heavenly Father will bring forth the kingdom in all the fullness of miraculous power and inaugurate the era of the fulfilled and victorious reign of the Divine will. Until then, God's faithful gather unobtrusively as a religious community—awaiting the kingdom of God, while fulfilling the Divine will among themselves and in the world as much as is provisionally possible.

Out of this fundamental message there arose a new religious community that distinguished itself from other religious communities by its Christ-cult—the worship of God as incarnate in Christ. With that, and by reason of its religious and liturgical unity, this community became a new sociological entity. From the very beginning, there was a definite sociological ideal in this new entity that enabled it to form and to implement its self-image, namely, the ideal of a combination of radical religious individualism with an equally radical religious socialism. It was only natural that this ideal should radiate from the narrowly religious sphere into the relations of secular life and activity, and mold them accordingly. Immediately conflict arose, not only with the social ideals of the alien society of late antiquity, which surrounded it, but also with the varied natural sociological laws and the actual demands of social life. The challenge now was to understand and to overcome this conflict.

In the process of solving this problem, *three major types* appear from the start, which in later history become increasingly accentuated and mutually antagonistic. They are connected with various approaches toward the sociological structuring of the Christian religious idea; indeed, their basic character can be grasped only in this frame of reference.

The most important and central sociological form assumed by the Christian idea is the *church-type*. The essence of the church-type is that it considers salvation as something given with the divine decree, as something that in principle is already realized. Independent of personal achievement and perfection, all salvation is based on the grace that has been embodied in the religious community by means of a redemption both finished and consummated. The point is to lay hold of the salvation that is available there, but to do so without self-righteousness and sanctimony. Renouncing self and laying hold of salvation, the devotion of faith gives rise to a perfection of the disposition, which is the only perfection desired and from which all other things follow of themselves by inner necessity. That is why the basic idea is that of grace—of a redemption that is already consummated in Christ's death, which faith has only to make its own. But necessary to this objective salvation is also an objective guidance and embodiment that are not contingent on the subject. This is the church established by Christ, with its apostles and their priestly successors, and with the sacraments instituted by Christ and permeated by his living presence. This idea gave rise to Catholicism with its constant reinforcement of the objective principle, with its dogma of redemption through the God-man, with its investment of this redemption in the church as the institution of salvation and grace.

Despite the simplification of dogma and the elimination of the strong emphasis on personal achievements and works (which had in the meanwhile regained currency), and despite the stress on personal assurance, this idea of the church was carried on by the two main confessional traditions of Protestantism. For Protestantism, too, Christianity is the institution of salvation and grace—the church that receives redemption from Christ and mediates this salvation to the individual. This mediation is effected entirely on the basis of dedication to this objective entity, not by virtue of personal achievement and the perfection of a Christian morality; the practical effects of a Christian disposition remain ever imperfect. Salvation rests on devotion to the objective institution of grace that is entrusted with the word and the preaching office. The inevitable shortcomings of the Christian conduct growing out of this devotion are the result of the ever-present sin that has ruled over everyone since Adam; these can only be abominated but never, really and completely be done away with.

Because of this whole inner structure, the church-type can forego insistence on strict Christian perfection; it can compromise with the existent structures of the world and society as they obtain in the state of sin; and it can recognize social and ethical structures that are less than Christian but very useful (for the time being) in the discipline and organization of the sinful world.

The second sociological form of the Christian idea, the *sect-type*, is distinctly different. Characteristic is its rigoristic demand for an unconditional application of the evangelical ethic and, in particular, of the Sermon on the Mount. It does not give in to the general state of sinfulness and does not build on an accomplished redemption and an objectively available grace. On the contrary, it demands the actual overcoming of sin, the living up to the divine commandments; and it believes in the full redemption only of those in whom grace has become a recognizable force supporting the practice of a Christian life. To the sect, the religious community is not a general, all-inclusive institution into which one is born and whose powers of grace reach out by means of the influence of the church, the clergy, and the sacraments. The sect seeks to gather mature and personally convinced Christians into a holy community that regards the preaching of the gospel, the sacraments, and the institutional community merely as means for the implanting and fostering of the religious life, with no miraculous power independent of the subject and subjective achievement. It rejects the priesthood and upholds lay religion. Insofar as it has priests, redemptive power is attributed to them as personally holy individuals, not simply by virtue of their office. For the sect-type, the sacraments are not channels for the acquisition of a subsisting treasury of grace but ways to consecrate and confirm a state of holiness based on a conscious act of the will.

The sect in this sense is already part of the primitive Christian movement prior to its evolution into a national or state church, which brought with it the clear emergence of the church-type. It comes to the foreground in the Montanist and Donatist movements, lives on in the medieval Waldensians and kindred groups, and continues to subsist in an incalculable number of new forms from the sects of the Reformation period down to the present time. Catholicism has assimilated a segment of its motives, insofar as the monastic orders represent within the church some of the ideals of the sect. A special offshoot of the sect-type is to be found in the Franciscans, who lost their original character as a result of their forced integration into the church. Luther also struggled with the sect-type as he came to grips with the ideals of the Sermon on the Mount. The sects and religious communities of our time give this type a latent but no less significant power within the whole of present-day society. It can be easily understood that the sect-type was bound by its very nature to despise the national and state church, that is substitutes the voluntary association for the institutional church, and particularly that it avoids and rejects compromise with the culture, the educational norms, and the less-than-Christian standards of life of the secular world. It goes without saying [that the sect-type] is bound to be as hostile to compromise and culture as the church-type of both traditions is sympathetic. Its strict Christian radicalism is bound to clash with natural sociological laws and with competing social ideals; in such clashes its particular sociological character will assume definitive form and impress itself on the total life of the community.

Enthusiasm and *mysticism* constitute a third type. Mysticism aims at the immediate, present, and inward quality of religious experience, at the immediate relationship with God that leaps over or complements traditions, cults, and institutions. The historical and institutional is to mysticism merely a stimulus and a means towards the inner, timeless intercourse with the divine. Mysticism in this sense already found expression in primitive Christian enthusiasm, in the doctrine of the possession of the Spirit that directly reveals or fulfills and continues the mysteries of the Godhead. Paul's religiosity, in particular, is deeply penetrated by a mysticism of this kind, which stands in deep inner tension with his ideas concerning redemption, salvation, and institution. But it was only with the assimilation of Neo-Platonic mysticism that the consolidation of Christian mysticism was achieved. According to the Neo-Platonic conception, a latent presence of God remains in the finite spirits as they emanate from the Divine. This presence is a seed or spark of the divine essence which, through the contemplation of the mysteries of this ground of being, carries the soul upward to substantial union with the divine, and back again.

These thoughts were often taken up where inward feeling was left unsatisfied by the objective character of cult, dogma, and institution.

The Christian framework of ideas was here regarded as liberating and awakening the divine ground in the soul, which, once quickened, experiences in its own inner life the revelation and presence of God. Mysticism is interwoven with the whole history of Christianity. It may appear in the enthusiastic-pneumatic mode; or in the Pauline mode, where history and the written word are transcended through inner union with a timeless Christ; or, finally, in a pantheistic Neo-Platonizing mode. Mysticism remains the more Christian the more it accentuates the personal character of God and of the goal of human life. It deviates from Christianity in the measure that it emphasizes the Neo-Platonic concept of God as unpredicated, static, absolute Being, and the submersion of the human personality in God.

But the truth is that mysticism is concerned strictly with the immediacy of union with God. Its manifestations are basically different, therefore, from those of the spirit of the sect, which is at pains to stay close to the letter of the historical word, to the actual sayings of the Lord, and to the organization of the holy community. The only common element is the indifferent or hostile attitude toward the world, because the divine Spirit rises far above the sensual, the worldly, and the finite. Mysticism, too, readily uses the injunctions of the Sermon on the Mount to express victory over—and exclusion of—the natural assertion of the self. But the mystics understand this victory differently; not as the rigorism of holiness but as the mortification of the natural impulses of the flesh, and as the liberation that consists in the suprasensual surrender of spirit to Spirit. Their indifference to the world may find expression in libertine as well as in ascetic forms. This is why the sociological significance of mysticism is quite different from that of the sect-type. Ultimately, mysticism is a radical, non-communal form of individualism. Independent of history, cult, and outward means of communication, the Christian stands here in immediate communion with Christ or with God. But his religion exhausts itself in this immediate encounter and in its practical consequence of commitment to a suprasensual life oriented to transcendence. Social relations are limited to the natural bond between individual kindred souls, based on similar experiences and a common understanding. No common cultus, no organization needs to issue from it. The sociological form assumed by such mysticism is found in the life of the hermit, or in the monastic community to the extent that it is imbued with a mystical ethos, or again in the small circles of Friends of God, of the Quiet in the Land, of Philadelphians and Brethren. Associated with mysticism is a limitless toleration that sees the same essential motive at work in all religion and looks upon every attempt to forge its external means into a coercive purity and inwardness of its life. The mystics' attitude of universal love is based on the coincidence of all creatures in the inner life of the Godhead and leads to the conquest of egoism and particularism. Apart from this general attitude of love, the relationship of mysticism to the secular world is essentially that of indifference to, and abstention from, all concerns and forms of life incompatible with the mystical life of God. The latter forms and concerns belong to the world and the flesh, which are either tolerated impassively for as long as they endure or denied for oneself and one's circle.

For each of these three main types, the task of coming to terms with natural necessities and non-Christian ideals of social life takes on a different form. The most important among them from a general historical standpoint is, of course, the church-type. It posses the greatest power of propagation, extension, and organization. It tends to coincide with the total life of the state and society. It takes up into itself, as far as possible, the secular culture and morality. However, it also represents a uniquely powerful religious idea, that of grace and freedom, which upholds the Christian attitude of trust in God and in the victory that overcomes the world, irrespective of the degree to which the Christian commandments are rigorously applied. The question is first of all, therefore: What relationship has the church formed to the non-Christian realities and ideals of social life, and how has it been able to do so with inner, conceptual motivation?

The answer to this question is, in short, that it has done so by developing the concept of Christian natural law and by gaining mastery over all those non-Christian elements with the help of this natural law. A word of clarification is in order. The natural law or, more precisely, the idea of a moral natural law, which is the source of all legal and social rules and institutions, is a creation of Stoicism. The Stoics had derived this idea from their perception of law that rules the whole world, and it was through their particular application of this world-law to the self-assertion and operation of the mind that they constructed ethcial and legal rules. In doing so, they increasingly relinquished their pantheistic principles and characterized the moral natural law in an almost theistic way as the expression of divine will. We see here a move in the direction of the Judaeo-Christian idea of an ethos uniting all people and deriving from the will of God. Even more important, however, are the substantive similarities. The Stoic legal and social philosophy, like the whole of Stoic ethics, is a product of the dissolution of the ancient *polis* and of the cosmopolitan horizon created by the world-empire. The ethics deduced from the general laws of reason supersede the positive laws and customs; the individual endowed with divine reason takes the place of the national and domestic interest; the idea of humanity without distinction as to state, region, race, or color displaces that of single political loyalties. This ideal of humanity is construed as a community of totally free people, obedient to the divine law of reason alone and not subject to instinctive desires. There would be no coercion, no differentiation of power or social class, no private property—which gives rise to such differentiation—but a free community based on mutual respect and love and ultimately on the fact that everyone is ruled by the divine law of nature.

But the Stoics could not help seeing that this is an ideal construction, not practicable in the world's present state. Consequently, they worked out the distinction between an absolute and a relative natural law. The former was realized only in the Golden Age at the beginning of human history, either incipiently and germinally or as a complete expression of the ideal. But its full realization was thwarted by the rise of human passions: greed, the lust for power, egoism, and violence. The moral reason therefore had to find ways to safeguard the ideal as best it could while taking into account these practical conditions. This was done through the development of an ordered political power, the establishment of property, the devising of a code of law guaranteeing natural rights, the institution of marriage and family, and the just settlement of social inequities. The positive law, which takes into account the particularities unforeseeable by reason, must conform to the ideal natural law to the extend that this is possible within the state of sin. The universal law of nations is already a rationally effected compromise between the positive law and the law of reason, which to be sure, still requires rational articulation. As is well known, these ideas passed over into Byzantine formulations of Roman law.

Stoic philosophy, then, had already considered scientifically and dialectically a problem posed for Christians by their ethics. Stoicism and Christianity in their origins were analogous in many respects. Both were products of the interiorizing, individualizing, yet also universalizing tendency that accompanied the collapse of the civil morality and national customs of antiquity. In face of a world that had lost its vitality, both were concerned to regenerate it through a religious idea. It is only natural that Christians, although differing it many ways from the Stoics, adopted the Stoic mode of dealing with this common problem. Christians identified the ideal freedom of the children of God and the community of unconditional love with the absolute law of nature of the Stoics. Just as the Stoics saw their ideal realized only in the Golden Age at the beginning of human history, so Christians believed theirs to be fully actualized only by their first progenitors in the Garden of Eden. The Stoic dominance of reason over the instinctive drives, and the Stoic doctrine of a humane fellowship of free and equal persons under the divine law, seemed essentially to be identical with the Christian teachings of sanctification and love.

Consequently, Christians could also take over the Stoic doctrine of the relative natural law. Just as the Stoics taught that it was lust for power, egoism, and greed that had destroyed the original harmony, equality, and freedom, so Christians, with the help of their Bible, traced the corruption back to the wickedness of the original man. From the Fall arose the necessity of work, and with it, private property and the institutions of marriage and family to regulate the now-awakened sexual passion. From the crime of Cain came the order of justice and retaliation. The founding of the state by Nimrod marked the beginning of law, authority, and princely power. The confusion of tongues in connection with the destruction of the Tower of Babel meant the division of mankind into nations. Ham's wickedness established slavery, on which a major portion of the economic order has been grounded ever since. In Stoicism, reason transformed the new institutions of society into instruments of discipline, order, and propriety; in Christianity, the evils mentioned were counteracted by God who turned these products of sin into means for the punishment and healing of sin. Yet they not only serve to regulate, discipline, punish, and combat sin; they also lay the foundation for an inward, personal morality through the creation of a civil and economic order.

Christendom, however, did not renounce the absolute natural law as completely as did the Stoics; it is preserved in, and identified with, the Lord's commandment in the Sermon on the Mount, which is meant for true and genuine Christians as distinct from the mass of average Christians. This distinction introduced a famous and far-reaching cleavage into Christian moral philosophy. The strict Christianity of the Sermon on the Mount, on the one hand, is not regarded as the unconditional duty of all, but merely as a collection of counsels for those who, because of their life situation and individual inclination, are qualified and called to the full realization of the Christian ideal. The toned-down Christianity of the masses, on the other hand, allows them to stay with the regualtions and activities of the relative natural law and to realize only as much of the strict Christianity as is possible under the circumstances. The latter represents a compromise of strict Christianity with the demands of actual life and involves a relative appreciation of the moral and legal institutions of the non-Christian and pre-Christian environment. Such a compromise was only possible for the church-type because the church tied salvation not to strictly personal achievement but to the objective means for the attainment of institutional grace. In this respect the two classes of Christians became one again. Their unity related to the main concern, while their division related to what was no more than an important side-issue, namely, the question of the degree of personal holiness subjectively achieved. It is obvious that the concept of relative natural law is very closely related to that of the church, its objective holiness, and its redemptive power independent of subjective achievement.

Thus the consequential concept of a Christian natural law came into being. The two-sidedness of this concept, which stems from its origin and comes to the fore in a very contradictory manner at different times in its later historical development, needs to be pointed out from the start. On the one hand, the stress can be laid on the relativity of this relative natural law—that it was occasioned by sin and that its function is the punishment of sin. In that case (as in Augustine) the state, law, property, and the whole of culture appear as the work of sin. For this reason the church, as in the Gregorian controversy, can intervene at will in these sin-oriented institutions that are wholly subordinate to it. The need for discipline and order will then also gain special prominence. The natural law of the church appears as a glorification of authority, which teaches humble submission to force and subordination (modified only by patriarchalism) to the ruling powers in the sphere of the state, the family, the feudal system, and serfdom. In this connection it appears as divine punishment and divine intervention in history, and often takes on the positivistic air of an arbitrary divine institution.

On the other hand, one can emphasize the naturalness and reasonableness of natural law, now seen as emanating from the light of nature, reason, and of the order of creation, as the rational substructure of the church and of the morality of grace; reason, its source, would still be valid even if God did not exist. Thus there arises a rational doctrine of the state, society, law, and economy that follows ancient social philosophy wherever possible and that regulates the whole of secular life by itself, deferring to the church only where the church's interventions is justified and made necessary by the positive law of God. At the same time, the democratic, egalitarian, liberal, socialistic, traits of the natural law are thrown into relief. Thus it is possible for the ecclesiastical natural law to proclaim revolution against godless rulers and even, under certain circumstances, to sanction tyrannicide. It can teach popular sovereignty and Christian democracy, and champion a Christian socialism that borders on communism. Gregory VII, for instance, on the one hand condemned (to the glory of the church) the political institutions of natural law as creations of sin, while on the other he mobilized Christian democracy and the sovereign power of the people against godless authorities not fulfilling the goal ascribed to them by reason.

Not all the characteristics of Christian natural law were to emerge in the ancient, pre-medieval church. Secular culture and Christian rigorism were still basically in tension, with monasticism providing the only outlet. In the medieval church and culture, however, where the religious and the secular, the ecclesiastical and the worldly fused into one great unity of life and monasticism was assimilated to the point of becoming an ecclesiastical élite, the natural law understandably attained its full significance. St. Thomas gave it the scientific form that has lasted to the present, feeding a never-ending stream of Catholic literature on constitutional law. The essence of this cultural morality of the church is the gradual ascent from nature to grace. 'Grace presupposes and perfects nature' is its true watchword, which makes it possible to develop the natural order of the relative natural law as the substructure of the whole ecclesiastical culture and to regard the course of history, in which the legal order has taken form, as indirectly established by God working through the natural course of events. Thus all creations of the positive law acquire divine status and are valued, first of all, as penalty and remedy for sin. Even these institutions conditioned by sin and the peculiarities of purely positive human law dictated by local conditions were assimilated to the absolute and rational law as far as possible, and all forms of life contradictory to it were, at least in theory, kept at a distance.

The mood of subordination to the prevailing powers and institutions and resignation to the existing inequalities, even to the point of recognition of serfdom and slavery—with a paternalistic relationship requiring obedience on the one side and a sense of care and obligation on the other—appear as the import of natural law. But this same natural law presently changes into a highly revolutionary and radical principle of criticism of all those powers, laws, and institutions which no longer fulfill their rational purpose of maintaining discipline, order, and harmony or even obstruct the saving work of the kingdom of mercy, the church. In this case it is not only permissible but even obligatory to replace the law that is contrary to reason by a reasonable one. In such a rational critique, arbitrariness and anarchy are forestalled only by virtue of the fact that it is always the church which ultimately passes judgement on the legitimacy of resistance and of the new order. The Christian character of the law newly constituted by criticism or revolution is conditioned, however, by the fact that in the development of its rational goals, the conditions of humanity's sinful state and the supremacy of the church are taken into account. In this sense, the law of nature or natural law is all-powerful and the lever for all cultural progress as understood by Catholicism up to the present time. Consequently, natural law is still being proclaimed at the great gatherings of Roman Catholics as the principle of culture, freedom, and progress; being distinguished, however, from any purely rationalistic, revolutionary, and abstract ideal of progress which fails to appreciate the conditions of humanity's sinful state and the relativity of all natural law.

The concept of Christian natural law is not the exclusive property of Catholicism. Just as the older Protestantism of both traditions— the Lutheran and the Calvinist—maintained the concept of the church and the idea of a unified, church-dominated national culture and of a Christian society, it also felt the need of compromising with the given, factual situation and the secular, moral-juridical institutions. Protestantism, like Catholicism, met this need with the help of the concept of Christian natural law. The ideas developed here are still a force in our society today. But the concept of natural law underwent certain changes here which varied considerably in the two traditions.

Lutheran ethics differs from Catholic ethics above all in that it does not recognize the double morality, the distinction between a lukewarm mass-Christianity and a monastically inclined élite. For precisely this reason it also does not recognize that hierarchical structuring of society with its steps leading from nature to grace, from the forms of life ruled by natural law to the realm of grace in the church. It insists on the complete uniformity and fundamental equality of morals for all Christians, allowance being made only for purely individual and qualitative differences. It cannot, therefore, set the natural and the Christian law side by side but must draw one into the other. It has to realize the Christian law immediately within and by means of the forms of life ruled by natural law. It accomplishes this by means of its famous doctrine of vocational ethics. In accordance with natural law, society is divided into a system of vocations and classes that are carefully maintained with all their distinctions, privileges, and duties. Vocational activity within the framework of this system of social stations is thus the contribution of the individual to the well-being and welfare of the whole. All that is needed now it that this vocational division of labor, based on natural law, be inspired by the spirit of Christian love. The preaching of the word breathes this spirit into society, bringing with it a free inward disposition. Thus Christian brotherly love becomes a reality precisely within the context of the work of the vocations. The faithful fulfilment of one's vocation is the means of showing a God-given love to one's neighbor in family, state, society, and economic life, and thus working out the grounds of one's own existence is a blessed fellowship with God through the treatment of one's neighbor.

Natural law sees to it that there are no vocations within this system that cannot be reconciled with the Christian spirit. It therefore excludes big business, speculation, and a credit economy, as well as any revolutionary spirit that might upset the social class structure. The postlapsarian natural law recognizes the state, power, law, capital punishment, property, commerce, etc., but only to the extent that they are reasonably apt to foster peaceful, quiet conduct, pleasing to God. It is therefore of the greatest importance to uphold this natural law in a thoroughly conservative way, as the structuring of a mutually supportive system of society that is given once and for all. The relative natural law of Lutheranism is, consequently, extremely conservative. This conservatism is to be seen also in the particular elaboration of the natural law. To safeguard uniformity and order, the legitimacy of power and authority must be emphasized to the maximum. This takes place above all by stressing the relative character of the natural law and by emphasizing the fact that it is conditioned by humanity's sinfulness.

Sin must be checked by force, and for that reason the natural law requires an extreme emphasis on the divine status of the ruling authority. The essence of authority is power and the right to shed blood, and the authorities are at liberty to use such power against any revolution. Resistance to the ruling authority would be a contradiction in terms and is consequently, intolerable—not only from a Christian point of view but also from the standpoint of natural law. The exercise of authority with whatever harshness it may require is, therefore, actually a Christian vocation, a Christian fulfilment of the demands of natural law in the spirit of brotherly love. It is only natural that under these circumstances the behavior required by a vocation sanctioned by natural law sometimes clashes sharply with what is required by the Christian attitude of love. It is not easy to view the soldier and the hangman as executors of the Sermon on the Mount. Here Luther makes a distinction between the ethics of office and vocation imposed by the postlapsarian natural law and the radical ethics of love, of an inner, purely personal Christianity which is to be practiced in the private, non-official activities of life. The duality of relative natural law and strictly Christian ethics is now laid into the heart of each individual. The result is that the Lutheran natural law has become a radically conservative glorification of the ruling authorities and a patriarchal submission to the system of classes and vocations; the personal, inner Christianity of the heart really has basically nothing to do with political and social conditions except to submit to them and to practice the ethic of love as best it can. This has continued to be the character of Lutheranism down to the present: a radically conservative, patriarchal natural law that glorifies power coupled with a narrowly religious disposition that is ultimately indifferent to political and social matters. Under present-day circumstances this indifference spells the political and social impotence of the Lutheran churches.

Very different and in many respects wholly opposite was the development of Christian natural law in Calvinism. To be sure, Calvin at first built chiefly on Lutheran premises, and his respect for authority was hardly less than Luther's. But from the very beginning, Calvin believed in a closer concurrence between the claims of natural law and of Christianity. In trying to realize the ideal of a truly Christian society in Geneva, he was forced all along the line to go further in assimilating the natural law to Christian ideas, and Christian demands to those of natural law. The organization of an actual community necessitated the mitigation of the strictly Christian ideals and an increased and more direct use of the institutions of natural law. Thus there was a mutual assimilation with respect to content. The way and the means to this was the identification of the ethics of the Old and the New Testament. Calvin did not recognize the distinction between the Christianity of the heart and the ethics of office and vocation, which made Luther's social ethics so idealistic but also so passive and indifferent.

Calvin wanted to build a Christian society and consequently had to apply natural law in a more direct and positive way to the establishment of a Christian commonwealth. Hence he laid greater emphasis on the rational, critical, and positively constructive value of natural law and deduced from it the right to resist an unreasonable and godless government. In such a case one should of course be as loyal as possible. When the proper authority fails to function properly, the right of revolution devolves only upon the authorities and officials next below it. When there are no inferior authorities, or when they too fail, logic would suggest no other appeal but to the sovereignty of the people. During the French, Dutch, Scottish, and English conflicts, Calvinism proceeded to cross this narrow bridge to the radical natural law of democracy, the sovereignty of the people, and the rational ordering of society by individuals. To be sure, the official view continued to be that no revolution and no rational organization of society should do more than restore the Christian order of life and the rule of true authority. Besides, Calvinist natural law retained the basic recognition, derived from relative natural law, of the disparity and consequent gradations of very unequal rights and duties; it gave emphasis to the duties over the rights imposed by natural and divine law.

On the whole, however, the specifically relative traits of natural law were continuously pushed into the background, while the abstract and absolute features were brought increasingly to the fore. Anglo-Saxon Calvinism, in making the transition from the state-church to the free-church system, even adopted the natural law scheme of the voluntary contract of individuals as the structuring principle for the church. Anglo-Saxon Calvinism has ever since made common cause with the liberal and democratic parties. The mainstay of the English Liberals are the Dissenters of the Calvinist middle classes. In America, the individualism of the churches has established the most intimate ties with political individualism, even though the outward institutions have remained totally separated. As a result, Calvinists today are supporters of liberal causes, participants in the anti-slavery and peace movements, and reformers of public life in the sense that they promote a practical rationality based on natural law and the participation of individuals in community enterprises.

Such are the developments of natural law in the large arena of the churches and confessions. But natural law is not wanting on the soil of the sects either. The fusion of Christian law and natural law had become so commonplace that even the sects did not fail to make this identification. It was bound to be an advantage to the sects to be able to appeal to the ancient, aboriginal demands of nature and reason as well as to the law of Christ. However, the meaning and function of natural law were quite different on the soil of the sects from what they are within the churches. The churches were mainly interested in the postlapsarian relative natural law in order to be able both to recognize and to regulate the given political, social, and economic orders under this legal title. This was a matter of course for the established national and territorial churches that dominated the entire culture. The interest of the sects was completely different. The sects attack the very idea of a universal church-dominated culture and of a mass-Christianity; they bring mature and conscious Christians into voluntary religious communities. There is little they can do, therefore, with the means of compromise provided by relative natural law. The full accent, for the sects, lies rather on the absolute natural law and its identity with Christ's strict law of love. Freedom, equality, common property, equal rights for man and woman, as was the case with Adam and Eve orginally: that is the natural law of the sects which they demand in the name of reason as well as of Christian revelation.

To be sure, two different tendencies must also be distinguished within the sect-type. There is the group of passive and long-suffering sects on the one hand, and on the other that of the aggressive sects bent on reform. The former represents the norm, though the latter is by no means a rare exception. Since the sect adopts above all the principles of the Sermon on the Mount, it is disposed to bear patiently the suffering and evil of the world, oppression and persecution, mockery and hostility, and to renounce vengeance and violence in accord with the words of the Lord. The sect demands the complete separation of the religious from the political community; for faith, it demands freedom from all external pressure; and when persecuted, it does not resist but rather seals its Christian testimony by martyrdom. The Christian law is here oppressed by the world, deprived of dominance and triumph, without general and public recognition. Such recognition is not expected until the end-time, with the establishment of the millennial kingdom at Christ's return. Natural law and the law of Christ will not really trimph, therefore, until the end-time. Christians, meanwhile, keep the law of revelation in their small circles and within the limitations imposed by their status as a suffering and oppressed sect.

The validity of the relative natural law for the non-Christian world of the state and society is not exactly denied, and from time to time it is even acknowledged. But here, too, Christians suffer passively and patiently under forms of life that are alien to them, and refuse either completely or in some measure to participate in office-holding, the administration of law, war, capital punishment, the taking of oaths, or the worldly way of life. The positive meaning of natural law is here reserved for the future. In the present it finds expression only in the equality, freedom, and brotherliness of the members of the religious community in their mutual relations. In modern times, as the sects have been less oppressed and persecuted, they often demonstrate a strong affinity for the democratic and Christian-socialist parties.

The transition from the passive, long-suffering sects to the aggressive, reforming type occurred wherever the pressure of persecutions or spiritual enthusiasm made the coming of the kingdom of God seem near. Now it is said that since the return of Christ is imminent, the days of suffering passivity are over, and the moment for the establishment of the kingdom of God and of nature has come. The peasant bands of Fra Dolcino proclaim this message, the Joachite literature promises it, the reformations of the Hussite Taborites, of the Anabaptists of Münster, and of individual groups of Independents are based on this. Radical democratic and socialistic or even communistic ideas emerge as a result. Such thoughts, based on the gospel and natural law, also played a role in the Peasants' Wars. But the point in question is always the absolute law of nature and of reason. Naturally, there are threads here that lead to modern socialism. Modern Christian socialism, in particular, is completely analogous—only it dispenses with the eschatological foundation and speaks instead of a re-creation of the world to be brought about by God, and of a proclamation of divinely willed progress in the great social movements of the time. But democratic socialism has connections with these ideas, too. The English revolution produced forerunners of socialism; and these ideas, present also in Catholicism, prepared the way for socialism in the person of Saint-Simon. Present-day Marxist socialism to be sure, has broken off all inner connections with this absolute Christian natural law of freedom and love; it has based everything on the class struggle instead of on love, and on the natural laws of economic development instead of on the divine world government.

Our third type, mysticism, has the least to do with Christian natural law. As a radical individualism of immediate religious experience, mysticism is not tied to organization. It can just as well adapt to existing organizations as disregard them, since it has no vital interest in them. Hence it does not need to compromise with the relative natural law, as does the church; nor does it need to look for the fulfilment of the absolute natural and revealed laws, as does the sect. Basically, where it does not associate itself with the sect—as is often the case—it is indifferent toward natural associations or organizations and tolerates them as they are. In one respect, however, even mysticism has an important, factual significance for natural law—without, however, its using this term and without incorporating its contributions in the conceptual framework of natural law.

The peculiar characteristic of consistent mysticism is that it sees all historical, liturgical, and dogmatic values purely as forms and reflections of the religious process that is basically the same everywhere. Christianity is the working of Christ in us, of the divine principle contained in Christ. Hence it is everywhere the same principle that is at work in all the various forms of historical Christianity, with only relative, outward differences. Indeed, the deeper non-Christian piety also has its roots in this principle, in the Christ in us, whom the heathen themselves do not perceive to be the Christ. The inner light is therefore identical with the divine order of reason; it also is identical with the light of nature. Hence arises not only, as in the sect, the demand for civil toleration, for non-interference by state authorities in religious controversies, and for the leaving of these matters to the purely spiritual powers; but more importantly, the idea of freedom of conscience originates here as a requirement of essential human nature, and as the right of all relative religious truth to subsist and express itself for the sake of the kernel of truth contained in it.

This inner light and its diffusion in all men is often connected with the natural moral law, which is viewed also as the essential element of every positive ethic and system of law. Yet this freedom of conscience is, to my knowledge, not designated within these circles as a constitutive element of what, after all, is always the ethical-legal natural law. It seems to me that it was only under the influence of the Enlightenment theory of natural law or of the rights of humanity (when all the legal implications of reason were given structure) that this freedom of conscience was included juridically among the natural rights of all people. Freedom of conscience itself, however, has its origin in the circles of mysticism, and in sectarianism insofar as the latter is fused with mysticism. The natural law of the church, on the other hand, had—exactly like Rousseau's program of the rights of man—designated the outward unity of culture and religion as the reasonable demand of natural law. The mystical idea is first presented in rationalistic and juridical form by the American constitutions. It cannot be overlooked, however, that already in Spinoza's *Theologico-political Tractate*, the demands for toleration, which are connected with the mysticism of the inner word, the Christ in us, and the law and light of nature, are closely related to demands for freedom of scientific thought, which appears as a human right that is not to be abrogated by the social contract. It was not for nothing that Spinoza lived for years with the Rhijnsburg Collegiants. To be sure, even he still deemed it necessary to balance these modern ideals, which were suspected of threatening anarchy, with the idea of the unity of culture in church and state. Just before him, Hobbes, too, felt that it was the task of philosophical sociology to give a new, modern foundation to this political-ecclesiastical unity of culture.

Now the focus shifts to the modern classical natural law of the eighteenth century. It marks the beginning of a new, modern conception of sociology, independent of ecclesiastical and religious criteria, which not only dominates the instinctive self-awareness of all community but has also deeply penetrated the juridical and factual construction of all modern institutions. In place of supernatural, divine foundations and conjunctions in the secular and ecclesiastical sphere, there now emerged the ideal of a radical reconstruction based on the voluntary association of individuals. The intent was to follow rational considerations of how the community should serve the individual, and to make this idea the basis of juridical theory. This is undoubtedly something new, not only in relation to the church-culture and its relative natural law but also relative to the eschatological enthusiasm of the sect.

When one considers the interrelationships that have been shown thus far, however, the probability suggests itself of a strong continuity between the secular natural law of classical antiquity and the natural law of the church on the one hand, and between modern radical movements of social reform and ancient Christian and Hellenistic ideas (which these movements seem to transform) on the other. The secular natural law is also an ideal legislation that in many ways represents an almost utopian contrast with the actual natural laws and conditions of society. It, too, is founded on a strong religious faith in the purposefulness of the world, in the victory of the good and reasonable—a faith that is to be seen as an echo and transformation of Christian-Jewish-Stoic theism. The continuity between the culture of the Enlightenment and the Christian-ecclesiastical culture is greater at all points than may appear to the generations involved in the battle—or to those who share the modern aversion to ecclesiastical culture.[1] The difference lies only in its optimism and this-worldliness, in the replacement of all supernatural revelation by the capacities of a logically articulated reason and universal moral predispositions; that is, in the consistency and radicalism with which a single idea is allowed to dominate the whole construction. Practically, however, and to a certain extent also formally and conceptually, the store of ancient ideas is continued and transformed. The still unwritten history of liberalism and of the *Weltanschauung* of natural law would have to take this factor into account at all points. The other influences and causes that help shape modern secular natural law are of course not disavowed. The urge toward emancipation in the middle class, the rationalism of the absolute state, the analogy of the general rationalistic-mathematical way of thinking: all these are of great significance. But these points of contact require an exposition of their own. Only the impact of ecclesiastical natural law was to be considered here.

The connection between ecclesiastical and modern secular natural law is easily traceable in the great thinkers who have shaped the modern world. Even Hobbes defined his ideal as the coincidence of the Christian moral law with the natural law as he construed it; the latter, to be sure, he developed more according to an Epicurean pattern, ignoring the Fall and taking no account of the Stoic-Christian tradition. But the general formulations of the questions he raises even in connection with his entirely new construction are, after all, suggested to him by the ecclesiastical doctrine of natural law. Grotius, consciously following Stoic and Scholastic models, extended the sway of the absolute and purely rational natural law, reducing the Christian moral law to the status of particular (not rationally necessary) counsels and supererogations, much as Catholicism does. Pufendorf obviously embedded the new findings in the old, while Locke identified the ethical and juridical natural law, which he construed in his own free and independent way, with a Christianity newly understood. Christian Wolff, notwithstanding his extension of the natural law, still finally maintained its definite identity with the Christian moral law. Natural law as carried out by the lawyers has retained the old distinction between an absolute and a relative natural law, it differentiating between an abstract, purely conceptual natural law and a hypothetical one that takes the particular circumstances into account. It is also evident that the more radical Calvinist development provided the first foundation and impulse for the new theories, while Lutherans and Catholics followed only slowly. No less worthy of attention is the prominence and effectiveness of the Stoic elements in the ecclesiastical natural law, which achieved an independent development by being able to link up with Roman law as well as with the church.

It is not possible to pursue this subject any further here. Research in this area has not yet progressed very far, as the history of philosophy is still not accustomed to the elucidation of the sociological elements in philosophical thought. But the general outlines of the relationship have now become clear. Something else can also be perceived now. Modern secular natural law is an ideal, similar to the Christian and Stoic social ideal; an ideal legislation that appealed initially, it is true, to the structure of the historical process in the founding of society, but that has become increasingly aware that it is really an ideal and not a sociological law immanent in nature or history. Rousseau, and especially Kant, clearly state that it is an evaluation of society in terms of ideal criteria and not an explanation of the actual process of society's coming into being. So here, too, one becomes aware of the conflicts between the ideal and the natural laws of society—in a manner reminiscent of Stoic-Christian natural law. The old Christian ideal emerged in conjunction with the individualistic and pessimistic disintegration of ancient society. But it very soon exposed the other side, its antagonism to the demands of nature. The modern ideal of natural law arose with the destruction of the old feudal ties and the emancipation of free vital energies, but very soon revealed its antagonism to the naturalness of society. Modern thought, however, no longer sees resistance caused by sin; but difficulties that are visualized in terms of the natural laws of genetics, of group psychology, and finally of sociology. Therefore, both the secular natural law of today and liberal idealism encounter, *mutatis mutandis*, the same struggles and difficulties as the old Stoic-Christian ideal.

Note

1. This is one of the main objections I have raised against Günther's book, *Die Wissenschaft vom Menschen; Ein Beitrag zum deutschen Geistesleben im Zeitalter des deutschen Rationalismus* (see my review in *Historische Zeitschrift*, Vol. 103). The Enlightenment appears to me indeed to be the first breakthrough of modern culture. But it seems that the Enlightenment itself, along with certain new motives, has its roots in the re-interpretation and transformation of the older religious ideas that are not only Christian but also include something of Stoicism and Neo-Platonism. I have nothing to say concerning the explanations with which Lamprecht accompanies this book by his pupil. My opinion concerning Lamprecht agrees completely with that of W. Goetz in the *Archiv für Kulturgeschichte* (Vol. 8).

18

On the Possibility of
a Liberal Christianity

'A liberal Christianity' is the motto of all those who see in the modern world a fundamental and radical change in all the practical and theoretical foundations of life, yet cannot and will not abandon the religious and ethical ideals of Christianity. They are conscience-bound to the Christian life-world, and their realization that its strengths are indispensable precisely to the modern world compels them to elaborate and to develop the Christian ideal in relation to the present and the future. In doing so, they can appeal to the inner freedom inherent in these strengths for life provided by Christianity, as well as to those in every age who have preceded them in this endeavor. But their task is nevertheless essentially new, and beset with great internal and external difficulties. The great question is whether a religious life-world that has assumed a definite form in the course of thousands of years is at all capable of assuming new forms; and if so, whether it would retain the strength and vitality to maintain itself and to condition a culture that has need, above all, of health and strength, of seriousness and depth. The number of those, moreover, who devote themselves to this task with a truly religious strength and practical success is not very great. Those interested only in the present (*Die Modernen*) look upon the very effort as mistaken, and the pragmatists (*die praktisch Handelnden*) tend to prefer the historic church and its tradition. So there is sufficient occasion for self-reflection and self-criticism.

Essentially, a liberal Christianity could be defined in terms of two characteristics: first, it replaces the tie to an authoritative church by an inwardness that derives, freely and individually, from the strength of the common spirit of the tradition; and secondly it transforms what has been the basic idea of historic Christianity, namely, the idea of a miraculous salvation of a human race suffering from the mortal infection of sin, into the idea of a redemptive elevation and liberation of the person through the attainment of a higher personal and communal life from God. Insofar as this liberal Christianity shares the general presuppositions (with respect to both substance and methodology) of the modern mind, it is also very much more likely to be influenced by it and to come into conflict with it than is the Christianity of the church, which sets aside precisely these basic methodological presuppositions and replaces them with its own authoritative and specifically Christian methodology. The whole inner situation of such liberal Christianity, consequently, gives rise to the fundamental question whether a Christianity thus based on new foundations and presuppositions is or is not at all inherently viable. The most important question is not the practical one, whether such a Christianity can find its place and take root in the churches. The most essential, penetrating, and difficult question is whether it is possible and viable in and of itself, or whether it is merely the last echo of a disintegrating Christian piety.

The best way to answer this question is to try to make clear to ourselves what are the most important antinomies and tensions affecting it. Then it must be shown whether these can be resolved or not. The cases of conflict to which we must accordingly address ourselves are the following four: (1) The collision of Judaeo-Christian theism and personalism with modern monism and antipersonalism; (2) The greater difficulty of connecting the Christian life-world with the cult of the person of Jesus (which, as divine revelation that redeems us and lifts us to a higher level, constitutes, after all, the sole bond of a specifically Christian community); (3) The greater difficulty of maintaining the Christian morality of love and regeneration, both in face of the modern preoccupation with immanence and in relation to the indispensable virtues of courage and justice, which regulate the struggle for existence; and (4) The disappearance of any common cultus as a result of the religious individualism rampant today, which cares only about self and, accordingly, results in an infinite fragmentation.

1. Personalism vs. Monism

The first of these cases of conflict is evident to all. Although its motivations and implications may differ greatly, monism is for many what the present calls for, and it is somehow present even in the most subtle ramifications of the modern idea. It is motivated, in the first place, by rationalism itself, which reduces (as it did for the Eleatics) all intelligible reality to the affirmation of identity; and which accordingly makes univocity (*die Einheit*) a postulate of reason, while denying the existence of a possible irrational actuality. In the second place, there is the idea of law, which has been developed strongly in the natural sciences and which regards the uniformity, at least, of a law that links the many to one another as the metaphysical formula of the world. Both of these motivations can be interpreted in an idealistic as well as in a materialistic sense, depending on the fundamental orientation of one's life towards the totality of things. A further motivation for monism derives from understanding art in terms of a natural pantheism, where the unconscious coincidence of nature with the artistic spirit is regarded as the essence of the beautiful, and the beautiful thus understood as the secret formula of the world. Finally, there is also a religious motivation, namely, the soulful mysticism of identity, which interprets religious experience as the becoming conscious of the identity of a particular being with the universe acting in and through it, and which tends to derive its conceptual supports from monistic speculations on univocity. The effects of all this are as variegated as the motivations: an innerworldly utilitarianism that realizes the unity of the generic consciousness, a quietistic mysticism, an aestheticizing naturalism, a relativism that changes anything into everything and robs every particular of its direct relationship to the Absolute, and a pessimism that sublates individual striving and leads to self-transcendence through culture.

Now these various currents are confronted by Prophetic-Christian personalism as faith in attainable, eternal, and absolute values of the person; in the subsistence of an absolute standard of the true and the good as over against all creaturely groping, seeking, and erring; in the anchoring of the ideal values of the person in a deity whose own being is somehow akin to them; and in the possibility of the perfection of the person in community with the personal life of the Deity. It is a deliberate dualism, which separates the world of absolute truths and values from the world of the searching and struggling creature, and which sees the purpose of the latter in precisely this kind of toil. It is a deliberate anti-rationalism that regards the existence of things as a incomprehensible miracle, explicable only by reference to the positive will of God; it sees every particular actuality, despite its ties to the whole, as at the same time an incomprehensible new creation with an actuality all its own. For this very reason it is optimistic with respect to the ultimate goal, in that it sees in the absolute values the ultimate meaning of the actual; and sees in their realization through the creature that has become involved in God's creative activity the final end of the toil of the spirit, which goes beyond and transcends physical and corporeal existence.

Such personalism can well appropriate to itself such views as the eternity of creation, the immensity of the world, the plurality of spiritual realms, the tie-in of every particular creation with the total nexus, and the immanence of the will of the divine creator in the world emanating from the Divine. What always remains, however, is the irrationalism of creation—of the macrocosm as well as of the microcosm—and the dualism of God and the world, of the absolute and the relative, of the eternal goals of life and a nature that rises to them only through freedom. Even immanent theism remains a radical irrationalism, dualism, and personalism, and all the more so as suffering and sin must be viewed even here not merely from the standpoint of a process that can be understood in terms of causality and of the total nexus, but as the natural antithesis of the world to the supreme values that are to be striven for.

But modern thought does not contain a single decisive refutation of all this. Rationalism would properly imply monism only if the interpretation of the world in rationalistic categories were the only permissible one, or if the concept of a uniform and universal cosmic law were, in fact, clear and viable and exhaustive of every actuality. In truth, however, irrationalistic motifs are as strongly represented in modern thought as rationalistic ones, and the tendency of the concept of law toward a mythological hypostatization is universally recognized. To make the recognition of anything dependent upon its rationalizability is no more than an enormous prejudice that is being successfully resisted, today as always, by life itself. All that is left of the tendency of thought towards uniformity and rationalization, then, is the idea of an immense correlativity, continuity, and interconnectedness, which, in their totality as well as in their individual and ever new particularities, are always irrational.

The presupposition of the religious, theistic, and personalistic stance toward the actual is accordingly unimpaired. It is indeed, the indispensable precondition of all faith in the subsistence of absolute values and standards, and in the attainability of absolute personality values. What must be left behind is the anthropomorphic form according to which this ground of the world had its own delimited existence apart from the world, and the anthropomorphic limitation of the goals, which interprets them as the eudaimonistic objectives of purely human well-being. But every idea of an absolute truth and an absolute good, indeed, even of the beautiful, and ultimately of being and reality itself, requires a ground for its actuality, in which and for which—apart from creaturely errors and illusions—it has its being. There is an essential connection, accordingly, between the Prophetic-Christian idea and our innermost convictions about life. An attitude of mere pessimism and relativism is not scientific but has its practical cause in certain moods of life; it always cancels itself when it is thought completely through, inasmuch as it depends on a comparison with the absolute standards whose subsistence it denies. Unable to comprehend belief in the objectivity of these standards, this attitude prefers to break the energy of life or to reduce life to trivialities that make it possible to forget those lofty standards. The overcoming of suffering, sin, and the relativity of our existence through the idea of a divine love that seeks us, educates us through struggle and the process of becoming, heals our pangs of conscience, and brings out the inner destiny of our being, affords an infinitely more solid stance toward life. It also avoids the fatal contradictions posed for the stance of radical pessimism and relativism by its own presuppositions.

Under these circumstances, there can be no question of the Prophetic-Christian idea of God being dissolved by modern life or replaced by modern thought. It remains, today as always, the center and support for every assertion of absolute personal life-values. Even as in antiquity, when Platonism and Stoicism received their world-historical power only from this idea of God, it still brings together all impulses and strivings for a spiritual content of life transcending the flux of life. For anyone who wants such a content and feels obligated to want it, there is but one religion of personalism, and that is the religious life deriving from Jesus and the Prophets.

2. The Christian Life-World and the Person of Jesus

The second point involves greater difficulties. Here the object of the church's faith, as it is delineated in the gospel and in the dogma of Christ, has been modified in a number of respects; it has been humanized, but at the same time burdened with many critical difficulties; and it has raised the more general problem of how eternal truths can be anchored in historical facts, and how these facts can be given a direct religious interpretation. Moreover, the whole idea of a world-redeemer has been adversely affected by the impression that the geocentric and anthropocentric view of the world is no longer tenable. Where the existence of mankind on earth is conceived as extending hundreds of thousands of years into the past and into the future, and where great intellectual and cultural systems are seen to rise and fall, it is impossible to regard this single person as the center of the entire history of all of mankind. All these impressions have made it impossible to continue to deify Jesus and to assign to him an absolutely central position. But the attempt, associated especially with liberal theology, to transfer to the human Jesus the role of a universal world-redeemer traditionally assigned by the church to Christ, is wholly impossible and fraught with intolerable contradictions.

Yet it is also true, that there is no other way to hold together the Christian community of spirit than through the common confession of Jesus; that it is impossible to keep alive the distinctively Christian idea of God apart from seeing its life-giving embodiment in Jesus; and that all the greatest and most characteristic ideas of Christianity—the idea of a grace that grasps and conquers us, of a certitude available to us, and of a superior power (*Kraft*) that elevates and overcomes us— depend on a religious appreciation and interpretation of Jesus as divine revelation. To separate the Christian belief in God in every respect from the person of Jesus would mean to cut this belief off from all its historic roots, from every means of expounding and illustrating it, from any greatness exceeding the measure of the average individual; and thus ultimately to dissolve the belief itself.

But such a separation is, again, not at all the necessary consequence of modern thought. Modern thought recognizes the axiom that the most profound and contentful religiosity is precisely not the spontaneous experience of any and every subject, which everywhere repeats itself in the same way. Such experience is characteristic only of a vague mysticism, devoid of both form and content, which is sterile for that very reason. Some sorts of symbols and embodiments, personal descriptions and demonstrations of superior religious power, are needed by every religiosity going beyond the average, whether it be that of Plato, the Stoics, Kant, Fichte, or any superior human being whose manner of life exudes religious power. The situation is not basically different in the case of Jesus' significance for Christianity. He is the embodiment of superior religious power, embellished in ever new ways in the course of thousands of years, whose heartbeat is felt throughout the whole of Christendom, even as the vibration of a ship's engine is felt in every nook of the whole ship. This is why he himself will always keep on living wherever the Prophetic-Christian belief in God is alive; and why this belief will rise to its full power and certitude, beyond the weakness and poverty of the average, only by having such a person to look up to. But if this be so, then the figure of Jesus will remain alive and inseparable from the power of the Christian belief in God. The core of all true and genuine Christian piety will remain, so long as there is such a piety, a Christ-mysticism in which every believer experiences a personal emanation from this central point; and where the faithful unite ever anew in the religious interpretation and veneration of Jesus as the divine revelation that enables us to transcend ourselves, and that has increased in power through the centuries in which it has made its impact upon world history. Apart from this core, the personalist belief in God would itself fade away and die.

But such a Christ-mysticism is not at all impossible now. What is to keep believers from making Jesus, surrounded and interpreted by the chorus of Old Testament Prophets and the great religious figures of the Christian era, the object of their believing imaginations? [What is to keep us from] confessing him as the source of our religious strengths and certainties? The critical study of the biblical texts (*Quellen*) cannot, after all, call the main features of Jesus' preaching and personality into question, and to tie the religious strengths of the followers to the great and powerful paradigmatic figure is not, after all, inconsistent with the religious idea. On the contrary, in all religions the dependence on the great paradigmatic figures is increased in proportion to the greatness of the life that is to be appropriated, so that the latitude afforded for original religious production is limited and most energy is consumed in devotion and empathy. There is really no insuperable difficulty here, however vacillating and uncertain people today may have become in their feelings.

One thing, however, the believer will have to forego—namely, to construe Jesus as the center of the world or even of human history, and to base his essential significance on this construction. The immensity of the world leads us to assume an infinite plurality of spiritual worlds; the human world that has arisen out of the biological evolution on earth is but one out of many and must perceive itself as within the nexus of a vastly larger cosmic life. There can be no question, therefore, of a cosmic position or significance of Jesus. But it is also difficult to think of Jesus as the culmination of humanity and thus to expect the religious strengths that became manifest in Jesus ultimately to conquer all of mankind. The enormous extent of human history, the possibilities of large-scale changes and of interruptions in the evolutionary chains, varieties in soul-capacity (*Beseelungsmög-lichkeit*) among various cultures and human groups—all this makes it probable that there are still other religious life-contexts with their own redeemers and paradigmatic figures.

It is also conceivable, of course, that the whole world of European-Christian culture will again perish and that some hundreds of thousands of years from now some new, great religious structures will arise. In that case, Jesus would simply be the religious center of the European-Christian world, with the religious life emanating from him and the Prophets (and encompassing the attainments of antiquity) constituting the appropriate and distinctive religious foundation of its existence, which would be shared with the rest of the world as long as other nations and races could be drawn into its life. The health and survival of European-Christian cultural life would accordingly depend on the maintenance of its religious foundations; and conversely, Christianity's own survival would perhaps depend on this cultural life. The truth of Christianity would be unaffected by all this if we are indeed justified in recognizing it as the most inward, profound, and active of all the available religious forces. Any truth that might come later would have to include the Christian truth; but in that different existential context it would not need to be connected with the person of Jesus but would link up with other symbols and paradigmatic figures.

For us and our existential context, however, (that is, for our own life and for our expansionary drive) the religiosity exemplified and embodied in Jesus—that is, the higher humanity emanating from him—would still remain the deepest and strongest source of the kind of life, for which we are destined and which is possible for us. We would perceive ourselves as standing in the sight of God, within the great circle of light radiating from Jesus, and our task would merely be truly to experience and to grasp God (having first been grasped by God) in this way that has been ordained for us. We would not need to be disturbed because there are still other circles of light, with other sources of light, within the great divine life of the world; or by the possibility that in future ages, perhaps after new ice ages and in completely new structures, there may arise new circles of light of this sort out of the depths of the divine life. The eternal truth of God has its particular historical form for every circle and for every general stance. Whatever is contained in this particular historical form can never, insofar as it is actually truth, become untruth. It will be included in every future truth, the more so as the future truth is more mature and profound. Every epoch stands immediately before God, and we stand immediately before God precisely as gathered together in the circle of light radiating from Jesus. It is a delusion to think that there could ever be a new religion for an epoch so deeply rooted in Christianity and in the kindred religious forces of antiquity. Our epoch will stand and fall with its religion, and its great existential question will be whether it will be able to preserve its own religious potency and at the same time share it, together with all of its cultural attainments, with the great nations that are making their first appearance on the world scene. Philosophical atheism, galvanizations of Platonism or Stoicism stripped of their Christian admixtures, or a merely witty anarchy of aphorisms will not be sufficient to enable it to survive.

Understood in this way, Christian theism and personalism, Christian belief in an elevation and redemption to a higher kind of humanity born of God, may indeed be linked to a religious appreciation and interpretation of Jesus' person; there is nothing impossible about it from the point of view of modern thought. In no way is it any longer the christological dogma of the church; but it is the innermost motif of that dogma, namely, the Christ-mysticism of an inner bond by which the community is united with its head, from whom the members derive life and strength, and whose representation as the revelation and symbol of God constitutes the chief element of a properly Christian cultus. A distinctively Christian cultus of this kind would be impossible without it, and a religion without cultus would be a dying religion. Christian theism is not a dying religion, but the firm support of all personal humanity (*alles persönlichen Menschentums*). But then our highest human strengths and convictions remain bound up, as far ahead as we are able to see, with devotion to the historical totality of life which has its point of departure in Jesus. Practically speaking, we need not be disturbed by something we cannot possibly see or even conceive; and theoretically, we could say to ourselves that something that is itself true will not be able to invalidate any truth available to us today that has actually proved to be true.

3. Christian Morality

Precisely from the practical point of view, namely, where the depth and stability of personal life is concerned, Christianity appears to be a constitutive part even of all modern religious life. But new difficulties now arise, again precisely from the direction of the ethical and the practical. (This is the third of the four cases of conflict mentioned above.) The Christian ethic is almost completely a religious ethic, which derives personhood exclusively from God; its individual morality is, accordingly, an ethic of self-sanctification for God, and its social morality is an ethic of the community of all the children of God, in God. The ultimate goal of individual action is thus a kind of personhood filled with the import of eternity, and the ultimate goal of communal action is a kingdom of divine love which overcomes the law (*Recht*), coercion, and the struggle for existence. This is perfectly logical and consistent. For the earthly self can only be overcome in transcendence (*im Ueberirdischen*) and a common bond to which all are subordinated can be found only in the sphere of the divine. But the goals of action thus become supramundane and transcendent, even though this transcendent community with God may be attained already in this life. Such action thus also becomes noticeably antithetical to an immanent humanism (*Humanität*) that merely seeks to render both nature and community more noble and spiritual. At the same time, however, this morality goes beyond the average conditions of life, which constitute no more than a regulating and disciplining of the struggle for existence by means of coercive organizations and utilitarian community formations, law (*Recht*), and justice; as well as beyond the average opportunities of life, which require above everything else technical, economic, and intellectual work, courage and bravery, victorious power and energetic self-assertion. Christian morality contradicts the instincts of modern immanentism and of the modern deification of the actual. Even intrinsically, moreover, it appears to be utopian, and to blind itself to its own impossibility by a pharisaic self-righteousness and an exaggeration of the omnipotence of evil.

These difficulties are undoubtedly there; and they are not being noticed for the first time today. They have been there from the beginning and have always been overcome only by means of compromises. But we are, to be sure, more strongly aware of them today. Cultural productivity has tremendously increased the significance of the here-and-now for everyone, the picture of an interconnection according to law of all the contents of the world absorbs immanence into the unity of the divine life, and an extremely fine aesthetic culture transfigures the world and our senses. At the same time, the connection between human existence and the great basic law of the struggle for existence, and our awareness of the infinite, complicated contingencies of human existence with respect to both nature and the social conditions, shows the dependence of all human life on very earthly circumstances. [This connection also shows] the impossibility of overcoming the inhibitions and distresses flowing from both nature and the laws governing the movement of social life with a mere good will and the inwardness of the disposition.

There is no doubt about all this. But there is, equally, no doubt about the profound thrust of the ethical personality beyond the merely temporal—toward a timeless and eternal import of life, and about the drive toward a supreme, purely personal morality, where people are inwardly united by a mutuality of disposition and by a community of free, inner understanding that transcends law, power, coercion, and struggle. The idea of continued personal development after the death of the body still points in the same direction even today. If indeed there is ever to be an actualization of absolute values above and beyond the merely relative values of everyday existence, then such an idea can only be implemented by means of another idea—namely, that of a further development and perfection after the death of the body, so that the seeds and beginnings of a higher existence, which are derived from the life in God, may be brought to fruition through a definitive return into the divine life. What is involved here is nothing other than the problem of absolute values itself, the overcoming of relativism. If it is true that personhood is attained only through the reception of absolute values into the natural life of the soul, then the problem of the person is likewise incapable of solution apart from the idea of an ultimate perfection after the death of the body, however many the difficulties and obscurities surrounding this point may be. Every affirmation of an ultimate, absolute being requires a doctrine of last things also with respect to the temporal development of the human spirit. Every affirmation of an absolute value beyond the relative values implies a transcendence also in the metaphysical sense. But human action and the human affect for life thus acquire a touch of the supramundane.

It is precisely this feature that is stressed by Christian piety which has implanted it most deeply in people's souls. Thus it truly corresponds to the ultimate demand of the practical-moral consciousness. Only it must be acknowledged that this is the highest, ultimate demand, which can only be asserted after the earlier, more immediate demands have been met. Since it always presupposes lower stages of morality below and beside itself, it can never singly and exhaustively determine morality. Its work cannot begin until nature's raw drives, instinctive group loyalties, and the jungle of the struggle for existence have either been broken or transformed and ennobled through cultural work and organization, through law and order, through intellectual and social discipline. A true morality that unites persons with one another and perfects them in their ultimate depths can come into play only after the conditions have been brought about which enable a person to rise above mere nature. It can be understood only as a supreme and ultimate stage of morality, which may indeed illumine the earlier stages with its gentleness but which may not reach its completion until the conditions of earthly life have been overcome. It will be free to act in full accord with its ideal only toward those who for their part recognize the ideal; toward others, it will have to have recourse to lower, tougher standards. It will always have to compromise with these tougher, more robust moral forces that have been created by the struggle for existence. Insofar as it is itself still struggling and searching, it will be characterized by a hardness and strictness, a flexibility and inchoateness, that are absent or superfluous in its purest form. It will be able, especially, to make immanence and the world of the senses a part of itself, in order to learn to be bored with mere secular work by engaging in secular work, and to sublimate sensuality by cultivating the senses. It will be able—and will need—to perceive itself as developing out of its preliminary stages, and thus will never need to enter into a pure and radical antithesis to them, if it learns to understand and acknowledge in them those elements that point upward to itself. It will no longer perceive itself as a conversional break with the world, but in rising above mere immanence it will be conscious of an inner continuity that cuts across the antithesis. The freedom and inclination of a morality that seeks above all else to be the unfolding of a life drawn from God, and the uniting of souls in God, will take care to see that every individuality should undergo this development in its own way and, in the end, form in its own way the synthesis of innerworldly and transcendant life.

All this is possible, much of it is actual. Schleiermacher, especially, has sought in this sense to lead the Christian ethos into the various moods and contexts of modern life, and has mediated between them. This renewal of Christianity as the religious ethos of the person and the personal community is even more prominent in the formulations of Christian ethics emanating from the modern social movement. In this new situation, Christianity becomes once again the message of the kingdom of God and of the infinite worth of the soul. The compromises with the morality of the world, which an earlier Christianity had effected in its own way, must then, to be sure, be effected once again in a new way. Here we are face to face with the great, vital tasks of the future. The task posed by the earliest Christianity now is posed again on a different basis. In the nature of the case, the morality of a highly-strung intellectual and material culture cannot be an absolutely simple one, but must be mediating and accommodating. The distinction (which is made in every culture) between the highest religious life-values with their corresponding life-style and secular goods and achievements with their corresponding innerworldly ethic has been merely intensified here and carried through, in both directions, to its ultimate conclusion—or, in any case, to what appears today to be the ultimate conclusion. In practice, this means the emergence of onesidedly oriented groups and infinitely varied compromises in individual life-style. Theoretically, however, a conceptual connection must be found that would lead upward, from one to the other, by means of inner mediations and transitions, without dissolving the antitheses themselves into a mere concept of immanent ethical development. The antithesis must remain. It constitutes the great life-tension from which life derives all its greatness and depth. At the same time, it must be inwardly bridged and overcome. But precisely this is what the ethic of a liberal Christianity is all about.

4. Individualism, Community, and Cultus

Now all this would be of little help if the cohesiveness and effective power of the Christian cultic community had actually broken down. A religion without cultus could not hope to be anything other than a dying religion, since it is cultus that makes vivid the shared imports of life and strengthens, by way of mass-psychology, the religious feelings and ideas. This brings us to the fourth point. And here the situation is indeed very difficult, especially for a liberal Christianity. The great historic denominations have an effectual cultic community, however much it may have been shaken in certain respects (especially in Protestantism). The fact is that they have such a cultic community because they originally were, and still are, something more than cultic communities. They originated as institutions of redemption and salvation competing for recognition as the one truly saving institution of Christianity. For them, Christianity is a supernatural community founded by God through Christ, endowed with an absolute, infallible truth and with ordained bearers of this truth; and they accordingly have come to view this community as the supernatural core and basis of all community-formation. They have sought to dominate society, either forcibly and directly, or indirectly, through the miraculous power within them. Either way, the result has been that the most varied political and social means were employed to further their dominance and cohesion. In this way, the cultic community acquired a power that was based on the idea of an absolute truth and of its own vocation to dominate the whole of society. In part, this idea is still alive today; in part, the fact that a common cultus is taken for granted is its after-effect.

But for a vast number of people today the power of this sociological construction has broken down. Radical and mystical communities, from the Anabaptists to the Pietists and the modern sects, have pointed in this direction; there the inwardness and personal quality of religious certainty becomes an illumination that differs from individual to individual, and the community becomes an association of those who voluntarily commit themselves to such a truth. The ultimate implication is an inwardness that renounces every kind of community. The analogies of scientific knowledge and certainty, which was understood as the autonomous making-sure-for-oneself apart from tradition, pointed in the same direction; since religious and scientific thought were so closely intertwined, the latter was bound also to affect the former. Then there was the whole new sociology of the age of individualism and natural law, which derived all community from the voluntary coming together of consenting individuals (in contrast to the objective and supernatural institutions and bonds of previous times) and, accordingly, recognized freedom from the community as the logical consequence of dissent. Dissent from the ecclesiastical tradition was not stimulated by the whole movement of religious criticism and skepticism, and inner opposition to all church establishment and its absolute truths was stimulated by the increasing widespread perception that here, too, there could only be relative truth or degrees of approximation to an ultimate truth.

All these factors have given rise to a religious subjectivism and individualism that turns even the religious communities into voluntary associations and normally reserves fully the freedom and flexibility of one's personal religious conviction. At least on this point, Liberalism and Social Democracy are agreed, and the whole world of modern thought is filled with the most brittle kind of subjectivism in matters of religion. It is also particularly a characteristic of liberal Christianity to be so strongly cognizant of personal conviction, of the relative and subjective character of all religious knowledge, and of its intertwining with science and criticism, that there can be no longer any question of an actual community or of a common spirit capable of action. But this leads also to the loss of the cultic community, which cannot subsist apart from the actual community and which today, has in in any case, lost much of its simple effectiveness—either by being tradition-bound or by facile re-interpretations of the tradition.

Whether this consequence of the previous development is

unavoidable and permanent—this is the question on which the viability of a liberal Christianity depends. To answer the question negatively, one might point out that the great tide of individualism and natural law has generally run its course. A new sociology is starting to take over in all areas. While it is not about to renew the old supernatural institutions and bonds, its conceptual apparatus of organic community structures nevertheless does affirm the priority of the whole over the individual, of the community over its members, of the common spirit over the subjectivities, of educational formation over a ready-made autonomy. Liberalism is everywhere giving way to Socialism. Only in the religious sphere has the individualism of Liberalism maintained itself also in Socialism. But when Socialism declares religion to be a private matter, it is animated by the hope that this delusion will thereby be destroyed. Meanwhile, Socialism preaches on its own behalf a metaphysics and dogmatics every bit as ruthlessly all-encompassinhg as any church ever did. What is true in this position is that a strong community requires shared metaphysical convictions; and this perception cannot fail to have its effect also in the religious sphere, where it originally received it most powerful implementation and where it was exploded only by the reaction of the liberated individual against the coercion of a thousand years.

Here—like anywhere else—it is impossible for the autonomy of personal conscientious conviction to mean a radical abandonment of tradition and a completely momentary spontaneity. It is always a matter of insights received from others (*überkommenes Erkenntnisgut*) and historically formed life-forces (*Lebensmächte*) that are not to be replaced by new insights of one's own; rather, they are to be personally appropriated and elaborated through life. But if this is true generally, it is all the more true in the religious sphere that there can be no infinitely varied individual insights and new constructions, but only a working-through and an internalization of the historic forces (*der historischen Mächte*). But then the common spirit and the tradition, and the common vessel of both of these, the organized community, regain their proper significance. All the relativism and all the subjectivism in the world can only mean, after all—unless they aim at an all-consuming skepticism—that the last word has not been spoken in any religion or denomination, that we are always only moving towards the absolute truth, that it is always a question of proximate values (*Annäherungswerte*). But then a special, comprehensive significance attaches to the highest proximate values; for they accordingly bear in themselves something of the power (*Kraft*) of the Absolute, and they create a bond of equality—not, indeed, an equality of achieved possession but a common point of departure and an identical direction of human striving.

The radical individualism that remains today in the religious sphere as a vestige of the age of individualism and rationalism threatens, because of the weakening of the self-confidence of reason, to turn into anarchy and skepticism. But it must first live out all of its implications, destroying all community where there is the strongest natural desire for association (*Zusammenschluss*) and for a common bond beyond the merely human, and arousing the passionate antipathy of all religion that is naturally conscious of its drive toward community. Only after driving into the arms of the historic churches all those conscious of their need for contact and community, after driving these churches into a united and determined counter-attack, and after uncovering the whole chaotic disruption of the modern spirit in all its depths—only then will the radical individualists perceive the absurdity of their position and return to the common enjoyment of the inheritance. Then even a liberal Christianity will perceive once again the necessity of an organization and of a common cultus that illustrates and represents the inheritance, and will be able to attract those who are wearied and pained by the excess of religious individualism. Conversely, the pressure of the encircling anti-individualistic structures—socialist, bureaucratic, and capitalist—must first be fully established and perceived. Only then, the free individual (confirmed by religion and metaphysics, as one will be within liberal Christianity and its cultic community) will be properly appreciated in one's significance for the preservation of freedom and of an individualism now taken too much for granted. Then it will also be necessary once again to understand the organizations in which alone such an individualism can grow and maintain itself. It will be evident once again that one must not saw off the limb on which one is sitting.

It is difficult to predict what form such a reconstruction will or might take. The system of privileged, politically co-ordinate territorial churches now prevailing in Europe represents a compromise between the old system of ecclesiastical uniformity and the modern plurality of religious convictions. It is unlikely to last another hundred years, and the re-ordering of these matters will be one of the great tasks facing the future leaders of church and state. But only such a re-ordering will get the problem of the religious life moving again and enable those involved with it to show their true vitality. Only then will the question of the incorporation of a liberal Christianity into these organizations become a live issue. Only the future can tell whether liberal Christianity will assume a new form of its own, or whether at least the large Protestant churches will be able to vouchsafe to it the freedom and congregational autonomy that would truly give it adequate scope. In Europe, there is at the moment no possibility of separate organizations. All that can be sought is a breathing space within the established churches; and even a liberal Christianity has, after all, close ties to the basic import of these churches. Their Protestant organization, moreover, has given rights of citizenship to critical scholarship and to the subjective religious life. No one would voluntarily renounce these rights. For the foreseeable future, the objective can only be to gain freedom of movement within Protestantism for a relatively liberal Christianity, yet not to lose or to deny the great historical sense of kinship with the creation of the Reformers.

We may look upon the task we are setting for ourselves as intrinsically possible, even though we must not underestimate the enormous difficulties. For its fulfilment, we must look largely to the future. What we can confidently expect is that the inner impoverishment of the present and the need for the strengths of faith will necessarily compel people to acquire or to regain religious foundations for their life. The theologians, professional philosophers, and religionists, who are generally charged with these matters, at least among us in Germany, are not by themselves able to provide these. They can do no more than to keep the spark glowing, to prepare for the future, and to break their bread for as many as come seeking it. Those who become anxious and dejected under these circumstances must cling to the inner assurance that is the foundation of all religion, that God is the Lord of the world and of history, that even the present changes and situations are created and fulfilled by God, and that we, with the movement of our own life, stand in the movement of God's life. Whatever may become of our search for a liberal Christianity, God sits on the Divine throne (*im Regiment*) with God's truth prevailing. What counts is not that we save Christianity but that we trust in the victory of God. What we perceive to be the truth binding our conscience cannot be wholly false and must point toward the future. We may devote ourselves, therefore, seriously and faithfully to the task that we comprehend, and leave the rest to God. For the present is no more without God than any other time ever was.

19

Max Weber

That which his friends thought incredible and impossible has come
about: Max Weber is actually dead. Let these words, then,
approximate what I had wished to say at his burial, above all about
the human impression of his total personality. I am not in a position
at this moment to evaluate his scholarly achievements, even though
all his writings are known to me and readily come to mind. But what
is scholarly accomplishment as compared with the total impact of this
powerful personality?

Max Weber was one of the few great men in the Germany of our
generation, one of the very few persons of real genius I have met in
my life. He sprang from a family endowed with a high concentration
of extraordinary intellectual gifts, but also burdened by severe nervous
disorders. He was closely related to the Baumgartens, the Jollys, and
the Hausarts. His mother was a most impressive figure, a longtime
leader of the women's movement and of social welfare activities.
Equally distinguished by goodness, discernment, and energy, she was
unforgettable—one among thousands. Her children must have
resembled a lion's brood, requiring infinite goodness and skill to
become what they have become. A portrait of Max Weber is
incomplete without the portrait of this remarkable mother. But no
less remarkable has been his wife, who has become a most effective
champion of the women's movement's second generation. She has
succeeded in retaining the more feminine and motherly elements in
this movement, the housewife along with the woman of distinction.

Weber grew up among great and unusual people, open and
ingenuous, who were linked together by the greatest tenderness and
truthfulness. Their abundant wit and taste was coupled with a kind of

goodness, considerateness, and refinement of mind reminiscent of the very best times of old German culture, which in the age of the superman has become almost old-fashioned. The marvellous house of his grandfather, located on the banks of the Neckar, was the center of family life. It had sheltered Gervinus and Hausrat; Treitschke and Häusser had spent many hours here as close friends of the family. Here Weber spent his most productive years, despite much sickness, and constituted, together with his wife, the center of attraction for all intellecutally interested youth. Unforgettable times these were, in the Heidelberg of men like Jellinek, Albrecht Dieterich, and Windelband. It was not for nothing that Count Keyserling visited Heidelberg every year to enjoy German culture before going on to London and Paris; for here he received an abundance of ideas that he could take with him on his philosophical trip around the world. And there were countless others, Germans as well as non-Germans, who did as he did.

A man like Weber could not fail to have a strong impact on others, and a large circle of friends—closer and more distant ones—gathered around him. He himself had no great need of the fellowship of others, but others had of his. To my knowledge, a strongly affective friendship linked him only to Paul Göhre. It ended early and abruptly, for reasons unknown to me. All his other relationships were based on common objective interests. Thus he had close relations with Friedrich Naumann, in particular; Weber's sociological and political insights became part and parcel of Naumann. Naumann's synthesis of modern social and power politics with a deep religiosity, which amazed many, was the fusion of his paternal inheritance and his own innermost being with the more externally appropriated teachings of Max Weber. Through Naumann, Weber's ideas have already exerted an historic influence on the German people. Among the philosophers, Weber's closest friend was the keenest logician of contemporary German philosophy, Heinrich Rickert, and the latter's pupil, Emil Lask. He was also close to Simmel. He identified himself with this Neo-Kantian school with a rigor I often found perplexing. But he also contributed significant ideas of his own to this school, not only through his shrewdly argued publications, but also through these scholarly friends. Regarding national economics, he carried on an exchange of ideas, especially with Werner Sombart, that lasted for several decades and was greatly enlivened by ethical controversies. If Sombart's work revolves around the concept and problematics of 'capitalism,' it seems legitimate to suppose that Weber played an important role in shaping Sombart's conception of the problem. That is to say, the modern universal-critical conception of history goes back, to a considerable extent, to Max Weber as well as to Karl Marx. Concerning myself, I will only take note of the fact that for years I experienced the infinitely stimulating power of this man in daily conversation and that I am conscious of owing to him a large part of my knowledge and skill.

Then there is the countless number of those whose relations to Weber were less close. During his time in Berlin an assistant judge and *Privatdozent*, he came to know the whole world of the politically prominent of the great Bismarck era. After that, he visited Berlin again and again until the very end, in order to maintain or renew contact with the leading figures of the various political groups. On his numerous trips he established contact with the leading minds of foreign countries. During the war, he was one of the few German authorities found more or less acceptable abroad. His participation in the drafting of the Versailles Memorandum concerning the dogma of German war guilt was motivated by the respect he had thus won. But he maintained various relations with poets and artists as well as with politicians and scholars. He was an admirer of Max Klinger and at the same time sought to acquire a feeling for the most modern art. Stefan George drew closer to him in recent years, and it is difficult even to think of the Heidelberg circle of George's admirers apart from the many stimuli provided by Weber, even though he insisted on regarding their undertaking as anachronistic—admirable, but powerless—in an era of class struggle, capitalism, and social reconstruction of the most basic kind.

Now what was at the core of this man, whose virtually magic influence radiated thus far and wide? Having begun his professional career in jurisprudence and commercial law, he turned to national economics, and finally he died working on a great work about sociology. His pioneering philosophical-methodological researches enriched philosophy as well as his own discipline. By separating from his major works such special problems as the cultural significance of Calvinism for the economic ethics of the world religions, he opened up new vistas to the life of the mind. Terribly handicapped by a severe nervous ailment, he nevertheless stimulated and accomplished more than ten people in good health and of more than average intelligence.

All this, despite its power, its profoundly, and its rigorous adherence to the scientific method, still belonged to the external side of his life. In his inmost soul he was a political man, a born ruler and an ardent patriot, whose saw his country headed in the wrong direction and who passionately desired to give it leadership; but who, in view of the conditions of the time, could not expect actually to provide it. During the

Wilhelmine era he did not want to dissipate himself in the service of the parties, already played out, and after the collapse [of 1918] these same parties were unable to recognize and to utilize his power. He was not a dogmatic democrat. For him, democracy was merely what fate had decreed for the modern world; it represented the loss of much that was beautiful and transcendingly great. He saw its only advantage in its raising up of segments of the population that under other systems are simply crushed, and hence the possible emergence of new leaders, who the spent old aristocracy and the short-sighted and well-sated intelligentsia could no longer be expected to produce. He was no socialist, but he regarded the rise of manual labor to a share in government as an irrevocable result of modern technology and modes of production. Hence he looked up the return to something like the social bonds of the Middle Ages as inescapable, and upon the treatment of the Social Democrats by the old ruling classes as at the same time shameful and stupid. He foresaw the coming of times when free individuality would be completely stifled by guilds and trade associations. He fought for a state that would maintain the relative possibility of liberalism, that is, of wealth and of freedom of individual movement itself. His approach to the state was not at all metaphysical or ethical; he looked upon it as a mere means by which the nation and the rich abundance of its life might be expressed, and which, since it changes with changing conditions, might be constructed in different ways at different times.

To save the life of the nation in a terribly threatening world situation and in face of a mad internal self-delusion, and to organize it anew, regardless by what means: this was the great pathos of his soul. In all political and social matters he was a complete relativist and recognized only two absolutes: faith in the nation and the categorical imperative of human dignity and justice. The last few years must have brought terrible anguish to his soul. His most recent pronouncements breathe a spirit that I did not recognize in him to this extent in the past; I can only designate it as heroic skepticism. With him, as with F. Th. Vischer, morality was simply taken for granted.

The nation did not recognize or utilize this treasure of potential leadership. In this respect he remained a Raphael without arms and hands. And since he could not be a politician and would not be a demagogue, he returned to the world of scholarship. Here death has taken from his hands a most promising and valuable piece of work. He had faults; they were the faults of persons great and strong, and there is no point in reassuring the Philistine by such a concession. His life, like that of his people was a tragedy; but he did not like to stir a tragic interest in others or even in himself. Duty, in the strict and simple sense of Kant, sufficed to give his life meaning. He had only contempt for the modern expressions of subjectivity, interestedness, and the super-human; he did not join the prevailing trend towards religion. A Stoic aura of greatness and hardness surrounds him like Shakespeare's Brutus, but still several degrees harder and more heroic. To him, too, apply the closing words of 'Julius Caesar,' behind which I want to conceal every personal sentiment of shock, of friendship, and of gentle, respectful awe in face of this combination, still basically strange to me, of skepticism, heroism, and moral strictness:

> The elements
> So mixed in him that nature might stand up
> And say to all the world, 'This was a man.'

20

My Books

Self-portrayals on the grand scale, such as these pages present, have their risky but also their useful aspect. The risky side is self-evident and repelled me at first, to be sure. But the publisher knew how to make the useful side very persuasive; in spite of all the author's errors and misunderstandings of himself, an authentic self-interpretation could ease the reader's start and eliminate many errors and misunderstandings on the part of interpreters. There is surely something to this. But it involves me in certain difficulties. I have no system, properly speaking, and in that I am different from most other German philosophers. Of course I keep one in the back of my mind, as a basic presupposition, but only to correct it constantly as a result of specific research. I cannot display the system in such an unfinished condition. I can only explain the sequence of my books—which in the case of a systematically oriented person is in itself a kind of system.

My desire for knowledge was from early youth directed towards the historical world, very much as was the case with Dilthey. This impulse was fed and nourished by diligent teachers in my school, a Bavarian humanistic *Gymnaisum* of the old style with marvelously few class hours. At home I was encouraged to investigate the natural sciences, since my father was a doctor who gladly would have made a medical practitioner of me also, and who pushed me at an early stage into scientific observation and collection. There were skeletons, anatomical compendia, electrical machines, books of plants, books about crystals, etc. Thus it came about that I learned from the beginning to view all problems in the history and philosophy of culture within the context of a scientific world-view, and sensed at the same time that the interpretation of both worlds was a burning theoretical and practical problem. Moreover, that was the time of the cultural lies of Nordau, of the speeches of Dubois-Reymond, of Scherr, Hellwald, and others. At that time, in the 1880s, Darwinism became popular as a philosophy. In short, there was opportunity enough to defend a position, and I soon became acquainted with that vacillation between materialism and idealism of some sort, which was customary in those years.

When I entered the university in 1884, I was vacillating as to my field of professional training. Jurisprudence appeared to me as a key to the understanding of history, which I early conceived to be conditioned by institutional types. But of course that was not motivation sufficient for the actual study of law and for a civil-service career. I was also fascinated by classical philology, in which our school had taken us to an unusual depth; but experiences with the schoolmasters of that day had shown all to clearly that Hellenic ideals of life cannot be realized today. Philosophy as such was then in no condition to be attractive; in medicine my interest was purely theoretical. So I studied theology. At that time, theology alone seemed to offer an approach both to metaphysics and to unusually exciting historical problems. Metaphysics and history were in fact the two extremely significant areas that simultaneously and jointly aroused my interest. This led almost automatically to the systematic study of religion, which places both sets of problems in intimate cross-fertiliztion. But the systematic study of religion meant theology. The practical consequences for my own career could then follow however they would. A naturally vigorous religious drive seemed to guarantee that everything would somehow or other work out.

I have never regretted the years that I dedicated to theology—quite the contrary. Theology was then, as historical theology, one of the most interesting, exciting, and revolutionary of disciplines. From the field of Old Testament we were gripped by Wellhausen, Kuenen, and Reuss, three of the very greatest researchers of the century. In New Testament studies we cut though all the customary apologetic to the school of Baur with its bold ideas, and above all to Karl Weizsäcker. In church history, Hase stimulated our minds, and Harnack was beginning to build a new organic and developmental view. All of this opened vast horizons; and when I begun to teach in Göttingen there grew up, in intimate contact with prominent men like Bousset, Wrede, Hackmann, Gunkel, and Albert Eichhorn, a religious-historical thought-world uniting great vistas with the most refined individual issues. Now no further progress could be made without the aid of philology. So we learned from Lagarde and the classical philologists, and the historical world became fabulously colorful and interesting. But of course all of these historical pursuits were for me only means; the end was the penetration of the religio-metaphysical consciousness. My teacher Albrecht Ritschl was a keen logician, a highly systematic thinker, and an original personality in the grand manner. I am grateful to him for an introduction to the psychology and logic of the growth of Christian dogma such as one could hardly have found anywhere else.

But while the study of dogmatic theology made clear to me how unintelligible European intellectual history is without knowledge of the theological components which for long ruled everything, for me the practical quest for the justification of religious commitment in face of a naturalism that was carrying all before it always remained central. On this point, however, my theology professors did not have much to say. They belonged to an era in which people were more naïve and guileless in these matters; a steadfast faith—which was sometimes, to be sure, mere unctiousness—was then more certain of itself than we young people could be. In these questions my Erlangen teacher, Gustav Class, had at the very start pointed me toward Lotze, and with this direction I at once combined study of the original writings of Kant, Fichte, and Schleiermacher. But Lotze was the controlling spirit at first. I was not to get to know him personally, for just as I came to Göttingen he moved to Berlin. But in those formative years I read his books again and again. Later, there came a correspondingly strong influence from Dilthey, whose new psychology interest me most of all because it moved in the direction of individuality and the new psychic entities, which Lotze also stressed, even if it did not provide a satisfactory solution. Studies in the history of philosophy and in the writers of antiquity and those of the seventeenth century reinforced the insights acquired, and, at first, resulted in a psychological theory that assured the substantial reality of the life of the spirit as over against the physical world and made the immediate inner assurance of the ideal dimension of life utterly independent of all naturalism. The evidence for this theory seemed to me to lie basically in the self-certainty of experience. All conflict with the natural sciences was avoided by assigning a different methodology to the cultural sciences and accepting the fundamentally idealistic interpretation of the physical world advocated by Leibniz and Lotze.

Given these fundamental principles, the two great groups of problems, religious and intellectual history in the historical area and the psychology and evolution of the spirit in the systematic area, were closely related. That this sort of 'intellectualistic' (*'verstehende'*) psychology, with its strongly metaphysical orientation, would have to defend itself against an experimental and physiologically oriented psychology was of course clear to me. I did not doubt, however, that a psychology of this type would prove useful in dealing with the facts. My problem thus become the construction of a general history of the development of the religious spirit on the basis of its rootage in the common life; a history, moreover, that would recognize and evaluate the special place of Christianity within this universal development. Now, this was obviously one of those superhuman problems with which inexperienced youth begins. The methods of rigorous scholarship acquired in technical studies and in psychology soon made clear to me that such a plan cannot be carried out—or at least, not until all preliminary work has been completed. So I kept on delaying its execution and undertook, first, to describe this development of the religious spirit in Christianity itself within the narrower context of merely European cultural history, in order thus to understand its contemporary situation in as clear and unbiased a manner as possible. That was still a superhuman undertaking, but at that time the state of theology seemed to demand such great synthetic undertakings rather than the more circumscribed work of the specialists. In this respect, too, theology was then one of the most interesting of disciplines. Here more than in other fields, general scholarship continued to be cultivated; although it had to be looked for, one could at least find it. Since then, the situation in theology has changed. Theology today is only interested in practical matters and has abandoned the historical and systematic study of religion in the struggle for its own survival. Such theology interests me only in terms of social psychology and history.

I had to limit my field of inquiry still more. Despite thorough studies of Christian origins, the early church, and the Middle Ages, I was especially fascinated by the emergence of the modern situation and its problems. Here I immediately encountered the struggle of the essentially traditional religious forces with the new spiritual forces that found expression above all in philosophy. This struggle provided me with a focal point for my reflections and dominated my first publications. In the first, *Melanchthon und Johann Gerhard*, I posed the problem of the philosophy of the Reformers. Its discussion showed the thoroughly medieval character of the thought of the Reformation. Ancient Stoic elements, always at home in the church but now quickened by the Renaissance, had been employed to simplify medieval thought-patterns. Dilthey grappled with this theme at the same time and came to exactly the same conclusions, although neither of us knew anything of the other at that time. These early reflections gave rise to further questions, such as the dating of the beginning of the total intellectual situation of modern times, marked as it is by the emergence of an autonomous secular education and culture alongside the education and culture that continued to be dominated by theology. My studies indicated that it was the Enlightenment that first shaped the impulses and consequences of political, social, and economic secularization, of the Renaissance, and, above all, of the great philosophy of the eighteenth century into a power in public life, a way of life, a culture, and an educational system. The Enlightenment drove the supernatural powers of church and theology into the background and reduced them to their narrower practical sphere.

These matters were treated in a series of highly laborious and ponderous articles that are interred in the mass grave of the *Realencyklopädie für protestantische Theologie und Kirche*. These articles had certain points of contact with contemporary works of Dilthey, into which I now plunged and from which I sought to learn whatever I could. It was mainly he who led on to the problems of the end of the Enlightenment and of German idealism, themes that I then dealt with in the same encyclopaedia. Finally all these studies, deepened by a renewed study of the Reformers and of the Orthodoxy that followed, enjoyed a kind of rejuventation and resurrection from the 'mass grave' in the big book that became a section of Hinneberg's *Kultur der Gegenwart* under the title, *Geschichte des Protestantismus*. In the process they also became, I hope, somewhat more elegant and smoother in style. I was then seeking more and more to overcome my fear of my German colleagues, lest I should compromise myself through too great an emphasis on literary form and make myself ineligible—because unscholarly—for many honors. The treatise is a large book indeed and will appear shortly in independent form in Teubner's press.

Parallel to these historical studies, the systematic ones in the philosophy of religion were carried forward. The nature of the problem here required that my studies should include general psychology, the theory of knowledge, and the philosophy of history. It became a basic conviction of mine that religion, as an experience of consciousness, had first to be studied from a psychological point of view, the most varied concrete expressions of religion being at least tentatively included. The various components and manifestations of religion must be analyzed. Only then is it possible to discuss the truth-content and the relative value of the various concrete, historical religions. This basic conviction led quite naturally to the question of the transition from psychological descriptions and analyses to critical studies of value and truth-content, and hence to the problems arising out of the relationships of psychological analysis to recognition from the point of view of the theory of validity. Here Dilthey ceased to be of much help, for as he himself recognized, he was weak at precisely this point. Pure psychologists had little more to offer, even Wundt, whom I valued especially highly for a long time. It became clear to me that the matter before me could not be mastered by psychology and history alone. Even Eucken, whose strongly metaphysical interpretation of psychology at first seemed to me to be serviceable as a bridge, could not satisfy me for long.

There was no other way. I had to plunge deliberately into the un-psychological [*antipsychologistische*] theory of validity. At this time, as a result of studies of this sort I entered into close personal relations with Windelband and Paul Hensel and independently of them I was very strongly moved and furthered by Rickert's sharp logic. Now I saw all these problems in a new light. This change in my approach to the problem appears in my lecture in St. Louis on 'Psychology and Epistemology in the Systematic Study of Religion' (1905) and my study of 'The Historical Element in Kant's Philosophy of Religion' (1904). An extended paper on the philosophy of religion followed in the Kuno Fischer *Festschrift* of 1906. Its point of view ultimately embraced the whole scope of philosophy. It proposed a systematic study of religion that would comprehend al these problem-levels, rather analogous to the way in which the task of a general theory of art was described at that time. Today I know that in this paper I came very close to the phenomenological school, and under its influence I would today express many things quite differently. The task stood in a certain continuity with my historical writings in that the latter recognized and formulated the modern state of the problem as it emerged from the disintegration of the supernatural church theology and the displacement of dogmatics by the philosophy of religion. The historical writings could indeed be designated as the result of insights into the history of the evolution of the modern spirit.

At the center of the problem as it was now envisaged stood the question of the legitimacy of Christianity's claim to validity. I dealt with these questions in the book, *The Absoluteness of Christianity and the History of Religion* (1902). At this point I had to come to grips with the relationships of the historically relative and the substantively absolute; that is, with the key issue in all philosophy of history as I had learned to understand it through exposure to critical historiography. This book contained the germ of everything that was to follow. It was bound to lead to further studies as to what today can be called Christianity in view of its extraordinary historical variations and its inner crisis. Unfortunately, I hardly found time to carry out in more than partial detail the program I had sketched. I regret this the more, since I find offensive and seek to avoid as much as possible the empty braggadocio of announcing programs. But there were indeed a number of unfinished places in the program. The Neo-Kantian doctrine of validity, in particular, represents a deliverance and a clarification over against mere psychology; but its tendency to make all objectivity into a product of the subject, differentiated from the mere contingency of the average product only by its a priori necessity, stood in simple, flat opposition and contradiction to the very idea of religion which was to be proven true by means of this doctrine. To make all knowledge so completely dependent on the subject, and to transform all reality into productions of the subject, is to contradict directly all natural sense of reality. Something was bound to be amiss here.

Now the whole complex of ideas was once again set in motion, at first on the systematic side. The 'philosophy of validity' had somehow to be a passageway to metaphysics, which could be developed out of it and which would then have to sublate the one-sided subjectivism that was merely a preliminary view of the situation. The results of these reflections are now in the process of taking shape; but I cannot bring myself to reveal them as yet. I would only suggest that the solution seems to me to lie approximately in the direction of Malebranche, Leibniz, and Hegel. In a preliminary way, I have simply collected the various tokens of the progress of my thought, groping its way through these logically closely related studies, in the second volume of my *Collected Writings* (1913). I would like to take this opportunity to comment that this title is intended to indicate only the revision and systematic organization of previously published works. A reviewer suggested that one does not normally publish his *collected works* so early, but rather waits until after death. Since self-revelations are always somewhat in the nature of self-recommendations, I do not want to neglect this opportunity to justify myself.

Yet there was still another reason that prevented me from undertaking the task of working out a philosophy of religion and hence a philosophical system. On the historical side, too, the whole problem again entered a state of flux. That is, I was virtually swept back into historical studies concerning the essence and history of Christianity by certain new perspectives that now obtruded upon me. Practical tasks of social politics, reflections on political and social affairs, the whole process of coming of age politically (a process that occurs exceedingly late, if at all, in the typical German): the combination of these factors greatly changed my apperception of the problem of intellectual history, which suddenly seemed vastly more complicated and dependent. Aroused by these impressions, I threw myself into sociological studies—which, admittedly, provide less a ready-made insight than a new way of viewing the problem. All the notions of a philosophy of history and a theory of evolution, which had previously been so one-sidedly ideological (as with Hegel and Dilthey), and which were bound to play an important role in any philosophy of religion, were transformed. All previous solutions turned into new problems.

At the same time I came under the spell of a very powerful personality, Max Weber, who had long since accepted as matters of course the wonders that now were only beginning to dawn upon me. It was through this new association that the Marxist teaching concerning a substructure and a superstructure came to grip me with the greatest force. Not that I unhesitatingly accepted it as correct. But it contains a problematics that can never be successfully avoided, even if it has to be answered case by case. The problem was now stated something like this: To what extent are the appearance, the development, the modification, and the modern impasse of Christianity sociologically conditioned, and to what extent is Christianity itself an actively formative sociological principle? These were extraordinarily difficult questions, regarding which very little useful preliminary work had been done. Yet no one who had grasped this problem could any longer think of the history of Christianity purely in terms of the history of dogma or of the history of ideas. This time I dropped every programmatic preparation and instead of merely getting ready to, I actually plowed into an indescribably laborious task. The invitation to review a miserable book by Nathusius on *The Social Task of the Evangelical Church* made me conscious of my ignorance, and ours, about these matters, and instead of writing a review I wrote a book of nearly a thousand pages. This became a history of the culture of the Christian church, a complete parallel to Harnack's *History of Dogma*, in which I regarded religious, dogmatic, and theological factors simply as the background of social-ethical forces or the reflection of sociological surroundings, the precise determination varying from period to period. In order to put some limits to a subject all too large, I contended myself with elucidating these matters only by reference to the social teachings of the church and the sects; that is, their ethical doctrines and their theories of society. To do more exact research into the actually prevailing conditions would have been beyond my strength because of the size of the whole undertaking. My work showed the original impetus, vastly powerful, of the ideal of an eschatological utopia; it also showed how its force was partly broken by the changing secular environment and by compromises, new revolutions, and side-currents; and finally, it showed how the Christian church-culture was deprived of its dynamic by the triumph of modern political, economic, and social conditions. For that reason, the book only goes as far as the eighteen century.

The book appeared in 1911 with the title *The Social Teachings of the Christian Churches and Sects* [Eng. tr., 1923] as the first volume of my *Collected Writings*, the first sections having already appeared in the *Archiv für Sozialwissenchaften*. When I finished, I felt rather uneasy. I had ventured a great deal. Shortcomings and gaps are easy to see afterwards. Anglicanism, to name the most glaring deficiency, had not been given independent treatment. But a truer picture of historical reality had been attained; truer, that is, than supernaturally-ecclesiastical and ideologically-modern portrayals were able to convey. A very important supplement to it, and one very close to my heart, was contributed by the study, *Augustine, Christian Antiquity, and the Middle Ages* (1915), which really should be followed by new studies of the intellectual history of the Middle Ages. Without it, the whole modern intellectual world, above all the religious history of Europe, cannot be understood. (Here I was happy to meet Konrad Burdach.) So far, I have been unable to carry these studies further.

All these developments had taken me somewhat beyond the confines of the theological discipline. I had devoted myself to the educational tasks of the theological faculty with the warmest regard for the great subject matter and with human love for my students. I viewed all dogmatics as something practical, where the obscurity and uncertainty of human knowledge play an especially important role, yet whose main value can be communicated to human hearts as a burning and driving power. My positive views are contained in the articles 'Revelation,' 'Faith,' 'Redemption,' Grace,' and 'Predestination' in *Religion in Geschichte und Gegenwart*. I was unable, for obvious reasons, to bring myself to write a dogmatic theology. So it is understandable that in 1915 I accepted an invitation to join the philosophical faculty of the University of Berlin as a philosopher. This was amidst the excitement of a war that also laid claim to the pens of the scholars. Through my studies of social teachings, I had become familiar with important aspects of the political and social views and attitudes of the Anglo-Saxons. I had become familiar with political matters in the course of eight years as university representative in the upper house of Baden. This led to a rather full participation in war-time journalism. The fact that I was able to observe the great historical events, at least in part, very close to their source afforded me a deep and vital impression of the nature of historical destinies, developments, and catastrophes in a way that no study of books and documents could give.

But these factors exerted only a secondary influence in my decision to turn now toward basic studies in the philosophy of history. These latest studies lay, as already indicated, in the direction of my earliest interests. More than anything else, my philosophy of religion needed clarification concerning the nature of the historical development of religion and concerning proper criteria of judgement. The attempt actually to trace the historical development of religion in a select period brought me right to the center of all sociological problems; and in thus moving beyond religion to civilization as a whole, I, like Schleiermacher, found myself obliged to bring philosophy of history and ethics closer together. From all these considerations there grew up in me, as basic to my present situation, concern for the theoretical and philosophical aspects of history—its relation to empirical professional research on the one hand, and to a theory of cultural values, or of ethics, on the other. This is the problem that I pointed up immediately in many of the articles of my second volume and—in this point fully following Schleiermacher—began to answer. Here, too, programs had to give way to actual implementation. For this purpose I devoted myself to a thorough critical examination of the theories of the philosophy of history advanced in the last hundred years, in all cases studying the sources. I also sought to substantiate my own systematic thought, above all in conversation with Rickert and Windelband, who seemed to me to afford the most useful foundation in the contemporary situation. The results are in good part published separately in the *Historische Zeitschrift*, *Kantstudien*, Schmoller's *Jahrbuch* and *Logos*. Then I brought together and elaborated these studies in another large work, the third volume of my *Collected Writings*, with the title *Historicism and its Problems* (1922).

The now available volume is only the first of the work. It deals logically and methodologically with the problem of the philosophy of history, in that it begins with the logic of empirical historical research and inquires for the path that would lead from here to a philosophy of history—or, stated differently, how the way to valid cultural values is to be found when one starts with the historically relative. It is the old question of the absolute taken up in a much broader perspective and oriented to all cultural values, not simply to the religious position. This approach leads to a thoroughgoing analysis of the theory of value in its relation to historiography, and to an equally thoroughgoing analysis of the concepts of historical evolution. The various theories of German and non-German philosophers and the practical attitudes of historians are reviewed. Such a review reveals the profound difference between West European and German historiography. It also shows the need for a philosophy of history that takes an activist position. Philosophical contemplation of the panorama of history is not enough. The volume concludes with the transition to the foundation for such an activist philosophy of history, which is rooted in the analysis of what it means to be European, though admittedly one must at the same time keep an eye on the non-European world for purposes of comparison.

The second volume is then to present the analysis, announced here, of what it means to be European; and to develop from this analysis, using the point of view of ethics and the philosophy of civilization, the proper positions for today. It is to be the most comprehensive of all of my studies and go far beyond the original religious starting point of my work. If life and strength stay with me, I would like ultimately to return to religion and to finish my philosophy of religion. The latter is my first love; even in the synthesis of contemporary culture, which is to be based on the philosophy of history, the religious element remains central. Without this there is no naïvete and no freshness.

What about the system that seems to be required of every philosopher? It naturally keeps on growing throughout this process. For all my works up to now have only resolved specific issues, very concrete particular questions, that had to be settled before the system itself could emerge. After the first youthful dreams of a system, I committed myself to a way of thinking that proceeds from positive knowledge and that is saturated with reality. Such a way of thinking must first settle many concrete questions of detail, just as a philosopher operating from the background of natural science must go through a great many particular scientific studies and had best be disciplined for a time in one of its branches. To be sure, such work can only have philosophical meaning and significance when it is undertaken with the conscious aim of clarifying or substantiating an important part of the system. In short, it requires a systematic philosophical foundation that will dictate what kinds of questions are asked and in what direction the results will be pointed. But on the other hand, the systematic foundation itself will also be greatly advanced and

influenced by this progressive clarification of individual issues an
presuppositions. To be sure, a system that keeps on reforming itse
will not be quickly finished, and it will suffer from a certain liabilit
and it is bound to strive for precision, sharpness of outline, an
universality. But since it can only grow up out of a constar
intercourse with the object—out of devotion to the real—and sinc
there is a hidden relation and affinity of the human spirit with th
reality from which its principles of order must be derived, the syster
cannot be deduced by pure logic from certain basic perceptions. I
must grow up with the whole work, in a continuous mutual correctio
of thought and life. Of course, such a view of the role of the syster
rests on a certain view of the nature of thought and its relation to lif
matters about which there has been, and continues to be, muc
dispute. But such a fundamental view of theoretical thinking is itself
vital part of the system, and it can only arise out of extensive person;
engagement in the problems of the various positive disciplines. A
least for my part, I would see in such a basic orientation one of th
chief tasks of the system. But I cannot discuss these matters her
because they have only reached the stage of academic lectures and a
not yet ready for communication to the public.

Such a system would necessarily revolve around logic, epistemolog
and psychology, which together seem to me to constitute the strictl
scientific center of all philosophy. But logic requires today a totall
new treatment that would focus attention on the relation of gener;
formal logic to the logic of the empirical sciences and would seek t
overcome the conflicts and contrasts of the empirical world by som
sort of metalogic or empirical dialectic. Such a metalogic is absolutel
essential. Thinkers who work only with the principles of formal logi
never arrive at the world of actual existence, as mere empiricists, the
fail to achieve unity and system. Only metalogic supplies this lack
and metalogic leads immediately into metaphysics. Here also lies th
real problem of modern doctrines of intuition. I do not know whethe
it will be possible for me to work through these matters with th
thoroughness that would be necessary for the complete elucidation o
the systematic background that I have in mind. When we reach th
ultimate essentials, human life is wont to give out, and nearly all of u
leave the body of our work uncompleted. If one begins in the thirtie
to reflect on how many of the plans will yet be obtainable in thi
life—while not long ago the possibilities had seemed unlimited!—the
a feeling arises that never again leaves, the feeling of the impossibilit
of completing the tasks that have been outlined. Even collaboratio
with other scholars provides no comfort here. Human thought, whicl

must penetrate the abstract and universal *via* sense perception, introspection, and memory, can never transcend the accidental and limited character of its starting points. At best, it can intuitively grasp, at a few points, the unifying thread that presumably unites everything. But it is difficult to reduce this thread to logic and system.

Finally, I do not want to suppress a further thought concerning the system. Naturally the philosopher needs a system; the system is what distinguishes a philosopher. Readers or those who want to understand, need to be able to discern this systematic orientation, because only thus can the presuppositions and directions of thought taken by the author be intelligible. Special studies devoted to particular topics may become meaningful only by reference to the system. The system is what makes comparison with other philosophers possible. It enables the philosopher to be placed within the general outline of possible philosophic positions. But all these advantages can be attained by a precise indication of the place within the system and an accurate exposition of the systematic background at the appropriate points of particular research. For today a system is basically a personal concern of the author, the exact reconstruction and presentation of his intellectual background and his capacity for philosophic thinking.

But a detailed presentation of the system itself is really desirable only in exceptional cases. Outlines of great systems are rare in the history of philosophy; they are grouped in a few great families. Generally speaking, the last hundred years have seen no truly new system; for the most part, old systems are combined and adapted. Yet there are many extremely important developments of single themes. Presumably there are not many more actual philosophical systems than there are political or religious systems, or artistic styles. The so-called systems of modern authors are means to understand their actual main works, which are directed to particular themes; they are instruments of control for themselves and others. It goes without saying that outstanding, brilliant, and instructive materials are to be found among them. But there is nothing remotely resembling the great systems of antiquity or of the seventeenth, the end of the eighteenth, and the beginning of the nineteenth centuries. In this sense, everything that we do today is the work of followers (*Epigonenwerk*), even if it is not dead and superfluous. My teacher Paul de Lagarde was accustomed to call the admirable Lotze the 'most epigonous of the epigones.' That is without doubt an injustice, and yet it contains a kernel of truth—indeed a kernel of truth that applies in some degrees to all of us, at least in so far as we try to think systematically. The new paths and breakthroughs today lie above all in the particular disciplines, wherever these are complemented by a philosophical mind and a universal perspective. Only from them (if one may think of a calming down again of the contemporary world confusions) will new systems emerge, sometime, somewhere. But within these particular disciplines there is movement enough and problems are approached in a new way. Here we are certainly not mere followers. The logical and systematic consequences of these new approaches will certainly develop with time. Perhaps the philosophical system will then again be something more than the requirement of a personal intellectual neatness and acceptance of responsibility.

To be sure, a critic might conclude that I am making a virtue of necessity, and that the whole history of my books that I have given here is evidence of how much need I have for such self-vindication. It might be said that this is in fact a history of books and not of a system. For my part, I wanted to show the opposite, that there is in fact an underlying thought that gives a certain unity to these various books. Only this demonstration can serve, in my opinion, to excuse the fact that I have dared to say so much to the reader about these books.

Index